STUDY GUIDE *to accompany*
PBS Adult Learning Service
TELEVISION COURSE

# Joseph Campbell

*Transformations
of Myth
Through Time*

STUDY GUIDE *to accompany*
PBS Adult Learning Service
TELEVISION COURSE

# Joseph Campbell

# *Transformations of Myth Through Time*

George deForest Lord    *Bodman Professor of English,*
*Yale University*

Peter Markman    *Professor of English, Fullerton College*

Roberta H. Markman    *Chair, Department of Comparative Literature,*
*California State University, Long Beach*

Robert Merrill    *Professor of Literature, The Catholic University*

Charles S. J. White    *Chair, Department of Philosophy and Religion,*
*The American University*

**Harcourt Brace Jovanovich, Publishers**

San Diego    New York    Chicago    Austin    Washington, D.C.

London    Sydney    Tokyo    Toronto

# Preface to Students

**Y**ou are setting out on a very exciting experience. You are going to learn a great deal about the mythologies that human beings have created over the long span of our development from a man who made the study of them his life's work. What makes Joseph Campbell particularly captivating is his ability to make those mythologies, many of them from very early periods of human culture, relevant to the lives of people living in the midst of the complexities of twentieth-century civilization. As you will see throughout the *Joseph Campbell: Transformations of Myth Through Time* television course, he can do this because those myths, for him, were not merely stories and images to be studied, but fascinating revelations of human needs and potential belonging to people in every age. Furthermore, he has the gift of making accessible to his students the inner experience of each of the mythic systems he discusses.

In addition to teaching you about Campbell's special insights into how myths reconcile human beings to the mysteries of life, the television course will also expose you to the ideas of other scholars who have made the study of mythology the focus of their work. This variety of perspectives will allow you to gain a deeper understanding of mythology's role in human history.

It will require some effort on your part to understand the factual information presented in the units of this *Study Guide* and by Campbell in the television programs, especially in areas with which you have little previous experience. It may also be necessary for you to rethink a number of definitions and ideas you have taken for granted. For example, on the simplest level, you will have to realize that the word "myth" can have a weightier meaning than our culture usually gives it, and that the term "hero" can refer to exploits of both men and women. On a more profound level, you may be encouraged to think more deeply than you have about religion — both your own and that of others.

We believe that the effort you put into *Joseph Campbell: Transformations of Myth Through Time* will be well worth your time. You have a thought-provoking, challenging, and enjoyable term of study ahead. As Campbell says in the television programs for this course, "Doors will open where you never expected them to be."

## Goals for *Joseph Campbell: Transformations of Myth Through Time*

This television course is an introduction to the study of the world's mythologies. Through the course's several components — this *Study Guide*, an *Anthology of Readings*, and 14 television programs — we hope to help you gain:

- an understanding of how myths have been transformed through myriad cultures throughout time
- an understanding of the relationship between myth, religion, and culture
- the ability to recognize underlying similarities and the wide range and variability of human cultures
- the ability to recognize and appreciate that there are and have been many equally valid myths and religions throughout the history of civilization

■ a broad cross-cultural background against which to view modern myths, cultures, and religions

■ an understanding of myths as reflections of both universal and ethnic ideas

■ a heightened awareness and appreciation of different religions both within our own culture and in the rest of the world

■ an introduction to thoughts and symbols from significant mythologies which can provide background for the study of literature, music, and art

## The Study Guide

This *Study Guide to accompany Joseph Campbell: Transformations of Myth Through Time* is both an integrating tool and a major text to aid you in the successful completion of this course. It provides information to supplement Joseph Campbell's lectures presented in the television programs, and it guides you through the range of essays and articles that appear in the *Anthology of Readings*. (See Appendix C for a list of the readings.)

At the beginning of each unit, we have set forth a study plan. Based on the experience of other students in television courses, the plan proposes that you read each unit in this book and the referenced selections in the *Anthology of Readings* before you watch the assigned television program. (Actually, you will find it most helpful to read each unit both before and after watching the television program.) The Unit Preview, Points to Look for in the *Anthology of Readings*, and Points to Watch for in the Television Programs will help you focus on the most important elements of each week's study. After you have read the *Study Guide* unit, seen the program, and read the required selections from the *Anthology*, you will be well equipped to undertake the assignments at the end of each unit.

The assignments in your *Study Guide* are designed to help you use the content of this course to think about and learn from the world's mythologies. Through this course, you will learn about the wide-ranging mythologies of the world, what they have in common, and how they differ. You will become acquainted with how different cultures develop concepts of life, death, and god. The *Study Guide* and the television programs refer frequently to the fact that many of the same ideas take various forms in the several cultures you will be studying. In the assignments at the end of each unit you will often be asked to compare a particular mythology with the myths in your own life in order to understand more fully the basis for relationships among the world's mythologies.

We hope that you will be able to respond to the assignments in a variety of ways. Most of the assignments can provide the basis for writing or for study and reflection. Even if you are not required to hand in all of these assignments, you will find it interesting and useful to react to them in your journal and to use your responses as the starting point for further study and writing.

Also, at the beginning of each unit, we have identified and defined a glossary of terms for that unit. These terms, along with other terms that seem particularly useful or potentially troublesome, are included in the General Glossary in Appendix B.

To further aid your study of mythology, there are brief bibliographies accompanying each unit, and a General Bibliography in Appendix A.

## The Anthology

Your *Study Guide* integrates all the course materials and provides substantial additional information. Each unit will contain references to selections in *Transformations of Myth Through Time: An Anthology of Readings*. This volume, specially prepared for the television course, is a self-contained collection of essays and articles by leading mythology scholars, including John Blofeld, Mircea Eliade, Marija Gimbutas, Roger Loomis, Wendy Doniger O'Flaherty, Walpola Sri Rahula, and Heinrich Zimmer. The readings were selected by the *Study Guide* authors and the television course's National Academic Advisory Committee. These readings complement, elucidate, and offer counterpoint to Joseph Campbell's televised lectures. You will be asked to read selections from the *Anthology* as you work your way through the units.

## The Course Journal

You will see in each unit's study plan that we recommend you keep a course notebook or journal, writing your responses to, and comments and summaries of what you watch and read. Although you may have an assumption that you should take notes during your viewing of the television programs, as you would if you were listening to a classroom lecture, you will find that the television medium does not lend itself to this practice. First, you will miss a good deal of the content if you do not really watch the visual images. Second, the pace may be too fast for you to take good notes, even if you devote yourself to it. Thus, you will find it more useful to watch the programs closely first and then to summarize what you have learned in your notebook afterwards. You may find it helpful, as many other television students do, to make audiotape or videotape copies of the television programs as you watch so that you can review them later.

You should also use your journal to record questions and concerns that you can raise with your instructor later. We hope that your notebook will come to be a good companion in your study and that you will be able to write freely and fully in it, recording your own thoughts and reactions, as well as noting the content of the course.

## The Television Programs

*Joseph Campbell: Transformations of Myth Through Time* features 14 hour-long programs. The Introductory Program is "The Hero's Journey," an award-winning biographical film. The next 13 programs were selected from over 50 hours of Campbell's lectures. For the first time, a scholar's major lectures are preserved on tape. These programs, compiled and edited by California filmmakers Stuart L. Brown and William Free, combine Campbell's penetrating lectures with presentations of related art works and artifacts.

## A Final Note

*Joseph Campbell: Transformations of Myth Through Time* television course is a significant resource for the study of mythology. It offers a unique opportunity to study with Joseph Campbell—author, teacher, and storyteller—as he explores the origins and meanings of the world's mythologies, folklores, and religions. We have enjoyed our work with these important materials. We hope that you will too.

# Acknowledgments

The authors take full responsibility for the information in the *Study Guide* but wish to acknowledge the contributions of the many people who helped to complete it. For their dedicated commitment to preserving the work of Joseph Campbell through their production of the television programs for this course, we would like to thank Stuart Brown and William Free. To Laurance S. Rockefeller we express our appreciation for providing the funding that made this course possible. We thank Dee Brock and Jinny Goldstein of the PBS Adult Learning Service for their advice and support during the development of the *Study Guide*. We thank Diane U. Eisenberg and Megan Scribner, of Eisenberg Associates, for designing, developing and coordinating the television course materials. Additionally, we gained very valuable suggestions and insights from the members of the National Academic Advisory Committee for this television course. We also would like to thank the staff at Harcourt Brace Jovanovich: Leslie Leland, Ken Fine, Don Fujimoto, and Avery Hallowell.

Finally, we thank our families and friends for their support and understanding as we worked against formidable deadlines.

# Contents

# List of Illustrations

PETER MARKMAN
ROBERTA H. MARKMAN

# The Hero's Journey:
## *The World of Joseph Campbell*

## UNIT STUDY PLAN

1. Read the material in this unit both before and after you view "The Hero's Journey: The World of Joseph Campbell"; respond to what you have read by summarizing the material and then interpreting it. Observe the difference in your observations before watching the television program and afterwards.
2. Write a summary of Joseph Campbell's interpretation of the hero's journey in your course notebook or journal.
3. Read the selections for this unit in the *Anthology of Readings*. These selections include the works of Joseph Campbell, Bill Moyers, and Mircea Eliade.
4. After reading the selections, comment in your notebook on what you have read. Show the relationship between the readings and the essay in this unit.
5. Complete the assignments at the end of this unit as specified by your instructor.

## POINTS TO WATCH FOR IN THE TELEVISION PROGRAM

1. Notice Campbell's references to metaphor, both implied and direct, and study the connections he makes between myth and metaphor.
2. Notice what Campbell suggests is the main function of mythology.
3. Consider Campbell's evaluation of the works of James Joyce and C. G. Jung.
4. Make a list of the stages that Campbell mentions in the hero's journey.
5. Consider why Campbell feels that the inner life must direct one's outer life. Notice how this connects with mythology and metaphor.

## POINTS TO LOOK FOR IN THE *ANTHOLOGY OF READINGS*

1. Note in the selection from Campbell's *The Inner Reaches of Outer Space: Metaphor as Myth and as Religion* the various levels on which metaphor can function. It is im-

portant to understand the basic relationship between the external and internal worlds in the structure of metaphor.
2. Observe carefully the four functions of mythology as Campbell describes them in *The Inner Reaches of Outer Space,* and note the essential differences between them.
3. Notice in the "Introduction" by Bill Moyers to *The Power of Myth,* Moyers speaks of Campbell's emphasis on the relevance of myth for today's world and on myth's ability to teach us about "the *experience* of being alive." Moyers points out that to Campbell "a myth is a mask of God, ... a metaphor for what lies behind the visible world" (13). Notice that, in this instance and in others, Moyers captures the essential assumptions underlying Campbell's thinking.
4. Notice the various categories of myth that Eliade suggests in the excerpt from *Patterns in Comparative Religion.* Notice particularly his discussion of the "myth of divine androgyny" and the way the masculine and feminine principles are used "to express—in biological terms—the coexistence of contraries, of cosmological principles (male and female) within the heart of the divinity" (18). Notice how Eliade relates the drama of the death and resurrection of vegetation to the concept of divinity and the idea of the fundamental unity of life and death. Consider how his statement "in no case can a myth be taken as merely the fantastic projection of a 'natural' event" (20) relates to the idea of the importance of understanding myth as metaphor. Consider also the relationship Eliade sees between myth and history.

## UNIT GLOSSARY

**Anthropology**: Literally, the study of humankind, "anthropos," but better described as the scientific study of humanity and culture.

**Apotheosis**: Deification; as Campbell often used it, the realization of one's own inner divinity, the God within.

**Archetype**: According to C. G. Jung, a primordial image in the collective unconscious of the human race.

**Epiphany**: A moment of revelation of divinity; as James Joyce used it, a sudden spiritual manifestation revealing the nature of reality.

**Ethnology**: The branch of anthropology that analyzes and interprets data regarding human life in specific cultures.

**Exegesis**: Critical exposition or interpretation, especially of religious texts.

**Monomyth**: James Joyce's term for the underlying basic myth from which all particular myths derive. Campbell uses the term to describe his paradigm of the hero's journey.

**Multivalent**: Having many meanings on a variety of levels, used in connection with metaphor and symbol.

**Paradigm**: Example or pattern; the fundamental pattern underlying seemingly different specific cases.

**Upanishads**: Metaphysical dialogues commenting on the Vedas, among the primary texts of Hinduism. For further discussion of the Upanishads, see Unit 5.

**Adolf Bastian (1826–1905)**: Pioneering German ethnologist whose work foreshadowed parts of present-day anthropology.

**Leo Frobenius (1873–1938)**: German anthropologist and archaeologist who specialized in the study of prehistory, especially that of Africa, developing a comprehensive theory of humankind's early development.

**James Joyce (1882–1941)**: Irish novelist, born in Dublin, who spent most of his adult life on the Continent. His development of a complex, highly symbolic, punning style and a "stream of consciousness" technique enabled him to deal simultaneously with the inner and outer lives of his characters. He is best known for *A Portrait of the Artist as a Young Man* (1916), *Ulysses* (1922), and *Finnegans Wake* (1939).

**Carl Gustav Jung (1875–1961)**: Swiss psychiatrist who postulated two areas of the unconscious, the personal and the collective, the latter consisting of archetypal images common to all humanity and symbolically expressive in dreams of inner reality.

**Thomas Mann (1875–1955)**: German novelist, born in Lübeck, who left Germany in 1933 and lived in the United States from 1936–52. His novels, based on myths or told from a mythic perspective, deal generally with the artistic temperament and its relationship to society. He received the Nobel prize in 1929 and is best known for *Death in Venice* (1912), *The Magic Mountain* (1924), *Doctor Faustus* (1951), and the tetralogy *Joseph and His Brothers* (1933–43).

**Oswald Spengler (1880–1936)**: German philosopher whose *The Decline of the West* (1918) sets forth the view that every culture passes naturally through a cycle of life similar to a human life.

## UNIT PREVIEW

This Introductory Unit will familiarize you with the basic ideas that form the foundation of Joseph Campbell's thought. The unit will also help to explain his unique approach to mythology. In addition, you will be given insight into the life of Joseph Campbell and his scholarly accomplishments:

**The Importance of Metaphor**: It is important to understand Campbell's approach to myth and metaphor and to understand clearly his interpretation of the word "metaphor."

**The Four Functions of Mythology**: Campbell has articulated four functions of mythology: 1) the mystical function, 2) the cosmological function, 3) the sociological function, and 4) the psychological function, the last of which he considers to be at the root of the other three.

**The Stages of the Hero's Journey**: In his work *The Hero with a Thousand Faces*, Campbell has outlined the basic stages of the journey that most heroes in the world's mythologies have taken. The hero must depart from his or her familiar surroundings and venture forth on unchartered paths, pass through a period of trials and victories, and return to the world with the boon of enlightenment. Campbell's monomyth of the hero's journey can be applied not only to the study of mythology, but to the lives of individuals, to works of literature, and to an understanding of the creative process.

**The Life and Scholarly Contributions of Joseph Campbell**: Joseph Campbell's life and scholarship can be understood in terms that parallel the stages of the hero's journey: separation, penetration to a source of power, and a life-enhancing return through the publication of his work.

# UNIT ESSAY

### Myth and Metaphor

In the television program for this unit, "The Hero's Journey," Campbell illustrates the importance of understanding metaphor in order to grasp his statement that myths are true in contrast to the radio talk show host who insisted myths were lies. In an exchange with Bill Moyers during the televised interview series, Campbell explained, more completely, the necessary relationship between myth and metaphor, a relationship that must be understood by anyone hoping to come to terms with his approach to mythology and religion.

CAMPBELL:    Every religion is true one way or another. It is true when understood metaphorically. But when it gets stuck to its own metaphors, interpreting them as facts, then you are in trouble.

MOYERS:    What is the metaphor?

CAMPBELL:    A metaphor is an image that suggests something else. For instance, if I say to a person, "You are a nut," I'm not suggesting that I think the person is literally a nut. "Nut" is a metaphor. The reference of the metaphor in religious traditions is to something transcendent that is not literally anything. If you think that the metaphor is itself the reference, it would be like going to a restaurant, asking for the menu, seeing beefsteak written there, and starting to eat the menu.

For example, Jesus ascended to heaven. The denotation would seem to be that someone ascended to the sky. That's literally what is being said. But if that were really the meaning of the message, then we have to throw it away, because there would have been no such place for Jesus literally to go. We know that Jesus could not have ascended to heaven because there is no physical heaven anywhere in the universe. Even ascending at the speed of light, Jesus would still be in the galaxy. Astronomy and physics have simply eliminated that as a literal, physical possibility. But if you read "Jesus ascended to heaven" in terms of its metaphoric connotation, you see that he has gone inward — not into outer space but into inward space, to the place from which all being comes, into the consciousness that is the source of all things, the kingdom of heaven within. The images are outward, but their reflection is inward. The point is that we should ascend with him by going inward. It is the metaphor of returning to the source, alpha and omega, of leaving the fixation of the body behind and going to the body's dynamic source.[1]

Campbell makes much the same point in a somewhat different way in *The Inner Reaches of Outer Space: Metaphor as Myth and as Religion*, the book that grew out of his realization that metaphor is widely misunderstood.

> A mythology is … an organization of metaphorical figures connotative of states of mind that are not finally of this or that place and time, notwithstanding that the figures themselves initially suggest such localization. My magnificent master and great friend of many years ago, Heinrich Zimmer (1890–1943), had a saying: "The best things can't be told; the second best are misunderstood." The second best are misunderstood because, as metaphors poetically of that which cannot be told, they are misread prosaically as referring to tangible facts. The connoted messages are thus lost in the symbols.[2]

The "best things," the most fundamental truths about the meaning of life, must be conveyed by metaphor because they cannot be fully explained through logic. Logical explanations can convey only partially the full truth communicated by the mythic narrative, as anyone who has been involved in an attempt to "explain" the meaning of a great work of literature or art must realize. An explanation or a synopsis can never be substituted for the full work. For this reason, the texts underlying the world's major religions are mythic stories rather than logical essays, and the truths of the great religions have always been communicated through the mythic images of great art. Theologians and others attempt to analyze and interpret these stories and images logically, but, as any examination of the history of such exegeses and the widely differing interpretations of the same story or image reveal, their success is limited at best since those logical interpretations can convey only a part of the whole truth of the story.

For Campbell, the truth was in the myth, not in the logical interpretation. Although he spent a great deal of his writing and speaking career explaining myths, as you will see in this television course, he also spent a lot of time telling the stories of the myths. You will notice that he tells these stories in such a way that they become meaningful to you and other listeners. He can do this because he understands the myths' meanings and can help those stories convey their meanings to you as he recreates, in the living moment of telling the story, the metaphors of which they are composed. Underlying the work of Joseph Campbell, then, is the fundamental assumption that it is as metaphor that myth is true, that myth is relevant, and that mythology is capable of the change that enables it to remain meaningful in spite of new scientific developments and changing human needs. Taken solely as literal fact, or merely as an entertaining story, mythology loses its relevance and power, becoming what Campbell calls "petrafact," or dead myth.

As Campbell never tired of pointing out, myths are true despite the current use of the term to mean something contrary to fact. Surely, what has kept the texts of the major religions and such mythic works as Homer's *Odyssey* and Sophocles' *Oedipus Rex* alive through the centuries is that they have been read metaphorically, and thereby allowed to speak to each new generation in its own relevant and meaningful terms. Twentieth-century writers who were especially important to Campbell, such as Thomas Mann in *Joseph and His Brothers* and James Joyce in such novels as *Ulysses* and *Finnegan's Wake*, exploited exactly this metaphoric nature of myth to express their political and social concerns and to enable modern readers to develop their own self-awareness through a metaphoric identification with the heroes they created. Like Campbell, these two great authors realized that the story of Joseph in Genesis or the wanderings of Ulysses in Homer's *Odyssey* could be the basis for their own stories because these heroes' journeys ultimately must be seen as metaphorically taking place within man even though, literally, they take place in the outer world. Beyond time and place, these are the stories of Everyman and every time. For that reason, when we read them as metaphor, these great masterpieces are able to speak directly to us as we allow our own thoughts to merge the traditional symbol of the hero and his journey with the imaginative new creation.

## What Is Metaphor?

But exactly what is a metaphor? Like most other students, you probably have learned that a metaphor is an implied comparison bringing together two essentially dissimilar things, as in the example Campbell used with the radio talk show host, "he is a deer." But the comparison must be implied. "He runs like a deer" is not a metaphor because it simply points out a similarity between the two dissimilar beings. The metaphor, on the other hand, unifies the two, at least momentarily, into a single entity. We know, of course, that in everyday life men and deer are not unifiable. They are quite different, quite separate beings. But beneath the surface there is a potential unity, and it is that potential that metaphor realizes. At the moment of perception, and perhaps only for that moment, there is no longer a separate "he" and a separate "deer." For that magical, metaphoric moment, "he *is* a deer." To understand both the importance and nature of metaphor, it is essential to comprehend the complexity of that relationship between the two things being compared, because in their momentary unity, they transform each other. The man becomes deerlike and the deer becomes manlike within the mind perceiving the metaphor. The factual reality of the everyday world recedes for a moment and allows the mysterious inner world, from which come dreams and myths, to emerge.

It is precisely the transformative power of metaphor that we can see in such a simple example that enables metaphor to link the external events of more important stories to their inner meanings, their inner metaphors. The ascension of Christ, to which Campbell refers in his conversation with Bill Moyers, is a good example. Through the power of metaphor, we are able to understand that Christ's literal ascent in the biblical account may be taken to mean that "Jesus went inward" and furthermore, that "we should ascend with him by going inward." The metaphor has tied the "facts" of the literal story of Jesus to their inward meaning and then linked those two levels of the story with the reader's own personal reality. In this way, the metaphor can awaken responses in the reader of which he might not have thought himself capable. The ability of metaphor to link the outer, factual level of reality to the inner, personal level enables the outer manifestations of experience to speak directly to the unconscious layer of the psyche, to unite inner and outer in the same way they are united in a dream. The metaphor thus provides a dynamic link at the point where the inner and outer worlds meet, exactly as the metaphor of Christ's ascension does. It uses images from outer experience to reveal inner reality, and it is precisely this ephemeral aspect of the metaphor that helps create the aura of magic that one associates with myths.[3]

When a metaphor is functioning in this way, it evokes a powerful, immediate response from the listener or reader. In this sense a metaphor is somewhat different from a symbol which calls forth, in the mind of the listener or reader, a meaning he or she already knows. The symbols of Christ on the cross or the Buddha beneath the Bodhi tree, as examples, cause the viewer to think of ideas; as symbols they do not join the viewer's inner world to the outer world in which the figures exist. But the same figures of Christ or the Buddha may act as metaphors if the viewer makes the comparison between himself or herself and that figure, thereby creating exactly that sense of unity. When used often over a span of time, metaphors can become so common that they no longer call up an image of the things being compared. These are called clichés or dead metaphors,

indicating they no longer have the power to generate a flash of meaning in the perceiver's mind. As dead metaphors they merely state an idea. Saying "he is a tiger," is, today, virtually the same as saying "he is ferocious" because the listener, as he hears it, no longer imagines a real tiger with all the particular ferociousness of that unique animal. When a metaphor becomes the same as everyday speech, it has died, for a true, living metaphor is clearly not an expression of a literal truth.

A metaphor cannot be equivalent to external reality as a factual statement is because, as Campbell points out, the metaphor expresses what is otherwise inexpressible. As the example of Christ's ascension suggests, an entire story or myth can be seen as metaphoric. By representing invisible or inner experience by means of external, visible events, the myth gives form to what in itself is beyond form and thus provides insight into the mysteries of life. What is created is what James Joyce called an epiphany, a window into inner experience; it is the point at which the outer world evoked by the story of the myth and the inner world of the profound meaning of the myth meet. The only possible response to the insight we experience when those two come together allowing us to transcend the everyday level of reality for a moment is "Wow!"

That "wow" is what we feel when a myth or a great work of art "hits" us. The ability to create a work of art that gives us that feeling is why Campbell considers artists as today's mythmakers. The modern work of art or the ancient myth, by expressing a profound truth brought to consciousness through metaphor, heightens and celebrates our sense of life. It does so by elevating a human situation or ordinary experience, such as the life of Christ or the life of the Buddha, to cosmological status. It allows, in other words, the particular human situation to become a revelation of the order of the universe. And our own identification with the metaphor enables us to see ourselves as part of that macrocosmic or universal level of existence. Our own mundane experiences open up to disclose dimensions beyond themselves, becoming larger than life, and we thus gain access to a spiritual level of existence. As Campbell suggests in his conversation with Bill Moyers, and as he indicates in his discussion of Christ and the Buddha in Unit 6, it is through this power of metaphor that we are able to discover the Buddha or the Christ within ourselves.

As Campbell points out, in the myths "images are outward, but their reflection is inward."[4] What we must do to make the myths our own is to follow what he called "the way of the mystic and of proper art [which] is of recognizing *through* the metaphors an epiphany beyond words."[5] For it is through a metaphoric reading of myths, and mythic literature and art that one can move from the literal reference of the character or event in the story to the inner realm where the true adventure takes place. It is both the function and beauty of metaphor to bring together those two realms, the outer and the inner, in which we all exist.

## The Four Functions of Mythology

In discussing the essence of mythology and making clear its fundamental relationship with metaphor, Campbell wrote,

> It is not something projected from the brain, but something experienced from the heart, from recognitions of identities behind or within the appearances of nature, perceiving with love a "thou" where there would have been otherwise only an "it." As stated already centuries ago in the Indian Kena Upanishad: "That which in the lightning flashes forth, makes one blink, and say 'Ah!' — that 'Ah!' refers to divinity.". . . The life of a mythology derives from the vitality of its symbols as metaphors delivering, not simply the idea, but a sense of actual participation in such a realization of transcendence, infinity, and abundance as this (*Anthology* 6–7).

That sense of participation constitutes what Campbell considers the most fundamental of the four functions of a mythology, the mystical function, that of "opening the mind and heart to the utter wonder of all being" (*Anthology* 7). Or to put it another way, of reconciling "waking consciousness to the *mysterium tremendum et fascinans* of this universe *as it is*."[6] Such an opening or reconciliation allows the individual to perceive reality mythologically, to see with the inner eye as well as the physical eye. By seeing in that new way, one gains an understanding of his or hew own relationship to that mysterious ground of all being, usually called god, which supports not only the cosmos "out there," but the microcosmic life of the individual "in here." Seeing in such a way gives one a mystic sense of the harmony of the universe and the relatedness of all its components.

The second function of a mythology, the cosmological function, follows from the first. Perceiving reality with the inner eye reveals a different world from the one normally seen. It is a people's mythology that details and interprets that world, showing how every feature of that world is related to the whole. In explaining this function, Campbell often refers to the distinction made by nineteenth-century ethnologist Adolf Bastian, between the apparently universal themes and motifs found in all mythologies, which he called *elementargedanken* (elementary ideas), and the images drawn from the local environment and culture through which these elementary ideas were expressed in specific myths. Thus, the local images, which he called *völkergedanken* (ethnic ideas), made the mystical insight — the *elementargedanken* upon which the mythology was founded — widely available within the culture. The local images, then explained for the people of a particular culture how the mystical harmony of mythology's first function could be seen and appreciated in terms of the world as they knew it. This second function of a mythology explains why mythologies from different parts of the world seem very different from each other, but actually convey the same fundamental ideas.

A mythology's third function is sociological, "the enforcement of a moral order; the shaping of the individual to the requirements of his geographically and historically conditioned social group"[7] and the validation of those requirements. The mythology binds the individual to his or her own group by proclaiming the rightness of the particular culture's way of doing things. "For those in whom a local mythology still works, there is an experience both of accord with the social order, and of harmony with the universe."[8] This function follows naturally from the first two since interpreting the mystery of the universe (the first function) in terms of images drawn from the local environment (the second function) naturally would lead to the perception that the way of life of the local culture somehow was ordained as correct by the gods.

Finally, a mythology has a fourth function, this one psychological and lying "at the root of all [the other] three as their base and final support."[9] Campbell calls this function pedagogical and describes it as responsible for "conducting individuals in harmony through the passages of human life, from the stage of dependency in childhood to the responsibilities of maturity, and on to old age and the ultimate passage of the dark gate."[10] Closely related to Campbell's conception of the hero's journey, this function of a mythology serves to enable the individual to realize his or her full humanity as it serves "to foster the centering and unfolding of the individual in integrity, in accord with himself (the microcosm), his culture (the mesocosm), the universe (the macrocosm), and that awesome ultimate mystery which is both beyond and within himself and all things:

> Wherefrom words turn back,
> Together with the mind, not having attained."[11]

## The Hero with a Thousand Faces

When Joseph Campbell examined the world's myths from a metaphorical point of view, he was struck by the themes they seemed to share. In *The Hero with a Thousand Faces*, his first book on myth that grew out of this realization, he demonstrates that, dressed in a thousand different masks and costumes and given a thousand different tasks to perform, the various heroes of the world's myths all undergo similar metaphoric journeys or quests. Although no hero experienced the journey in exactly the same way as any other, Campbell found that the basic pattern or paradigm of the hero's journey existed in all cultures. In all of them the hero set out on a journey or quest to a strange, adventure-filled land; overcame a series of similar trials and obstacles; and finally was able to return to the world fully conscious of his experiences on the journey. He returned home from his trials and victories armed with the knowledge that made possible the conquest of the forces threatening the world to which he returned.[12]

On the basis of this paradigm, Campbell defines the hero as "the man or woman who has been able to battle past his personal and local historical limitations to the generally valid, normally human forms. Such a one's visions, ideas, and inspirations come pristine from the primary springs of human life and thought."[13] In other words, to set out on the quest which is his destiny and for which he is now ready, the hero must leave his home, his tradition, and each and every aspect of the life he grew up with and through which he feels secure. The hero must die to the world to know the experience of going inward to be born again,[14] for the true journey is inward even though it must be expressed metaphorically as "overground." The object of the quest is "to return to [the world], transfigured, and teach the lesson he has learned of life renewed."[15]

**The Departure**: In leaving his familiar surroundings, the hero responds to a call to adventure that acknowledges his special destiny and lures him to the dark forest or the mysterious mountain, the heretofore unknown realm of adventure, of both treasure and danger. The hero may refuse the call, as some do, but if he accepts the challenge and sets forth on his way, he will receive "unsuspected assistance that comes to one who has undertaken his proper adventure."[16] This assistance often comes in the form of a protective figure who appears mysteriously and provides the hero with the mental and physical tools he will need to confront the dangers that lie ahead. In his passage from the familiar surroundings of home into the regions of the unknown, the hero will have to overcome the dangers put in his way by the guardians of that strange, new realm. These dangers may be involved with the world of the night or symbolic death in some other form, but whatever the encounter, the hero must pass through a symbolic death to be spiritually reborn. In this stage, the hero's adventures in the world must be seen, according to Campbell, as metaphorically inward. He should be seen as engaged in conquering the outside influences that have kept him from understanding the life force that lies buried within him.

**Trials and Victories:** The symbolic death of the first phase of the journey separates the hero completely from his former life, and he now passes into a period of awesome trials and great victories won in part through the efforts of the protective figure whom he had met earlier. The path he must follow is a perilous one. Each experience along the way demands courage and sacrifice, but rewards his efforts with revealing moments of illumination.

The ultimate adventure during this stage of the journey is the mystical marriage with the Goddess of the World, a composite of mother, sister, mistress, and bride. She is a complex and powerful symbol of nourishment and protection as well as of death and destruction. According to Campbell, her complexity and importance to the hero comes from the fact that "woman, in the picture language of mythology represents the totality of what can be known. The hero is the one who comes to know."[17] Thus "the meeting with the goddess (who is incarnate in every woman) is the final test of the talent of the hero to win the boon of love which is life itself enjoyed as the encasement of eternity."[18] On the other hand, if the hero is a woman, she is fit, at this stage of the journey, to become the consort of an immortal. Another difficult challenge that arises

at this stage of the journey requires the hero to form a union with his father who, like the mother figure, is both powerful and complex. Like the mother, the father also represents both good and evil and, in addition, poses a threat to the son for mastery of the universe. Once the union takes place, however, "the agonies of the ordeal are readily borne; the world is no longer a vale of tears but a bliss-yielding, perpetual manifestation of the Presence."[19]

By the time he has reached the end of the perilous path of trials and victories characteristic of this stage of the journey, the hero comes to realize that his outer victories must be matched by inner ones, for it is only within himself that all of the opposing forces he has encountered finally can be reconciled. That final recognition makes clear that even the gods which seem outside are really projections from within. By conquering those outside forces, the hero becomes their equal, and his attainment of that state is suggested metaphorically in many mythologies by his deification.

**The Return with the Boon:** If he has been fortunate in his quest, the hero has received this ultimate boon of perfect illumination. He has reconciled all the opposites and has experienced the union of his individual consciousness with the universal will. Having died to his personal ego, he has been born again, thus reliving metaphorically the creation of the world and thereby becoming one with it. He realizes fully, as Campbell puts it, that "the essence of oneself and the essence of the world . . . are one."[20] At that point in his journey, the hero has overcome all the obstacles to self-knowledge and to knowledge of the universe and is ready to return home, to reintegrate himself with the society he had left to undergo his solitary adventures. When seen metaphorically, this return, Campbell says, "is indispensable to the continuous circulation of spiritual energy into the world, ... from the standpoint of the community, [it] is the justification of the long retreat, [but] the hero himself may find it the most difficult requirement of all."[21]

Campbell gives several reasons for this difficulty. First, the hero may not want to return. Once he has reached the goal of supreme enlightenment, the problems of the world he has left behind may no longer concern him. "There is danger that the bliss of this experience may annihilate all recollection of, interest in, or hope for, the sorrows of the world."[22] Second, he may not be able to make the return. If he refuses to submit to the initiatory tests and grasps the boon from powers that can destroy him, he may be weakened and deprived of the power he needs. Finally, if he does return, he may be misunderstood completely by those he has come back to help since they have not undergone his trials and, thus, cannot understand his hard-won wisdom. But whether or not he is successful in restoring society, the hero has "been reborn in identity with the whole meaning of the universe."[23] He is free to act and to move between the two worlds of the microcosm and the macrocosm because he has come to understand the relationship that exists between them. "The godly powers sought and dangerously won are revealed to have been within the heart of the hero all the time,"[24] and the hero has discovered that they are one:

> The two — the hero and his ultimate god, the seeker and the found—are thus understood as the outside and inside of a single self-mirrored mystery, which is identical with the mystery of the manifest world. The great deed of the supreme hero is to come to the knowledge of this unity in multiplicity and then to make it known.[25]

**Applications of the Monomyth:** The monomyth of the hero's journey, which Campbell distilled from the tremendously varied myths of the peoples of the world, can be seen as a pattern, not only in those ancient myths, but in the heroes of today's literary masterpieces on the screen, the stage, or in the pages of a book, and even in the lives of creative people in the arts and the sciences. All of these lives, actual and literary, can be more fully appreciated when, according to Campbell, one views them from the perspective of the hero's journey because we become aware in that way that the creative process itself follows the paradigm of the journey. The creative person must first answer the call to create and accept the challenge of the creative act. That challenge involves undergoing agonizing trials and overcoming difficult obstacles before the outer form of the finished product and the inner feelings of the creative person's idea can become integrated in the book, painting, theory, or composition that is the result of the creative process. Only through that product of the imagination, difficult as it is to create, can the insight of the creative person be communicated to the world. As Campbell knew and as we all must realize, that boon, in all its various forms, holds the key to our survival: Only the creative person who has gone beyond the "safe" ideas already known to his group can see the way to the resolution of today's problems and the creation of a "new" world based on a fresh interpretation of the universal values. It is such a creative thinker who has undergone his or her own hero's journey who would be able "to see through the fragments of time to the full power of original being."[26] Such seeing, Campbell described as a function of art, but he felt it was a function not always served by today's art.

For that reason, he was saddened somewhat by the loss of mythologized thinking in today's world, by the failure of many today to understand the inner meanings of even their own myths. But he did not despair entirely because he knew that the spiritual continued to exist in myths and works of art and could come alive at any time through a metaphoric reading of their images. Those external images retained their power to awaken the images within, thereby becoming transparent to transcendence and again giving us a sense of the sacredness of life and of ourselves. He felt assured that there always would be those who would answer the age-old call:

> Not all, even today, are of that supine sort that must have their life values given to them, cried at them from the pulpits and other mass media of the day. For there is, in fact, in quiet places,

a great deal of deep spiritual quest and finding now in progress in this world, outside the sanctified social centers, beyond their purview and control; in small groups, here and there, and more often, more typically, by ones and twos, there entering the forest at those points which they themselves have chosen, where they see it to be most dark, and there is no beaten way or path.[27]

## Joseph Campbell: The Hero As Scholar

One of Campbell's remarks, as he was being interviewed by Bill Moyers in the PBS series, "The Power of Myth," sets forth his approach to the scholarship that was his life's work.

> People say that what we're all seeking is a meaning for life." I don't think that's what we're really seeking. I think that what we're seeking is an experience of being alive, so that our life experiences on the purely physical plane will have resonances within our innermost being and reality, so that we actually feel the rapture of being alive. That's what it's all finally about, and that's what these clues help us to find within ourselves.[28]

These "clues," of course, were the mythic facts, themes, and images upon which his scholarship was founded, clues that revealed not only the inner reality of the peoples who created them, but the spiritual potential inherent in the human psyche. Campbell's scholarly work had as its primary aim the goal of allowing those myths that humanity created to continue to speak to the human spirit.

It is through this approach to his scholarship that Campbell's life and work must be understood, and it is in this way that his life and work can be seen to follow the same mythic pattern he himself delineated in *The Hero with a Thousand Faces*: the pattern of separation from the world, penetration to a source of spiritual power, and a life-enhancing return, the pattern that all creative lives ultimately follow. Later, in a discussion of the various ways in which the hero's journey might be undertaken, he said of himself, "I prefer the gradual path — the way of study. My own initiation into the mythical depths of the unconscious has been through the mind, through the books that surround me in this library."[29]

That is, of course, the way of the scholar, a way Campbell embarked upon early in life. Fascinated by Indians as a young boy, he had soon read all the children's books on the subject in the new public library near his home, and at the age of ten or so started to read, of all things, the annual reports of the Bureau of Ethnology in which the well-known anthropologists of the day detailed the lifeways of the Indian tribes. In them he "began noticing great parallels between the Indian myths and his Bible stories [of his Catholic upbringing] about virgin births, resurrection, floods, and creations."[30] Needless to say, few ten-year-olds do that kind of reading, and not many readers of those annual reports, of any age, notice the parallels that struck Campbell so strongly. His life's work had clearly begun, although he did not yet know it. The essence of that long campaign of work, which was to continue for three quarters of a century, already was apparent. He was not reading merely about Indians; in his mind he was one — he already had announced to his startled grandmother when he was five that he had Indian blood in him — but he was then, and always remained, an Indian while continuing to be himself. Thus he was enabled to experience fully, through reading and study, the inner, mythic reality of human beings very different in background and circumstance from himself.

His formal preparation for the scholarship that was to be his life's work began with the study of cultural history at Columbia University and continued with two postgraduate years of studying the Arthurian romance, one year at Columbia and one at the University of Paris. Then he abandoned that formal study, moved to the University of Munich and plunged into the study of Sanskrit and Eastern thought while simultaneously devouring the novels of Thomas Mann and James Joyce and the works of Oswald Spengler and Leo Frobenius to which he had first been exposed in Europe. These generated within him what was to be a life-long excitement. At the end of his life, as he was working on the vast compendium of his knowledge, the *Historical Atlas of World Mythology*, projected to be four large volumes, and simultaneously on the comparatively miniscule *The Inner Reaches of Outer Space: Metaphor as Myth and as Religion*, which would contain the very essence of his thought, he was using his spare time to brush up on his Sanskrit and Japanese. The excitement engendered in those early years in Europe never left him.

Returning to the United States during the Great Depression when there were no jobs to be had, he "went to the woods," as he put it, spending five years reading. But it was not casual reading; it was more in the nature of research. And, in fact, it was the research on which his long career as a scholar was most fundamentally based. Knowing how Campbell read makes this clear. As he read a book, he took detailed notes on its contents, and when he had finished the book, he prepared a one-page summary of those notes, placing the notes in a file folder with the summary page on top. By the end of his life, he had a number of filing cabinets filled with such folders, but the ultimate "filing cabinet" was his mind. This painstaking, disciplined reading fixed the information in his mind and enabled him to develop an understanding of large amounts of information that otherwise would have been impossible. As any conversation with him revealed to those who knew him, and as the interviews with Bill Moyers made clear to a great number of people, Campbell had a vast amount of information at his command, and he understood what he knew. There was never any fumbling; that was the result of the discipline reinforced so strongly during those five years of reading in solitude, a solitude from which he emerged to begin his career as a teacher-scholar that was to last until the very end of his life.

The pattern of Campbell's hero's journey is apparent.

First, *Separation* — leaving home for Europe; leaving the security of directed postgraduate study for his own intellectual interests; leaving the communal scholarly life for the solitude of the woods.

Then, *Penetration to a source of power* — the five years of solitude in the woods, a time of communion, through books, with those he called his great teachers: the primitive myths, Hinduism, Spengler, Frobenius, Jung, Mann, and perhaps most of all, Joyce, who, Campbell once said, "had been a Catholic [as he himself had been] and found a way out without losing his symbols,"[31] as Campbell himself was to do through scholarship, the way of study.

Finally, *A life-enhancing return* — the emergence from the woods to a life of teaching, scholarship, and writing through which he shared with countless numbers of people the boon he discovered through the works of those great teachers.

That boon of knowledge was to be shared with the world in a number of ways, most directly, perhaps in the books and articles he wrote. The first to enunciate clearly what were always to be his two major themes — the hero's journey and the metaphoric nature of myth — was *The Hero with a Thousand Faces*, published in 1949. Significantly, two books testifying to the diversity of his interests came before that one. The first, *Where the Two Came to Their Father: A Navaho War Ceremonial*, written with Maud Oakes and Jeff King, tied the American Indian mythological material that had fascinated him since his youth to the mythologies of other cultures, especially those of India. The second, *A Skeleton Key to Finnegans Wake*, written with Henry Morton Robinson, presented a detailed analysis of James Joyce's complex and fascinating last novel. During that same period he was editing for publication in four important works the notes left at the untimely death of the great Indologist Heinrich Zimmer, a man Campbell often described as his great friend and teacher, the first person he knew who considered myths as metaphoric of life-enhancing inner possibilities.

The diversity of his scholarly interests during this early period was to continue as he later edited the *The Portable Arabian Nights* and *The Portable Jung* for the Viking Press, as well as the six volumes of the Jungian *Papers from the Eranos Yearbooks* and a collection of essays entitled *Myths, Dreams, and Religion*. Meanwhile, he was writing his own books: the four volumes of *The Masks of God*; two volumes of collected essays: *The Flight of the Wild Gander* and *Myths to Live By*, and *The Mythic Image*. Finally, in the last four years of his life, as capstones to that long career, came *The Inner Reaches of Outer Space: Metaphor as Myth and as Religion*, containing, in small compass, the very essence of his thought; and the first two volumes of the vast four-volume *Historical Atlas of World Mythology, The Way of the Animal Powers* and *The Way of the Seeded Earth*, an encyclopedic compendium of his knowledge. The titles alone of these works suggest both the diversity and the continuity of Campbell's interests as they focused again and again on the writers and concerns that had fascinated him in those early years in Europe.

And they suggest as well his constant awareness of the importance of inner reality: of the identity of the images of dream and myth, of the identity of the world of the gods and the world we enter nightly in sleep, of the similarly metaphoric nature of the images to be found in both, images whose meaning must therefore be seen as metaphoric of the mystery-shrouded ground of being that projects us all. That ability to understand and identify with the inner realities of all of the peoples of the world, as revealed to us in their myths, is the boon that Joseph Campbell, the scholar as hero, has brought back to the world. Rather than a body of information regarding the mythologies of the world (although he surely gathered such a body over the course of his writing career) or a set of theories regarding the nature and development of myth (although the theories he advanced are an invaluable aid to the student of myth), his true legacy resides in his awareness of the essential mystery at the heart of mythic thought, the mystery within which the meaning of human life is enclosed.

Campbell strongly felt that we must not merely learn from him, or anyone else, what the myths have to teach. Rather, we must each set out on our own inward hero's journey with those myths as our guides, conquer our own dragons, penetrate to a source of power for ourselves, and return, as he did, with the boon of understanding. When asked, as he often was, how a person might do this, he generally responded, "Where is your deepest happiness, your innermost bliss? Find that within yourself and follow it!" Mythology, he knew, was crucial in that respect.

> Mythology is poetry, it is metaphorical. It has been well said that mythology is the penultimate truth — penultimate because the ultimate cannot be put into words. It is beyond words, beyond images, beyond that bounding rim of the Buddhist Wheel of Becoming. Mythology pitches the mind beyond that rim, to what can be known but not told. So this is the penultimate truth.
>
> It is important to live life with the experience, and therefore the knowledge, of its mystery and of your own mystery. This gives life a new radiance, a new harmony, a new splendor. Thinking in mythological terms helps to put you in accord with the inevitables of this vale of tears. You learn to recognize the positive values in what appear to be the negative moments and aspects of your life. The big question is whether you are going to be able to say a hearty yes to your adventure, ... the adventure of the hero — the adventure of being alive.[32]

Joseph Campbell clearly said that hearty yes to his own adventure and allowed humanity's myths to provide the guideposts along the way as he traveled in his own life, the way of the scholar, as he sought the enlightenment that he finally would return to the world in his writings and lectures.

## ASSIGNMENTS FOR STUDY, WRITING, AND ANALYSIS

1. Consider the stages of the hero's journey. Do you know someone whose life seems to have followed these stages? To what extent has your own life reflected these stages? Have you ever experienced a sense of destiny about some important quest you feel you must make? In what areas of your own life have you moved away from society to embark on an unchartered path?

2. To what extent does the idea you formerly had of how mythology functions compare with the four functions of mythology described by Campbell? In your own experience with mythology, which of the functions have been important? Rank the functions in order of your evaluation of their importance. What are some of the myths that you can identify in our society and what functions do they serve?

3. Discuss the meaning of metaphor and write a paper to demonstrate how the concept of metaphor relates to the power of mythology.

4. Consider a major myth or fairy tale that you know. Show how it can be interpreted metaphorically and made relevant to your own life today. What does it say about the human condition?

5. Tell a story that uses external reality to express an inner experience and then analyze its metaphor.

6. Explain why you think that interpreting the Virgin Birth or the Promised Land metaphorically adds to or detracts from the basic concept involved.

7. What conclusions can you come to about the life of a scholar after reviewing the brief biography of Joseph Campbell in this unit and viewing the television program "The Hero's Journey?" Think about the discipline, the background, and the dedication required to accomplish the kind of work that Campbell has done.

## FURTHER ASSIGNMENTS FOR WRITING AND REFLECTION

1. Analyze a great novel or film using the paradigm of the hero's journey as the focus of your interpretation. To what extent does the hero of the novel or film experience the stages of the hero as described in this unit? Is there another character who refuses the call to adventure?

2. In what works with which you are familiar is there a search for the father, a symbolic death, and rebirth? Discuss why these are essential in order for the hero to return with the boon. If you have studied Melville's *Moby Dick* or Homer's *Odyssey*, you might consider them in this regard.

3.  From the background you have received in this unit, ana-
    lyze the following quotation from Campbell's work, *The
    Flight of the Wild Gander*: "Mythology is misread then as
    direct history or science, symbol becomes fact, metaphor
    dogma, and the quarrels of the sects arise, each mistaking
    its own symbolic signs for the ultimate reality — the local
    vehicle for its timeless, ineffable tenor."[33] "Vehicle" here
    means the statement made by the metaphor, while "tenor"
    refers to its meaning.

4.  Consider the implications of looking at religious belief as
    myth and therefore, as metaphor. Analyze the story of
    Joseph in Genesis 28, the story of Christ from birth to
    crucifixion, the Book of Job, the Garden of Eden, etc. To
    what extent does the symbol open up by being analyzed as
    a metaphor? Does it enhance or detract from the spiritual
    essence of the concepts involved in the stories?

## ENDNOTES

[1] Joseph Campbell, *The Power of Myth* with Bill Moyers, ed. Betty Sue Flowers (New York: Doubleday, 1988) 56–57.

[2] Joseph Campbell, *The Inner Reaches of Outer Space: Metaphor as Myth and as Religion* (New York: Alfred van der Marck Editions, 1986) 21.

[3] Roberta H. Markman, "The Fairy Tale: An Introduction to Literature and the Creative Process," *College English* January 1983: 33.

[4] Campbell, *Power of Myth* 56–57.

[5] Campbell, *Inner Reaches* 21.

[6] Joseph Campbell, *The Masks of God: Creative Mythology* (New York: The Viking Press, 1968) 4.

[7] Campbell, *The Masks of God* 4–5.

[8] Campbell, *The Masks of God* 5.

[9] Joseph Campbell, "Mythological Themes in Creative Literature and Art," *Myths, Dreams, and Religion* ed. Joseph Campbell (New York: E. P. Dutton & Co., Inc., 1970) 141.

[10] Joseph Campbell, *The Way of the Animal Powers*, vol. I of *Historical Atlas of World Mythology* (New York: Alfred van der Marck Editions, 1983) 9.

[11] Campbell, *Creative Mythology* 6

[12] It should be noted at this point that although Campbell generally uses the masculine pronoun "he," in his discussion of the mythological hero's who undergo the hero's journey, a usage which we follow in this section for clarity in moving back and forth between his and our writing, his work generally makes clear the fact that he does not see the role of the hero as limited to men. His use of the masculine pronoun stems from customary usage and the fact that the myths generally, though certainly not always, cast males in the hero's role. As Campbell knew, however, this should not be seen as normative, and the reader should understand "he or she" wherever "he" is used in this way.

[13] Joseph Campbell, *The Hero with a Thousand Faces* (Cleveland: World Publishing Co., 1956 [originally published 1949]) 19–20.

[14] Campbell, *The Hero* 91.

[15] Campbell, *The Hero* 91.

[16] Campbell, *The Hero* 36.

[17] Campbell, *The Hero* 116.

[18] Campbell, *The Hero* 118.

[19] Campbell, *The Hero* 148.

[20] Campbell, *The Hero* 386.

[21] Campbell, *The Hero* 36.

[22] Campbell, *The Hero* 36.

[23] Campbell, *The Hero* 386.

[24] Campbell, *The Hero* 39.

[25] Campbell, *The Hero* 40.

[26] Campbell, *The Power of Myth* 228.

[27] Joseph Campbell, *The Flight of the Wild Gander* (New York: The Viking Press, 1969) 226.

[28] Campbell, *The Power of Myth* 3.

[29] Sam Keen, "Man and Myth: A Conversation with Joseph Campbell," *Psychology Today* July 1971: 37.

[30] Donald Newlove, "The Professor with a Thousand Faces," *Esquire* September 1977: 102.

[31] *Newlove* 132.

[32] Campbell, *The Power of Myth* 163.

[33] Campbell, *The Flight* 73.

## UNIT BIBLIOGRAPHY

### The Major Works of Joseph Campbell

*Where the Two Came to Their Father: A Navaho War Ceremonial*. Given by Jeff King, text and paintings recorded by Maud Oakes, commentary by Joseph Campbell. Bollingen Series, I. First edition: Richmond, Va.: Bollingen Series, Old Dominion Foundation, 1943; second edition: Princeton, N.J.: Princeton University Press, 1969. Campbell's commentary, indicative of what was to come in his career as a writer and scholar, focuses on the points of comparison between the Navaho myth and other myths of the world. He discusses this material in Unit 2 of this television course.

Campbell, Joseph. *The Flight of the Wild Gander: Explorations in the Mythological Dimension*. New York: The Viking Press, 1969. This book consists of a series of chapters that were originally published as separate essays over a 24-year period. In these essays, Campbell sought to interpret what he thought of as the "mystery of mythology."

———. *The Hero with a Thousand Faces*. Bollingen Series, XVII. New York: Bollingen Foundation, 1949; reprinted in various editions. Campbell's first major, sustained work, and still probably his most widely read book, *Hero* delineates the paradigm of the hero's journey through a wealth of examples from the world's mythologies.

———. *The Inner Reaches of Outer Space: Metaphor as Myth and as Religion*. New York: Alfred van der Marck Editions, 1986. Deals centrally with the role of metaphor in the understanding of mythology and provides a view of the essence of Campbell's approach to the study of mythology.

———. *The Masks of God: Creative Mythology*. New York: The Viking Press, 1968. Examines modern culture and its development from the Middle Ages in terms of the Human potential of creating new myths.

———. *The Masks of God: Occidental Mythology*. New York: The Viking Press, 1964. Examines the mythologies of the West–of Greece and Rome, the Levant, and Christian Europe.

————. *The Masks of God: Oriental Mythology*. New york: The Viking Press, 1962. Examines the mythologies of the Orient as they developed into the religions of Egypt, India, China, and Japan.

————. *The Masks of God: Primitive Mythology*. New York: The Viking Press, 1959. Examines the roots of mythology in human biology and evolution, and the beginnings of mythology in preshistoric human development.

————. *The Mythic Image*. Bollingen Series, Princeton, N.J.: Princeton University Press, 1974. A handsomely illustrated book, especially in the hardcover edition, that documents Campbells idea that "imagery, especially the imagery of dreams, is the basis of mythology" and provides a psychological reading of myths through the discipline of Kundalini Yoga.

————. *Myths to Live By*. New York: The Viking Press, 1972. A series of essays growing from lectures given by Campbell at the Cooper Union Forum that trace the mythological development of humanity. They focus particularly on the ways in which myths meet enduring human psychological needs.

————. *The Way of the Animal Powers*. vol. 1 of *Historical Atlas of World Mythology*. New York: Alfred van der Marck Editions, 1983; republished in two parts in 1988 by Harper and Row. Traces the development in time and space from the Paleolithic, one of the earliest mythologies of the hunting and gathering peoples of the world as they are manifested in narratives and images.

————. *The Way of the Seeded Earth*. vol. 2 of *Historical Atlas of World Mythology*. New York: Harper and Row, 1988–1989; to be published in three seperate parts. Continues the Historical Atlas, covering the mythologies of the planting peoples who flourished before the advent of civilization and of some contemporary planting cultures.

Campbell, Joseph and Henry Morton Robinson. *A Skeleton Key to Finnegans Wake*. New York: The Viking Press, 1944. Provides an outline of the basic action of Joyce's novel and explicates its complex allusions, images, and mythic themes.

# NOTES

**NOTES**

**NOTES**

PETER MARKMAN
ROBERTA H. MARKMAN

# In the Beginning:
*Origins of Man and Myth*

## UNIT STUDY PLAN

1. Read Unit 1 in the *Study Guide*.
2. Watch Program 1: "In the Beginning: Origins of Man and Myth."
3. In your course notebook or journal, write a summary of Joseph Campbell's interpretation of the earliest forms of mythology in the television program. As soon as you have finished watching the program, make a note of points that may be unclear, as well as your own reactions and observations.
4. Read the selections for this unit in the *Anthology of Readings*. These selections include excerpts from works by Mircea Eliade and Joseph Campbell.
5. After reading the selections, comment on what you have read in your notebook.
6. Complete assignments at the end of this unit as specified by your instructor.

## POINTS TO WATCH FOR IN THE TELEVISION PROGRAM

*This television program was delivered as a lecture by Joseph Campbell in Santa Fe, New Mexico, in 1982.*

1. Notice the relationship between Jane Goodall's experiments with chimpanzees and Campbell's conclusions about the human condition.
2. Pay attention to the distinctions that Campbell makes between male and female symbolic values.
3. Be aware of the progression of the development of human beings through the earliest periods of civilization and the various changes manifested in that progression.
4. Consider the significance of the early burials and the presence of the cave bear skulls and shrines as they are indicative of the beginning of ritual. Note Campbell's important observation that the art in the caves is stylized and abstract rather than realistic.
5. Notice how Campbell substantiates his claim that the caves and the cathedral are in the category of sacred ground, a magic realm.
6. Consider what Campbell says about the dualities of male-female, good-evil, ignorance-illumination, and the relationship these have to mythology.

## POINTS TO LOOK FOR IN THE *ANTHOLOGY OF READINGS*

1. Notice how Mircea Eliade builds his essay from *Patterns in Comparative Religion* on what he identifies as the pattern associated with lunar symbolism, "moon-rain-fertility-woman-serpent-death-periodic-regeneration." Note his contention that these items, like all symbols, are meaningful only as parts of the pattern in which they exist.
2. Notice Campbell's descriptions of the four functions of mythology in the selection from *The Way of the Animal Powers*, that has been discussed in the Introductory Unit. Pay attention to the way he establishes the historical and geographical factors involved in the rise and diffusion of specific myths and mythological systems.
3. In the selection from Campbell's *Myths to Live By*, note the changes he identifies in the mythological thinking of different cultures, as well as the particular symbolic associations, with the bear, fire, and woman that have been made in those cultures. Notice also his explanation of how the environment bears on the mythological thought of the culture.

## UNIT GLOSSARY

You will note that in this Unit and those following we will use B.C.E. (before the common era) and C.E. (of the common era) in place of the commonly used B.C. (before Christ) and A.D. (*anno Domini*, in the year of the Lord) since much of the discussion relates to cross-cultural phenomena.

**Desacralized**: Without spiritual or sacred implications.

**Iconography**: The representation of religious or legendary objects by conventional images and symbols.

**Liminal**: Related to the threshold between two states of being.

**Matriarchy**: A social organization marked by the supremacy of the mother in the clan or family, the legal dependence of husbands or children, and the reckoning of descent and inheritance through the female line.

**Neophyte**: A new convert involved in a ritual experience.

**Paleolithic**: A period of the prehistoric era known as the Stone Age. Historians have divided the prehistoric times into the Stone, Bronze, and Iron Ages. The Stone Age was further divided into Paleolithic, Mesolithic, and Neolithic on the basis of the kind of hunting done and the types of artifacts used.

**Patriarchy**: A social organization marked by the supremacy of the father in the clan or family, the legal dependence of wives or children, and the reckoning of descent and inheritance through the male line.

**Shamanism:** A religious phenomenon, most clearly characteristic of Siberia and Central Asia, in which a religious figure or medicine man called a shaman, moved through a trance into the supernatural for the purpose of healing or resolving the problems of his or her people.

## UNIT PREVIEW

In this unit you will be introduced to some of the basic concepts in the study of mythology and to the periods that mark the beginning of humanity's mythic consciousness.

**The Temple Caves of the Paleolithic**: Many mythic meanings are discernible in the paintings of these caves, such as the concept of a divine essence, the beginnings of initiatory rituals, and the sense of the mystery-dimension of human residence in the universe.

**Shamanism**: The role of the shaman is that of a religious specialist who derives his or her power directly from the supernatural; the shaman is able to (and needed to) bridge the gap between the mundane lives of the people and the mysteries of the invisible world.

**Initiation**: The stages of initiation take neophytes from their existing social role through a precarious passage or period of liminality to a final reintegration into the society in which they will play a new role.

**Lunar and Solar Symbolism**: The characteristics that are identified with the lunar and solar systems become the symbols that help to determine the implications of masculine and feminine principles, basic ingredients in the study of mythology.

## UNIT ESSAY

### The Well of the Past

The "Prelude" to Thomas Mann's tetralogy *Joseph and His Brothers* begins: "Very deep is the well of the past. Should we not call it bottomless? Bottomless indeed, if—and perhaps only if—the past we mean is the past merely of the life of mankind. For the deeper we sound, the further down into the lower world of the past we probe and press, the more do we find that the earliest foundations of humanity, its history and culture, reveal themselves unfathomable."[1] Those earliest foundations that we always are tempted to seek do, indeed, seem unfathomable. Campbell remarks, in referring to Mann's "Prelude," that even the earliest civilizations, of which we have only scant knowledge, "are but the foreground of the long backward reach of the prehistory of our race—there rest the centuries, millenniums, even the centuries of millenniums of primitive man, the mighty hunter, the more primitive root and bug collector, back for more than half a million years. And there is a third depth, even deeper and darker below that—below the ultimate horizon of humanity. For we shall find the ritual dance among the birds, the fish, the apes, and the bees."[2] The beginnings of the mythic impulse seem impossible to find. From Campbell's point of view, that impulse originated far back in the evolutionary chain, much farther down in the "well of the past" than our instruments of vision, our ways of study can enable us to see.

### The Temple Caves of the Paleolithic

The burials and cave bear shrines of the Middle Paleolithic (130,000–40,000 years ago) to which Campbell refers in the television program for this unit provide the earliest evidence of ritual by human beings. They give us the first hint of the mythic thought that presumably accompanied such ritual, but it is not until the creation of the great painted temple caves of the Upper Paleolithic (40,000–10,000 years ago) that we can begin to discern, however dimly, the outlines of that early mythic thought. Campbell describes them in the following way:

> The idea of a temple as distinguished from a chapel or shrine—namely, of an enclosed area in which all the forms are of vision—was conceived and first realized in the great painted caves of southwestern France and northern Spain, and most marvelously in those termed by the Abbé Breuil the "Six Giants": Altamira, Font-de-Gaume, Les Combarelles, Lascaux, Les Trois Frères, and Niaux. As in Chartres Cathedral the mystery of the hidden history of the universe is revealed through the imagery of an anthropomorphic pantheon, so here, in these temple caves, the same mystery is made known through animal forms that are at once in movement and at rest. These forms are magical: midway, as it were, between the living species of the hunting plains and the universal ground of night, out of which the animals come, back into which they return, and which is the very substance of these caves.[3]

That revelation of mystery is the first function of a mythic narrative or a mythic image, as you will remember from the Introductory Unit. In this case, a sequence of carefully arranged mythic images constitutes what may have been something like a narrative text, but unfortunately it is one that we cannot yet "read" in any detail.

Through reading backward from the myths and tales of recent hunting cultures, however, Campbell suggests that certain meanings seem discernible in the paintings of the caves:

> Among these [meanings] we may number that of the animals killed as being willing victims, that of the ceremonies of their invocation as representing a mystic covenant between the animal world and the human, and that of song and dance as being the vehicles of the magical force of such ceremonies; further, the concept of each of the animal world as a kind of multiplied individual, having as its seed or essential monad a semi-human, semi-animal magically potent Master Animal; and the idea related to this, of there being no such thing as death, material bodies being merely costumes put on by otherwise invisible monadic entities, which can pass back and forth from an invisible other world into this, as though through an intangible wall.[4]

The paintings reveal, through metaphor, the Paleolithic conception of a mythic ground of being, thus fulfilling what Campbell considers the first function of a mythology.

But Campbell and others believe that those great painted caves served another mythic function as well, playing an important role in the initiatory ritual through which boys became men, assuming their social role as hunters and beginning their spiritual lives. It was in these caves that the mysteries of life were revealed to them, and that they first began to develop their own relationship to the realm of mystery that provided life and food but required death as the price of creating and sustaining life. Campbell, in the television program for his unit, quotes Kühn's description of his visit to the great cave of Les Trois Frères in 1926, and that description suggests why one might see the caves as sites of initiatory ritual. First going through a number of galleries, Kühn's party finally came to

> a very low tunnel. We placed our lamp on the ground and pushed it into the hole. . . . The tunnel is not much broader than my shoulders, nor higher. I can hear the others before me groaning and see how very slowly their lamps push on. With our arms pressed close to our sides we wriggle forward on our stomachs, like snakes. The passage, in places, is hardly a foot high, so that you have to lay your face right on the earth. I felt as though I were creeping through a coffin. You cannot lift your head; you cannot breathe. . . . And so, yard by yard, one struggles on: some forty-odd yards in all. Nobody talks. The lamps are inched along and we push after. I hear the others groaning, my own heart is pounding, and it is difficult to breathe. It is terrible to have the roof so close to one's head. And it is very hard: I bump it: time and again. Will this thing never end? Then, suddenly, we are through. . . . It is like a redemption.[5]

As such a description makes graphically clear, the act of entering the sacred ground of the cave's great painted hall would have provided those boys of Paleolithic times with a very real sense of a death like separation from the everyday world of their childhood. It also might have recalled the sensation of birth as they emerged from the dark, constricted tunnel into the light and space of the great sanctuary. They were being prepared for the literally awe-inspiring scene that suddenly would appear before them as they entered into the dim, torch-lit hall:

> The hall in which we are now standing is gigantic. . . . From top to bottom a whole wall is covered with engravings. The surface has been worked with tools of stone, and there we see marshalled the beasts that lived at that time in southern France: the mammoth, rhinoceros, bison, wild horse, bear, wild ass, reindeer, wolverine, musk ox; also, the smaller animals appear: snowy owls, hares, and fish. And one sees darts everywhere, flying at the game. . . . Truly a picture of the hunt; the picture of the magic of the hunt.[6]

As Kühn's description suggests, the art of the caves immersed the young initiates into the world of the hunt, the world in which they were destined to live as adults. In this world, they would play the time-honored role of killing the animals that offered themselves as "willing victims" according to the plan of the gods for the maintenance of the life of the human community. The ritual accompanying the hunt would guarantee the rebirth of the animals and the continuance of the cycle of life and rebirth through which both animal and human life continually would be created and sustained. The mystery at the heart of that cycle was both the real subject of these paintings and the focus of the initiation ritual.

That initiation was not only to the neophyte's future social role as hunter. As Mircea Eliade indicates, initiation, above all, reveals the sacred.

> And, for the primitive world, the sacred means not only everything that we now understand by religion, but also the whole body of the tribe's mythological and cultural traditions. . . . Through initiation, the candidate passes beyond the natural mode—the mode of the child—and gains access to the cultural mode; that is, he is introduced to spiritual values. From a certain point of view it could almost be said that, for the primitive world, it is through initiation that men attain the status of human beings; before initiation, they do not fully share in the human condition precisely because they do not yet have access to the religious life.[7]

Thus these young men were being initiated into their mythology on a level that they had not realized before. The mystery at the heart of life in the world, and at the heart of their own being, was revealed to them through these teeming herds of supernatural beasts decorating the walls of the great caves. These animal messengers testified to the fluidity of the movement of the life force from the inner, mysterious reaches of the spirit, characterized by the darkness of the cave, to the outer world of nature, the everyday world of light and the sun, of the hunt and of life in the human community. These young men were here to be made aware of the continuity between those two worlds. They were to learn that the natural world is but a manifestation of the only true reality, that of spirit, and that this true reality is to be found deep in the darkness of the cave, deep in the dreams of the night, deep in the trance of the shaman.

## Shamanism[8]

In that large hall of the cave at Les Trois Frères,

some 15 feet above the level of the floor, in a craggy apse—watching, peering at the visitor with penetrating eyes, is the now famous "Sorcerer of Trois Frères." He is poised in profile in a dancing movement. . . . but the antlered head is turned to face the room. The pricked ears are those of a stag; the round eyes suggest an owl; the full beard descending to the deep animal chest is that of a man, as are likewise the dancing legs; the apparition has the bushy tail of a wolf or wild horse, and the position of the prominent sexual organ, placed beneath the tail, is that of the feline species—perhaps a lion. The hands are the paws of a bear. The figure is two and a half feet high, fifteen inches across. "An eerie, thrilling picture," wrote Professor Kühn. Moreover, it is the only picture in the whole sanctuary bearing paint—black paint—which gives it an accent stronger than all the rest.[9]

"But who or what is this man—if man he is?"[10] asks Campbell. The answer to that question has been debated for a long time. Is the figure the representation of a god, an Animal Master who presides over the depicted beasts and who offers the flesh of their real counterparts on the plains to the hunter in return for ritual obeisance? Or does the figure represent a costumed shaman or medicine man who, through ritual and trance, is able to enter the darkness of the world of the spirit inhabited by these fabulous beasts? We can never know for certain the answer to that question, but perhaps, as Campbell suggests, the precise answer is not as important as our realization that this figure, whether god or man, surely acts as a link, a mediator between the two worlds.

If we were to see him as a god, he would fit precisely the description of a certain category of the supernatural described by the anthropologist Edmund Leach. Interestingly, Leach's approach is based on a somewhat different set of assumptions than those of Campbell.

Religious life is everywhere tied in with the discrimination between living and dead. Logically, *life* is simply the binary anti thesis of *death*; the two concepts are the opposite sides of the same penny; we cannot have either without the other. But religion always tries to separate the two. To do this it creates a hypothetical "other world" which is the antithesis of "this world." In this world life and death are inseparable; in the other world they are separate. This world is inhabited by imperfect mortal men; the other world is inhabited by immortal nonmen (gods). The category god is thus constructed as the binary antithesis of man. But this is inconvenient. A remote god in another world may be logically sensible, but it is emotionally unsatisfying. To be useful, gods must be near at hand, so religion sets about reconstructing a continuum between this world and the other world. But note how it is done. The gap between the two logically distinct catego-

ries, this world/other world is filled in with tabooed ambiguity. The gap is bridged with supernatural beings of a highly ambiguous kind—incarnate deities, virgin mothers, supernatural monsters which are half man/half beast. These marginal, ambiguous creatures are specifically credited with the power of mediating between gods and men. They are the objects of the most intense taboos, more sacred than the gods themselves. In an objective sense, as distinct from theoretical theology, it is the Virgin Mary, human mother of God, who is the principal object of devotion in the Catholic church.[11]

Although Leach takes the view of the anthropologist concentrating on the "logical" development of spiritual thought as opposed to Campbell's more psychological view, there is a striking concurrence between Leach's views and Campbell's in terms of the "supernatural monster" that is the Sorcerer of Les Trois Frères. For both, that figure's essential function is mediation between the other world of the spirit and this world of daily reality, and both regard that function as highly important to the people who created the image. Both see that figure as essential to the explanation of the mystery of death, of the paradox that life feeds on death. But Leach regards such images of "supernatural monsters which are half man/half beast" as a species of gods, while Campbell finally concludes that the figure in the cave at Les Trois Frères is more likely a shaman. Perhaps it does not matter since the "god" Leach describes appears at the interface between spirit and matter, just as it is the function of the shaman to cross that same interface. At that point of transition—and the sacred space of the sanctuary in the great cave at Les Trois Frères provided just such a point—the features of man and god merge and the usual distinctions no longer hold.

Our knowledge of shamans and shamanism does not come from these caves, however. It is derived from ethnographic studies of the natives of Siberia and Central Asia. The term "shaman" is employed by anthropologists to describe religious specialists of the tribal peoples of that area who derive their power directly from an experience of the supernatural. This experience of the supernatural, gained through a period of intense psychological crisis, sets the shaman apart from the priest who functions within the context of an institutionalized religious organization and whose power derives from and is expressive of his place within that organization. The naturally individualistic shaman is, in Campbell's view, the perfect spiritual mediator for nomadic hunters. The priest, on the other hand, more adequately fits the requirements of the settled village life of agriculturalists. This difference will be discussed in greater depth Unit 3.

In his definitive study of shamanism, Mircea Eliade defines the term as it fits the Siberian and Central Asian practice as a "technique of ecstasy" since the shaman's "ecstatic experience is considered the religious experience par excellence." Through trance, the shaman "is believed to leave his body and ascend to the sky or descend to the underworld," the two planes of spirit enveloping the world of nature on the earth's surface.[12]

But as he notes, the term "shamanism" has been used to describe a similar kind of religious experience occurring throughout the world. Rather than a religion, shamanism, in this sense, would be described more precisely as a form of mysticism that exists "within a considerable number of religions." The person fitting the description of the shaman within those religions is "the great specialist in the human soul; he alone 'sees' it, for he knows its 'form' and its destiny."[13]

The ecstatic or mystical experience reveals to the shaman the reality of the hidden world of the spirit and, in this way, can be clearly related to the visions painted and engraved during the Paleolithic period on the walls deep within the great temple caves. As Campbell suggests in the television program for this unit, the initiatory ritual that probably took place within those caves opened to the awed youths a reality similar to that revealed in the individual shaman's ability to break through the normally impenetrable barriers that separate the planes of matter and spirit. The shaman's was an ecstatic personal experience with practical uses for his or her people, the hunting and gathering, nomadic peoples of the Paleolithic period and later times. As magician, diviner, or curer, he or she was uniquely capable of bridging the gap between the mundane lives of the people of the community and the mysteries of the invisible world that could give those lives purpose, direction, and meaning, and through which the ailments and problems of the individuals and the community could be resolved.

Perhaps the most fundamental assumption of shamanism holds that all phenomena in the world of nature are animated by a spiritual essence. In the shaman's world everything is alive, and all life is part of one mysterious unity by virtue of its derivation from the spiritual source of life—the life force. Each living being is merely a momentary manifestation of that eternal force. The commonality of the life force makes possible, within the shamanic context, the primordial capability of magical transformation from one form of life to another. Through this transformation, the shaman can explore the myriad dimensions of the material and psychological worlds, and through the concomitant liberation from the limitations of his own body, he can venture into the world of the spirit—the proper domain of his own spiritual essence.

A second assumption of shamanism follows directly from this first one. In the shamanistic universe, the soul or the individual spiritual essence, is separable from the body in certain senses or under certain conditions. The spirit can become autonomous and function free from the body. Thus, human beings are not necessarily limited to or by their physical existence; they are capable of moving equally well in each of the two equivalent worlds of which they are a part—that of nature and that of spirit. This equivalence of matter and spirit makes the common distinctions between dream and experience, this world and the afterworld, the sacred and the profane insignificant because the shaman demonstrates that the only true reality is spirit, albeit spirit temporarily garbed in the material

trappings of the world of nature. Just as the spirit of the shaman can transform itself into other forms of natural life, so it can leave the physical body entirely and "travel" unfettered in the spiritual realm. It is there, of course, that the shaman finds what is needed to cure the ailments and solve the problems of his or her people. This is one of the shaman's primary functions in a world that believes that the cause of everything in nature is to be found in the world of the spirit.

This belief in the separability of matter and spirit concurs with a third basic assumption, that the universe is essentially magical rather than bound by what we would call the laws of cause and effect as they operate in nature. Since material realities are the result of spiritual causes, in order to change material reality, the spiritual causes have to be found and addressed through ritual and shamanic visionary activity. The magical universe consists of two levels of spiritual reality, one above and one below the earthly plane. The three levels are connected by a central axis, often represented by a world tree, a "soul ladder," or stairway that links the planes of spirit and matter and provides the pathway for the shaman's spiritual journeys.

These assumptions constitute the core of shamanism. They suggest the fundamentally spiritual nature of humanity. The shaman is the mediator between the visible and the unseen worlds, the point of contact between natural and supernatural forces. Significant among the supernatural forces are the figures of the shaman's ancestors, the clear embodiment of death and the life after death. In linking the natural with the supernatural, the material with the immaterial, and life with death, the shaman establishes an inner metaphysical vision of the primordial wholeness of cosmic reality. Having left his or her body through a symbolic death, traversed both the realms of life and death, and returned to tell the tale, the shaman comes back from his or her visionary experience, which closely resembles the paradigm of the hero's journey. (For a discussion of the hero's journey, see the Introductory Unit.) The shaman resumes his or her natural form in the material world in order to communicate that experience, and by sharing that vision of the world of the spirit with the community, assures their health and well-being.

## Initiation

Campbell believed that a people's mythology serves to conduct the individual in harmony through the stages of a normal life. Perhaps the most important of those stages involves the movement of the individual from youth to adulthood, from the stage of dependence on parents for survival, to independence, and ultimately to becoming a parent. This movement, generally referred to as initiation, links the ritual through which it is accomplished to the mythology of the culture, since the mythology contains the culture's idea of what it is to be an independent, mature human being. Myths describing the creation of man and woman, for example, are metaphorical descriptions of the nature of humanity as perceived by the culture. The use of these myths in initiatory ritual serves the pedagogical function of guiding the individual through the life the particular culture deems the proper human life ordained by the gods at the moment of creation. Therefore, creation may be seen, metaphorically, as occurring each time a new adult is "created" through the ritual of initiation.

Those rituals through which youths are initiated into their societies as full-fledged, autonomous members have been studied widely by scholars in a variety of disciplines. A large body of material regarding initiatory practices throughout history by now has been assembled. Recently, the work of one of the early theorists in this field, Arnold van Gennep (1873–1957), has been reemphasized in the work of the North American symbolic anthropologist Victor Turner, whose main subject of research and theoretical writing has been initiatory ritual. For Turner, van Gennep provided a theoretical framework for understanding that ritual.

In their most basic form, initiation rites involve three stages: separation from the existing social role; passage through a precarious time in which the initiate is no longer what he was, but is not yet what he will be; and final reintegration into society in his new role. In short, he has died as a child and has been reborn an adult. He is different from what he was, and in primitive societies especially, that difference is often physical as well as mental. As Campbell said in an interview with Bill Moyers: "In primal societies there are teeth knocked out, there are scarifications, there are circumcisions, there are all kinds of things done. So you don't have your little baby body anymore, you're something else entirely."[14]

The middle of the three stages, what Turner calls the liminal stage, is of particular interest in the study of mythology since it is during that stage of the ritual process that the myths are presented.

> Liminal entities are neither here nor there; they are betwixt and between the positions assigned and arrayed by law, custom, convention and ceremonial. As such, their ambiguous and indeterminate attributes are expressed by a rich variety of symbols in the many societies that ritualize social and cultural transitions. Thus, liminality is frequently likened to death, to being in the womb, to invisibility, to darkness, to bisexuality, to the wilderness, and to an eclipse of the sun or moon.[15]

This temporary existence in the "no-time" and "no-place" of the liminal state is necessary since only the temporary removal of initiates from their culture's everyday assumptions about the nature of reality will enable them to accept the deeper, more profound wisdom that reveals the basic structure and nature of the ultimately spiritual universe in which they exist.

That deep structure is revealed through the myths. As Eliade puts it,

> the experience of initiatory death and resurrection not only basically changes the neophyte's fundamental mode of being, but at the same time reveals to him the sacredness of human life and of the world, by revealing to him the great mystery, common to all religions, that men, with the cosmos, with all forms of life, are the creation of the Gods or of Superhuman Beings. This revelation is conveyed by the origin myths. Learning how things came into existence, the novice at the same time learns that he is the creation of Another, the result of such-and-such a primordial event, the consequence of a series of mythological occurrences, in short, of a sacred history.[16]

From Campbell's perspective, such a comment would only need to be qualified by the realization that in many, perhaps most, societies, the realization of the neophyte that he is the result of a sacred history is presented as metaphorical, as was discussed in the Introductory Unit. That is, the initiates are made to realize that they themselves are sacred; that they carry within themselves the essence of life and therefore they exist in a sacred manner, as life itself. They come to the realization that the world around them is not what it seemed to their youthful eyes before their initiation. That world they saw then was merely appearance, now they "see" beneath the surface to the true reality of the world of spirit. This is the world they have entered and in which they will live out their days before their own return to spirit through "the ultimate passage of the dark gate."[17]

That was the realization, no doubt, of the boys conducted into the liminal reality of the great sanctuary at Les Trois Frères so long ago, a realization that they were to share with all of the boys and girls who would come after them in the long march of human history. It is only recently in the industrialized societies of the modern world that such initiatory ritual has begun to disappear, a disappearance that is a part of the larger process of what Eliade has called the desacralization of modern life. He, Campbell, and many others have been concerned with the problems for this "brave, new world" that they see resulting from that desacralization. They have tried to understand how human beings will live as purely historical beings in that desacralized world. Perhaps, in Campbell's view, the symbols of mythology can be interpreted psychologically and in that way continue to support humanity in this new world. As Campbell says in the beginning of the television program for this unit, "Getting into harmony and tune with the universe, and staying there, is the simple function of mythology."

## Lunar and Solar Symbolism

One might well argue that a study of lunar and solar symbolism would provide a key to understanding all the major aspects of duality that one encounters in most mythological systems, particularly that of the male and female principles which, as we will see, have long been associated with those heavenly bodies. As Campbell says in the television program for this unit, the rock carving known today as the Venus of Laussel indicates that by the time it was carved, about 20,000 B.C.E., humanity already had recognized "counterparts between the celestial and earthly rhythms of life," particularly in connection with the moon. Similarly, in *The Masks of God: Primitive Mythology*, he points out that the lunar cycle has been in great part responsible for a "life-structuring relationship between the heavenly world and that of man. . . . It has been a force and presence even more powerful in the shaping of mythology than the sun, by which its light and its world of stars, night sounds, erotic moods, and the magic of dream, are daily quenched."[18] Eliade adds that "even in the Ice Age the meaning of the moon's phases and their magic powers were clearly known. We find the symbolism of spirals, snakes and lightning—all of them growing out of the notion of the moon as the measure of rhythmic change and fertility—in the Siberian cultures of the Ice Age" (*Anthology* 28).

But the solar cycle has been extremely important as well, and in some areas—Egypt, particularly, but also in Asia and in primitive Europe—what has been thought of as sun-worship attained sufficient importance to become a dominant force.[19] In fact, Campbell has shown that later among "the shaman-guided peoples of Siberia—the high deity of their pantheons is typically the Sun; and in the folk legends of those areas, as well as in those of the tribes of North America, the testing father, master of all the trials and terrors to which young heroes are subjected, is again the Sun. The Sun, then, is both the testing father and the model of the hunter's as also of the warrior's, given task. His solar rays are his darts and spears."[20]

As Campbell suggests in the television program for this unit, it is not enough to recognize that both lunar and solar cycles have been basic to the symbolism of mythological systems. One must be aware that it is only through their combination that true awareness can emerge. He shows in the television program that the mystic marriage in Greek mythology between the parents of Achilles, Thetis and Peleus, depicted on a red-figured urn from the fifth century B.C.E., involves the union of the lunar serpent power representing life and the solar lion power representing consciousness in the female, Thetis. The marriage initiates the man, Peleus, into this combined power representing the total energy of life. Through that initiation, Peleus dies to the limitations of his own limited ego and is reborn, through the female, to what Campbell calls "the knowledge of the transcendent, becoming transparent to transcendence." Thus, male and female, sun and moon, lion and serpent, conscious and unconscious awareness are joined in the metaphoric, mythic image.

In most mythological systems, lunar symbolism is associated with the biological stages of life in general, but even more particularly with the feminine principle. As Campbell has noted "there is actually a physical influence of the moon upon the earth and its creatures, its tides and our own interior tides, which has long been consciously recognized as well as subliminally experienced. The coincidence of the menstrual cycle with that of the moon is a physical actuality structuring human life and a curiosity that has been observed with wonder."[21]

While the sun always seems to be itself and never changing, "the moon, on the other hand, is a body which waxes, wanes and disappears, a body whose existence is subject to the universal law of becoming, of birth and death. The moon, like man, has a career involving tragedy, for its failing, like man's, ends in death. For three nights the starry sky is without a moon. But this 'death' is followed by a rebirth: the 'new moon.' The moon's going out, in 'death' is never final. . . . It is reborn of its own substance, in pursuance of its own destined career" (*Anthology* 28). In fact, while the moon appears inexhaustible in its own regeneration, it does go through the stages of death, whereas the sun passes through the underworld and emerges unchanged, not seeming to experience the condition of death. Thus, the moon is related to the rhythms of life and is connected to all the spheres of nature governed by the laws of recurring cycles such as those of the waters, rain, plant life, and fertility. For this reason, probably, many of the fertility gods are also deities of the moon, and the moon often is seen as comparable to animals, like the bear, that go through rhythmic life cycles and those, like the bull, whose horns resemble the shape of the crescent moon.

With such a strong affinity to the biological order of things, the moon, because it also is related to the laws of change, growth, and decline, seems closer to human life than the sun, which although also expressive of rebirth, does not manifest the phases of dying in quite the same way. It guides men's souls through the underworld and returns with them the next day at dawn, a return which is, therefore, also suggestive of resurrection, making its death seem more symbolic than biological. However, because the death of the moon comes after the physically apparent stages first of growth to the full moon and then decline to the point of the disappearance, or "death" of the moon, it can be seen as analogous to the seasons of the year and to the stages in the span of man's biological life. But that "death" is, of course, only temporary, as the moon regenerates itself during the time of its disappearance and returns on the fourth night to begin a new life cycle. That, in fact, has been a primary source of humanity's hope for immortality. As Campbell reminds us, "we celebrate the mystery of that mythological death and resurrection to this day, as a promise of our own eternity."[22]

## Masculine and Feminine Principles

In a discussion of myth as metaphor it is important to keep in mind the difference between masculine and feminine *principles* and masculine and feminine *roles*. In all cultures, the *roles* of men and women, to a great extent, have been determined and defined by society's economic, ethical, political, social, and spiritual beliefs, and to some extent by biology. Women, after all, bear children while men do not. Masculine and feminine *principles*, on the other hand, must be considered as energies within all of us, male and female, so that the union and synthesis of these principles, as suggested in the mystic marriage of Thetis and Peleus are essential for life to continue. The need for this union can be seen in the earliest folk myths that depict the world as created from a single, undifferentiated egg or a single figure. The unified "one" splits to become two. Similarly, Teiresias, the Greek seer capable of a profound understanding of the mystery of life, is both male and female, appearing first as masculine, then as feminine, and then again as masculine.

The strong association of fertility with the moon led to lunar-related rituals that would insure both the growth of plants and the passage of the soul through the land of the dead to be followed by rebirth. Such associations go a long way toward explaining why, when matriarchy was superseded by patriarchy in the course of human development, the moon came to be associated with the feminine principle and the sun with the masculine. Eliade reminds us, "there is no such thing as a symbol, emblem or power with only one kind of meaning. Everything hangs together, everything is connected, and makes up a cosmic whole" (*Anthology* 29). It should be clear then, for example, that the moon is not adored for itself "but in what it reveals of the sacred, that is, in the power centered in it, in the inexhaustible life and reality that it manifests" (*Anthology* 31).

All that is associated with the moon becomes part of its multiple levels of meaning and in turn contributes to the symbolism associated with the feminine principle. Because it receives its light from the sun, for example, it can be seen as "passive" and can be equated in that way with the passive nature of the feminine principle and the mystery or occult side of nature rather than with the sun, which is symbolically responsible for the active life of the manifest world. The moon's close association with those aspects of the night that suggest mystery (particularly the mystery of motherhood): dream and the unconscious, ambivalence, "becoming," and the imagination, also contributes to the mystique of moon symbolism just as "the mysterious (one might even say, magical) functioning of the female body in its menstrual cycle, in the ceasing of the cycle during the period of gestation, and in the agony of birth—and the appearance, then, of the new being; these, certainly, have made profound imprints on the mind."[23]

A striking and beautiful manifestation of the association of the feminine with the moon that Campbell discusses in the television program for this unit and that has been mentioned above can be seen as early as 20,000–18,000 B.C.E. in the carving called the Venus of Laussel. This striking female figure is portrayed with her left hand resting on her obviously pregnant womb and her right hand raised, bearing aloft the horn of the waxing moon marked with thirteen lines which, as Campbell remarks, "is the number of nights between the first crescent and the full moon." In his book, *The Way of the Animal Powers*, Campbell adds that "the left hand laid on the belly may

have been significant of the womb as the vessel of birth and rebirth, which in its monthly mystery is matched by the measures of the moon."[24] Examples of these connections abound in the world's mythologies especially in the innumerable myths in which the father is the sun and the mother is the moon. Campbell retells a particularly striking Blackfoot version, "Scarface," in *The Way of the Animal Powers*.[25] The same mythic association is made by the African Pygmies as the feast of the new moon is reserved exclusively for women, while the feast of the sun is celebrated exclusively by the men who are identified with the sun as are their javelins with its rays.[26] The light of the sun is similarly analogous in many mythologies to the light of conscious knowledge as it operates in the manifest daylight world. This solar symbolism often is associated with the male hero in his opposition to the father. Thus, heroes often become identified with the sun itself so that the sun comes to symbolize heroism and courage and therefore action, intellectuality, and willpower. By extension, this symbolic connection accounts for the gold crown's "symbolizing the secular power as well as spiritual authority of the character on whom it sits."[27]

Thus, it is completely understandable that the nineteenth-century German philosopher, Friedrich Nietzsche, in his *Birth of Tragedy*, gives the attributes of the feminine principle, such as awe and blissful ecstasy akin to the condition of drunkenness, to Dionysius, the Greek god of wine. According to Nietzsche, the "ecstasy of the Dionysian state, with its annihilation of the ordinary bounds of existence"[28] represents the joy of universal harmony. On the other hand, as one might expect, Nietzsche associates form and reason with the masculine Apollo.

Although the following listing of opposed characteristics is far from complete, it perhaps can serve to give a sense of the duality suggested in the myths and tales that make the relationship of masculine and feminine their concern. Since neither of the principles has meaning outside its relationship to the other, as principles they must be held in tension in the process of their interaction. The many myths concerned with the dynamics of their relationship repeatedly suggest the necessity of that integration in order for the creative process of life to continue. Both men and women, according to this view, must bring themselves "into harmony with the two astral rhythms," thereby "unifying the sun and the moon" in their own lives and bodies (*Anthology* 43). Such an inner integration of the masculine and feminine principles would result in the transcendence of which Campbell often speaks, truly making each man and woman "transparent to transcendence" and thereby making true human fulfillment possible through the unification of all of the human powers and potentials which might at first glance seem opposed.

| *Masculine* | *Feminine* |
|---|---|
| Sun | Moon |
| Apollonian | Dionysian |
| Intellect, reason | Feeling, soul, mystery |
| Movement, action | Being, passivity, in process of becoming |
| Outer form | Inner, intuition, impulse |
| Mind-related, logical | Earth-related, creative |

It must be pointed out that the division of these principles into two categories in no way should be seen as constituting a value judgment; both principles are essential to the ongoing creative process of an individual or a culture. Ideally, they must be integrated so that neither is dominant and they function in harmony. You only have to hear a musical composition whose form is intellectually perfect (the masculine principle) but which lacks feeling and a sense of mystery (the feminine principle) to know how dull and uncreative such a work can sound. On the other hand, a musical work embodying feeling but lacking an essential form can be impossible to relate to. The same need for a harmonization of the opposing principles can be seen symbolically in fairy tales. Often there is a great threat to the land that is, in effect, lacking the feminine principle. The prince must find and marry a princess to unite the masculine and feminine principles and restore harmony and productivity to the land. Male and female, sun and moon, intellect and emotion must work in harmony, both in the outer world of nature and in the inner world of humanity, for the creative process of life to continue.

## ASSIGNMENTS FOR STUDY, WRITING, AND ANALYSIS

1. Write a paper in which you analyze the difference between realistic and abstract expression in art, noting Campbell's emphasis on the latter. What effect does abstraction have in terms of universal versus specific implications?
2. Consider the implications of ritual and its importance in society. What rituals have you experienced and what has been their effect as to changing your perspective about the human condition or your own role in society?
3. Analyze the process of initiation. What experiences have you had in your life that you could consider initiatory? What effect have these experiences had on your life?
4. Campbell has said in several of his works that the artist is today's shaman. After reading the section on shamanism in this unit, explain how this might be so.
5. Discuss the difference between masculine and feminine *roles* and masculine and feminine *principles*. Illustrate your discussion by using some examples of each from your own experience.

6. After reading Edmund Leach's quotation on page 18, how would you describe the difference in the approaches of Campbell and the approaches of an anthropologist like Leach to the material they discuss? What could you say about the differences in their assumptions?

## FURTHER ASSIGNMENTS FOR WRITING AND REFLECTION

1. Read and research the book *Treasures of Prehistoric Art* by André Leroi-Gourhan (see Unit Bibliography, page 24) or another text recommended by your instructor, on the temple cave of Lascaux and describe how the mystery of the hidden history of the universe is revealed through the imagery that was found there.
2. Identify what figures or institutions in today's world serve the function of the shaman. To what extent is this role needed today?
3. Consider a fairy tale with which you are familiar, such as "Hansel and Gretel" or "Cinderella," in terms of masculine and feminine *principles* and show how their integration results in a "transcendence of the cosmos."
4. What initiation experiences do you wish you had experienced in your life that you apparently missed?
5. What would a historian understand of our culture by studying the iconography that he or she would find in our religious institutions, in our art museums, or in our advertisements? Would the abstract works be more revealing than the realistic in terms of our basic beliefs? Consider why or why not.
6. What would a shamanic experience have meant to you during a particularly crucial time in your life? Can one have one's own shamanic experience, do you think, or does it have to come through an outside source?
7. Do you think that there is any validity in considering feminine and masculine *principles* in terms of your own experience with the question of feminism? Why is it important in that regard to differentiate between *roles* and *principles*?

## ENDNOTES

[1] Thomas Mann, *Joseph and His Brothers* Tran. H. T. Lowe-Porter (New York: Alfred A. Knopf, 1948) 3.

[2] Joseph Campbell, *The Masks of God: Primitive Mythology* (New York: The Viking Press, 1959) 6.

[3] Campbell, *Animal Powers* 60.

[4] Joseph Campbell, *Myths to Live By* (New York: The Viking Press, 1972) 41.

[5] Campbell, *Animal Powers* 75.

[6] Campbell, *Animal Powers* 75.

[7] Mircea Eliade, *Rites and Symbols of Initiation: The Mysteries of Birth and Rebirth* Tran. Willard R. Trask (New York: Harper and Row/Harper Torchbooks, 1958) 3.

[8]Portions of this discussion are drawn from Peter T. Markman and Roberta H. Markman, *Masks of the Spirit: Image and Metaphor in Mesoamerica* (Berkeley and Los Angeles: University of California Press, 1989).

[9]Campbell, *Primitive Mythology* 308–10.

[10]Campbell, *Primitive Mythology* 310.

[11]Edmund R. Leach, "Anthropological Aspects of Language: Animal Categories and Verbal Abuse." *Reader in Comparative Religion* Eds., William Lessa and Evon Z. Vogt 4th ed. (New York: Harper and Row, 1979) 158.

[12]Mircea Eliade, *Shamanism: Archaic Techniques of Ecstasy* Tran. Willard R. Trask (New Jersey: Princeton University Press, 1964) 4–5.

[13]Eliade, *Shamanism* 5–8.

[14]Campbell, *The Power of Myth* 8.

[15]Victor Turner, *The Ritual Process: Structure and Anti-Structure* (Ithaca: Cornell University Press, 1969) 95.

[16]Eliade, *Rites and Symbols of Initiation* 19–20.

[17]Campbell, *Animal Powers* 9.

[18]Campbell, *Primitive Mythology* 58.

[19]Mircea Eliade, *Patterns in Comparative Religion* Tran. Rosemary Sheed (n.p.: Sheed and Ward, Inc., 1958) 124.

[20]Campbell, *Animal Powers* 79c.

[21]Campbell, *Primitive Mythology* 58.

[22]Campbell, *Primitive Mythology* 143.

[23]Campbell, *Primitive Mythology* 59.

[24]Campbell, *Animal Powers* 67–68.

[25]Campbell, *Animal Powers* 234–35.

[26]However, although the duality is generally as described above, there are also important exceptions to be noted. In Germany and Japan, for example, the sun is a goddess and the moon is a god. There is also a German myth that Campbell retells about a moon brother who pursues his sun sister; when he finally is able to catch her, there is an eclipse. "This myth was known to the North American Indians, as well as to the northern Asian tribes, and may indeed be of immense age." See Campbell, *Primitive Mythology* 393–94.

[27]Campbell, *Primitive Mtythology* 448.

[28]Friedrich Nietzsche, *The Birth of Tragedy*, Tran. Clifton P. Fadiman, in *The Philosophy of Nietzsche* (New York: The Modern Library, 1927) 984.

## UNIT BIBLIOGRAPHY

Campbell, Joseph. *The Way of the Animal Powers*. Vol. 1 of *Historical Atlas of World Mythology*. New York: Alfred van der Marck Editions, 1983.

———. *The Masks of God: Primitive Mythology*. New York: The Viking Press, 1959. These two works by Campbell contain his most complete treatment of humanity's earliest mythology.

Eliade, Mircea. *Shamanism: Archaic Techniques of Ecstasy*. Tran. Willard R. Trask, Bollingen Series, LXXVI. Princeton, N.J.: Princeton University Press, 1964. The definitive work on the subject by a noted historian of religions who shared many of Campbell's basic assumptions.

Goodall, Jane. *In the Shadow of Man*. Boston: Houghton Mifflin, 1971.

Köhler, Wolfgang. *The Mentality of Apes*. New York: Random House/Vintage, 1959. Originally published 1925. These two works provided Campbell with much of his information regarding apes and chimpanzees.

Leroi-Gourhan, André. *Treasures of Prehistoric Art*. New York: Harry N. Abrams, n.d. Contains a comprehensive, illustrated study of the Paleolithic cave paintings by an expert in the field.

Turner, Victor, *Dramas, Fields, and Metaphors: Symbolic Action in Human Society*. Ithaca: Cornell University Press, 1974.

———. *The Ritual Process: Structure and Anti-Structure*. Ithaca: Cornell University Press, 1969. These two works contain the essential aspects of Turner's thought regarding the structure of ritual, generally and specifically the ritual process of initiation.

van Gennep, Arnold. *The Rites of Passage*. Tran. Monika B. Vizedom and Gabrielle L. Caffee. Chicago: University of Chicago Press, 1960. Originally published in French in 1909 but not translated into English until 1960, this work provided a basic theoretical framework for the work of Turner and other recent symbolic anthropologists.

# NOTES

# NOTES

PETER MARKMAN
ROBERTA H. MARKMAN

UNIT 2

# Where People Lived Legends:
## American Indian Myths

## UNIT STUDY PLAN

1. Review the discussions of the functions of mythology and of the hero's journey in the Introductory Unit.
2. Read Unit 2 in your *Study Guide*.
3. Watch Program 2: "Where People Lived Legends: American Indian Myths."
4. In your course notebook or journal write a summary of Joseph Campbell's interpretation of the myths of the Native Americans. As soon as you have finished watching the program, make a note of points that may be unclear, as well as your own reactions and observations.
5. Read the selections for this unit in the *Anthology of Readings*. These include excerpts from works by Barre Toelken, Sam D. Gilly, Joseph Campbell, and Alfonso Ortiz.
6. After reading the selections, comment on what you have read in your notebook. Show the relationship between the readings and Campbell's insights into the myths of the Native Americans.
7. Complete assignments at the end of this unit as specified by your instructor.

## POINTS TO WATCH FOR IN THE TELEVISION PROGRAM

*This television program was delivered as a lecture by Joseph Campbell in Santa Fe, New Mexico, in 1982.*

1. Notice how Campbell uses the mandala from Yeats to indicate the cycles in the stages of life, and observe the connection between the mandala and American Indian mythology.
2. Notice the symbolic implications of the sun as compared with those of the moon.
3. Consider the basic assumptions underlying Chief Seattle's view of nature as expressed in the speech Campbell quotes.
4. Pay attention to how colors and directions are used in the sand paintings that Campbell describes and in the legends that he tells.
5. Make a list of the mythic images to which Campbell refers throughout his lecture, noting the significance that he gives to them.
6. Notice how and to what extent the legend of "Where the Two Came to Their Father" relates to other parts of Campbell's lecture in the television program—

particularly the earlier discussion of the tensions between society and the individual—and to Campbell's concluding remarks concerning Black Elk's idea that "the central mountain is everywhere."

## POINTS TO LOOK FOR IN THE *ANTHOLOGY OF READINGS*

1. Notice how Joseph Campbell analyzes the details of Black Elk's story to seek out the universal aspects found within it. Campbell then compares these to the motifs in other very diverse myths, such as the myth of Christ crucified and archaic myths from the Near East, to show how these universal motifs are shared by other mythologies of other times and places.
2. Consider how Campbell's discussion of the symbols involved with Navajo sand painting is meaningful only in terms of a metaphorical understanding of the ritual involved. This understanding enables him to compare its significance to other mythologies. Notice also how he differentiates between the universals of myth and the local and historical metaphorical images through which these universals have been given.
3. Pay attention to how Toelken stresses the importance of understanding a whole new set of concepts, codes, patterns, and assumptions if we are to learn anything about the Navajo, and by extension, any other religion. Note that he differentiates between what a culture is taught to see and how it actually does see reality. He shows us that we must learn how to look at a culture before we can hope to see it.
4. Notice how Sam Gill uses his description of the Navajo sand painting and the Hopi Kachina ceremony to show Native American appreciation for the power of symbolization and to demonstrate that the material forms involved in both of these examples are meaningful only in the degree to which they manifest the sacred. Consider, then, the importance of studying the transformation of the material to the sacred through ritual in all mythologies.
5. Notice, in Alfonso Ortiz's telling of the Tewa Creation Myth, the complexity of the Tewa cosmology. Consider how it brings time, space (including the physical geography of the entire area), color direction, ritual all into the same pattern. It also shows how people are always in the process of "becoming", particularly as each group of humans is matched by a parallel category of supernaturals.

## UNIT GLOSSARY

**Axial tree**: A symbol of absolute reality, that is, of the center of the world. See "world axis" below.

**Cosmogony**: The creation or origination of the world or universe or a theory of the origin of the universe.

**Cosmology**: A study of the universe as an orderly system.

**Kachinas**: The masked gods of Pueblo ritual, who appear especially in dances of the winter season.

**Liminal**: Reference to the threshold between two states of being.

**The long body**: The body in its entire course of existence from birth to death as opposed to the physical body existing at any given moment.

**Mandala**: The Sanskrit word for a circle symbolic of the cosmic order.

**Petrafact**: A myth that has become "petrified"; one that is no longer alive for the culture in which it exists.

**World Axis**: The imagined axis linking the earth's surface with the lower world (hell) and the upper world (heaven) at the metaphoric center of the earth. The world axis is often metaphorically a tree, with its crown in the upper world and its roots in the lower.

**Yahweh**: The Hebrew name for God in some books of the Old Testament.

## UNIT PREVIEW

In this unit you will be introduced to the Native American mythological tradition through a few key mythic motifs drawn from that tradition and exemplified in specific myths. You will be shown how these motifs appear within the tradition and how they illustrate Campbell's "functions of mythology" and "hero's journey" as those concepts are described in the Introduction. It should be noted that the placement of this unit in no way suggests that Native American mythology is seen as "primitive" or the equivalent of the myth and ritual of prehistoric humanity. Rather, the contemporary manifestations of Native American mythological tradition reveal important links to earlier myths of that traditions.

**The Shamanic Origins of Native Americans**: The ancestors of the native peoples of the Americas began coming across the Bering Straits land bridge as long as 40,000 years ago, bringing with them a body of mythic belief associated with shamanism which was to provide the foundation for the native mythological tradition of the Americas.

**The Ritual Initiation to the Stages of Life**: Some Native American rituals are designed to help the individual initiate pass harmoniously through the stages of life from birth to death and experience the return to the realm of the spirit.

**A Native American Version of the Hero's Journey**: The Navajo tale of "Where the Two Came to Their Father" is a North American version of the hero's journey. We see the hero brothers as they proceed from their miraculous birth to the call to adventure. They experience many trials, but aided by helpers, they finally attain a union with their father, the sun, through which they gain an understanding of themselves. This final enlightenment is the boon that they take back to the world and thus save it from threatening monsters.

**Native American Creation and Emergence Myths**: Native American creation and emergence myths, read metaphorically, can be seen to conceptualize the nature of reality held by Native American peoples.

**The Ritual Use of Myth, American Indian Sand Paintings**: Many of the Native American legends can be read in the Navajo sand paintings that represent the created world. They provide an opening to the world of the spirit that makes healing and initiation possible.

## UNIT ESSAY

### The Sacred Circle of the Mandala

Campbell begins his discussion of the Native American mythological tradition in what might seem at first a strange way. Neither William Butler Yeats nor the mandala that Campbell discusses is obviously connected to that tradition. But, as we can see from the television program for this unit, there are very important relationships that illustrate both the underlying connections between seemingly divergent mythological traditions and the sophisticated nature of the Native American mythology. What we see in these connections is an illustration of the title of this entire series of lectures: *The Transformations of Myth through Time*. For the mandalas of the Oriental tradition, the sacred circles of the Native American tradition, and the cyclical diagram which the twentieth-century poet, William Butler Yeats, drew from sixteenth-century European alchemical tradition are all transformations of a single, fundamental, mythological idea.

The mandalas are especially interesting because they clearly illustrate the connection between a mythic image presented in a work of visual art and a mythic narrative presented as a story. As this course will illustrate over and over again, myths are communicated in mythic images just as often as they are in narrative form. The two forms, of course, are not opposed, but complementary. They work together to communicate the metaphoric essence of the myth. As you have seen in Campbell's discussion of the pollen painting in the television program, mythic images often contain episodes of a narrative myth and are often used in the telling of the myth, especially when it is told in the context of a ritual as is the case with "Where the Two Came to Their Father."

The image from Yeats that Campbell uses in the television program for this unit to discuss the tension between the society and the individual is essentially a mandala, "the Sanskrit word for a circle, but a circle that is coordinated or symbolically designed so that it has the meaning of a cosmic order."[1] The mandala is a geometric diagram, often quite complex, that divides the wholeness of a circle into symbolic segments. Any particular mandala is an attempt to coordinate a particular—personal or cultural—order with the cosmic order, which is precisely the function of Yeats's image. In personal terms, individual mandalas, serving as instruments of meditation, provide a way of understanding inner experience. The forms of individual mandalas are as varied as the experiences of the individuals from which they are derived. Mandalas serving ritual functions for an entire culture, on the other hand, display a more limited number of archetypal and widely recognizable motifs. These mandalas express the transformational nature of life in a less individual way. "In a very elaborate Buddhist mandala, for example, you have the deity in the center as the power source, the illumination source. The peripheral images would be manifestations or aspects of the deity's radiance."[2] (For further discussion of the mandala in Oriental mythology, see Unit 9.)

The mandala's use in establishing a relationship between an individual's psychic life and the universal order was explored in great depth by the psychologist C. G. Jung, who came to believe that mandalas derived by individuals from their dreams and representing their innermost psychic realities were paths leading ultimately to self-understanding and a harmonious relationship with reality. He saw them as cryptograms corresponding to the nature of the psyche and felt that through such drawings he could observe the dynamic transformations of the psyche. Jung also came to believe that these individual mandalas, derived from individual dreams and visions, corresponded to the most basic of the religious symbols of humankind.

Mircea Eliade, on the other hand, saw the mandala in its cultural role. For him it was the *imago mundi* (image of the world) representing the cosmos in miniature and repeating the cosmogony, the creation of the world. The mandala served one of the most important and sacred functions of mythology: "Its construction is equivalent to a magical recreation of the world."[3] Black Elk, the Oglala Sioux visionary, suggests why this general truth is particularly relevant to Native American mythology:

> Everything an Indian does is in a circle, and that is because the Power of the World always works in circles, and everything tries to be round.... The sky is round, and I have heard that the earth

is round like a ball.... Even the seasons form a great circle in their changing, and always come back again to where they were. The life of man is a circle from childhood to childhood, and so it is in everything where power moves.[4]

Significantly, we find in most of the Native American mythological tradition that the cross, conceptualized as within a circle—the form of the mandala—symbolizes the four world corners in representing the four-fold shape of the cosmos. According to Hultkranz,

> the symbol first appears in the Mississippian culture (700–1700 A.D.), a culture that was inspired from Mesoamerica and brought many new features in religion, ritual, and symbolism to the southeastern, prairie, and plains provinces of North America. Indeed, the whole of this vast area shows the sacred circle design in the most diverse functions.... The Sun Dance lodge of the plains [for example] was thought to be a replica of the sacred universe, with the middle post as the *axis mundi*.[5]

That *axis mundi* is the the center of the universe, the all-important opening to the sacred world of the spirit. Throughout the dwellings and sacred structures of Native Americans, conceptualizations of human life, of the cosmic structure, and of representations of space and time were all constructed in the form of the sacred circle—the mandala.

That this is so, and that in all cultures the mandala serves this function to a greater or lesser degree suggests the universality of the symbolism inherent in that sacred circle. It is significant that in the largest sense, the earth itself may be considered a mandala inside of which various formations and transformations are continually taking place, as in the multiple images that emerge one after another with each turn of a kaleidoscope. The earth's transformations, like the kaleidoscope's, consist of forms within forms—all of them in motion.

Campbell often speaks of the earth itself as a sacred circle and of the need for new myths to bring a sense of wholeness and harmony to the peoples of the earth. In talking with Bill Moyers on the PBS series "Power of Myth" Campbell said, "When you see the earth from the moon, you don't see any divisions there of nations or states. This might be the symbol, really, for the new mythology to come. That is the country we are going to be celebrating. And those are the people we are one with." And as if in implicit recognition of the closeness of this conception to the mythic thought of the Native American peoples, Moyers responded: "No one embodies that ethic to me more clearly in the works you have collected than Chief Seattle."[6] Moyers refers here to the words of Chief Seattle that Campbell read in this unit's television program: "As we are part of the land, you too are part of the land. This earth is precious to us. It is also precious to you. One thing we know: there is only one God. No man, be he Red Man or White Man, can be apart. We *are* brothers after all." To Campbell, as to Chief Seattle, the earth is one: "The chosen center may be anywhere. The Holy Land is no special place. It is every place that has ever been recognized and mythologized by any people as home."[7] It is the center of any and all mandalas.

## The Native American Mythological Tradition

One of the great difficulties in discussing the American Indian and the mythological tradition embodied in the words of Chief Seattle comes from the incontrovertible fact that while there certainly were and are American Indians, there is no "American Indian." That is to say, the peoples who populated this continent before it was conquered by the Europeans were quite different from each other in many important respects. The essentially European concept of a unitary American Indian culture did not and does not exist in reality. According to some authorities, before the Conquest, there were as many as 2,000 separate cultures, many of them speaking mutually unintelligible languages. Among these cultures there was a wide variety of life-ways; there were hunters, gatherers, and planters—each with varying degrees of sophistication; there were highly developed religious and social systems and comparatively rudimentary ones. So great in number are the differences between the various Indian groups, that scholars find it very difficult to generalize about the Indian as a whole. Many, in fact, contend that studies should be limited to particular groups.

And yet, there is the constant temptation to generalize because one feels that there are some fundamental similarities between most Native American cultures which set their members apart from their fellow Americans who exist within an essentially European culture. From the perspective of the study of mythology, the similarities are apparent. Stith Thompson, in the introduction to his important collection of tales of the North American Indians, first discusses in some detail the differences between the myths and tales of each of the regions of North America, but then he says:

> After due consideration is given to the differences in the various areas, however, these will be found not nearly so striking as the likenesses. Generally speaking, though proportion varies, the same classes of tales are found everywhere on the continent. The practised reader immediately recognizes a tale as characteristically American Indian, whether it comes from California or Labrador. In spite of the intrusion of stories from the whites during the past few centuries, the body of older American Indian tales is very clearly established. These tales have been here for a very long time—long enough for the incidents to travel over the entire continent.[8]

They *have* been here a long time. The ancestors of the native peoples of the Americas began coming across the Bering Straits land bridge perhaps as long as 40,000 years ago, bringing with them not only their hunting and gathering life-ways and their primitive tool kits, but the body of mythic belief associated with shamanism that we have discussed in Unit 1 of this course and that is discussed further in Unit 9. As Campbell points out: "in any broad review of the entire range of transformations of the life-structuring mythologies of the Native Americans, one outstanding feature becomes immediately apparent: the force, throughout, of shamanic influences."[9]

In this he concurs with Mircea Eliade who, in his definitive work on shamanism, indicates that "a certain form of shamanism spread through the two American continents with the first waves of immigrants."[10]

There are two fundamental impulses in Native American mythic thought attributable to the shamanic background. First, there is a reverence for nature, for all the life forms of the world around us, because nature is for them a visible manifestation of the invisible world of the spirit, what Europeans call God. Second, there is a consistent belief that natural events have spiritual causes. If a person becomes ill, mentally or physically, the essential cause of that illness is to be found in a disequilibrium in the world of the spirit. Success or failure in worldly endeavors results primarily from spiritual rather than natural factors. And it is the shaman, whatever he or she is called in a particular group, who is able to enter the spirit world through trance to discern the cause of the natural problem and effect its solution.

## The Stages of Life

As Campbell suggests in this television program during his discussion of the picture from Yeats's book, *A Vision*, one of the primary functions of a mythology is to guide an individual harmoniously through the various stages of a normal human life. Campbell calls these stages "the long body," and defines it as the period "from infancy to engagement in the world and on to disengagement in old age, after which the mystery occurs of death, the ultimate term to the no less tremendous *mysterium* of birth—between which terms there will have been so many minor cycles of sleep (with dreams) and waking."[11] This is true of the mythologies of all cultures, of course, but the means by which that guidance is achieved and the particular modes of movement through the universal stages vary from culture to culture.

In the native mythologies of the Americas, the stages of human life are always depicted as parts of the cyclical pattern drawn from nature. Death is a return to the source from which life springs. It is the prelude to renewal rather than an end. The death which closes the life of the individual is but one of many deaths that occur in the course of a normal life. Initiation, the passage from youth to adulthood, is illustrative of this truth because the initiate must die to youth in order for the adult to emerge. As Victor Turner has shown, the ritual through which this movement is made possible, especially in traditional societies, is structured precisely in terms of the metaphoric death and rebirth of the initiate. "Such rites characteristically begin with ritual metaphors of killing or death marking the separation of the subject from ordinary secular relationships ... and conclude with a symbolic rebirth or reincorporation into society"[12] as the newly born adult ultimately becomes one who administers the ritual. These stages might well be seen as closely related to those of the hero's journey.

Two examples drawn from the multiplicity of such Native American rituals are illustrative. Among both the Algonquian peoples of the Northeast and the Athabascans of the Northwest, both of whose mythologies contain remnants of their hunting heritage, the initiation of young men was accomplished through a solitary fast undertaken in the wilderness. In the deathlike trance state engendered by the privations he willingly underwent, he would experience a vision of a guardian spirit, usually in animal form, which would shape and protect his adult identity. The shaping power of such a vision is clear from Joseph Epes Brown's comment: "The Indian actually identifies himself with, or becomes, the quality or principle of the being or thing which comes to him in a vision. . . . In order that this power may never leave him, he always carries with him some material form representing the animal or object from which he has received his 'power.'"[13]

Among the Hopi of the Southwest, on the other hand, initiation is tied to the agricultural cycle as can be seen in the initiation of Hopi children into the kachina cult, the beginning of their religious life. (For an original account of this initiation, see pages 79–87 in Leo Simmons *Sun Chief: The Autobiography of a Hopi Indian*.) Brought up to view the masked kachinas as gods and to believe that they would become kachinas after they died, the children are abruptly exposed to the unmasked kachinas—their elder brothers, fathers, and uncles—at the end of the Powamu ceremony, a ritual of world renewal directly related to planting and the rebirth of the agricultural cycle. Of the effect of that unmasking, Sam Gill says:

> In one sharp and sudden blow, the expectations so carefully nurtured [in the children] are forever shattered. For the moment only pain and bitterness take its place, ... but even with the disappointment, life goes on. But once initiated into the kachina cult, religious events can never again be viewed naively. Unforgettably clear to the children is the realization that some things are not what they appear to be. This realization precedes the appreciation of the full nature of reality. (*Anthology* 101 ).

As Turner points out, ritual is necessary to protect the initiate during the liminal period of the passage, the period in which he or she is betwixt and between the two stages of life, existing for the moment in no-time and no-place without an identity. But that ritual serves to guarantee that the initiate will pass from his or her identity as an unformed youth into that of the role assigned by the society, following what Campbell calls the right-hand path, that of the society's ideology.

## The Hero's Journey: A North American Version

**Beginnings**: The Navajo tale of "Where the Two Came to Their Father" that Campbell discusses at length in the television program for this unit is a North American version of the hero's journey. This story, as retold from anonymous sources by Jeff King to Maud Oakes, concerns two hero brothers whose mother, Changing Woman, also a hero although not the focus of the story, is born miraculously as are all great heroes. Darkness is her mother and Dawn, her father. Found at the peak of Mountain Around Which Moving Was Done by Talking God, who heard her first cry, she is entrusted to First Man and First Woman to be brought up under the direction of the Holy People. Upon reaching maturity, she in turn gives birth miraculously, again at Mountain Around Which Moving Was Done, to two sons who represent two aspects of the hero: the "split image" of light and dark manifested in the mother's parents. The mountain that is the scene of all of these miraculous births symbolizes the center of the earth, the world navel. At the age of twelve, these two hero sons born at the center of created reality embark on the hero's journey foretold by their miraculous birth, the initial stage of which is the crossing of the first threshold.

**The Call to Adventure**: The response of the two hero sons to the call to adventure results in a separation from the existing social condition that has formed their lives. They set out into unknown regions in search of their supernatural father, the Sun. This quest for the father is a common theme in American Indian myths. It appears also, for example in "The Woman Who Fell from the Sky," a northwestern legend that serves as an interesting comparison to the southwestern "Where the Two Came to Their Father." In each of these legends the hero brothers follow the pattern of the hero's journey. In each legend the two brothers are symbolic of the polarities associated with the sun and the moon. The sun represents form, outer orientation, and strength, while the moon suggests sensitivity and emotion, inner-directed personality, creativity and formlessness or change (for a fuller consideration of this dichotomy, see Unit 1). But, whereas the brothers in "Where the Two Came to Their Father" function in harmony and are companion brothers, the split heroes, Flint and Sapling, in "The Woman Who Fell from the Sky" are contending brothers. Their positions are antagonistic from the beginning: Flint would make things difficult for mankind; while Sapling would make them easy.

In the former legend, the older brother born of the sun, who will come to be known as Monster Slayer, is a master of action. The moon's child, Child Born of Water, is relatively weak and shy and so slightly developed that he seems on the surface to be only a shadow of his older brother. However, it is not until the quest is fulfilled that we, or even he, will know his real identity. In "The Woman Who Fell from the Sky," Flint, who kills his mother, is related to stone, which represents eternal form. Sapling, who represents the creative and transformative process of Spring, with the restorative warmth that accompanies growth, builds a bridge across a lake to join two worlds. Sapling's search for the father is clearly a quest for the knowledge of his destiny and of what it means to be alive. Flint will remain removed from the regenerative influence of his father. He is frozen in the congealing ice of winter like the ice giants who threaten the world.

**Trials and Symbolic Death:** The next stage of the journey involves initiation by symbolic means through the various confrontations and trials which the heroes must undergo. As Campbell's paradigm of the hero's journey suggests, helpers appear to the boys when they are needed. In "Where the Two Came to Their Father," the brothers are first threatened by Sand Dune Boy whom they overcome by flattery. Then they must suffer the consequence of not heeding potential helpers such as Old Age and, therefore, face the limitations of their own mortality. As a result, they learn to go beyond the kinds of fears that normally limit the actions of life. Then, finding themselves alone in the dark on an unchartered path, they are ready to encounter Spider Woman, another manifestation of the mother figure who symbolizes their rebirth. She nourishes them with an inexhaustible supply of food and provides them with medicine for courage and a live eagle feather to protect them from danger. The feather in American Indian folklore is a "symbol of the wonderful ascending power of … purified nature."[14] It is bestowed on them now because they are spiritually prepared to make use of it.

**Atonement:** Now the two hero sons have come to another stage of the hero's journey, for they have the resources necessary to transcend death and to experience rebirth. Still, they face many tests: they must overcome Cutting Reeds, Rock That Claps Together, Cat Tail People, and others who threaten them. In each case helpers appear: Rainbow Man helps them cross the rocks, Little Wind and the feathers they received from Spider Woman help them overcome Cat Tail People, and Water Bug People. But still more difficult trials follow before they can experience the "at-one-ment" with their father, the Sun, who will initiate them into the knowledge of their proper character and estate. He imposes the most difficult of the trials before he can recognize them as his sons and give them their names. His dual nature is manifested both by his formidable fury in the trials he puts them through and by his kindness as seen through the actions of his daughter who tries to protect them. When the Sun finally recognizes them as his sons, he gives them names: the older, whom he calls "my son," is named Monster Slayer; and the younger, "his grandson," is named Child Born of Water. These are the names that give them their true identities.

In "The Woman Who Fell from the Sky," it is only Sapling who goes through all the stages of the hero's journey. The first stage of his journey is initiated by his attempting to recover an arrow he has shot. The search for it brings him to the hidden domain of his father who is waiting for him with a gift of a bow and arrow and two ears of corn.

**Apotheosis and Return with the Boon:** Thus, in both legends it is through the recognition of the father that the heroes reach an apotheosis; they come to know who they are and what they must do. In "Where the Two Come to Their Father," as the two split into four, it becomes clear that they have reached the wholeness that includes all directions and all polarities, a condition that represents an expansion of consciousness and brings the boon of illumination and freedom for which they have been seeking. In fact, throughout the legend there are numerous references to the four directions and their four colors. Important among those references is the room full of sparklings of all colors, a reference to created reality, into which their father ultimately takes them. Their entrance into the room is metaphoric of their attainment of total glory, extending into and encompassing all that is possible in time and space. That glorified state is also symbolized by the gift of another feather from the Sun. This feather is symbolic now of enlightenment and indicative of the spiritual preparation to make the return journey to the realm of the mother and of the earth people whom they will save from the threatening monsters which represent the things that must be overcome in the course of man's daily life. They return with the boon that will restore the world.

Sapling, on the other hand, creates man and woman, and he breathes life into the "inert clod" that Flint had created. He names the Sun as the Great Warrior and the moon as Our Grandmother, and thus effects the marriage of the Sun and the Moon. Subsequently, he subdues the terrifying and threatening thunder-god. His expansion of consciousness and the growth of his spiritual position extend to the creation of the world.

While the adventures of these hero brothers are told as incidents in the external world, they are clearly metaphoric of the quest into the inner self and reveal the dual nature of reality in what Campbell calls "a cosmic dialectic." The heroes must come to know who they are and bring that awareness into the world of being. With the insight that has enabled them to restore themselves, they are in a position to restore the world for others. Campbell has said that "the landscape of the myth is the landscape of the human spirit,"[15] and it is clear that "Where the Two Came to Their Father" and "The Woman Who Fell from the Sky" provide insight into the human condition. Such legends enable us to understand on a metaphoric level the relationship of humanity to nature and of human life to the transcendent realm with which it seeks to unite in harmony in order to partake of its power.

## Creation Myths

Like all myths, creation myths may be read in more than one way. They may be taken literally, as an account of events that happened in a more-or-less actual way long ago, at the beginning of time. Or they may be seen as metaphoric statements about the nature of reality. In our own culture, some people regard the Judeo-Christian myths as factual accounts of the creation of life, while others see those accounts as metaphoric; and the conflict between these two groups is often bitter. This conflict within our own culture reflects a universal human problem which Campbell addresses in the Introductory Unit throughout his work. Seeing such myths as factual makes them "historic" and gives them a locus in time and space. Seeing them as metaphors for the entrance of life into the previously non-alive world, on the other hand, enables the individual to participate in the creation, since his or her own life is then as much a new creation as is that of the first man or woman. Each creation of life renews the mystery of creation whereby the transcendent ground of all life somehow—in a way which cannot be explained logically—enters into the created world. Seeing the myths as metaphoric opens them up for the individual and makes them, in Campbell's terms, "transparent to transcendence," rather than limited to a historical reference.

Barbara Sproul, in explaining why she feels that creation myths must ultimately be seen as metaphoric, says that of all myths, "only creation myths have as their primary task the proclamation of … absolute reality and the description of its relation to all other, relative realities."[16] By its nature absolute reality is "eternal (not temporal), independent (not dependent), active (not reactive), and unchanging (constant)."[17] An idea of such an absolute reality, completely alien to human experience, can only be held and communicated through metaphor. Of all myths, then, those depicting the creation of the world and the beginning of life might be seen as the most powerfully metaphoric. Regarded as metaphors, the varied creation stories of the Native American peoples have in common the depiction of humanity as an integral part of the world of nature, and that natural world is seen as the manifestation, through transformation, of the essence of spirit. Men and women, thus, are part of nature, and the whole package of nature is a visible manifestation of God.

As Campbell points out many times in his work, including the television programs for this course, this view is fundamentally different from the Judeo-Christian metaphor, which sees humankind as estranged both from God and from nature. Cast from the Garden, Adam and Eve enter the world of nature, not as creatures of that earthly world, but as overlords whose God-given dominion over nature enables them to use it for their own purposes. In the different attitudes of Native Americans and European-Americans toward the relationship between man and nature, we can see that creation myths do, indeed, stand as metaphors for a people's view of the essential nature of reality.

Though the Native American creation myths conceptualize humanity's relationship to nature in a similar way, this should not suggest that those myths are all the same. They are, in fact, quite varied.[18] (See Alfonso Ortiz's selection in the *Anthology of Readings* for a creation myth of the Pueblo Indians.) In some, such as the Earth Diver tales found primarily in the Northeast, land is created from the primordial waters through the efforts of an animal who succeeds, often at the cost of its own life, in bringing from beneath those waters a bit of mud from which both earth and humankind can be formed. In others, such as the myth of the "Woman Who Fell from the Sky" of the Eastern Woodlands tribes and many others, the creative principle descends from above. In both cases, the myth depicts the forces and materials necessary for creation as coming from the timeless world of the spirit enveloping the earth. In other Native American creation myths, land is formed from the waters simply as the result of a command of the gods. A well-known example can be found in the *Popol Vuh* of the Quiche Maya of Guatemala, but there are many others. Still another motif to be found in these creation myths involves the earth and its various life forms arising from the body of the god. Sometimes creation occurs either through a dismemberment of the body of the god or through growth from the body that becomes the earth itself. In a fascinating series of myths of the southwest, the natural landscape emerges from a spider god as a web does from a spider.

The above summary of the various modes of creation in Native American myths indicates several things. First, in most cases creation is accomplished through natural forces operating through natural creatures for the worlds of nature and of the spirit are neither opposed nor mutually exclusive in the Native American mind. Second, when the earth and its creatures are formed of or out of the body of the god, the relationship between the worlds of spirit and nature is similarly indicated, nature being merely a visible, temporal manifestation of the invisible, timeless world of the spirit. Third, a number of the myths locate the creative principle in the heavens above the earth's surface or in the sea beneath the surface. This three-level cosmic structure, with the earth enveloped within the upper and lower spiritual worlds, is a familiar feature of shamanic mythic systems which see the creatures of the earth as material manifestations of spiritual realities. Such a view also sees nature and spirit as essentially one.

## The Material World and the Realm of the Spirit: The Emergence Myths

Nowhere is the view of the material world on the earth's surface as a layer between the spiritual realms more powerfully portrayed than in the varying emergence myths of the Pueblo peoples and of the Navajo and Apache of the Southwest. Campbell emphasizes the importance of the emergence myths in the television program for this unit.

> For many Indians in the United States, even beyond Arizona and New Mexico, The Emergence is the premier myth. People know it and respect it, just as Euro-Americans respect the Book of Genesis. This feeling extends to lawyers, teachers, novelists, and other professionals who have entered the mainstream of modern American life. For them the sacred text embodies a concept of profound religious significance, and many still treat it as an article of faith. One cannot speak of The Emergence as a relic of the Indian past.[19]

In the Navajo version, for example, First Man and First Woman were brought into existence in Black World, the first of the four successive worlds which their descendants must traverse, emerging from each to the one above after an arduous struggle. Only in the fourth world, the world of our reality, do the Navajo clans and the present way of life come into being, and their emergence into being takes place in the local landscape. This emergence recognizes "features of the local landscape as mythological images," as Campbell points out in the television program.

All of the creation and emergence myths illustrate "the mystery of that cosmogonic sleight of hand by which the one became and continues to become the many, and by which the timelessness of eternity is reflected in the changing scene of time."[20] In the southwestern emergence myths, that flowering of the one into the many metaphorically occurs at the point of emergence, the center or navel of the world. That is the point at which movement between the planes of spirit and matter can take place thereafter because it is the point of the original emergence of matter from spirit. As Campbell discusses in the television program, that metaphoric point of emergence, identified always with a specific spot in the local landscape, assumes great importance as the point at which passage between the planes of matter and spirit can take place. For that reason, the emergence myth and the place of emergence play a vital role in healing and initiatory ritual, linking the present reality to that of the timeless realm of the spirit, the only true reality in Native American thought. Barre Toelken explains this point:

> To many native Americans the world that is real is the one we reach through special, religious means, the one we are taught to "see" and experience *via* ritual and sacred patterning. Instead of demanding proof for the Otherworld, as the scientific mind does, many native Americans are likely to counter by demanding proof that *this* one exists in any real way, since, by itself, it is not ritualized (*Anthology* 93–4).

The significance of that point at which movement between the planes of matter and spirit can take place, as well as its essentially metaphoric nature, is nowhere better explained than in Campbell's discussion of Black Elk, the Oglala Sioux visionary, in the television program for this unit and in his interview with Bill Moyers. At the age of nine, Black Elk, psychologically troubled and attended by a shaman, experienced a powerful vision, both initiatory and healing, prophetic of the troubles that would come to the Sioux and instrumental in shaping his own life. Campbell explains:

> The vision was an experience of himself as going through the realms of spiritual imagery that were of his culture and assimilating their import. It comes to one great statement, which for me is a key statement to the understanding of myth and symbols. He says, "I saw myself on the central mountain of the world [comparable in its centrality to the points of emergence we have been discussing], the highest place, and I had a vision because I was seeing in the sacred manner of the world." And the sacred central mountain was Harney Peak in South Dakota. And then he

says, "But the central mountain is everywhere." That is a real mythological realization. It distinguishes between the local cult image, Harney Peak, and its connotation as the center of the world. The center of the world is the *axis mundi*, the central point, the pole around which all revolves. The central point of the world is the point where stillness and movement are together. Movement is time, but stillness is eternity. Realizing how this moment of your life is actually a moment of eternity, and experiencing the eternal aspect of what you're doing in the temporal experience—this is the mythological experience.[21]

The emergence myths, like the creation myths, when properly regarded, enable men and women to open themselves to transcendence, to move beyond what Campbell calls "a religion of worship" to "a religion of identification with the divine."

## The FourFold Division of the Created World

Another way of seeing the significance of the central point symbolized by the point of emergence or by Black Elk's central mountain comes through the realization that all of temporal and spatial reality is conceptualized in Native American thought as organized around that central point. That organization is fourfold, each of reality's quarters being identified with a color, a direction, a point on the sun's course, and a god. When the Sioux smoke the calumet, ritually puffing smoke in each of the four directions and then straight above, they are embodying this conception in ritual. Similarly among the Yaqui and Mayo of northern Mexico and the southwestern United States, masked pascola dancers open the pahko ritual by symbolically locating themselves in the center of the world by referring to those directions. Felipe Molina describes the dancers of Arizona as they finish dancing to the *tampaleo* and start to bless the ground:

> They stood toward the East, home of the Texans, and they asked for help from *santo mocho'okoli* (holy horned toad). Each *pahkola* marked a cross on the ground, . . . [and] then they stood toward the North and said: "Bless the people to the North, the Navajos, and help me, my *santo bobok* (holy frog), because they are people like us," and they marked another cross on the ground. Still they stood towards the West and said: "Bless the *Hua Yoemem* (Papagos) and help me, my *santo wikui* (holy lizard)," and they marked another cross on the ground. Finally they stood towards the South and said: "To the South, land of the Mexicans, bless them and help me, my *santo behori* (holy tree lizard)," and they marked the last cross on the ground.[22]

While the quadripartite nature of created reality can be seen everywhere in Native American mythic thought, nowhere is its beauty and sophistication more apparent than in the spiritual thought of the most highly developed culture in the Americas whose thought is still available to us, that of the Aztecs of the Valley of Mexico before the Conquest. It is now clear to scholars that that body of mythic thought is vitally linked to the mythological traditions of the native peoples of what is now the United States.

For the Aztecs, the process of creation finds its mythic embodiment in the metaphoric unfolding of the unitary divine essence, Ometeotl, into levels of reality more and more accessible to mankind through ritual. The unfolding of the unitary Ometeotl into male and female entities is followed by a further unfolding which brings into being Tezcatlipoca, Smoking Mirror, generally considered the most significant and most powerful of the gods accessible to man through ritual. But just as Ometeotl, the ultimate ground of being, is at once unitary and dual, similarly Tezcatlipoca is mysteriously unitary, dual, and fourfold. As half of a duality, Tezcatlipoca, Smoking Mirror, finds his opposite in Tezcatlanextia, Mirror Which Illumines. One is associated with the night and the other, the day. But Tezcatlipoca is, in addition, fourfold, a quadripartite manifestation of the divine, each of whose four aspects is associated with a color, a cardinal direction, a primary point on the sun's diurnal course, and a separate deity.

These four deities are: Quetzalcóatl, the white Tezcatlipoca associated with the west and sunset who was widely seen as the creator of human life; Xipe Tótec, the red Tezcatlipoca associated with the east and sunrise and with the creative power which provided man's sustenance, the corn; Huitzilopochtli, the blue Tezcatlipoca, the warrior of the south associated with the zenith position of the sun who was responsible for the creation and maintenance of the Aztec state; and the black Tezcatlipoca, the warrior of the north and the nadir position of the sun who is Tezcatlipoca himself. He is defined, in short, by the spatial and temporal parameters of the created world. The metaphoric meaning is clear: in that sense, at least, Tezcatlipoca *is* that world. And the process of unfolding is also clear; Tezcatlipoca, a manifestation of Ometeotl, exists simultaneously as the unitary being who unfolds into four, as one unit of a duality, and as one of the four divisions of the unitary Tezcatlipoca. This majestic metaphor that depicts the divine essence manifesting itself through successive unfoldings into human reality, defined for the cultures of the Valley of Mexico the relationship between man and god. And it is the clearest, most complete, and most sophisticated example left to us of the typical Native American metaphor for the relationship between matter and spirit, man and god, multiplicity and unity.

## The Ritual Use of Myth: Healing through the Sand Painting

As Campbell demonstrates in the television program, the emergence myth and its related conceptions of the central point at which matter and spirit meet and the fourfold division of time and space play a central role in Navajo healing ritual. Most basically, healing is accomplished by the Navajo through the construction of a "painting" illustrative of an incident from myth by placing colored sands and other natural materials on the ground in one of many traditional patterns. When the

painting is complete, the patient is placed on it. Meanwhile, a healing ritual is enacted by the singer who is a shamanic healer. Such a way of dealing with illness might seem strange to those of us who are accustomed to physicians and hospitals with all of their scientific backing, but as Toelken points out wellness, a far larger concept among the Navajo than our idea of physical health, can be assured only through "reestablishing his relationship with the rhythms of nature. It is the ritual as well as the medicine which gets one back 'in shape,' (*Anthology* 88).

Campbell describes the healing (or initiatory) process as follows:

> Neighbors and friends have assembled, and for a period of one to five continuous nights and days of chanting, prayer, and metaphorical acts, the patient or initiate is ceremonially identified in mind and heart and costume with the mythological protagonist of the relevant legend. He or she actually enters physically into the painting, not simply as the person whose friends and neighbors have solicitously assembled, but equally as a mythic figure engaged in an archetypal adventure of which everyone present knows the design. For it is the archetypal adventure of them all in the knowledge of their individual lives as grounded and participative in a beloved and everlasting pattern. Moreover, all the characters represented in the ceremonial are to be of the local landscape and experience, become mythologized, so that through a shared witnessing of the ceremonial the entire company is renewed in accord with the nature and beauty of their spiritually instructive world.[23]

It is important to recognize that the ritual repeats the process of creation as revealed in the myth (*Anthology* 97–8). In the Navajo creation myth, the life forces created in the world were arranged through the placement of colored objects on the floor of a ceremonial hogan by First Man so that a world of harmony and beauty in which everything had its proper relationship to everything else was created. In that sense, the sand painting is metaphoric of the created world and can be instrumental in restoring harmony and proper relationship to the life of the patient. Each of the myriad traditional designs of the paintings reflects a design imparted to a mythic hero who was himself being cured, and the materials used in each are curative of the hero/patient's illness. And as was the case in the creation myth, the final removal of the materials which made up the painting represents the necessary transition from the spiritual world of the ritual moment to the temporal world of nature. In that transition, the boon of wellness, of proper relationship, has been brought to the world of humankind: not only to the patient, as Campbell points out, but to the community as well.

The sand painting and its accompanying ritual are illustrative of the fact that "material symbols exist and are meaningful only in the degree to which they manifest the sacred" (*Anthology* 102). They exist as openings to the spiritual realm, points of contact between this world and the all-important other world. They reveal the fundamental assumption underlying all Native

American mythic thought: the experiential world can exist only through the constant support of the invisible spiritual world. Or, as Black Elk put it: "I looked about me and could see what we then were doing was like a shadow cast upon the earth from yonder vision in the heavens, so bright it was and clear. I knew the real was yonder and the darkened dream of it was here" (*Anthology* 102).

## ASSIGNMENTS FOR STUDY AND ANALYSIS

1. Consider the two masks that Campbell discusses in the television program. Describe the mask that you feel society has asked you to wear, and then describe the mask that you consider to be your individual mask. Write an essay about the tension that you have experienced from the conflict between them.
2. Consider your own attitude toward nature and divinity. Write a brief essay in which you discuss the relationship between human beings and nature from that point of view.
3. Consider the implications of deciding (1) that god and nature are one or (2) that god is separate from the world. What necessarily follows from each of these assumptions? Incorporate your answers in an essay.
4. Can you think of any nonmedical parallels in our society to compare to the process of healing among Native Americans? Discuss them.
5. Write an essay about the role of ritual in your own life. What rituals have you experienced? How have they affected you?
6. Consider the stages of life that Campbell discusses. Of which stages in your own life have you been aware? In the lives of others around you? What effect has that awareness had? Write an essay considering your answers to these questions.

## FURTHER ASSIGNMENTS FOR WRITING AND REFLECTION

1. Write an essay based on Sam Gill's selection in the *Anthology of Readings* and further research into the kachina ceremony, showing how it reflects the Native American world view as expressed in the various components of this unit.
2. Write a comparative study of the nature of God in Genesis 3 with the relationship of god to humanity and nature as expressed in Native American mythology.
3. Compare and contrast several creation or emergence myths from various areas of North America, noting to what extent and how they express similar or different concepts regarding the nature of the human condition.

4. Campbell says in the television program for this unit that "the function of ritual and the myth is to let you experience it here. Not somewhere else a long time ago." Consider to what extent mythology and ritual function for the American people here and now. You might want to read Campbell's book, *Myths to Live By* and the last pages of *Hero with a Thousand Faces* to learn more about his ideas regarding this subject.

## ENDNOTES

[1]Campbell, *Power of Myth* 216.

[2]Campbell, *Power of Myth* 216–17.

[3]Mircea Eliade, *Myths, Rites, Symbols: A Mircea Eliade Reader* Ed. Wendell C. Beane and William G. Doty, vol. 2, (New York: Harper and Row, 1975) 376.

[4]John G. Neihardt, *Black Elk Speaks* (Lincoln: University of Nebraska Press, 1961) 164–65.

[5]Ake Hultkranz, *The Religions of the American Indians* Trans. Monica Setterwall. (Berkeley: University of California Press, 1979) 28.

[6]Campbell, *Power of Myth* 32.

[7]Campbell, *Inner Reaches* 32.

[8]Stith Thompson, *Tales of the North American Indians* (Bloomington: University of Indiana Press, 1966) xxii.

[9]Campbell, *Animal Powers* 253.

[10]Mircea, Eliade, *Shamanism: Archaic Techniques of Ecstasy* 333.

[11]Campbell, *Animal Powers* 9.

[12]Victor Turner, *Dramas, Fields, and Metaphors* (Ithaca: Cornell University Press, 1974) 273.

[13]Joseph Epes Brown, *The Sacred Pipe: Black Elk's Account of the Seven Rites of the Oglala Sioux* (New York: The Crossroad Publishing Co., 1982) 45, n. 2.

[14]Joseph Campbell, "Commentary" *Where the Two Came to Their Father* 2nd ed. (New Jersey: Princeton University Press, 1969) 40.

[15]Campbell, "Commentary" 33.

[16]Barbara Sproul, *Primal Myths: Creating the World* (New York: Harper and Row, 1979) 6.

[17]Sproul 6.

[18]See Sproul 232–313, for a large assortment of these myths.

[19]John Bierhorst, *The Mythology of North America* (New York: Quill/William Morrow, 1985) 78.

[20]Campbell, *Primitive Mythology* 108–109.

[21]Campbell, *The Power of Myth* 89.

[22]James S. Griffith and Felipe S. Molina, *Old Men of the Fiesta: An Inroduction to the Pascola Arts* (Phoenix: Herd Museum, 1980) 41.

[23]Campbell, *The Inner Reaches of Outer Space* 94.

## UNIT BIBLIOGRAPHY

Bierhorst, John. *The Mythology of North America*. New York: Quill/William Morrow, 1985. A comprehensive guide to Native American mythology by a well-known editor and translator in the field.

Brown, Joseph Epes. *The Spiritual Legacy of the American Indian*. New York: The Crossroad Publishing Co., 1982. Religion and mythology of North American Indians.

Campbell, Joseph. "Commentary." *Where the Two Came to Their Father: A Navaho War Ceremonial*. Given by Jeff King, recorded by Maud Oakes. 2nd. ed. Princeton: Princeton University Press, 1969. Originally published 1943. Bollingen Series I. Contains reproductions of the sand paintings, a retelling of the myth, and an extensive commentary on both by Campbell in which he points out extensive parallels to the Oriental mythological tradition.

———. *The Flight of the Wild Gander: Explorations in the Mythological Dimension*. New York: The Viking Press, 1969. The essay "Mythogenesis" provides an exceptionally complete analysis of an American Indian legend.

———. *The Way of the Seeded Earth*. Vol. II of *Historical Atlas of World Mythology*. New York: Harper and Row, 1989. This volume provides a selection of Native American myths and analyses of those myths.

Capps, Walter Holden, ed. *Seeing with a Native Eye: Essays on Native American Religion*. New York: Harper and Row, 1976. A largely successful attempt to do what its title suggests—to allow us to see reality through the spiritual "eyes" of a Native American.

Eddoes, Richard and Alfonso Ortiz, eds. *American Indian Myths and Legends*. New York: Pantheon Books, 1984. A recent collection of myths and tales drawn from the Native American experience.

Hultkranz, Ake. *The Religions of the American Indians*. Trans. Monica Setterwall, Berkeley: University of California Press, 1979. A thorough and readable survey of the myth and ritual of Native Americans by a noted European historian of religions.

Markman, Peter T. and Roberta H. Markman. *Masks of the Spirit: Image and Metaphor in Mesoamerica*. Berkeley: University of California Press, 1989. Provides, in its second section, a lengthy discussion of Native American cosmogony and cosmology.

Neihardt, John G. *Black Elk Speaks: Being the Life Story of a Holy Man of the Oglala Sioux*. Lincoln: University of Nebraska Press, 1961. Contains descriptions of the visions of Black Elk, much admired by Campbell.

Simmons, Leo W. *Sun Chief: The Autobiography of a Hopi Indian*. New Haven: Yale University Press, 1942. An excellent firsthand account of the way mythology and initiation transform personal experience.

Thompson, Stith, ed. *Tales of the North American Indians*. Bloomington: University of Indiana Press, 1966. Originally published 1929. An excellent collection of Native American tales by a noted folklorist.

# NOTES

**NOTES**

# NOTES

PETER MARKMAN
ROBERTA H. MARKMAN

# And We Washed Our Weapons in the Sea:
## Gods and Goddesses of the Neolithic Period

## UNIT STUDY PLAN

1. Read Unit 3 in your *Study Guide*.
2. Watch Program 3: "And We Washed Our Weapons in the Sea: Gods and Goddesses in the Neolithic Period."
3. In your course notebook or journal, write a brief summary of Campbell's discussion of the goddess. As soon as you finish watching the program, write your observations, comments, and questions.
4. Review the discussions of the masculine and feminine principles in Unit 1.
5. Study the selections for this unit in the *Anthology of Readings*. These include excerpts by Anthony F. Aveni, Anne L. Barstow, and Marija Gimbutas.
6. Complete the assignments at the end of this unit as specified by your instructor.

## POINTS TO WATCH FOR IN THE TELEVISION PROGRAM

*This television program was delivered as a lecture by Joseph Campbell in Santa Fe, New Mexico, in 1982.*

1. Note the three main centers that Campbell identifies as matrices of the origin of agriculture and the domestication of the animals.
2. Note the similarities among the various examples that Campbell shows of the Mother Goddess as the primary mythological feature found in early archaeological sites.
3. Make a brief list of the various goddesses that Campbell identifies in the television program.
4. Consider the animals that are associated with the Mother Goddess in the cultures that Campbell discusses. Note especially how some—the bull, the snake, and the bird—are related to the goddess as the feminine principle.
5. Observe how the idea of the cosmic order was related to the invention of writing, mathematics, and precise observation of the heavens.

## POINTS TO LOOK FOR IN THE *ANTHOLOGY OF READINGS*

1. Notice that, in her study, *The Goddesses and Gods of Old Europe*, Marija Gimbutas makes an important point about the mythic imagery of the prehistoric era and how it tells us a great deal about the basic assumptions of the cultures of that time. This imagery is indicative of the way these cultures saw the relationship between nature and human life, as well as how they understood the structure of the cosmos. Gimbutas explains the purpose of the supernatural powers and why and how the various symbols came to be attached to those powers. Throughout the study, she shows how the pantheon of that early time reflected a society dominated by the feminine principle as expressed through the imagery of the goddess.
2. Anne L. Barstow's essay, "The Prehistoric Goddess," provides insight into the earliest manifestations of the goddess. In her discussion of the prehistoric goddess, Barstow relies on the discoveries made by the archaeologist James Mellaart at the site of Catal Huyuk (which Campbell refers to in the television program). As a feminist, Barstow is concerned with power; observe her definition of power here.
3. Anthony F. Aveni's introduction to his pioneering work on pre-Conquest Mesoamerican astronomy, "Archeostronomy and its Components," demonstrates the uses of astronomy throughout the ancient world, as well as the means by which archaeologists today are coming to understand the complexity of that ancient use.

## UNIT GLOSSARY

**Abstract Design**: A design that has only intrinsic form with little or no attempt at realistic pictorial representation.

**Aesthetic Field**: An enclosed area in a work of art that is separated from the space outside in which the work is organized.

**Gynocratic**: Related to the political supremacy of women.

**Libation Vase**: A vase from which a liquid was poured as a sacrifice to a deity.

**Maize**: Indian corn.

**Macrocosm**: The universe.

**Mesocosm**: A culture or large social grouping; that which exists between the universe and the individual human being.

**Microcosm**: The individual human being. The microcosm often is seen as a replication in miniature of the macrocosm.

**Minotaur**: A monster shaped half-man and half-bull.

**Pythagoras (c. 582–c. 507 B.C.E.)**: Greek philosopher and mathematician who believed that numbers were the essence of all things and that all relationships could be expressed and understood numerically.

**Trefoil**: An ornament or symbol in the form of a stylized leaf of a leguminous herb.

**Ziggurat**: An ancient Babylonian temple tower consisting of a lofty pyramidal structure built in successive stages with outside staircases and a shrine at the top.

## UNIT PREVIEW

In this unit, you will be introduced to several important mythological themes associated with the development of humanity as it moved from the simpler planting cultures of the Neolithic period to the emergence of the beginnings of the great city civilizations.

**The Continuity of the Goddess**: From the beginning, the goddess was associated with symbols of fertility and creativity, the most important of which was the moon. The preva-

lence of female rulership as early as 6500 B.C.E. and the continuing association of the goddess with such animals as the bird, the bull, the snake, and others resulted in a complex, composite image of the goddess in the Neolithic period and later.

**The Story of Inanna**: The Mesopotamian moon goddess, Inanna, provides an example of the power of the goddess and shows how such a mythological goddess embodies the feminine principle discussed in Unit 1.

**Temple Worship and the Priesthood**: The change from the individual religious experience of the hunting peoples to the more communal experience of the agriculturalists led to the development of a priesthood and the institution of temple worship in the emerging city civilizations throughout the world. Three results of this development were the growth of priestly ritual, an esoteric interpretation of mythological symbols, and the use of the newly developed art of writing to transmit priestly thought.

**Astronomy and Mathematics**: The search for order in the universe as a means of attaining insight into its spiritual mysteries led to and was aided by the discovery of the principles of astronomy and mathematics. Through those principles, humanity was able to discern an impersonal, abstract order in the universe.

## UNIT ESSAY

### The Rise to Civilization

In the television program for this unit, Campbell discusses the crucial stage in the development of humanity that was marked by the emergence of the great city civilizations, the forerunners of today's complex societies, from the simpler planting cultures of the Neolithic period. Campbell often characterized these changes as the movement from "the way of the seeded earth" to "the way of the celestial lights." Those Neolithic planters, living what Campbell calls in the television program "the timeless idyll of the nature religions," were a sedentary people living and working within the cultures of small, self-sufficient villages. They created a life-way revolving around the household and the planting field, and their rich mythologies reflected that way of life in their emphasis on the goddess and the fertility of the earth. But the foundation of this relatively simple life, the development of agriculture and the domestication of animals, also prepared the way for the evolution of the higher civilizations. For the "taming" of "wild" natural plant and animal life provided the necessary prerequisites for the gradual accumulation of wealth and the consequent diversification of human functions and roles within culture.

As Campbell points out in this television program, these developments took place separately in at least three different

areas of the world. Significantly, each of these developments took place in a similar way, both in material terms and in terms of what might be called the spiritual development of humanity, that is, in the areas of mythology and religion. The best understood of those evolutions from village to city cultures took place in Mesopotamia, in and around the Tigris and Euphrates valleys. By about 6000 B.C.E., the size of villages began to increase in connection with the development of irrigation. By about 3500 B.C.E., as the result of an evolutionary process whose full complexity is not completely understood, "the fundamental arts of all high civilization" were in evidence: "writing, mathematics, monumental architecture, systematic scientific observation (of the heavens), temple worship, and, dominating all, the kingly art of government."[1]

Such a list is particularly interesting because it indicates that due to those decisive developments in the Near East; the roughly contemporary, but apparently independent move toward civilization in the Indus Valley of India; the rise, somewhat later, of the Shang civilization of northern China; and still later, the growth of the Olmec of Mesoamerica and the Chavin of South America, led to a life similar to what we still know and live today. A closer look at that list reveals three areas that are of particular importance to the study of the transformations of myth through time because they are central to the evolution of human spiritual life: mathematics, observations of the heavens, and temple worship. It is vital to understand, however, that these developing civilizations did not break completely from the past. In their continued worship of the goddess, their roots in the farming villages of the Neolithic period can be clearly discerned.

## The Continuity of the Goddess

**The Prehistoric Goddess:** In his work, *The Way of the Seeded Earth*, Campbell speaks of the Paleolithic caves as wombs of eternal darkness. He observes that for prehistoric humanity "here in the dark of the womb of the pregnant earth is actuality, while above in the extended light world—which here seems remote and alien—are the appearances only of insubstantial phantoms." Consequently, he concludes that "the numerous female figurines of that same high period of the Paleolithic Great Hunt were surely personifications in human form of the indwelling power of that same mother womb. What their actual uses were can only be surmised: whether as fetishes to aid childbirth, as protectresses of the family hearths, or as personifications of the mystery already symbolized in the caves, to be implored in some way for the fecundity of the necessary herds."[2] Whether or not these figurines were symbolic of the Mother Goddess as such, they certainly suggest the veneration of maternity as a divine principle, since they all emphasize the breasts, the navel, the vulva region, and often the position of childbirth. The Venus of Laussel, discussed in Unit 1, was discovered in a late Paleolithic grave at Mal'ta near Lake Baikal in Siberia. She is portrayed with her left hand resting on her obviously pregnant womb while in her raised right hand she holds the horn of the waxing moon marked with thirteen lines. Significantly, at least twenty female statuettes of mammoth ivory were taken from that same Mal'ta site. To Campbell, such figures "suggest that a myth of some kind must have justified the cult of these Paleolithic 'Venus' figurines, whereby the necessary slaughter of the hunt became transformed into a ritual enactment, in the way of the animal powers, of the will in nature."[3]

There is sufficient evidence in the archaeological record to indicate that even in prehistoric times communal worship was expressed through the medium of the idol (*Anthology* 120), and that goddesses were worshipped even before male deities. In "The Prehistoric Goddess" in the *Anthology of Readings*, Anne L. Barstow writes that as early as 25,000 B.C.E., long before recorded history, there is evidence of the involvement of female figurines in sacred activities such "as in circles of stones found on floors of caves" (*Anthology* 112). By 6200 B.C.E., outline carvings of the goddess are found on a wall in the position of giving birth. Under the carvings are rows of "plaster breasts, nipples painted red, ... molded over animal skulls or jaws that protrude through the nipples." Barstow concludes that the goddess "already at her first appearance . . . is deity of

both life and death" (*Anthology* 116). From these earliest examples it can be seen that prehistoric humanity made "the obvious analogy of women's life-giving and nourishing powers with those of the earth" and thus associated the fertility of women "with an idea of the motherhood of nature."[4]

**Excavations at Catal Huyuk in Anatolia**: Campbell speaks in the television program for this unit of the important site at Catal Huyuk in Anatolia (now modern Turkey) and the excavations that were conducted there by James Mellaart. Those excavations yielded artifacts from as early as 6500 B.C.E. To Mellaart's reported astonishment, these artifacts made it clear that the ancient society that existed there was gynocratic, and its predominant deity was feminine throughout the Neolithic period and into later times. Interestingly, Mellaart also concluded that the society existing there was peaceful and harmonious; many scholars since have attributed that phenomenon to feminine domination. There is clear evidence that the goddess was associated with the sacred bull, and that the idea of bull-leaping came from the Anatolians of Catal Huyuk to Crete, where it underwent further development. Bull-leaping was not the only thing borrowed by the society of Crete from Catal Huyuk. The sacred double-axe motif, the Cretan symbol of the goddess, of matriarchal rule, and of imperial power, and suggestive of the sacred union of the Sky God and Earth Goddess, was found painted on the temple walls of Catal Huyuk. There also is evidence that funerary honors and ritual burial were accorded mostly to women, since there were far more buried female skeletons than male. Most male bones indicate that the bodies were simply thrown into a charnel house.[5]

So it is not surprising that the status of the women whom Campbell describes in this television program as so elegantly prominent in Crete was derived directly from Catal Huyuk where the phenomenon of goddess rulership was clearly prevalent. In both cultures, the association of the goddess with the bull clearly signifies goddess rulership, since the bull is worshipped for its strength and procreative power. The bull came to symbolize the earth and the humid power of nature because of its association particularly with rain, storm, and thunder, and with the generative power associated with the moon and rain clouds. Later, between 3500 and 2500 B.C.E. in Crete, the bull represented the reproductive force in nature partially because the bull's horns are shaped like the moon, which also represents death and resurrection.

**Venus of Vinca**: It is no wonder then that almost all of the images associated with the goddess are related to fertility and creativity. Gimbutas reminds us that "a farming economy bound the villages to the soil, to the biological rhythms of the plants and animals upon which their existence wholly depended. Cyclical change, death and resurrection, were ascribed to the supernatural powers and in consequence special provision was made to protect the capricious life forces and assure their perpetuation." (*Anthology* 119). The body of the Bird Goddess of the seventh to fifth millenium B.C.E., for example, contains the image of an egg, which symbolizes "a universal life source, not human foetuses."[6] As Gimbutas suggests, "the hybridization of woman and bird endows the figures with a greater dignity, the dignity of the supernatural."[7] This dignity surely is possessed by the numerous figurines that have been excavated, many of them by Gimbutas herself.

The Bird Goddess, the most important goddess of the Vinca people and known, therefore, as the Venus of Vinca, was portrayed with some features of a bird, such as a beak, but with human breasts, abdomen, and legs. In the Aegean and Balkan areas, the Bird Goddess often was portrayed as "a life-like erect phallus with small wings and a posterior of a woman, which, if seen in profile, is readily identifiable as a bird's body and tail."[8] Although each area portrayed this goddess in its own distinctive way, the basic relationship to fertility, life-generating cosmic forces, and the total embodiment of the feminine principle remained the same.

**The Great Goddess of the Neolithic Period**: Gimbutas explains that the Great Goddess or Mother Goddess or Fertility Goddess of the Neolithic period, as she was variously called, stood metaphorically for a more complex concept than her predecessors because she was "a composite image with traits accumulated from both the preagricultural and agricultural eras. During the latter she became essentially a Goddess of Regeneration, i.e., a Moon Goddess, product of a sedentary, matrilinear community, encompassing the archetypal unity and multiplicity of feminine nature. She was giver of life and all that promotes fertility, and at the same time she was the wielder of the destructive powers of nature. The feminine nature, like the moon, is light as well as dark."[9] This Great Goddess often is portrayed with a phallus-shaped head indicative of her androgynous nature.

Many of these figures of the Great Goddess are shown with their hands on their breasts, in a squatting position, with their genitals exposed, or with some other physical indication of their giving birth. Often there are two large eggs or circles on the back of the body or a double egg inside, all of which symbolize, as does the moon, the process of "becoming." Other symbols associated with the goddess continue this theme. Gimbutas describes the dog as the goddess's principal animal because of its lunar character (suggested by its being a nocturnal creature that often howls at the moon). The deer represents the cycle of regeneration because its antlers, which resemble branches on the tree of life and are shaped like the moon, are renewed regularly. The toad's shape is reminiscent of the female giving birth; the bee is a symbol of eternal renewal and immortality; the butterfly symbolizes the emergence of life from the dead chrysallis; and the bear's maternal devotion and cycles of hibernation relate to the phases of the moon. All of these are associated with the Great Goddess since they either appeared on or near her body or provided a form for the Goddess herself. Such is the case in a painted representation of the goddess with butterfly wings on a Minoan III vase from Knossos or a birth-giving goddess in the shape of a toad

engraved on the base of a Linear Pottery dish from Bohemia from the end of the sixth millenium B.C.E. (for illustrations of these objects, see Marija Gimbutas's *The Goddesses and Gods of Old Europe*, pp. 131 and 187). It should, however, be noted that while all of these are symbolic of the lunar cycle and in some way related to fertility and regeneration, often the goddess was flanked by male animals associated with physical strength and suggestive of her power, such as the leopards and lions in Anatolian and Mesopotamian representations.

**Inanna: The Mesopotamian Moon Goddess**: In the television program for this unit, Campbell discusses an impression made from a cylindrical seal from ancient Sumer (*c.* 2330–2150 B.C.E.) that he claims was thought to be a foreview of the fall in the biblical account of the Garden of Eden because so much of the mythology in the book of Genesis is largely an adaptation of Sumer-Babylonian myths. He points out, however, that although the Sumerian piece has symbols similar to those of the Garden of Eden, such as two figures on either side of an axial tree, a serpent rising up behind the figure on the right (who is thought to be a deity because of its horned crown), and the hands of both figures gesturing toward the tree as if to point out its importance, there is a very different spirit from that in the biblical account. The Sumerian spirit will be discussed later in this unit, but first it will be helpful to have some background on the Moon Goddess depicted with a crown on the Sumerian seal impression.

The Sumerian tree, known as the Hullupu-tree, is a date palm that was an important source of nutrition for the ancient people of Mesopotamia and was related to the Moon Goddess known as Inanna "Queen of Heaven" or "Lady of the Date Clusters" by the Sumerians. This same goddess was known as Ishtar by the Semites living in Sumer. According to the Sumerian scholar, Samuel Noah Kramer, "Inanna played a greater role in myth, epic, and hymn than any other deity, male or female."[10]

In *Inanna, Queen of Heaven and Earth*, Diane Wolkstein discusses the story of the goddess as it was reconstructed and translated by Kramer from the fragmentary original Sumerian cuneiform texts. She notes that Inanna had rescued the Hullupu-tree from perishing by taking it to a place where she herself could cultivate it. The goddess wanted the tree, which "embodies the dual forces of the universe . . . consciousness and unconsciousness, light and darkness, male and female, and the power of life and the power of death,"[11] so that she could have a shining throne and a bed made from it. But a serpent who could not be charmed made its nest in the roots of the tree, an Anzu bird set its young in the branches of the tree, and the dark maid Lilith built her home in the trunk of the tree. None of them would leave it. Even when Inanna took the tree into her own garden, they remained. Finally, after much weeping, Inanna convinced her brother Gilgamesh to help her. He finally rid the tree of these demons, and it was moved from her garden to the city where he carved her a throne and a bed from it.

According to the story, Inanna could not have the throne or the bed until the tree was moved to the city and "shared between Inanna and Gilgamesh; woman and man, goddess and mortal. Contact with the tree brings Sumerian man and woman to a closer understanding of life's forces: the world's creation and its human echo, woman's sexuality and her emerging consciousness."[12] Sitting on a throne made from the Hullupu-tree, the goddess Inanna would understand all the meaning inherent in the tree itself—the meanings of life and death, consciousness and unconsciousness and all of the dualities that, when fully understood, make possible a full understanding of the human condition. Later on in the spring when Inanna was betrothed to a shepherd, Dumuzi, they would sleep in that bed made from the sacred, magical tree. She and Dumuzi, who became her king and husband but whom she sometimes called brother, came to know the secrets of those dualities that relate to love and sexuality.

**Genesis and the Story of Inanna: A Comparison**: In the television program for this unit, Campbell compares the story of the tree as told in the story of Inanna with that of Adam and Eve in Genesis. In both Genesis and the story of Inanna, the tree has the connotations of duality, such as of good and evil, and in each, the tree acts as a key to the understanding of the meaning and mystery of life. In Genesis 3:6 we are told that Eve ate of the tree because "the tree was to be desired to make one wise." But that act, as we know, estranges her from the Lord and results in her being punished, whereas as Campbell says in this television program, there is no idea of a fall in the Sumerian story. The tree in that account is the provider of what is essential to a creative life; Inanna has only to wait until the demons are destroyed to begin the process of awakening. No estrangement or punishment follows, only creativity and becoming. Thus, the story of Inanna exemplifies, once again, the goddess as part of the process of becoming, as a symbol of fertility, while the story in Genesis emphasizes instead a lesson taught by a god outside of the human world, a god from whom humankind is estranged.

Inanna's is not the only ancient story in which the tree serves the goddess and humanity. In Homer's *Odyssey*, the bed that reveals the secrets of the relationship of Penelope and Odysseus is one made many years before from a sacred olive tree, and it is through Odysseus's identification of the bed that he and his wife are reunited in a creative relationship that will symbolically enable Ithaca to continue to grow and thrive. In such stories, but not in the biblical account, we can see the necessity of the union of male and female principles that were discussed in Unit 1.

**From Goddesses to the Virgin Mary**: It seems clear that the characteristics and the role of the Great Goddess represent the female principle, that is, the principle of creativity, of regeneration, and of power over life and death. And it is clear that she was worshipped in various ways, as, for example, the source of wisdom and the guardian of fertility. Whether as

the Lady of the Beasts, the Lady of the Date Clusters, the Earth Mother, Isis, Ishtar, Nut, Hathor, the Mesoamerican Coatlicue or Tonantzin or as the epitome of the great goddess reborn, the Virgin Mary, she was the symbol of fertility, of motherhood, and of the assurance of continued plant, animal, and human life. As Campbell suggests,

> A number of the typical and apparently perennial roles of this mother-goddess can be learned, furthermore, by simply perusing the Roman Catholic "Litany of Loreto," which is addressed to the Virgin Mother Mary. She is there called the Holy Mother of God, the Mother of Divine Grace and Mother of Good Counsel; the Virgin most renowned, Virgin most powerful, Virgin most merciful, Virgin most faithful; and she is praised as the Mirror of Justice, Seat of Wisdom, Cause of our Joy, Gate of Heaven, Morning Star, Health of the Sick, Refuge of Sinners, Comforter of the Afflicted, and Queen of Peace; Tower of David, Tower of Ivory, and House of Gold.[13]

In many myths even the god descends from the female source and is called her son. Or in stories such as that of Inanna, the god is called her husband. Because the source of all life often is seen as female, it is certainly understandable that the earliest deities would have been identified with the moon and the female principle. Not until later, when changes in the law of kinship gradually transferred a great deal of social power and authority to males, did the goddess lose a significant portion of her authority to the male deity. But even then, as we can see in connection with the Virgin Mary, the goddess, symbolic always of the female principle, continued to celebrate the fertility and creativity that must exist if life is to continue.

## Mythology and the Rise of Civilization

**Temple Worship and the Priesthood**: While the cult of the goddess provides a thread of continuity binding together the mythic thought of prehistoric peoples with the thought of the newly developed civilizations, there are other areas in which those civilizations break with the prehistoric past. Temple worship, for example, is a result, at least in part, of the institutional consolidation of the movement from the shaman (individualistic religious specialist of the hunting peoples of the Paleolithic period and later times) to the priest (characteristic of the settled, communal life of agriculturalists). According to Campbell,

> the priest is the socially initiated, ceremonially inducted member of a recognized religious organization, where he holds a certain rank and functions as the tenant of an office that was held by others before him, while the shaman is one who, as a consequence of a personal psychological crisis, has gained a certain power of his own. The spiritual visitants who came to him in vision had never been seen before by any other.[14]

From the standpoint of the study of mythology, especially of the "transformations of myth through time," this difference is significant for several reasons.

**Priestly Ritual**: First, although myths function in several ways within a culture (see Introduction), each of those functions is dependent in one way or another on ritual (see the discussion of initiation in Unit 1 and the stages of life in Unit 2 for a review of the ties between the functions of myth and ritual). Such ritual, when performed or guided by the individualistic shaman, tends to focus on the participant as an autonomous individual and on his or her individual relationship to the mysterious well-spring of life experienced or contacted through the ritual process. Ritual conducted in a temple by a priestly member of the institution of the religious hierarchy sanctioned by the culture tends, on the other hand, to be communal in its emphasis, binding the individual to the community of communicants and to the society as a whole. Such priestly ritual favors the further development of the communal ethos within which it occurs and thus, functions as an integral part of the developing city civilization. Within such a civilization, as Campbell has observed, the individual no longer can know all of the lore of the society as individual members of the simpler hunting and gathering cultures could. Specialization is the hallmark of the urban civilization, and each individual must see himself or herself as a component part of the whole. The priest, of course, becomes the specialist of the sacred, in a different way from the earlier shaman. Through the priesthood, the lore of the sacred is preserved and transmitted.

**Myth as History and Myth as Metaphor**: Second, the development of a specialized priesthood leads to a predictable result. Within each of the highly developed religions of humankind there are, in a sense, two religions. One is the religion of the common people, those whose lives are devoted primarily to pursuits other than religion. That religion is generally rather simple, and the mythic tales that provide its foundation often are believed quite literally. Myth, in this context, is history, and, as we can see often today, if such mythic history conflicts with observable reality or the science of the time, tensions arise. There is another religion, however, that might be characterized as the esoteric religion of the priesthood. That religion, based on the same mythic foundation and observing the same rituals as the religion of the common people, often is extremely complex. This complexity arises from the priest's tendency and ability to read the myths on which the religion is founded as metaphor and symbol.

Marcel Griaule, who spent a significant portion of his life studying the complex religion of the Dogon people of Africa, finally came to precisely this understanding after years of field work.

> In African societies which have preserved their traditional organization the number of persons who are trained in this knowledge is quite considerable. This they call "deep knowledge" in contrast with the "simple knowledge" which is regarded as "only a beginning in the understanding of beliefs and customs" that people who are not fully instructed in the cosmogony possess.... But among groups where tradition is still vigorous, this knowl-

edge, which is expressly characterized as esoteric, is only secret in the following sense. It is in fact open to all who show a will to understand so long as, by their social position and moral conduct, they are judged worthy of it. Thus every family head, every priest, every grown-up person responsible for some small fraction of social life can, as part of the social group, acquire knowledge on the condition that he has the patience and, as the African phrase has it, "he comes to sit by the side of the competent elders" over the period and in the state of mind necessary. Then he will receive answers to all his questions, *but it will take years*.[15]

It is clear that in the archaic societies with which this unit is concerned, the priesthood, which developed and communicated this esoteric knowledge, was linked directly to the rulers of the societies. At times, in fact, the functions of priest and ruler were exercised by the same person. Thus, rulership became aligned with spiritual knowledge, and the ruler came to be seen as an emissary of the gods or as a god incarnate. What Campbell calls the "kingly art of government" and the priesthood were related developments in these archaic societies.

**The Impact of Writing**: A third significance of the development of temple worship and a specialized priesthood can be understood by realizing their connection with another hallmark of civilization—writing. The development of writing, probably in Mesopotamia in the fourth millennium B.C.E., brought with it the ability to keep the records of an increasingly complex society and to preserve the occurrences of a particular time and place, in essence, to create history. In addition, it permitted the development of a large, complex body of speculative thought, as one generation of thinkers was able to build on the thought recorded by the previous generation. Before the development of writing, myths existed in an oral tradition that was extremely conservative in its primary concern with the preservation of the tradition it communicated. The emphasis was on precisely learning and communicating the mythic lore. There was little room for innovation within such a tradition. The development of writing freed the mind from the task of preserving the tradition. Therefore, it favored the development of a body of speculative religious thought based on an exegesis of the mythic heritage that would have been beyond the capability of the traditional planting societies of the Neolithic period just as it would have been too complex for the individual shamans of the hunters.

Bruce Lincoln summarizes these changes, brought about by the development of a priestly tradition, in his comments on the priestly class of the early Indo-European societies. He says that "we may accurately view the priestly class as an elite intelligentsia, devoted not only to speculation on the nature of man and the cosmos, together with the performance of rituals attendant to such speculation, but also to the propagation of a social ideology encoded in the . . . myths." He notes that "these priests viewed themselves as discovering, articulating, and transmitting the most sacred and profound of all truths, in which were revealed nothing less than the fundamental structures of reality,"[16] and we might add that the societies that these priests served also regarded them as the keepers of the sacred.

## Astronomy and Mathematics: The Twin Keys to the Mystery of the Universe

Nowhere were those "fundamental structures of reality" more clearly revealed to the early priests than in the regularity in the movements of the heavenly bodies, which they were able to observe in the nighttime sky. In the selection from *The Skywatchers of Ancient Mexico* included in the *Anthology of Readings*, the archaeo-astronomer Anthony Aveni suggests that it is difficult for us today to appreciate the degree to which the ancients were preoccupied with astronomy because our own lives are so different from theirs. But as Campbell points out, the traces of that early fascination with heavenly order remain even today, "where the festivals of the religious year still follow the seasonal signs of sun and moon, kings and queens wear radiant celestial crowns, and to the God whose glory the heavens proclaim, there is daily lifted the Christian prayer: 'Thy will be done, on earth as it is in heaven.'"[17]

But where did that fascination with the regularity of the movement of the heavenly bodies begin? From the data archaeology provides, it appears that the priests of the temple compounds of ancient Sumer, of the cities now called Ur, Kish, Lagash, Shuruppak, Uruk, Ubaid, Nippur, and others like them in the Tigris and Euphrates valleys during the fourth millennium B.C.E., were the first to practice the "science of exact astronomical observation, which had been made possible by recorded notations." For them, "the measured movements of the seven visible celestial spheres—Sun, Moon, Mercury, Venus, Mars, Jupiter, and Saturn—along an apparently circular way through the constellations, led to the realization, altogether new to the world, of a cosmos *mathematically* ordered."[18]

Having discovered that the sun, moon, and visible planets moved through the heavens day by day and year by year in an order absolutely predictable through mathematical calculations, it must have seemed to those early skyward-gazing priests that they had discovered in mathematics the principle of order itself. Through this understanding of mathematics, they felt they were able to approach the workings of the divinity they worshipped. The somewhat later Greek mystic and mathematician, Pythagoras (c. 582 – c. 507 B.C.E.), believed that numbers were the essence of all things, and that even the relationship between human beings and the gods could be expressed and understood through mathematics. The seemingly magical manipulation of numbers could reveal the unchanging order underlying the changing forms of nature. The mathematically expressible abstract constants of the universe, such as the Pythagorean theorem we still learn today, thus expressed the mystical order underlying what might seem to the uninitiated to be the chaos of nature.

Having discovered what they took to be the essence of universal order in the mathematically comprehensible regularity of the movements of the heavenly spheres, the priests of ancient Sumer set about trying to replicate that divine order on earth. "The whole city . . . was now conceived as an imitation on earth of the cosmic order, a sociological 'middle cosmos,' or mesocosm, established by priestcraft between the macrocosm of the universe and the microcosm of the individual, making visible the one essential form of all."[19] That cosmic order "became the celestial model for the good society on earth: the king enthroned, crowned as the moon or sun, the queen as the goddess-planet Venus, and the high dignitaries of the court in the roles of the various celestial lights."[20]

Astronomy and mathematics of the ancient Sumerians were not practiced for scientific ends. Rather than attempting to discover physical laws governing the natural world, as do scientists today, the ancients wanted to discover spiritual laws functioning within the mysterious realm of the supernatural through which human beings could harmonize their lives with the divine order. Their astronomy created the first astrology, a system using "the orderly round-dance of the five visible planets and the sun and moon through the constellations of the zodiac"[21] as a means of understanding the past and prophesying the future. Time, according to their new understanding, was cyclical, and each segment of the cycle had particular characteristics that would determine the events and fortunes of both the society as mesocosm and the individual as microcosm.

Giorgio de Santillana and Hertha von Dechend, in *Hamlet's Mill: An Essay on Myth and the Frame of Time*, offer a fascinating but complex and often difficult study of the ancient knowledge of astronomical phenomena and the relationship of those phenomena to mythology. They summarize these developments in a way that captures, despite its difficulty, the awe with which this ancient knowledge must have been regarded then, in contrast to our temptation today to take such wonders for granted since they no longer speak to us of the transcendent. Our forebears, these two authors say, not only built

> time into a structure, *cyclic time*: along with it came their creative idea of Number as the secret of things. . . . Cosmological Time, the "dance of stars" as Plato called it, was not a mere angular measure, an empty container, as it has now become, the container of so-called history; that is, of frightful and meaningless surprises that people have resigned themselves to calling the *fait accompli*. It was felt to be potent enough to control events inflexibly, as it molded them to its sequences in a cosmic manifold in which past and future called to each other, deep calling to deep. The awesome Measure repeated and echoed the structure in many ways, gave Time the scansion, the inexorable decisions through which an instant "fell due." Those interlocking Measures were endowed with such a transcendent dignity as to give a foundation to reality that all of modern Physics cannot achieve; for, unlike physics, they conveyed the first idea of "what

it is to be," and what they focused on became by contrast almost a blend of past and future, so that Time tended to be essentially oracular.[22]

What these ancient seers had achieved, apparently for the first time in human history, was a conception of the cosmos as governed by a unitary law. This law might manifest itself in a multitude of ways in the natural world, but, in essence, it was mystically single and simple. According to Campbell, this law was known to the ancient Sumerians as *Me*; to the Egyptians as *Maat*; and later, in the Orient where its dictates still are followed, in Chinese as *Tao*, and in Sanskrit as *Dharma*.[23] It has since been superseded in the West, he believed, by a mythological understanding of reality rooted not in astronomy, but in psychology—an understanding that he has called the "Way of Man" and which manifests itself in the emphasis on individualism throughout the Western world today. That earlier emphasis on cosmic law, however, still can be seen as the underpinning of mythological thought throughout the Orient.

In the Orient still today, as must have been the case in ancient Sumer, "the first duty of the individual. . . . is simply to play his given role—as do the sun and moon, the various animal and plant species, the waters, the rocks, and the stars—without resistance, without fault; and then, if possible, so to order his mind as to identify its consciousness with the inhabiting principle of the whole."[24] In this way the individual, the society, and the gods could be seen as an integral whole functioning in harmony within the cycles through which time, life, and the heavens moved.

## ASSIGNMENTS FOR STUDY AND ANALYSIS

1. After reading the selections in the *Anthology of Readings* by Marija Gimbutas and Anne L. Barstow and this unit in the *Study Guide*, write an essay in which you consider the connections between the Great Goddess and the feminine/lunar principle as defined in Unit 1.
2. After viewing the television program for this unit and reading the Gimbutas selection in the *Anthology of Readings* in the *Study Guide*, consider the various symbols associated with the Great Goddess. Which of those symbols have similar connotations in our own society?
3. Discuss the relationship between the symbols associated with the goddess and an agricultural society. How would that relationship have an effect on the eventual change from a matriarchal to a patriarchal society?
4. Consider the Hullupu-tree in the story of Inanna and how it relates metaphorically to trees discussed in the other units in this telecourse. What does the use of these trees suggest about the relationship of humanity to nature? What does the story of Inanna suggest about this relationship?
5. Write an essay in which you explain how the desire to find order in the universe would be a stimulus to the study of

astronomy and mathematics. Point out as many kinds of order as you can, both natural and spiritual, that could be derived from that study.
6. Discuss the three developments that came with temple worship and a specialized priesthood. Show how and to what extent each has continued to influence the world in which we live. Which seems to you to have been the most important in the development of civilization?

## FURTHER ASSIGNMENTS FOR WRITING AND REFLECTION

1. Compare the attributes of the masculine and feminine principles and consider why the female deity would seem particularly important in an agricultural society.
2. Consider the implications of having a feminine deity rather than a male deity in a society. What effect would it have on the basic assumptions of a culture and on its mythology?
3. Review the various symbols associated with the Great Goddess. Which of them have similar associations in the world today? Which would not be acceptable to a feminist? Which of them do we still consider important feminine attributes? What can you say about the meaning of the changes that have taken place?
4. Consider which of the attributes of the goddesses discussed in this unit still are associated with the Virgin Mary. Write an essay about the way our society, or the various components of our society, evaluates these attributes in connection with women in general.
5. Write a brief essay explaining why it is important, from a feminist point of view, to trace mythology back to a time when "god was a woman." If you were writing a lengthy study from that point of view, how would you incorporate the information in this unit to make your point?
6. Write a brief essay showing how mathematics or astronomy is used to provide our society with a sense of universal order.

## ENDNOTES

[1]Joseph Campbell, *The Masks of God: Occidental Mythology* (New York: Viking Press, 1964) 6–7.

[2]Joseph Campbell, *The Way of the Seeded Earth*, Part 1: "The Sacrifice" vol. II of *Historical Atlas of World Mythology* (New York: Harper and Row, 1988) 10–11.

[3]Campbell, *Seeded Earth* 11.

[4]Campbell, *Primitive Mythology* 139.

[5]Elizabeth Gould Davis, *The First Sex* (Harmondsworth, Eng.: Penguin Books, 1971) 77 ff.

[6]Marija Gimbutas, *The Goddesses and Gods of Old Europe, 6500–3500 BC* (Berkeley and Los Angeles: University of California Press, 1982) 166, *see also* 107.

[7]Gimbutas 107.

[8]Gimbutas 135.

[9]Gimbutas 152.

[10]Samuel Noah Kramer, *From the Poetry of Sumer: Creation, Glorification, Adoration* (Berkeley: University of California Press, 1979) 71.

[11]Diane Wolkstein, "Interpretations of Inanna's Stories and Hymns," *Inanna, Queen of Heaven and Earth: Her Stories and Hymns from Sumer* by Diane Wolkstein and Samuel Noah Kramer, (New York: Harper and Row, 1983) 144.

[12]Wolkstein 145.

[13]Campbell, *Primitive Mythology* 139–40.

[14]Campbell, *Primitive Mythology* 231.

[15]Germaine Dieterlen, "Introduction," *Conversations with Ogotemmêli: An Introduction to Dogon Religious Ideas* by Marcel Griaule, (London: Oxford University Press, 1965) xiv.

[16]Bruce Lincoln, *Myth, Cosmos, and Society: Indo-European Themes of Creation and Destruction* (Cambridge: Harvard University Press, 1986) 164–65.

[17]Campbell, *Animal Powers* 10.

[18]Campbell, *Animal Powers.*

[19]Campbell, *Primitive Mythology* 147.

[20]Joseph Campbell, *Myths to Live By* (New York: Viking Press, 1972) 56.

[21]Campbell, *Primitive Mythology* 149.

[22]Giorgio de Santillana and Hertha von Dechend, *Hamlet's Mill: An Essay on Myth and the Frame of Time* (Boston: David R. Godine, 1977) 332–33.

[23]Campbell, *Myths to Live By* 65.

[24]Joseph Campbell, *The Masks of God: Oriental Mythology* (New York: Viking Press, 1962) 3-4.

## UNIT BIBLIOGRAPHY

Campbell, Joseph. *The Masks of God: Oriental Mythology*. New York: Viking Press, 1962.

————. *The Masks of God: Occidental Mythology*. New York: Viking Press, 1964. These two volumes contain the most complete account of Campbell's thought concerning the material in this unit.

Christ, Carol P. and Judith Plaskow, eds. *Womenspirit Rising: A Feminist Reader in Religion*. New York: Harper and Row, 1979.

Olson, Carl, ed. *The Book of the Goddess Past and Present: An Introduction to Her Religion*. New York: Crossroad, 1983. These two books contain a number of excellent essays, primarily written from a feminist point of view, dealing with the goddess in her various manifestations.

Frankfort, H., H. A. Frankfort, John A. Wilson, Thorkild Jacobsen, and William A. Irwin. *The Intellectual Adventure of Ancient Man: An Essay on Speculative Thought in the Ancient Near East*. Chicago: University of Chicago Press, 1946. These scholars, each of them preeminent at the time in his own field, discuss the earliest evidence of the movement from mythology to the speculative thought we know as philosophy and theology among the Egyptians, the Mesopotamians, and the Hebrews.

Wheatley, Paul. *The Pivot of the Four Quarters*. Chicago: Aldine, 1971. Wheatley, an urban geographer, discusses the ancient city as an organizing principle for the civilization in which it existed and considers its symbolic associations as well.

Wolkstein, Diane and Samuel Noah Kramer. *Inanna, Queen of Heaven and Earth: Her Stories and Hymns from Sumer*. New York: Harper and Row, 1983. A new and very readable translation of the myth with insightful comments about its meaning and the history of its discovery and decipherment.

# NOTES

# NOTES

# NOTES

PETER MARKMAN
ROBERTA H. MARKMAN

# Pharaoh's Rule:
## *Egypt, the Exodus, and the Myth of Osiris*

## UNIT STUDY PLAN

1. Read Unit 4 in your *Study Guide*.
2. Watch Program 4: "Pharaoh's Rule: Egypt, the Exodus, and the Myth of Osiris."
3. In your course notebook or journal, write a brief summary of Joseph Campbell's interpretation of the myth of Osiris.
4. Read the selections for this unit in the *Anthology of Readings*. These selections include excerpts from works by Henri Frankfort, E. A. Wallis Budge, and James Henry Breasted.
5. After reading the selections, comment in your notebook on what you have read. Show the relationship between the readings and the essay in this unit.
6. Complete the assignments at the end of this unit as specified by your instructor.

## POINTS TO WATCH FOR IN THE TELEVISION PROGRAM

*This television program was delivered as a lecture by Joseph Campbell in Sante Fe, New Mexico, in 1982.*

1. Reflect upon the experience that Campbell relates regarding his reading of Martin Buber. What does Campbell mean when he says that he didn't know what Buber meant by god? Note the several examples that Campbell offers to show how god is defined in various ways.
2. Make a brief list of the various gods and their symbolic representations that Campbell discusses. You will want to remember them when they are referred to in the remaining units of this television course.
3. Note the origin of the Sphinx and its relationship to the pharaoh, as well as the relationship between the pharaoh and Osiris.
4. Listen carefully to Campbell's retelling of the basic myth of Osiris and Isis. Consider the symbol of the tree in this myth.
5. Note Campbell's description of the judgement scene.
6. Consider Campbell's comparison of the monotheism of Ikhnaton and of Moses.
7. Notice how Campbell uses the art of the tomb of the Pharaoh, Ramses the Second, to reconstruct both the history and the mythology of the period, including the story of the Exodus.

## POINTS TO LOOK FOR IN THE *ANTHOLOGY OF READINGS*

1. Henri Frankfort writes in "The Egyptian Gods," the first chapter of his *Ancient Egyptian Religion: An Interpretation*, of the possibilities of looking at the gods and their symbols, the significance of the sacred animals, and the cosmic gods and their relationships to human problems in ancient Egypt.
2. E. A. Wallis Budge, in "Gods of Egypt" from *The Gods of the Egyptians*, provides an excellent background for the study of Egyptian mythology by explaining the relationship of the gods to nature and discussing the elements of magic prevalent in ancient Egyptian ritual.
3. James Henry Breasted, in his book, *Development of Religion and Thought in Ancient Egypt*, discusses the "Osirinization of the Hereafter" and provides the background necessary to understand the rituals by which the deceased entered into the world beyond. He quotes extensively from the Pyramid Texts, thereby helping his readers to become aware of the original source material.

## UNIT GLOSSARY

**Adze**: A cutting tool with a thin arched blade set at right angles to the handle.

**Atum**: The sun god in the aspect of the setting sun portrayed as the figure of an old man.

**Ba**: A combination of the soul and the intelligence in ancient Egypt.

**Martin Buber (1878–1965)**: Jewish philosopher whose theological writings have had a wide influence throughout the world.

**Sigmund Freud (1856–1939)**: Austrian pioneer of psychoanalysis. Author of *Moses and Monotheism*, which suggests as its thesis that Moses, considered one of the greatest Jewish historical figures, was not a Jew, but an Egyptian, and that Moses chose the Hebrews to be the inheritors of Ikhnaton's religion. Freud's psychoanalytic interpretation of the evidence makes fascinating reading.

**Johann Wolfgang von Goethe (1749–1832)**: German poet, dramatist, novelist. Author of *Faust*, a rarely performed play, completed just before his death and very important in the history of German literature. In the second act of the play, Goethe shows the price one must pay to achieve one's highest goals (in Faust's case, the innocent Baucis and Philomen must be killed).

**Hammurabi (2100 B.C.E.):** King of Babylonia, his code of laws is one of the most famous of ancient documents.

**Herodotus (c. 484–425 B.C.E.):** Greek historian known as the father of history. His work, the first comprehensive attempt at secular narrative history, is the beginning of the writing of history in the Western world.

**Ikhnaton:** King of Egypt from 1375 to 1358 B.C.E. He was the son of Amenhotep III and began his reign as Amenhotep IV. He changed his name when he attempted to unify political, social, and artistic life under a monotheistic cult centered around the sun god Aton. The priests opposed him and gradually he was brought to ruin, but his reign was one of the greatest for Egyptian art.

**Ka:** To the ancient Egyptian, a kind of "double" of the deceased that had been with the person since he was born, but functioned at his death to guide the individual in the realm of the dead. At death one was said to have "gone to his ka."

**Moses:** Lawgiver of Israel and the prophet who led his people out of bondage in Egypt to the edge of Canaan, the Promised Land. Through Moses, God gave the Ten Commandments, the criminal code, and liturgical law to the people. Therefore, they are called Mosaic law.

**Mycenae:** An ancient city in Greece that reached its height of development about 1600 B.C.E. Excavations here in 1876 helped to rewrite the history of Greece.

**Nefertite:** The Queen of Ikhnaton's rule. A statue bust of her is one of the greatest treasures of world art.

**Old, Middle, and New Kingdoms:** Historical division of ancient Egyptian civilization into its three primary phases. They lasted, respectively, from 2686 to 2181 B.C.E., 2133 to 1786 B.C.E., and 1567 to 1085 B.C.E. with intermediary phases between these periods.

**Papyrus:** Ancient Egyptians used the roots of this plant for fuel, the pith for food, and the stem for boats, cloth, twine, and sheets of writing material that also is called papyrus.

**Pharaoh:** The biblical title of the kings of Egypt

**Ra:** The sun god worshipped in Egypt. The concept of supreme rule became associated with the sun cults in Egypt through this deity.

**Syncretism:** The combination of different forms of belief or practice.

**Tutankhamen (c. 1355 B.C.E.):** King of ancient Egypt of the XVIII dynasty. He was the son-in-law of Ikhnaton and revised the latter's policy by returning to the worship of Amon. His tomb was opened in 1922 by Howard Carter.

## UNIT PREVIEW

In this unit you will be introduced to several important aspects of Egyptian mythology and its relationship to that of other cultures.

**The Myth of Osiris, Isis, and Horus:** This, the preeminent Egyptian myth, explains the importance of Osiris and his association with fertility. It provides the foundation for much of Egyptian mythological structure and thought, such as the preparation of the deceased for a blissful life beyond the grave.

**Death in Egypt:** The concept of death accounts for much of the important ritual and mythological thought in ancient Egypt and includes the idea of the ka and the ba associated with the deceased.

**Preparation for the World Beyond:** Because death did not mean the end of life, the preparation of the body was a vital consideration in ancient Egypt.

**The Pyramid Texts, the Coffin Texts, and the Book of the Dead:** These various and vitally important texts, which include funerary rituals, mortuary offerings, ancient religious hymns, magical charms, fragments of old myths, and prayers, provide us with a great deal of evidence regarding the world of ancient Egypt.

## UNIT ESSAY

### History and Geography

Any consideration of ancient Egyptian thought generally, and of that civilization's mythology specifically, must take into account the geography and the history of the land. Geographically, Egypt is unique. Its civilization developed, and continues even today to exist, entirely along the narrow ribbon of the Nile valley, bounded on either side by forbidding desert terrain that both isolated and protected Egyptian culture. Within those bounds, the Nile created a fertile valley capable of providing sustenance for life in abundance. The agriculture that brought forth that plentiful bounty from the earth supported a vast society of commoners, wealthy nobles, and pharaohs whose wealth must have seemed im-

measurable to the commoner. The agriculture was based necessarily on the cyclical changes in the river because rainfall was, and still is, essentially nonexistent. Large systems of irrigation and tight regulation of access to and use of water (which could only be accomplished by strong central rule) made social cohesiveness imperative. As all historians note, in times of strong rule, Egypt prospered. When it was lacking, Egypt faltered.

In the course of a year, the river on which life depended went through three stages. From June to September, the melting snows in the mountains of its origin in Ethiopia and Uganda raised the Nile to flood stage and the lands along its course in the valley were inundated, a flooding now controlled by dams. From October through February, the flood subsided, the fields

## CHRONOLOGY: A listing of events significant in the history of ancient Egypt

EXACT DATING OF EVENTS AT THIS REMOVE IN TIME IS ALMOST IMPOSSIBLE. DATES USED HERE ARE APPROXIMATIONS BASED ON THE MOST RECENT STUDIES.

| B.C. | Periods | Dynasties | | Politics and Trade | Culture and Society |
|---|---|---|---|---|---|
| 3200 | | | | Upper and Lower Egypt are united by Menes, the first Pharaoh, who builds his capital at Memphis | |
| 3100 | EARLY DYNASTIC PERIOD 3100–2686 | Dynasty I | 3100–2890 | Trade with Levant | Development of calendar and hieroglyphic writing |
| 3000 | | | | Expeditions to Sudan | Copper tools and weapons in use |
| 2900 | | | | Large irrigation and drainage projects are undertaken | Royal tombs built near Abydos and Memphis |
| | | | | | First known treatise on surgery |
| 2800 | | Dynasty II | 2890–2686 | Religious and political strife between Upper and Lower Egypt | Granite and slate statuary in use |
| | | | | Reunification under Pharaoh Khasekhemwy | Increased use of stone in building |
| 2700 | | | | | Skillful metal, ivory, wood and faïence work |
| 2600 | OLD KINGDOM 2686–2181 | Dynasty III | 2686–2613 | Djoser is outstanding ruler of this period | Large-scale building and sculpture in stone Step Pyramid built at Sakkarah |
| | | | | Lower Nubia under Egyptian rule | |
| 2500 | | Dynasty IV | 2613–2494 | Outstanding Pharaohs are Khufu, Khafre and Menkaure Wars waged against Nubians and Libyans; timber imported from Lebanon; copper mined in Sinai | Bent Pyramid of King Snefru built at Dahshur The Great Pyramids and the Sphinx built at Gizeh |
| 2400 | | Dynasty V | 2494–2345 | Gold and incense imported from Punt | Rise in importance of Heliopolis and its patron, the sun god Re Famed Pyramid Texts, records of funerary customs, inscribed in royal tombs Excellent sculpture in wood and stone for private patrons |
| 2300 | | | | Weakening of pharaoh's absolute power | |
| 2200 | | Dynasty VI | 2345–2181 | Internal strife grows during Pepi II's long reign Rise of feudal lords leads to anarchy | Feudal nobles build sepulchers in their own domains |
| 2100 | INTERMEDIATE PERIOD 2181–2040 | Dynasty VII | 2181–2173 | Many kings with short reigns; dissolution of royal power; social and political chaos | Ancient artistic tradition disrupted in wake of political turmoil; pyramids ransacked; tombs and statues destroyed |
| | | Dynasty VIII | 2173–2160 | | |
| | | Dynasty IX | 2160–2130 | Herakleopolitan rulers of Lower and Middle Egypt battle Theban rulers of Upper Egypt | Coffin Texts, later funerary writings, inscribed in tombs of nobles |
| 2000 | | Dynasty X | 2130–2040 | | |
| | | Dynasty XI | 2133–1991 | Reunification of Egypt under Theban Pharaoh Mentuhotep II, who establishes Thebes as capital | Artistic renaissance follows restoration of order Mentuhotep's mortuary temple built at Deir el Bahri |
| 1900 | MIDDLE KINGDOM 2133–1786 | Dynasty XII | 1991–1786 | Powerful pharaohs suppress feudal nobles, undertake large irrigation schemes, vigorously exploit Sinai copper mines, build advance outposts as far south as Third Cataract of the Nile. | Period of cultural splendor Development of portraiture Classical period of literature Temples and sculpture on colossal scale God Amon becomes prominent |
| 1800 | | | | | |
| 1700 | INTERMEDIATE PERIOD 1786–1567 | Dynasty XIII | 1786–1633 | Decay of central authority; seizure of power of Hyksos kings, who infiltrate from Asia | Decline of artistic standards and ideas |
| | | Dynasty XIV | 1786–1603 | | Disintegration of traditional culture under impact of Hyksos ideas and techniques |
| 1600 | | Dynasty XV | 1674–1567 | Under Hyksos rule, Egyptians introduced to powerful Asiatic equipment, including horse-drawn chariots Nubia and Lower Sudan regain freedom | |
| | | Dynasty XVI | 1684–1567 | | Improved spinning and weaving; bronze in general use New musical instruments—lyre, oboe, tambourine |
| 1500 | | Dynasty XVII | 1650–1567 | | |
| | | Dynasty XVIII | 1567–1320 | Egyptian Pharaoh Ahmose I ousts Hyksos Thutmose III expands empire to the Euphrates Other significant rulers: Hatshepsut, Amenhotep IV, (Akhenaton), Tutankhamen and Haremhab | Opulent craftsmanship, thriving literature Akhenaton fails to impose monotheism Elaborate tombs in Valley of Kings; temple of Amenhotep III at Luxor; temple of Hatshepsut at Deir el Bahri |
| 1400 | | | | | |
| 1300 | NEW KINGDOM 1567–1085 | Dynasty XIX | 1320–1200 | Pharaohs Seti I, Ramses II maintain Egyptian power, repel Hittite threat Under Merneptah, military power declines | Energetic building activity; temple of Ramses II at Thebes; Hypostyle Hall at Karnak; rock-cut temple at Abu Simbel "Books of the Dead" written on papyrus rolls |
| 1200 | | | | | |
| 1100 | | Dynasty XX | 1200–1085 | Rule of Ramesside Pharaohs (Ramses III-XI); invasions of Libyans and Sea Peoples repelled; loss of Asiatic dependencies; increasing poverty and lawlessness | Mortuary temple of Ramses III at Medinet Habu commemorates victories Tombs at Thebes looted |

| B.C. | Periods | Dynasties | | Politics and Trade | Culture and Society |
|---|---|---|---|---|---|
| 1000 | | Dynasty XXI | 1085–945 | Egypt divided; kings dependent on Libyan mercenaries | Completion of Khons temple at Karnak |
| 900 | | | | | |
| 800 | | Dynasty XXII | 950–730 | Kings of Libyan origin | Era of thriving craftsmanship<br>Bronze casting perfected<br>Skilled metal and faience work |
| | | Dynasty XXIII | 817–730 | Invasion of Palestine; Solomon's temple plundered<br>Growing dissension encourages invasion by Nubians | |
| 700 | LATE<br>DYNASTIC<br>PERIOD<br>1085–341 | Dynasty XXIV | 730–715 | Brief rule by Lower Egyptian king concurrent with Dynasty XXV | |
| 600 | | Dynasty XXV | 751–656 | Rule by Nubian pharaohs<br>Thebes sacked during Assyrian invasions | Nubian rulers foster study of the past<br>Beginnings of a cultural renaissance<br>New realism in sculpture |
| 500 | | Dynasty XXVI | 663–525 | Independence from Assyrians achieved;<br>Strong fleet; active commerce; trade with Greece | Arts of past imitated<br>Faultless incised inscriptions |
| 400 | | Dynasty XXVII | 525–404 | Persians conquer and rule Egypt, canal from Nile to Red Sea completed | Darius I of Persia commands codification of Egyptian law |
| | | Dynasty XXVIII | 404–398 | Persians expelled with Greek aid; Egyptian king enthroned | |
| | | Dynasty XXIX | 398–378 | Pharaohs from Delta rule briefly | Numerous monuments erected by Pharaoh Achoris |
| 300 | | Dynasty XXX | 378–341 | Last native pharaohs; reconquest of Egypt by Persians | Last flowering of native Egyptian art |
| 200 | PTOLEMAIC<br>PERIOD<br>332–30 | | | Alexander the Great conquers Egypt; on death of Alexander, one of his generals founds Ptolemaic Dynasty | Temple of Isis at Philae<br>Temple of Horus at Edfu<br>Temple at Kom Ombo<br>Temple of Hather at Dendera |

emerged from the water, and the planting cycle took place. Drought prevailed from March until June when the flood waters reappeared. In ancient times, the flooding period, called the Inundation, served two vital purposes. First, it brought an abundance of water to wet the parched earth, water that could be trapped in artificially constructed catch basins and used for irrigation throughout the growing season. Second, and equally important, the flooding river deposited rich black soil from its mountain sources on the valley's fields. In a literal sense, then, the river was the source of life for the Egyptians. The connection of Osiris with the Nile as a symbol of resurrection clearly had its roots in the geography of the land.

Throughout ancient times, Egypt was conceived as having two parts: Lower Egypt, dominated by the area where the Nile fans out into the Delta; and Upper Egypt, where the river runs its narrow course between deserts and through gorges. At first politically distinct, these two areas were joined early on (c. 3000 B.C.E.) under the rule of one pharaoh, traditionally known as Menes. Menes is associated with the Narmer Palette, a symbolically decorated, carved stone palette of the sort originally used in preparing cosmetics. He and the two dynasties that succeeded him in the next 400 years unified Egypt from their base in the Delta city of Memphis. They began the practice of constructing elaborate tombs for their afterlives that inspired the later pyramids, and set the stage for the prosperity of the period that was to follow their rule. The following period has come to be known as the Old Kingdom. It lasted from 2686–2181 B.C.E. and saw four dynasties of Lower Egypt rule in succession. This was the period of the Pyramid Texts,

hieroglyphic texts inscribed within the pyramids' tombs to aid the dead pharaoh in the afterlife. Mythic themes were consolidated into a powerful religion during this period.

Feuding between nobles, each with their own regional interests, drought, and external pressures, eventually led to a period of strife before the reassertion of strong unified rule in the period known as the Middle Kingdom. The ruling dynasties of this period, 2133–1786 B.C.E., were located at Thebes in Upper Egypt and inaugurated a period of large public works and cultural and artistic development. It was in this period that the god Amon became prominent. Following a second occurrence of dissension and foreign pressures, the period now known as the New Kingdom arose in 1567 B.C.E. and saw the beginning of foreign conquests and the building of an Egyptian empire that was to last through three dynasties until 1085 B.C.E. At that point, the gradual decline of Egyptian civilization began.

Even such a brief survey as this suggests the importance of the institution of the pharaoh to the integrity and development of Egypt. It is not surprising, then, that Egyptian mythology focuses a great deal of attention not only on the pharaoh's godly nature, but on the continuity of rule from pharaoh to pharaoh. The pharaoh, in a mystical sense, always existed; each individual pharaoh was but a manifestation of that spiritual reality. When the living pharaoh (identified with the god Horus) died, he became Osiris. The new pharaoh, who legitimized his rule by burying his predecessor as Horus buried Osiris, then became Horus. In this sense, the pharaoh never died; Horus lived and ruled eternally. Thus both Egyptian history, in its manifestation of the need for a strong ruler to unify the society and manage the production and distribution of food, and Egyptian geography, in its dependence on the Nile, played an essential role in the development of Egyptian mythology.

But one must realize that this mythology shares its major themes with the other great mythologies arising at that same time in the Near East. According to Campbell, "the myths of the dead and resurrected god Osiris so closely resemble those of Tammuz, Adonis, and Dionysos as to be practically the same . . . . The myth of Osiris, therefore, and his sister-bride, the goddess Isis, must be read as Egypt's variant of a common, late Neolithic, early Bronze Age theme."[1] What differs are the local forms of the universal ideas, what Bastian called the völkergedanken (discussed in the Introductory Unit). Those distinctive inflections can be seen in all the images and tales of Egyptian mythology.

## Osiris, Isis, and Horus

**The Myth:** Throughout the centuries of Egyptian culture, the most popular and probably the most important myth, as can be seen from the written and artistic evidence that remains, is the story of Osiris, his faithful wife Isis, and their son Horus. Although a full version of the entire myth exists only in the writings of Plutarch, a Roman of later times, there are numerous local Egyptian variants of each of the myth's episodes which, when put together, tell essentially the same story as the one recounted by Plutarch. A full version of the myth, taking into account all of those variants and the changes it underwent through the millenia of its development, would fill volumes, but the basic story is fairly straightforward and remains constant throughout its history. According to that story, Osiris was born of Nut, the Mother Goddess who is the vault of the heavens above the earth in Egyptian myth. Since it is Nut who devours the sun at evening and gives it birth in the morning, her bearing Osiris already suggests his identification with the sun. His father was Geb, the earth, suggesting his strong identification with fertility. Geb and Nut were also the parents of Seth, Osiris's envious brother, and of Isis and Nephthys. In due time, Osiris married Isis, assumed the throne of Egypt, and brought civilization to the land by teaching the cannibalistic inhabitants to grow crops, to worship the gods, and to obey the laws he provided. Turning his attention to the civilizing of the rest of the world, Osiris traveled through neighboring lands bestowing the benefits of civilization he had brought to his own people who in his absence were ruled by Isis.

While he was gone, his brother Seth, who had married Nephthys, perhaps jealous because he had not been given the throne in Osiris's absence, plotted against Isis's rule. As Campbell recounts in the television program for this unit, when Osiris returned from his travels, he was tricked by Seth into climbing into his own sarcophagus which was then sealed and cast into the floodwaters of the Nile. It floated down the river

to the Mediterranean, and eventually found its way to Byblos, a coastal city in Syria, where a tamarisk tree grew around it, reaching amazing size. The size of the tree attracted the local monarch who had it cut down and then erected as a pillar, still containing Osiris, in his palace. In the meantime, Isis searched for her lost husband. Using her intuition and the reports of observers, she traced the sarcophagus down the Nile, discovered it had entered the Mediterranean, and sought along the coast for the place where it had come ashore. Finally she found the palace and the pillar that now held Osiris inside of it.

In the television program, Campbell tells the details of her entering the palace as a child's nursemaid, suggestive of her maternal role in this myth and in Egyptian thought, and eventually being given the body of her husband. On the way back to Egypt with the body, Isis was able to revive Osiris sufficiently to be able to conceive a son with him. Upon her return, Seth discovered the body of Osiris, left unattended for a time by Isis, and tore it into fourteen, fifteen, or sixteen pieces which he then scattered all along the course of the Nile, hoping finally to be rid of his brother. But Isis, ever faithful, began her search for her husband anew, eventually finding all his parts but one, his penis which had been swallowed by a fish. Aided by Nephthys, Isis reassembled Osiris and revived him enough to enable him to enter the Land of the Dead where he became the ruler. As Campbell puts it in the television program, the dead Osiris is "the resurrected Osiris who is now the judge of the dead in the underworld."

While these events were taking place, Isis gave birth to Horus, Osiris's son, in the marshlands of the Nile Delta where she had sought refuge from Seth. As a baby, Horus was stung by a scorpion and on the verge of death. Isis appealed to the supreme god, Ra, for aid, and through the intervention of Ra, Horus was saved. Shortly thereafter, Isis contrived to learn Ra's secret name, and when she did, she attained Ra's supreme power for herself and her son and, by extension, for Osiris as well. But the jealous Seth still governed in Egypt, and as Horus was growing up in the marshlands, his dead father instructed him in warfare. When Horus attained manhood, he called together the supporters of Osiris and attacked Seth and his forces. After a protracted struggle and the intervention of other gods, Horus finally prevailed, primarily as the result of his own courageous actions, and became ruler of the two Egypts, Lower and Upper, united under one pharaoh.

**The Theme of Fertility**: The events of the myth suggest the fundamental connection in Egyptian mythic thought between Osiris and fertility. Born of the maternal sky and the paternal earth, he unites the two realms responsible for the growth of plant, animal, and therefore human life. Fittingly he acts as a culture hero to introduce to humanity the knowledge of agriculture, the bringing forth of life from the earth. Osiris was originally the focal point of a fertility cult that probably came from Syria into Egypt. Even before the earliest written records, his mythology and theology already seem to have been fully developed. Even in historic times, however, his fertility connections remain apparent because each year at the time that the flood waters of the Inundation began to recede from the fields, the Egyptians made clay figures of Osiris into which they pressed seeds that would germinate, causing a miniature field of grain to grow from the god's body. More grandiose figures of the same sort were found in pharaohs' tombs, indicating both the importance of the belief and its symbolic nature. In this sense Osiris was the mystic embodiment of the life-force that sprouted anew in each plant as the fields emerged each year from the Nile's flood.

The end of the agricultural cycle was related to Osiris as a guarantor of fertility as well. At the harvest, farmers lamented their cutting down the grain, symbolic of the god, and trampling him to pieces in the threshing. But as the myth foretold, the spirit of life embodied in the harvested grain, as in Osiris's being "grown into" the tamarisk tree or the dismembered Osiris, was not destroyed. It would rise again with the sprouting seeds of the next cycle. The same seemingly paradoxical union of life and death can be seen in the images of Osiris that survive. Depicted as a human figure showing only his hands and head emerging from a tight fitting, mummy like white garment emphasizing his passivity, his skin is colored black or green, colors associated with fertility in the Egyptian mind. Black was the color of the fertile soil deposited on the fields by the flooding Nile each year, and green, of course, was the color of the plant life that resulted from that fertility. Therefore, Osiris could be seen as both the cause of the fertility and the nourishing life-force resulting from it.

**Life, Death, and Resurrection**: It is clear that the Egyptians extended Osiris's fertility associations beyond their presumably original agricultural connection. As lord of the underworld, Osiris became the generator of life since death did not mean to them, as it often does to us, the end of life. The Egyptians, in fact, had an almost unique view of life and death as the result of their geographical situation. The Nile Valley, like the deserts surrounding it, was essentially rainless. Life existed only as far from the river's banks as the life-nurturing water extended. As noted Egyptologist John Wilson puts it, "the line of demarcation between life and nonlife is startlingly clear: one may stand at the edge of the cultivation with one foot on the irrigated black soil and one foot on the desert sands."[2] The river banks with their black soil and green vegetation were associated with life while the deserts represented death. But within the bounds of the vital riverbanks there was another separation of life and death. Daily, the rising of the sun into the cloudless sky separated the life of day from the death of night, and annually the cyclical change in the river brought life and then death to the crops. Their unique geography, then, gave the Egyptians two views of death. On the one hand it could be seen as two eternally distinct states—fertile riverbank and barren desert, a land of life and a land of death. On the other hand, however, life and death were parts of a single process through

which the life-force, whether symbolized as sun or river, could be seen to move. Osiris was that always resurrecting life-force for, as we have seen in the myth itself, he was directly associated not only with the Land of the Dead as its lord, but with the sun and the Nile. One of the Pyramid Texts makes this identification clear as it records King Ramses IV addressing Osiris: "Thou art indeed the Nile, great on the fields at the beginning of the seasons; gods and men live by the moisture that is in thee."[3]

In the earliest recorded times, Osiris was associated with the reigning pharaohs, but not with other mortals, as if to say that these pharaohs, like the sun and the Nile, would not die. They would live on in the Land of the Dead in the changed state of Osiris who had become and would remain spirit. In the course of the development of Egyptian spiritual thought, this identification of the dead with Osiris was broadened to include, first, the nobles associated with the pharaoh and finally, all human beings. According to this view, as Campbell points out in the television program, "when a person dies, he becomes identified with Osiris. The dead person is called Osiris, Osiris Jones, let's say, and he goes on an underworld journey to unite with Osiris." Thus, death is not death in the sense in which we have come to envision it, as the annihilation of life. Rather, in the words of Henri A. Frankfort, a noted scholar in the field of Egyptian art, "death is a mere phase of life."[4] As Campbell explains in his discussion of the weighing of the heart of the dead person against a feather, death was understood as the spiritualization of the material person, as a return to spirit from whence he came.

This conception of life and death applied to each succeeding pharaoh in a particular way. When alive, the pharaoh was identified with Horus, the final ruler in mythic times. But when he died, the pharaoh became assimilated with Osiris, Horus's father who had been the initial ruler. Thus, the identity of the pharaoh could be seen in two entirely different ways. Literally, the pharaoh was the particular man, or woman in a few instances, who sat upon the throne. Mythologically, however, the living pharaoh was Horus who, in some mysterious way, was at this point in time manifesting himself as this particular man. When the pharaoh died, becoming Osiris, Horus continued to rule in his manifestation as the next human ruler. In this sense as well, then, Osiris, both in himself and in his son, embodied the principle of the continuity of life through an eternal series of risings and fallings, of deaths and resurrections.

**The Perennial Duality**: In addition to its emphasis on the duality of life and death, the myth of Osiris is concerned with other dualities. The clearest and most important of these is embodied in the perennial antagonism between Seth and Osiris, which continues in the struggle between Seth and Horus. In both of these oppositions, Seth is depicted as the ferocious, malevolent one in contrast to the relatively peaceful, beneficent Osiris and his son. This contrast grows from one that is even more fundamental, for according to Frankfort, "Horus [with Osiris] and Seth were the antagonists per se—the mythological symbols for all conflict. Strife is an element in the universe which cannot be ignored; Seth is perennially subdued by Horus but never destroyed."[5] Seth was associated in the Egyptian mind with the "red land" of the deserts and therefore with the ferociousness and death of those barren lands. On the other hand, Osiris, and then Horus, was associated with the Nile, with agriculture, and with the peaceful life of the civilization that he brought to Egypt. In addition, Seth was associated with the sun at night as it ran its course on the nether side of the world, while Horus was associated with the daytime sun. This association probably was made, in part, as a result of the amalgamation of two separate gods named Horus, one the son of Osiris, and the other the son of the sun. This opposition had a historical dimension as well, since Seth was associated from the earliest times with Upper Egypt, while Horus was the god of Lower Egypt. After the unification of the two Egypts under a single pharaoh, that pharaoh was seen as Horus.

But as Campbell points out in *The Masks of God: Oriental Mythology*, that last opposition, as was equally true of all the others in the deepest sense, existed only on the surface. There was understood to be a fundamental unity under the surface of the myth. The evidence for this

> appears beneath the sands of Abydos, in the tombs of the pharaohs of Dynasty II, which are enormous. . . . On the seals of the seventh and last pharaoh of this line, Khasekhemui, the two antagonists, Horus the hero and Seth the villain of the piece, stand side by side, together and co-equal while the monarch himself is termed [by Petrie] "the appearing of the dual power in which the two gods are at peace." . . . Mythologically representing the inevitable dialectic of temporality, where all things appear in pairs, Horus and Seth are forever in conflict; whereas in the sphere of eternity, beyond the veil of time and space, where there is no duality, they are at one; death and life are at one; all is peace.[6]

Suggesting the vital importance of this fundamental unity, Campbell goes on to say that "this secret knowledge that there is the peace of eternal being within every aspect of the field of temporal becoming is the signature of this entire civilization."[7]

**The Holy Triad**: There are, then, a multiplicity of important themes to be found in the mythic cycle of Osiris, Isis, and Horus, and many of them, like the theme just discussed, are of fundamental importance to an understanding of Egyptian mythic thought and of Egyptian civilization. That multiplicity suggests the importance of this myth and suggests, at least in part, a reason for its lasting at least 2,000 years and becoming the preeminent myth of Egyptian culture. But there is another reason for its having captured so strongly the fancy of that culture. As we have seen, the democratization of the Osiris cult made that god the focal point of each person's hope of surviving death. But even more than that, the myth of Osiris grounded the hope of survival in the story of an honest, just man betrayed

by those he trusted. In his suffering, he was aided constantly by his ever-faithful wife, and then by his loyal son. For the first time in the development of the world's mythologies, the family unit becomes central, and it is through that unit that human beings can identify and interact with the mysterious world of the spirit.

The "sacred triad" of the Osirian family unites life and death, most notably in the conception of Horus by the "dead" Osiris and the living Isis. In the involvement of Seth, it unites good and evil, and in the passing of the kingship from Osiris to Horus, it unites youth and age in cyclical fashion. But perhaps the most striking unity is that of the male and female principles, discussed in Unit 1, joined here in the context of the creative family. Osiris emerges clearly as the male principle in his widespread worldly activity whereas Isis, often depicted in Egyptian art holding the infant Horus, appears as the epitome of the nurturing maternal power in the world. The mystical and sexual union of Osiris and Isis stands as a metaphor for the creative act that brings both new life and continuity to the world in the issue of that union, in this case Horus. This creativity, which assures the continuity of the life-force in the world, was a creativity not only of gods, but one shared in by all the worshippers of Osiris and Isis. They too could have children in and through whom they would live despite the injustices of life and its eventual end in a certain death. And if they shared the fate of Osiris in this sense, then they could share it in another, becoming united with him in spirit in the Land of the Dead. Thus, the myth of Osiris held out hope of deliverance from the vicissitudes of life for all humankind.

## Death: The Reality and the Myth

In the tombs of Egypt, as far back as the Neolithic period, tools and food have been found buried with the dead for use in an afterlife that would be a duplication of the best and most important experiences of earthly existence. Death was not to be ignored; it had to be prepared for with great concern. The tomb of a pharaoh probably took years to prepare under his supervision; the art that decorated its walls portrayed the activities he expected to continue in his afterlife, such as hunting, sailing, or harvesting. Figurines were found in the tombs representing those who would help the deceased carry out the tasks that the gods required of him. Henri Frankfort, however, insists that these provisions should not be considered as merely materialistic possessions placed in the tombs for comfort. They were there to provide sustenance for the deceased's spiritual needs, to help the person survive as a god in the beautiful world beyond.[8]

Actually, there were many different metaphoric views of the afterlife in Egypt. Some, particularly those associated with the sun cult, felt that the dead pharaoh went aboard the sun's heavenly boat and accompanied him across the sky in the day and underneath the earth through another sky at night.

According to the cult of Osiris, the dead pharaoh traveled to the underworld and became Osiris who was once an earthly king and was now lord of the underworld. The dead pharaoh would continue to rule as Osiris in this other world of the spirit. These two seemingly opposed views which, in fact, existed simultaneously, help to explain the kinds of preparations that were made for the deceased. There was, on the one hand, the belief that the dead continued to stay in or near the tomb and, on the other, the view that the deceased left the tomb to exist in a distant, beautiful realm.

As evidence of the gradual democratization of the belief in an afterlife, Egyptian noblemen began building their tombs close to those of the pharaoh so that they too could share his immortality. And later, by the time of the First Intermediate Period (2181–2040 B.C.E.), the period between the Old and Middle Kingdoms, even the ordinary people could share the blessings of immortality, and appropriate prayers and rituals became available to whoever could pay to have them performed or inscribed inside the coffin. As Campbell points out in the television program, then, even the commoner could become Osiris, lord of the underworld, who was always portrayed mummylike. "Becoming Osiris" came to mean simply "the dead one," and from the moment of death, the name of the deceased was prefaced with the name "Osiris." Since Osiris lived in all of nature, the deceased gained immortality by becoming part of nature and being absorbed into the dynamic process of the universe.

**The Ka and the Ba**: In the sculptured scenes in the tombs the deceased often was portrayed with another figure similar to himself. This figure was known as the "ka," a kind of double that would guide the individual in the realm of the dead. Actually the ka existed in that realm, and the dead were said to "have gone to their ka."[9] According to the Pyramid Texts, the ka was able to help the deceased by speaking to the gods on their behalf and by protecting them in other ways. Thus one of the Pyramid Texts reads: "How beautiful it is in the company of thy ka!"[10] Although the ka was one's double from the time of birth, it was only at death that the relationship between them became important.

On the other hand, the "ba" was related to the actual personality of a person and represented a combination of intelligence and soul. It often was symbolized by a bird with a human head and human arms hovering over the body or flying down a tomb shaft to rejoin the body. A person became a ba at death; hence, one of the Pyramid Texts says to the dead king, "thou mayest become a ba among the gods, thou living as (or 'in') thy ba."[11] Although "soul" is the closest word we have for the translation of "ba," for the Egyptians it was not a quality separate from the physical body as is suggested by the concept of the soul.

**Preparation for the World Beyond**: Because death did not mean the end of life and because the spirit was not completely separable from the body in Egyptian thought, it was essential that the physical body be carefully prepared for preservation after death. Bodies were mummified through a very elaborate process so that they would not decay and the relationship of soul and body would not be lost.

According to the ancient Greek historian Herodotus, it might take as long as seventy days to prepare the body of a noble person in order to preserve it. The process took place in a workshop called "the good house" or "the house of gold." After the body was washed in water from the Nile, various organs and the brain were removed and replaced with spices and resins and later on with balls of linen that helped to keep the features of the face intact. The heart was left in the body because it represented the source of intelligence. Various amulets were placed on the body, one of which was a scarab, the symbol of renewed life, which was placed over the heart. The body was then wrapped in layers of linen bandages before being placed in the coffin. It was believed that all of the materials used in embalming were grown from the tears that were shed by the gods when Osiris died; thus, their use in the embalming process bestowed the power of these gods on the deceased. James H. Breasted makes the point that the whole idea of preservation might have been influenced by the amazingly favorable conditions of climate and soil in Egypt conducive to the preservation of the human body.[12]

After appropriate mourning and funeral rites, the coffin, lying in a boat and pulled on a sledge by oxen and men, was taken to the tomb by an elaborate procession of mourners, many of whom were hired for the purpose. Servants in the procession carried items that the deceased would need in the afterworld, such as food, furniture, clothing, and paintings. Others carried statues of the deceased that represented his ka, which would live beside him in the tomb and would need to be nourished by the family of the deceased.

In the tomb, the mummy was placed upright, and the ceremony known as the "Opening of the Mouth" was performed. This ritual symbolized the event of Horus's visit to his father Osiris after he overcame Seth, avenged his father's murder, and finally succeeded to the throne. Horus, who represented good, came to announce his victory to his father and to give him his eye, the symbol of that victory, that Seth had snatched out in their battle. When he received Horus's eye, Osiris became a soul. Horus also came to touch his father's lips with an adze. The adze represented the Great Bear, for in an ancient myth Seth had opened the mouths of the gods with an adze and thereby had given them the power of command. This ceremony of the "Opening of the Mouth" resulted in the resurrection of his father's soul, and therefore the ritual was repeated in the burial rites in order to assure the same rebirth of the soul for others when they died.

In the period between 2686 and 2181 B.C.E., gilded plaster masks made from the face of the deceased were placed over the mummy's face, and the mummy was placed in a plain wooden coffin, or more rarely in a stone sarcophagus, that was finally put in a burial vault hollowed out in the rock underneath the desert sand. In later periods the embalming techniques and the rituals became much less elaborate.

**The Pyramid Texts**: The Pyramid Texts were found in the pyramids of the Old Kingdom (2686–2181 B.C.E.) beginning from about 2625 B.C.E. They were written in hieroglyphics and found on the walls, the passageways, and the chambers of the pyramids. Significantly, some of the texts contain material that goes back even before the two lands of Upper and Lower Egypt were united. Although the texts were meant to help the king through the transition from this world to survival in the next, they also speak about the daily life at that time, and, thus, a great deal can be learned about life in Egypt five thousand years ago. The texts insist that the deceased has not died and will not die. Essentially, they are concerned only with eternal life. In fact, Breasted claims that the word "death" never appears in the texts except in a negative way or when it applies to an enemy.[13] Generally, the subjects of these texts were taken from ancient books and include funerary rituals and mortuary offerings, ancient religious hymns and ritual, magical charms, fragments of old myths, and prayers on behalf of the dead king.[14]

Interestingly, these texts also contain the oldest references to the cosmogony and to the High God Atum:

> O Atum! When you came into being you rose up as a High Hill,
> You shone as the Benben Stone in the Temple of the Phoenix in Heliopolis.[15]

Another text refers to the creation of the first creatures and emphasizes the bisexual nature of Atum, or as R. T. Rundle Clark, an English Egyptologist, suggests, "the self-sufficiency of the High God": "Atum was creative in that he proceeded to masturbate with himself in Heliopolis; he put his penis in his hand that might obtain the pleasure of emission thereby and there were born brother and sister—that is Shu and Tefnut."[16] In addition, there are many references to the ka in the Pyramid Texts. These lines, for example, suggest that kas are not in this world, but in the sky:

> King N is on his way to that distant place of the *Ka*-Lords, where the sun is greeted every morning . . . to be the god of those who have [already] gone to their *ka*'s'[17]

Most of the funerary texts do not express an abstract philosophy about life after death. Instead they express, sometimes in detailed metaphoric imagery, a great concern regarding the survival of the deceased and the proper fulfillment of the requirements for that survival. Alternatively, they sometimes express a fear of death and the thought of darkness.

**The Coffin Texts and the Book of the Dead**: In the Pyramid Texts, it was only the pharaoh who was spoken of as being a god in the next world. However, by 2181–2040 B.C.E. the nobles had become independent of the pharaoh and by repeating the rituals and prayers, they too believed they would survive after death. They took over the ancient texts and had them copied in somewhat altered form inside the coffins in which they were buried. These now are known as the Coffin Texts. It was believed that one wealthy enough to have an inscribed coffin and the accompanying rituals at his or her funeral, also would become an Osiris in the hereafter. Gradually, even the common people had the privilege of sharing these keys to eternal life. This further democratization of the afterlife (from 1320–1200 B.C.E.) led to the texts being further altered and written on papyrus scrolls to be placed with the dead. In this form they are known as *The Book of the Dead* or *The Book of Coming Forth by Day*, referring to the soul's coming out of the tomb. The expressions and concepts in *The Book of the Dead* are similar to those of the Coffin Texts, but long explanations have been added giving a sense of communal ritual to what in the earlier texts had seemed very personal and moralistic.[18] *The Book of the Dead* contained many varieties of magic spells, such as one that would enable the deceased to assume any form he might choose for pleasure or convenience, a bird or a flower or any other living thing. It also expressed much about the idea of moral judgement and the idea of a conscience. One dead person says, for example, "The heart of a man is his own god, and my heart was satisfied with my deeds."[19]

**The Judgement**: In order to continue his existence as a god in the underworld, the dead person first had to be judged by Osiris. Dressed in a robe of feathers that symbolized justice, Osiris was seated on a throne in a hall of judgement and surrounded by forty-two judges, each with the feather of truth on his head, and each representing one of the forty-two provinces of Upper and Lower Egypt. Each judge was to examine a particular aspect of the conscience of the deceased. Many gods, including the sun god in the forms of both Ra and Atum, were present. The mummy of the deceased then was presented with *The Book of the Dead*, which had passwords written on it to enable him to enter into the "Hall of the Two Truths" where the seat of judgement was situated. After the deceased showed that he was completely pure, Thoth, the God of Good Judgement, who was represented by a baboon, stood by to record the verdict that would be announced by Anubis, just as he had done much earlier for Osiris and Horus.

On one side of the scale was a feather, the symbol of truth, and on the other side was the heart of the dead person; the heart represented the essence of his conscience and was a reflection of his virtues and faults. If the heart were really innocent, it would balance the scales with the truth and Thoth, the scribe, would record the verdict as to whether he deserved life in eternity or should suffer a second death, this one of complete extinction. If the scale balanced, the monster, Ammut, standing by to devour those with a guilty verdict, would be dismissed, and Osiris would announce to the deceased that he would be accepted into the world of the gods to enjoy a life of eternal bliss. Whenever the deceased had work to perform in the world of the gods, (where work had to be done just as it had to be done on earth), the little figures that were buried with him would do the tasks for him while he continued to exist happily in his new state. This procedure follows every stage of the Osiris legend in which Osiris, the redeemer who waited for his son to come from the earth, can be seen as representing the principle of good which, through his son Horus, overcame Seth, the principle of evil.

It can be seen clearly from *The Book of the Dead* that there was no concept of a "fall" in Egypt. The individual at death would be judged by Osiris, but as Campbell states it, "that was to be an affair touching the virtues of only that particular case. Mankind itself was not ontologically condemned, nor was the universe. . . . The inhabiting spirit of the mythology is wonder, not guilt."[20] This concern with a particular case can be seen in an account from *The Book of the Dead* given by Breasted. This account was originally three different records of a judgement that evidently at one time were independent of each other but were combined to become what is known as Chapter CXXV of *The Book of the Dead*. In the first account, a deceased person is purged of the wrong that he has done. He sees the face of the god and says:

> I am led (thither) in order to see thy beauty. I know thy name, I know the names of the forty-two gods who are with thee in the Hall of Truth. . . . I bring to thee righteousness and I expel for thee sin. I have committed no sin against people. . . . I have not done evil in the place of truth. I knew no wrong. I did no evil thing. . . . I did not do that which the god abominates. I did not report evil of a servant to his master. I allowed no one to hunger. I caused no one to weep. I did not murder. I did not command to murder. I caused no man misery. [He continues to enumerate many sins of which he was not guilty] I am purified four times, I am pure as that great Phoenix is pure which is in Heracleopolis. For I am that nose of the Lord of Breath who keeps alive all the people.... There arises no evil thing against me in this land, in the Hall of Truth, because I know the names of these gods who are therein, the followers of the Great Lord.[21]

In the second account, he addresses each of the gods by name and to each he declares his innocence of a particular sin. Ultimately, this is not a confession, but a declaration of innocence followed by a listing of all his virtues:

> I live on righteousness, I feed on the righteousness of my heart. I have done that which men say, and that wherewith the gods are content. I have satisfied the god with that which he desires. I gave bread to the hungry, water to the thirsty, clothing to the naked, and a ferry to him who was without a boat.... Save ye me; protect ye me. Enter no complaint against me before the Great God. For I am one of pure mouth and pure hands, to whom was said "Welcome, welcome" by those who saw him.[22]

The third account tells of Osiris sitting on his throne in the Great Hall. Isis and Nephthys stand behind him and the nine gods, headed by the sun god, are along the side. It is the latter who finally announce the verdict. Anubis is at the scales and Thoth, who is behind him, supervises the weighing and re-

cording of the result. The deceased makes a further appeal and Thoth finally announces the verdict: "Hear ye this word in truth. I have judged the heart of Osiris [the deceased]. His soul stands as a witness concerning him, his character is just by the great balances [scales]. No sin of his has been found."[23] The nine gods agree and the deceased is presented as Osiris Ani to Osiris by Horus. And after giving thanks and offerings, he enters the kingdom of the gods. Breasted makes the fascinating point that these accounts of 3,500 years ago "are the graphic expression of the same moral consciousness, of the same admonishing voice within, to which we still feel ourselves amenable."[24] If this is correct, it suggests that the "transformations of myth through time" have the foundation in the human psyche, essentially the same in all times and places, of which Campbell speaks throughout this television course.

## ASSIGNMENTS FOR STUDY AND ANALYSIS

1. Write an essay in which you compare the myth of Osiris, including Horus and Seth, with another myth that you know. Consider what basic assumptions in the culture account for the differences in the two myths.
2. Discuss the relationship between the geographical area and the idea of fertility in the mythology of Egypt; compare Egyptian mythology in that regard with the mythologies associated with the goddess in Unit 3.
3. Write a brief essay on the metaphorical implications of the fragmentation of Osiris's body by Seth.
4. Consider the myth of Osiris as the myth of the hero in the paradigm of the hero's journey as set out in the Introductory Unit of this *Study Guide*.
5. Compare the Egyptian idea of death with that of Christianity. What is your personal reaction? What do you feel would be the effect of the Egyptian concept if it were the common belief of our society? What basic changes would we see?

## FURTHER ASSIGNMENTS FOR WRITING AND REFLECTION

1. Write an essay in which you compare the basic concepts and assumptions regarding death in ancient Egypt with those of other mythologies with which you are familiar. Consider those concepts one finds in the Old and New Testaments, in Homer's *Odyssey* and *Iliad*, in Virgil's *Aeneid* , in Dante's *Divine Comedy*.
2. Evaluate the antagonism between Seth and Osiris. Why is it an important conflict to consider in any society, and in Egypt in particular? In what other mythologies with which you are familiar is there a similar conflict? Discuss these in a brief essay.

3. Write an essay in which you consider the various ways in which the concepts discussed in this unit are similar to or basically different from those in the Judeo-Christian tradition. Is it possible that one could be the outcome of the other?

4. Consider the relationship of one's philosophy about death to the way one lives his or her life. How does your own idea of death affect your life?

## ENDNOTES

[1]Campbell, Oriental Mythology 47-48.

[2]John A. Wilson, "Egypt: The Nature of the Universe," in Henri Frankfort, H. A. Frankfort, John A. Wilson, Thorkild Jacobsen, and William A. Irwin, *The Intellectual Adventure of Ancient Man: An Essay on Speculative Thought in the Ancient Near East* (Chicago: University of Chicago Press, 1946/ Phoenix Edition, 1977) 31.

[3]James H. Breasted, *Development of Religion and Thought in Ancient Egypt* (New York: Harper, Harper Torchbooks, 1959) 18.

[4]Henri Frankfort, *Ancient Egyptian Religion, An Interpretation* (New York: Harper, Harper Torchbooks, 1948) 21.

[5]Henri Frankfort, *Kingship and the Gods* (Chicago: University of Chicago Press, 1948) 21.

[6]Campbell, *Oriental Mythology* 81.

[7]Campbell, *Oriental Mythology* 82.

[8]Frankfort, *Ancient Egyptian Religion* 90-91

[9]Breasted 52-3.

[10]Breasted 54.

[11]Breasted 56.

[12]Breasted 49.

[13]Breasted 91.

[14]Breasted 93.

[15]Utterance 600, quoted in R. T. Rundle Clark, *Myth and Symbol in Ancient Egypt* (London: Thames and Hudson, 1978) 37.

[16]Utterance 527, quoted in Clark 42.

[17]Utterance 598, quoted in Clark 234.

[18]See John A. Wilson, *The Culture of Ancient Egypt* (Chicago: University of Chicago Press/ Phoenix Books, 1951) 118.

[19]Breasted 298.

[20]Campbell, *Oriental Mythology* 101-102.

[21]Breasted 300.

[22]Breasted 303-304.

[23]Breasted 305-306.

[24]Breasted 306.

## UNIT BIBLIOGRAPHY

Breasted, James Henry. *Development of Religion and Thought in Ancient Egypt*. Originally published in 1912, now available: New York: Harper and Row, 1959. A companion, in a sense, to Breasted's *History of Egypt*, this volume traces the development of the spiritual thought of Egyptian civilization through its successive historical phases.

———. *A History of Egypt*. Originally published in 1905, available today in paperback: New York: Bantam, 1964. Despite its age, still one of the most complete, definitive, and readable accounts of the growth of Egyptian civilization.

Budge, E. A. Wallis. *The Gods of the Egyptians or Studies in Egyptian Mythology*. 2 vols. Originally published in 1904, now available: New York: Dover Publications, 1969. Well illustrated and filled with fascinating detail, this book is still the most thorough account of the gods of ancient Egypt.

Campbell, Joseph. *The Masks of God: Oriental Mythology*. New York: Viking Press, 1962. Pages 49–102 of this book contain Campbell's most complete treatment of the mythology of Egypt. His extended discussion of the Narmer Palette is particularly important to this unit.

Clark, R. T. Rundle. *Myth and Symbol in Ancient Egypt*. London: Thames and Hudson, 1959. This study uses the texts of the ancient Egyptians—the Pyramid Texts, the Coffin Texts, and *The Book of the Dead*—to retell and to analyze the myths.

Frankfort, Henri. *Ancient Egyptian Religion*. New York: Harper and Row, 1948. A brief, well-organized, lucid, and thoughtful account of the fundamental assumptions and underlying ideas of the religious life and thought of ancient Egypt.

Wilson, John A. *The Culture of Ancient Egypt* (originally published as *The Burden of Egypt*). Chicago: University of Chicago Press, 1951. A cultural history of Egypt by leading Egyptologist of his time. In the selection "The Culture of Ancient Egypt," Wilson discusses the Egyptian myth of recreation.

**NOTES**

# NOTES

# NOTES

# The Sacred Source:
## *The Perennial Philosophy of the East*

## UNIT STUDY PLAN

1. Read Unit 5 in your *Study Guide*.
2. Watch Program 5: "The Sacred Source: The Perennial Philosophy of the East."
3. In your course notebook or journal write a summary of Joseph Campbell's interpretation of the origin of the world's earliest civilizations. In particular, emphasize that of India.
4. Read the selections for this unit in the *Anthology of Readings*. These include excerpts from works by Eliot Deutsch, F. R. Allchin, Surendranath Dasgupta, and Wendy Doniger O'Flaherty.
5. After reading the selections, comment in your notebook on what you have read. Show the relationship between the readings and the essay in this unit.
6. Discuss the special way that Joseph Campbell presents the fundamental notions at the basis of Eastern mysticism.
7. Complete assignments at the end of this unit as specified by your instructor.

## POINTS TO WATCH FOR IN THE TELEVISION PROGRAM

*This television program was delivered as a lecture by Joseph Campbell in New York City, in 1983.*

1. Pay attention to what Campbell refers to by the term "Elementary Idea." Notice the way in which Campbell associates his examples with each other.
2. Be sure that you understand the idea of the "Perennial Philosophy" and its relation to the early history of religion.
3. If you are unfamiliar with or unsympathetic to the theory of many gods in the universe, try to develop an understanding of why such a religious system could come into existence and even persist to the present day.
4. Have a clear idea of the geography of India, i.e., the location of the Indus Valley.
5. Pay attention to the history of the development of Hinduism in the Vedic period.
6. Take special notice of the ending of the television program for this unit. It is a lead-in to the beginning of the television program for the next unit.

## POINTS TO LOOK FOR IN THE *ANTHOLOGY OF READINGS*

1. Notice that in Professor Allchin's survey of the "The Legacy of the Indus Civilization" he has to be very tentative in his discussion of religion because of the absence of available written records. It is only about seventy years since the archaeological remains of the Indus Valley have been unearthed. New discoveries are still being made, though for the most part not so dramatic as in the beginning.
2. In reading the selection from *The Source Book of Advaita Vedanta*, you will be introduced to important examples of the formative literature of the Hindu-Buddhist tradition. Note the special meaning of the word shruti or revelation, as it is translated from Sanskrit. In connection with this, note the important place given the Upanishads by the great Hindu philosophers such as Shankara. In the Upanishads you would find the most important Hindu concepts about the Self and spiritual emancipation.
3. The selection from Surendranath Dasgupta refers to the teaching of Sankhya philosophy concerning the material world (Prakriti) and the spiritual entity (Purusha). Be aware that Prakriti and Purusha are the eternal *Reals* of Sankhyan thought. The Sankhyan terminology was nearly universally adapted to various aspects of Hindu metaphysics.
4. Wendy Doniger O'Flaherty is a significant interpreter of the comparative mythology of Hinduism. Hence, in reading her chapter on "The Interpretation of Hindu Mythology" you will have access to another approach to the sorting out of the meanings in the complex symbols and stories (myths) that cluster about the great god (perhaps the greatest in Hinduism according to O'Flaherty) Shiva. She has set out a fascinating network of interrelated themes that join the paradox of Shiva's eroticism with his asceticism. Some of these themes can be hypothetically projected backward upon the original religious materials that survive from the Indus Valley period, i.e., the Protoshiva (the horned ithyphallic deity of the stamp seals).

In the short selection from Dr. Doniger O'Flaherty's *Hindu Myths*, you will find an example of how the great Hindu deity Shiva touched the mythic imagination. The sage Mankanaka and Shiva both had great abilities as dancers, but it is unseemly and even dangerous for a mortal to compete with a god. Yet, an ascetic, through self-control, can earn the respect of, and a long lasting relationship with, a god.

## UNIT GLOSSARY

**Archetype**: A word similar in meaning to Campbell's "elementary ideas." It was used by the psychologist Jung to refer to a common psychic heritage of symbolic forms that all human beings share in the collective unconscious.

**Aryan**: Word meaning "Noble" in Sanskrit. This term is used by high-caste Hindus to refer to their ancient ancestors.

**Brahmanas**: The highest Hindu social caste—the priesthood. In ancient times this caste dictated the rules of religious and social behavior in Hinduism.

**Cycles of the Heavens**: The fascinating transit of the heavenly bodies according to strict laws of time and motion. According to Campbell, it was one of the earliest sources for the religious imagination.

**Lingam**: The phallic symbol of Shiva found in Indus-Valley religion and in contemporary Hinduism.

**Maya**: A common term in Hinduism to refer to the transitory, "illusory" nature of the material world. (It has some relationship to the philosophical issue of how you determine whether what you perceive with your senses really exists.)

**Mysticism**: A dimension beyond religion with the claim that a human being experiences union with God (or Spirit).

**Perennial Philosophy**: A concept linking together all mystical experience in spite of the religious and cultural differences in which mystics arise.

**Realm of Karma**: The world of cause and effect, i.e., samsara.

**Samsara**: The cosmic system of constant change because of the inexorable law of cause and effect. It refers to the constant recreation of the universe and the reincarnation of souls or life-stream entities.

**Sankhya**: One of the six classical Hindu philosophies, accepted by orthodox Hindus as authoritative.

**Sanskrit**: Alleged language of the Aryan invaders of India (*c.* 1800 B.C.E.) who introduced the special cultural perspective of religion that transformed Indian culture.

**Shiva**: One of the two principal dieties of Hinduism. (The other is Vishnu.) His symbols, the trident and lingam, are found in the earliest strata of Indian civilization.

**Symbol**: A word, picture, gesture (as well as other things) that open the religious imagination from the physical, mundane world toward the spiritual or higher world. (The word may have other meanings in other disciplines, for instance, literature.)

**Trishula**: The trident symbol of Shiva that, as Campbell points out, was also the symbol of Poseidon, the Greek god.

**Upanishads**: The literature of the first period of historical Hinduism that presented many of the ideas that led to the later Hindu emphasis upon spiritual emancipation as the final goal of religious life. The last writings of the Veda.

**Varna**: The Sanskrit word (basic meaning is "color") for the castes of classical Hinduism. Castes are social divisions determined by birth.

**Vedic**: Referring to the scripture, called the Veda, upon which the Hindu religion is based—also, the period from about 1800 to 600 B.C.E. when the Veda was completed.

## UNIT PREVIEW

This unit discusses the background of Indian religious history. Before civilizations began, there was a long formative period during which human beings developed elementary forms of technology and even began to experiment with artistic depictions. Gradually, the hunting and gathering technology gave way to agriculture. With the discovery of agriculture, larger and larger social groups began to appear. With the invention of writing in Sumer near the year 4000 B.C.E., true civilization could come into existence.

**The Perennial Philosophy**: Campbell adopts the terminology of Adolph Bastian to refer to certain common points that arise in the formation of systems of symbols and myths at the basis of religion. He calls these "elementary ideas." The elementary ideas occur universally throughout the history of religions and hence can be linked to a concept of the Perennial Philosophy.

**The Indus-Valley Civilization**: Although the Indus-Valley people possessed writing in the middle of the third millenium B.C.E., it remains undeciphered to this day. However, we can theorize about the religion of this period on the basis of comparisons of Indus-Valley artifacts with those of the ancient Near East at about the same time. Through such comparisons, scholars have come to believe that the formative notions of Hinduism arose at this time. The later Hinduism contains concepts from the Indus Valley as well as from the Indo-Aryan invaders who entered India after 1800 B.C.E.

**The Vedas and Upanishads**: The earliest documents of Indian religion are contained in collections of writings collectively called the Veda. The Upanishads are the last group of such writings. They generally reveal that the thought processes of ancient India gradually left behind the cruder ideas of sacrificing animals to maintain cosmic order. In their place, the Upanishads taught that the sacrifices were no longer necessary for those who had adopted an ascetic mode of life in the pursuit of moksha or spiritual emancipation. Meditation came to be an important part of the spiritual discipline of Indian religion in general. With the end of the Vedic period, the primary focus of popular Indian religion shifted toward the temple.

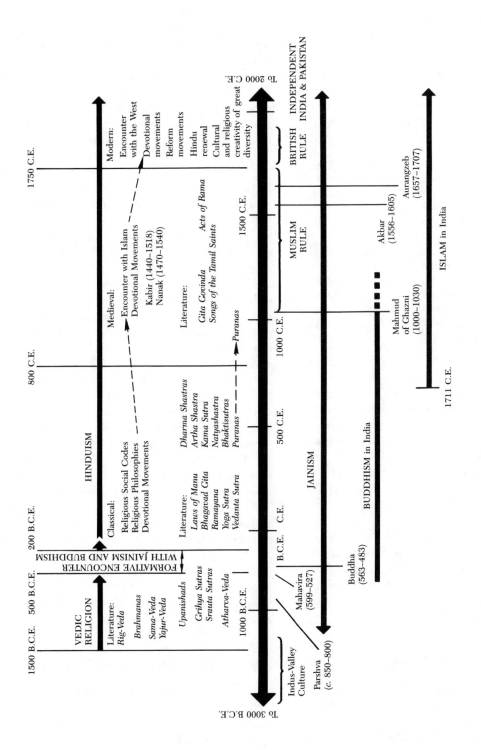

Chronological Chart of the Development of Religions in India

# UNIT ESSAY

## The Sacred Source: The Perennial Philosophy of the East

Joseph Campbell is interested in the way that myths and symbols organize the world of human action, culture, and history to provide a totality of meaning. Indeed, other scholars of religion have come to the same conclusion. Clifford Geertz, the ethnologist, has stated the case for the persistence of religion well into the scientific age when it was thought by earlier scholars of the modern period to have exhausted its purpose. Geertz writes:

> There are at least three points where chaos—a tumult of events which lack not just interpretations but *interpretability*—threaten to break in upon man at the limits of his analytic capacities, at the limits of his powers of endurance and at the limits of his moral insight. Bafflement, suffering, and a sense of intractable ethical paradox are all, if they become intense enough or are sustained long enough, radical challenges to the proposition that life is comprehensible and that we can, by taking thought, orient ourselves effectively within it—challenges with which any religion, however "primitive" which hopes to persist must attempt somehow to cope.[1]

Geertz epitomizes this insight in a memorable phrase: religion is the expression of "an acute and chronic cognitive concern."

Campbell, in the introduction to this unit's television program, discusses his own commitment to a theory developed by Adolph Bastian to the effect that there are certain "Elementary Ideas" that have formed the basis of human cultures and civilizations. These are similar to what psychologist Jung referred to as archetypes. In the history of civilizations, therefore, one can find these elementary ideas clothed in various garb, depending upon the way those cultures have developed their unique characteristics.

In the following five units, you will be concerned especially with some particular developments in the Hindu-Buddhist religions and their associates, subtypes, and cultural variants. Campbell fixes your attention first on the cultural horizon of the origin of the civilizations that gave rise to the dichotomy between East and West.

## The Origin of World Civilizations

Civilization is a somewhat ambiguous word as it is used in contemporary speech. If you look at the basis of the word, its meaning is linked to human city life. More characteristic still is the development of written language. The earliest use of written language has been associated with the Mesopotamian civilization of Sumer, where cuneiform writing appears early in the fourth millenium B.C.E.; writing begins in Egypt early in the third millenium B.C.E.; and there is written language in the middle of the third millenium B.C.E. in the Indus Valley, associated with the origins of Indian civilization. In the case of the Indus Valley, however, the number of written records is minimal and scholarship has not yet found a way to decipher the records. Civilizations develop in Middle America as early as the second millenium B.C.E. These seem to exhibit some of the characteristics of early civilizations in other parts of the world, though without the appearance of true writing. Nevertheless, there was a considerable sophistication in the use of mathematics in Middle American civilizations.

The earliest period in which there is evidence of religious behavior is much earlier in the human record than the first use of writing. The Neanderthal of *c.* 100,000 B.C.E. and the Cro-magnon of *c.* 35,000 B.C.E. have left such artifacts as religiously fashioned burial sites and cave paintings of presumed religious import. (For further discussion of these early religious rituals, see Unit 1.)

What Campbell implies in the discussion in the early part of the television program for this unit is that humanity crosses a line some millenia before the beginning of our era (the so-called Common Era, or C.E.). After that, religions shape their content to respond to certain widely held insights or experiences. These experiences draw human beings from the manipulation of the material characteristics of the human environment to an inward journey. In referring to the term "Perennial Philosophy," Campbell borrows from the thought of Aldous Huxley, who suggested that there are common, underlying mystical trends in all religions.

You have noticed that this course attempts to show how these common elements develop in unique features of religious expression, such as symbolism and mystical experience. The expressions of these common elements can be seen in religions that we know about from the ancient past as well as in comparisons between Eastern and Western religions.

In the case of the history of Hindu-Buddhist religion that follows, you will first need to know something about the early history of Indian religion. This will give you a context in which to appreciate some of the special topics in religion that Campbell emphasizes in the units that follow Unit 5.

## The Indus-Valley Civilization

Early in the twentieth century Sir John Marshall, a British archaeologist, unearthed the remains of two large, previously unknown ancient cities at sites named Mohenjodaro and Harappa, both located in present-day Pakistan. From the excavations at these sites, Marshall was able to establish the existence of an ancient civilization that was contemporaneous with the civilization of ancient Mesopotamia, (in the region of contemporary Iraq), although somewhat later in origin. He called it the Indus-Valley Civilization because these two ancient cities were located along or near the riverbed of the Indus River.

Archaeological investigations have continued since Marshall's time, and the spread of Indus-Valley cultural artifacts is discernible through a large part of the Northwestern section of the Indian subcontinent. However, no other cities comparable in significance to Mohenjodaro and Harappa have been found.

The Indus-Valley Civilization is generally regarded as the source of certain striking elements in later Indian civilization and religion. Most scholars now regard the Hindu religion, and such related religions as Buddhism and Jainism (discussed in Unit 6), as products of a streaming together of two originally distinct cultural expressions. One of these may have arisen in the Indus-Valley Civilization. The other and more conspicuous element is the Indo-European, or Aryan, that came into India with the Aryan invasion of India around 1800 B.C.E.

There is a curious lack of major religious monuments in Harappa and Mohenjodara. These city-states had a well-organized municipal life with such features as a sewage system, a well-designed grid-work of streets with special centers for civic functions, granaries, and a differentiation in status among the inhabitants on the basis of the size of their dwellings. One of the most striking buildings in Mohenjodaro contained a large receptacle or tank for bathing, but its precise religious significance cannot be determined. However, in later Hinduism, ritual bathing and the building of tanks for bathing near temples are common features.

Most of the theory about religious life in the Indus Valley is based upon certain limited categories of objects that survive that can be given religious interpretations. There is a sizable quantity, for example, of stamp seals, like those that Campbell points to in the television program, that contain both undeciphered writing and elegantly carved impressions of animals and what are thought to be male and female deities. In the absence of knowledge of the written language, you can well imagine that the interpretation of the images is pure conjecture. However, they bear a certain resemblance to materials found, for example, in Mesopotamia and elsewhere, as well as to later elements in Hinduism. So it may not be too farfetched to draw some inferences about the artifacts.

On one of these stamp seals is the image of an animal, perhaps a bull (bos indicus) with what appears to be a ritual vessel beneath its throat. More than one seal represents a seated, seemingly yogilike figure whose head is covered with a horned mask. Still other seals appear to show a female "goddess" figure flanked by animals, perhaps tigers. The last motif, especially, suggests parallels with icons of the goddess that come from ancient Mesopotamia and Anatolia (in the region of contemporary Turkey). In summation, however, we can only conjecture that the religion of the Indus Valley may have created the prototypes of such typical features of later Hindu-

ism as devotion to the mother goddess; a type of religious asceticism, suggested by the "yogi" figure—also sometimes assimilated to features of the god Shiva; acceptance of animals as symbolic embodiments of sacred meaning; and the use of ritual bathing. There are also phallic images among the artifacts, and these suggest aspects of later Shaivite and Tantric Hinduism. (These terms refer to the worship of Shiva and the yoga that builds upon Shiva's mystique. Units 7 and 8 discuss these matters more fully.)

There is evidence in the earliest scriptures of Hinduism, the Rig Veda, that the Aryan invaders had encountered a people whom they disdained and conquered. They criticized the "dasyus" or "slaves" for their phallic worship and lack of well-developed ritual life. Whatever the state of affairs may have been in that ancient setting, in later Hinduism some of the aforementioned elements rose to prominence when the religious forms of the Aryan invader began to fall into partial disuse.

## The Vedic Culture of India

What particularly interests Campbell in this period of the inception of Indian religion is that the myth and ritual of religion begin to be "interpreted." It is from such interpretations in India that we develop the profound philosophies and mystical theories that point toward a valuing of human life beyond the merely material elements of the cosmos.

However, you will need to know the general shape of Vedic religion as the source from which the later developments emerge. The Aryan invaders were an Indo-European speaking people: this means that they spoke a language whose structure linked them to the ancient Greek and Latin speaking peoples of the West. The theory is that the Indo-Europeans (called Aryans or "Nobles" in ancient Sanskrit literature) arose from a common geographical location in what is now the southwestern region of the Soviet Union. They originally were a nomadic, herding, warlike group that, in prehistoric times, entered upon a period of intensely dynamic expansion that led them to the farthest shores of Europe in the West and to India in the East, with stops all along the way. Hence, there are numerous peoples both in Asia and in Europe who can claim a common Indo-European origin.

You should keep in mind that language and its accompanying culture do not necessarily imply unity of so-called "race." However, the Nazis of modern times latched onto the term "Aryan" to support their theories of racial superiority. In this they evoked a degree of sympathy among certain Indians who were supportive of the view that the ancient Aryans of India were a superior race. In fact, the invasion of India around 1800 B.C.E. led to the blending of the ancient pre-Aryan race and culture of India with that of the Indo-European. This was a very productive union that eventually gave rise to Hinduism, one of the most significant cultural expressions in world history.

## Early Vedic Beliefs and Practices

The term Hinduism refers to the sum total of the religious history of the majority of the population of India from prehistoric to contemporary times. There are several distinct periods in the development of Hinduism, but Campbell touches mainly on the early Vedic Period (1800–600 C.E.) and the following Classical Period (600–1200 C.E.). In the latter, Indian civilization reached its peak in art, architecture, literature, science, and many other areas. However, later periods such as the Muslim Period (1200–1750 C.E.) and the British Period (1750–1947 C.E.) were also of great cultural and religious significance.

The Aryan warriors brought with them a religious system that had both mythological and ritualistic elements linked to a body of sacred literature. We call that literature the Veda, and through it we get a picture of the nature of the cosmos, the role of human beings in the cosmos, and how to relate to the deities. According to the Veda, the universe is populated with a large number of gods, chief among whom is the storm god Indra. Indra is one among thirty-three gods, the Adityas, who form the basic core of the Vedic pantheon.

Simply speaking, the Vedic world view is a three-part universe: (1) The lowest earth level where such deities as Agni (the god of fire) have their principal domain. (2) The midheaven, the realm of dynamic action where Indra (the storm god) accompanied by his warrior companions (suggesting the counterpart of Aryan life with its princes and common fighters) engage the cosmic dragon, Vritra, who withholds the rains, the sustenance of the earth. The destruction of Vritra releases the waters. Hence, Indra is the champion of the good cosmic forces struggling against the malevolent forces, such as Vritra, ranged against cosmic order and value. (3) The upper heaven is the abode of the calm deities of the sun and moon and the heavenly bodies whose movements reflect the great cycles of repetition according to very fixed principles. This last aspect of the universe, as Campbell points out, caught the attention of early religious thinkers in many parts of the world.

Besides those mentioned for the regions above, other important deities of the Vedic pantheon include Rudra who later is transformed into the great god shiva of classical Hinduism. His rival in significance, Vishnu, is also prominent in the Vedic pantheon. But both play a secondary role to Indra. In addition to the tri-level structure of the world, the Veda taught a principle of cosmic order, *Rita*, and the idea that the forces of positive being, Sat, were arrayed against the negative urge toward chaos, Asat. A mother principle, Aditi, was the genetrix ("mother" in the sense of female creator) of the pantheon of deities that numbered as many as 33 million.

Vedic ritual was inspired by the concept that the cosmos needed to be reinforced by periodic sacrifices in order to maintain itself against the negative forces. You will remember Campbell's comparison of the gods to a flock of birds sitting in the branches of a tree, waiting for someone to throw food on the ground so that they could fly down to eat. The Vedic priests offered elaborate ritual sacrifices, including animals, to bring sustenance to the gods, in particular to Indra. This was to help the gods in their constant struggle against the acosmic, demonic forces, typified by Vritra. Agni could be thought of as the mouth of the gods, because it was through Agni that the sacrifices were transmuted to the metaphysical realm. Indra was worshipped directly as were certain of the other deities. Whichever deity was the object of the sacrifice became the source of sustenance for all the other deities. This concept was referred to by Max Mueller and other historians of Indian religion as "Henotheism," a kind of monotheism in which one god serves for all the gods.

In the television program for this unit, Campbell points out that over time the process of interpretation introduced an unusual perspective into the way that the Brahmana priesthood viewed its relationship to the sacrifices. Since it was through the "magic" of the priesthood that the cosmos was sustained in a positive way for the welfare of both gods and human beings, the Brahmanas themselves became the speculative focus for the source of power in the universe. Through the sacrifice, the priests could be thought of as pulling the strings that made the universe function. Two other sections of the Veda, the Brahmana and the Arnayaka, develop this speculative aspect of priestly power and authorize the use of the sacrificial formulae for meditation by the Brahmanas. The Brahmanas apparently began to theorize that the forms of the cosmos existed within consciousness as much as externally.

## The Upanishads

The final stage of the development of Vedic thought before the end of the Vedic period gives birth to a type of esoteric literature called the Upanishads. In the television program for this unit, Campbell says that the word Upanishad means "to sit next to" in the sense of a student sitting close to a teacher to receive a private, or even secret, teaching. A number of Upanishads have survived to modern times and continue to be regarded as among the most significant writings on the mystical experience ever produced in world religions. Campbell refers to several of them, including the Katha and Chandogya.

It appears that this literature of the mystical experience was the culmination of the process by which the manipulative sacrificial religion of the early Vedic period gave way to a profound reinterpretation of the universe and humanity's role in it.

In addition to what you have already learned about the cosmology of the Vedic religion, you should be aware that, after the inception of the Brahmana and Aranyaka period around 1000 B.C.E., new ideas were advanced as to the nature of time and human society. The concept of time in particular underwent a profoundly expansionist change. The priests theorized that the universe was an unending process in which the cosmic structure was periodically destroyed and recreated. The concept of the Yugas and Kalpas (cosmic cycles) was propounded. (These comprised units of millions and billions of solar years.) Together with this concept, the teachers formulated the ideas of rebirth through samsara (the cosmic system of constant change and rebirth) and the idea that your actions were forever recorded in the account books of Karma, the impersonal moral law of cause and effect.

A rather complex view of human destiny in relation to the social order was also gaining currency. Already in Rig Veda X:90, the doctrine of a definite theory of creation was put forward stating that every person was born into a particular caste from the bodily parts of a great creator deity, Purusha. The castes were born respectively as Brahmanas (priests) from the head; Kshatriyas (warriors) from the arms; Vaishyas (merchants and small landed gentry) from the thighs; and the Shudras (peasants and servile classes) from the feet.

Each of the upper three castes, or the "twice-born" had to fulfill a heavy social responsibility, incorporating work with religious duty in the elaborate structure known as the Varna-ashrama-dharma system. It was theorized that at the culmination of the social process, some individuals might be able to undertake a rigorous meditative and ascetic discipline that could lead to Moksha or permanent release from the realm of transmigration. (Curiously, even Shudras or Untouchables could aspire to Moksha since anyone, including women, who formally adopted an ascetic way of life, thereby chose to leave the conventional social order.)

Thus, the Upanishads are significantly more pessimistic about the value of human life per se than appears to have been the case at the inception of the Vedic period when the boisterous Aryans sank their spear shafts for the first time into Indian soil and settled down gradually from their previous nomadic life. The complexity of life in the Indian setting led to the speculations and mystical experiments that produced the Upanishadic mystical philosophy.

The Upanishads (or the Vedanta, the summing up of the Veda) give the esoteric teaching about the true nature of the universe. The Katha Upanishad, for example, tells the story of Nachiketas, a young Brahmana boy, who finds the god of death Yama as his guru in the quest for the truth about human existence. Yama tells him that the deluded in this world are those who opt for a life of sensual enjoyment and are blind to the truth of the constant repetition of the human reincarnation and cosmic cycles. Only the wise, like young Nachiketas, will willingly give up the rewards of sensory life for the much greater fulfillment of the freedom that comes from complete emancipation from the realm of Karma.

## Later Hinduism

With the end of the Upanishadic period, at about 600 B.C.E., possibly due to the rise of Jainism, Buddhism, and new forms of Hinduism, Indian culture was poised to embark on the great multifaceted development that produced magnificent works of art and literature as well as extremely refined analyses and methods for the attainment of the ideal of spiritual emancipation. It is somewhat startling to recognize that the religious traits of Hinduism, that you have probably associated with the worship of elaborately carved images of deities in great stone temples, had not yet come into existence. The responses of Hinduism to Buddhism and the need to actualize the reality of the gods in iconic and literary form, gave birth to expressions that had not previously existed. An important new development, for example, was the incorporation of numerous goddesses and of a principle of the divine feminine into the pantheon and the philosophy/theology of later Hinduism. In the following units on Indian religion you will be looking more deeply into some of these special issues.

Campbell's thesis that the elementary ideas that come to us from the very origin of human existence take on ever changing shapes in the great religious traditions of the world is amply justified. The Hindu-Buddhist religious tradition in India and abroad is an especially rich source for the contemplation of many diverse aspects of the history of religions. Sharing unbroken continuity with the prehistoric, these religious traditions preserve many of the most ancient myths, symbols, and religious practices. However, in the modern Western world, often we can only know of this heritage in the spontaneously generated content of a troubled psychology; for example, as interpreted in the psychotherapy of Freud or Jung or in the opaque symbols of economic, political, or artistic creation. In other words, Campbell's elementary ideas function more and more in the prevailing scientific and secular imagery of contemporary life. It is important for you to notice, however, that the "elementary ideas" *do* survive even if in a changed form.

A particular value of Campbell's lecture style and the content of his presentation is that he has the gift of making accessible to his listeners the inner experience of the mythic system to which he alludes. Thus, although it may take considerable effort on your part to match the factual content of his talk on the origin of Indian mysticism with your own information and interpretation, you nevertheless have an immediate experience of the great significance of what he has to say. He is able to convey this significance to you directly in the act of performative utterance. This is another way of saying that in the case of Campbell, "the Medium is the Message."

## ASSIGNMENTS FOR STUDY AND ANALYSIS

1. In your own terms, explain what Campbell was referring to by the term, "elementary ideas." You may want to reflect on the following passage from Campbell's *Primitive Mythology* as a point of departure. "... Mythology is a rendition of forms through which the formless Form of forms can be known." (You should read the selection, "The Imprints of Experience" in the *Anthology of Readings* to get the whole context.)

2. What is the basis of our use of the term "civilization" as applied to the Indus-Valley culture of India? Read the selection in the *Anthology of Readings* on "The Legacy of the Indus Civilization" to understand the current sweep of research on the subject.

3. Who were the Indo-European (sometimes also called Indo-Aryan) conquerors of India? Discuss the general contribution they made to the foundation of Indian civilization.

4. Discuss the concept of "Henotheism" in the Vedic form of Hinduism in relation to the Vedic theory of the cosmos.

5. Review the passages in the *Source Book of Advaita* in the *Anthology of Readings*. What are some of the examples in Vedic literature that support the idea of "spiritual emancipation" in Indian religions?

## FURTHER ASSIGNMENTS FOR WRITING AND REFLECTION

1. Having read the material for this unit in the *Anthology of Readings*, how would you say that Eastern symbolism and mythology are used to resolve the issue that Clifford Geertz raises in his assertion that religions provide the most satisfying answers to humanity's ". . . acute and chronic cognitive concern"?

2. Keeping in mind the general Indian belief in the transitory nature of all phenomena in the material worlds, comment on the following bit of dialogue from the Chandogya Upanishad found in the selection from *A Source Book of Advaita Vedanta* in the *Anthology of Readings*:

"Bring me a Banyan fruit."

"Here it is, sir."

"Split it."

"It is split, sir."

"What do you see inside it?"

"A number of rather fine seeds, sir."

"Well, split one of them."

"It is split, sir."

"What do you see inside it?"

"Nothing, sir."

He said to him, "This very fineness that you no longer can make out, it is by virtue of this fineness that this Banyan tree stands so big.

"Believe me, my son. It is this very fineness which ensouls all this world, it is the true one, it is the soul. *You are that*, Shvetaketu." [Shvetaketu is the son and Uddalaka the father in this dialogue.] (74).

3. Indian philosophy in a more formal sense begins after the end of the Upanishadic period (*c.* 600 B.C.E.). Campbell mentions especially the Sankhya system of philosophy as one of these further developments. He makes the following statement about the Perennial Philosophy in the television program for this unit:

It's the basic idea of the philosophy, the Perennial Philosophy, that deities are symbolic personifications of the very images that are of yourself. And these energies that are of yourself are the energies of the universe. And so the god is out there and the god is in here. The kingdom of heaven is within you, yes. But it's also everywhere. And this is Perennial Philosophy.

Read the passage from S. Dasgupta on Sankhya philosophy in the *Anthology of Readings*. Discuss how the teaching of Sankhya relates to the insight about the Perennial Philosophy contained in the quotation above.

4. Wendy Doniger O'Flaherty gives you an exercise in the complex structuring of myth and symbol to show the paradoxical relationship between asceticism and eroticism in the figure of the great Hindu god Shiva. Discuss some of the important and necessary ways that myth transcends logic in the *coincidentia oppositorum* (simultaneous coexistence of logical opposites) of this myth and in religion generally.

5. Unit 5 is an introduction to the Hindu and Buddhist mythologies of India which spread to many other countries. By comparison, what is your view of the role of mythology in shaping the values of life of Americans and other Westerners? From what you know now do you see any conflict between the Eastern and Western world views? Do you think the Perennial Philosophy of Eastern thought (perhaps Western thought, too) can survive the continuing industrialization and modernization of the whole world?

6. Hinduism is the religion of the majority of the people who live in India. How does what you have learned about Hinduism in this unit relate to the impressions you have formed of India and the Indian people? For example, Mahatma Gandhi is one of the great ethical teachers of the modern age. The civil rights movement, advocacy for the homeless, and advocacy for animal rights find a point of origin in the Gandhian ethic. What relation do you see between the traditional Judeo-Christian ethical system of the West and the ethical insights developed or borrowed from Hinduism, particularly under the Gandhian inspiration?

7.  If there is such a thing as a Perennial Philosophy, how would its acknowledgment affect your own Western value system? Is a spiritual universalism harmonious with the Western world view?

## ENDNOTES

[1]Clifford Geertz, *The Interpretation of Cultures* (New York: Basic Books, 1973) 100.

## UNIT BIBLIOGRAPHY

Basham, Arthur L. *The Wonder That Was India*. New York: 1955. A comprehensive interpretation of Indian civilization from its origins onward with emphasis upon the classical period.

Chaudhuri, Nirad C. *Hinduism: A Religion to Live By*. New York: Oxford University Press, 1979. A personal statement of faith by a leading Indian author who specializes in interpreting India to the English-speaking world and vice versa.

Danielou, Alain *Hindu Polytheism*. New York: Bollingen Foundation, 1964. The typology of Hindu polytheism is outlined and annotated.

Embree, Ainslee T. *The Hindu Tradition*. New York: The Modern Library, 1966. An introduction to the main literary and theological periods in the history of Hinduism.

Hopkins, Thomas J. *The Hindu Religious Tradition*. Belmont, CA: Wadsworth Publishing Co., 1971. Thomas J. Hopkins reviews the basic Indian theories of the social order. The caste system of the Hindus describes the underlying dramatic situation in the social "universe."

Kinsley, David R. *Hindu Goddesses: Visions of the Divine Feminine in the Hindu Religious Tradition*. Berkeley: The University of California Press, 1986. A survey of the principal goddesses in the Hindu pantheon. Some Buddhist material included.

Kramrisch, Stella *The Hindu Temple*. Delhi: Motilal Banarsidass, 1976. The definitive study of the subject by the foremost authority in the field.

O'Flaherty, Wendy Doniger. *The Origin of Evil in Hindu Mythology*. Berkeley: The University of California Press, 1976. A penetrating study of its subject by the leading authority on Hindu mythology.

Radhakrishnan, Sir Sarvepalli. *The Hindu View of Life*. London: George Allen Unwin, 1961. A short meditation on some of the leading motifs in Hindu spirituality. The author, besides being a renowned philosopher, was President of India.

Walker, George B. *The Hindu World*. New York: Praeger, 1968. A two-volume, short encyclopedia on the Hindu religion. A unique reference work in the field.

# NOTES

# NOTES

# NOTES

CHARLES S. J. WHITE

# The Way to Enlightenment:
## *Buddhism*

## UNIT STUDY PLAN

1. Read Unit 6 in the *Study Guide*.
2. Watch Program 6: "The Way to Enlightenment: Buddhism."
3. In your course notebook or journal, write a summary of Joseph Campbell's interpretation of Buddhism in the television program. As soon as you have finished watching the program, make a note of points that may be unclear, as well as your own reactions and observations.
4. Read the selections for this unit in the *Anthology of Readings*. These include excerpts from works by Heinrich Zimmer, Walpola Rahula, Edwin A. Burtt, John Blofeld, and Henry Clarke Warren.
5. After reading the selections, comment on what you have read in your notebook. Show the relationship between the readings and Campbell's insights into the primary experience of the Buddha.
6. Complete assignments at the end of this unit as specified by your instructor.

## POINTS TO WATCH FOR IN THE TELEVISION PROGRAM

*This television program was delivered as a lecture by Joseph Campbell in New York City, in 1983.*

1. Interpret for yourself the distinction made between Theravada (Hinayana) and Mahayana Buddhism.
2. Be sure you have an idea of what Campbell means when he says about the Buddha after Enlightenment: "His body was there, but his presence was like the sun that has already set."
3. Consider what the purposes and meanings might be for the comparisons made between the Buddha and Jesus Christ.
4. Make clear in your mind the relationship between the historical Buddha (born Gautama) and the Buddhas and Bodhisattvas of mythology and philosophy.
5. Pay special attention to the parallel developments of new religious emphases (non-Buddhist) in the Middle East and China at about the same time as the rise of Buddhism.

## POINTS TO LOOK FOR IN THE *ANTHOLOGY OF READINGS*

1. Walpola Rahula is a Buddhist monk from Sri Lanka who worked for a number of years as a professor in the United States. It would be desirable for you to read the whole text of *What the Buddha Taught*. It will give you the clearest exposition of the full context of the Buddha's First Sermon as well as important additional discussion. "The Doctrine of No-Soul: Anatta" is the assigned reading from *What the Buddha Taught*. In it, you will notice that Rahula explains the Chain of Causation. It is very important to understand this theory to get the point of what the Buddha meant when he said all existence is suffering.
2. Notice that E. A. Burtt, in the "Parables of the Burning House and the Prodigal Son," gives you examples of the literary devices of the Mahayana to assist human beings to emancipation. In the case of the Prodigal Son, the son does not have the insight to recognize that his birthright is wealth and high social status because of the achievements of his father. The father stands for the Bodhisattva and humanity is the Prodigal Son. In the story of the Burning House, the point is that humanity is so distracted by the pleasures of the world that it takes drastic measures to attract humanity (the children) out of the burning house (the world of Samsara).
3. You should be aware, in the excerpt from Blofeld's *Bodhisattva of Compassion*, that Kuan Yin is a major figure in Chinese and Japanese Buddhism. You will get a fuller picture of the Buddhist pantheon and cosmology in Unit 9. Kuan Yin is linked to the Indo-Tibetan version of the Bodhisattva Avalokiteshvara. The full story of Kuan Yin (Avalokiteshvara) appears in the scripture called the *Saddharma Pundarika*. This is an enjoyable text to read, and you may reach fuller understanding of Mahayana Buddhism by looking at it.
4. Be sure that you grasp the point of Zimmer's comparisons and distinctions between Hinayana (Theravada) and Mahayana Buddhism. Because of the dramatic, even catastrophic, events in East and Southeast Asia in the past fifty years, the role of Mahayana is somewhat diminished. This has tended to bring the two branches of Buddhism closer together. An American named H. S. Olcott converted to Buddhism at the end of the nineteenth century and is renowned in the Buddhist world for his efforts at reconciling Hinayana (Theravada) and Mahayana. He designed the Buddhist flag widely adopted in the Buddhist world.

## UNIT GLOSSARY

**Akshobhya**: (Uhk-sha-byuh) The Dharmakaya (cosmic) Buddha of the East.

**Anatman or Anatta**: The Buddhist concept that there is no soul existing as an eternal element apart from the material world.

**Axis Mundi**: "The axis of the world." A mythological figure that can be represented by a tree, such as the Bodhi Tree under which the Buddha attained Enlightenment, a mountain, or any conceived center of reality. The Buddha is seated in meditation under the Bodhi Tree, therefore, it is at the center of the universe or is the center of the universe. Campbell has used the term "Immovable Spot" to refer to the same concept.

**Bhumi Sparsha**: (Boo-me Sparsha) "Touching the earth." The gesture used in depicting the Buddha in iconography wherein he touches or points toward the earth. This is to call mother earth as witness to his resolve to persist in his final pursuit of emancipation in spite of the temptations of worldly and material existence, symbolized in the temptations of the Buddha by Mara.

**Bodh-Gaya**: (Bod with a silent 'h' and Gai-a) The place in the contemporary Indian state of Bihar where the Buddha attained Enlightenment.

**Bodhisattva**: A term with two usages: (1) the previous births of Gautama before he became a Buddha; (2) in Mahayana Buddhism this term refers to the savior figure of mythology who stands on the brink of Nirvana but takes the vow not to be emancipated until all sentient beings are emancipated. In other words, in the second meaning, the Bodhisattva vows to save all beings.

**The Buddha Nature**: A theory, especially prominent in Mahayana Buddhism, that the whole universe is permeated by the essential characteristics of Buddhahood. This gives rise to the further theory that every human being is potentially a Buddha. It also implies that Samsara and Nirvana are the same.

**Dharma**: The Indian theory of socio-religious responsibility.

**Jainism**: (Jai-nism) The religion founded by the Jina, Mahavira, who was a contemporary of the Buddha.

**Karma**: The moral law of cause and effect, roughly equivalent to the Western adage: "As ye sow so shall ye reap."

**Little Ferry Boat and Big Ferry Boat**: Campbell's and Heinrich Zimmer's translations of the Hinayana (currently called Theravada by preference) and Mahayana respectively: the two principal types of Buddhism.

**Nirvana**: The condition of complete spiritual freedom or ultimate reality.

**Samsara**: The world of transmigration and the continuous cycles of the universe and its events, characterized by Dukkha or suffering.

**Stupa**: Originally a mound-shaped structure within which were preserved the relics of the Buddha. The Stupa was the inspiration in other parts of Asia for the temple structures of Buddhism such as the Pagoda.

**The Tao**: (Dao) A concept in Chinese religion and philosophy that there is an impersonal source from which everything that exists arises. It also is the source of order and harmony in human society and nature if understood properly.

**Yogi**: A term coming from Indian religion for the individual who attempts to control body and mind to become attuned to the inner spiritual center opening to ultimate reality.

## UNIT PREVIEW

In this unit, you will be introduced to the two principal types of Buddhism, commonly called Theravada (or Hinayana) and Mahayana. You will also learn about the life of Gautama, the founder of the religion, who achieved the status of a Buddha, the Emancipated One. His triumph over the material world is the story of a hero's journey leading to perfect spiritual freedom. You will also learn about other intellectual and religious developments that are related to Buddhism.

**The Relationship Between Jainism and Buddhism**: Jainism was a religious development parallel to that of Buddhism in ancient India. Both religions stood against the dominance of the Brahmanic Hindu priesthood. Jainism and Buddhism differ profoundly in their metaphysical theories but agree that there is no separately existing "soul" apart from matter. Jainism places great emphasis upon ascetic practices, and it appears that the Buddha attempted to follow the Jaina path before finding his own way.

**The Buddha's Enlightenment and his Religion**: The Buddha discovered the way to Nirvana. After his Enlightenment he lived for more than forty years and taught the way to emancipation to his followers, many of whom became monks and nuns in his Order. Several centuries after his death, his community split into two main divisions: Theravada (Hinayana) and Mahayana. These are sometimes called the Little Ferryboat and the Big Ferry Boat respectively. Theravada places its primary emphasis upon the monks or nuns who seek to attain Nirvana on their own. Mahayana idealizes the Bodhisattva figure who gives himself or herself wholly to the salvation of others.

**Buddhism and Its Early Parallels and Interactions**: At about the same time that the Buddha flourished, the great Chinese religious philosophies of Taoism and Confucianism came into existence. There are some similarities between the Chinese religions and Buddhism. From the West in the early Buddhist period, Alexander the Great initiated the first significant political, military, and intellectual contact with India and Indian spirituality. Subsequently, Ashoka, the great Buddhist emperor of India, promulgated Buddhism abroad by sending missionaries to Southeast Asia, Sri Lanka, and also toward the West.

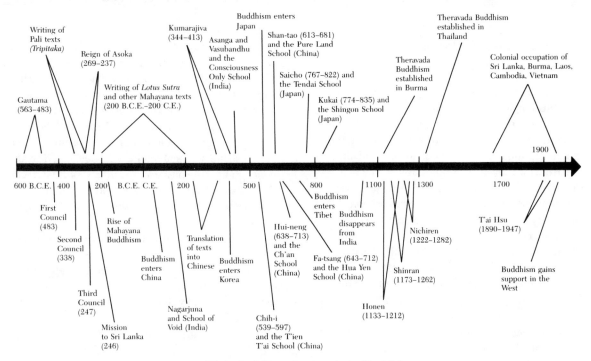

Gautama
(563–483)

Writing of
Pali texts
(Tripitaka)

Reign of Asoka
(269–237)

Writing of Lotus Sutra
and other Mahayana texts
(200 B.C.E.–200 C.E.)

Kumarajiva
(344–413)

Asanga and
Vasubandhu
and the
Consciousness
Only School
(India)

Buddhism enters
Japan

Shan-tao (613–681)
and the Pure Land
School (China)

Saicho (767–822) and
the Tendai School
(Japan)

Kukai (774–835) and
the Shingon School
(Japan)

Theravada
Buddhism
established
in Burma

Theravada Buddhism
established in
Thailand

Colonial occupation of
Sri Lanka, Burma, Laos,
Cambodia, Vietnam

1900

600 B.C.E. 400    200   B.C.E. C.E.    200        500        800      1100    1300        1700

First
Council
(483)

Second
Council
(338)

Third
Council
(247)

Mission
to Sri Lanka
(246)

Rise of
Mahayana
Buddhism

Buddhism
enters
China

Nagarjuna
and School of
Void (India)

Translation
of texts
into
Chinese

Buddhism
enters
Korea

Chih-i
(539–597)
and the T'ien
T'ai School (China)

Hui-neng
(638–713)
and the
Ch'an
School
(China)

Buddhism
enters
Tibet

Buddhism
disappears
from
India

Fa-tsang (643–712)
and the Hua Yen
School (China)

Honen
(1133–1212)

Shinran
(1173–1262)

Nichiren
(1222–1282)

T'ai Hsu
(1890–1947)

Buddhism gains
support in the
West

## Historical Developments in Buddhism

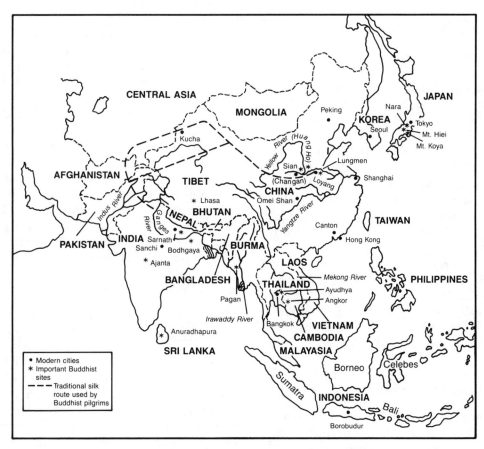

## Modern Asia with Historic Buddhist Sites

# UNIT ESSAY

## Buddhism in Relation to Jainism and Hinduism

As Joseph Campbell suggests in his discussion of Buddhism, this religion is closely linked to the Jaina religion, and you really should know about the Jaina theory of spiritual emancipation in order to interpret the Buddha's experience fully. Jainism (*ai* equals *eye*) and Buddhism differed from the religion of Hinduism, with which they were to some extent competitors, in several important ways: (1) These religions placed their principal emphasis on the possibility that every human being has the capacity to escape from the realm of rebirth and karma through an intensive effort at self-mastery. (2) Because of the first difference, the leadership of the religious community was the order of monks (and nuns) who provided the example for the laity of the possibility of self-mastery, even to the extent of becoming liberated from the world of matter. (3) Both religious movements rejected the traditional Brahmana priesthood as the final authority and the rituals of the priesthood as requisite for a good life in this world and the next.

## The Early Ascetic Tradition

At the beginning of Indian religious history in the Indus-Valley Civilization, there is evidence for the ascetic ideal. For example, on the stamp seals (discussed in Unit 5) there is the yogi figure who has been given the title, Proto-Shiva. This mixture of Indus-Valley (also called Dravidian) and Aryan elements that occurred after the Aryan conquest of India, which gradually developed throughout the second millennium B.C.E., incorporated the pantheon and rites of the deities of Indo-European origin with elements persisting from the Indus - Valley religious milieu. (We have discussed this formative period in Unit 5.) Prominent among these must have been an order or orders of ascetics that were the precursors of the Jaina and Buddhist orders.

It seems likely, scholars will tell you, that the Jaina Order was older than the Buddhist, and that it developed a materialistic theory of the universe that set it at odds with the Brahmana priesthood of the Hindus. Because of the type of materialism in the Jaina philosophy, it taught a rigorous asceticism that was its principal method for overcoming the bondage of rebirth.

## The Jaina Contribution

The Jainas continue to exist in India today as one of the most affluent communities, because their nonviolent credo tended to force the adherents into business and money-lending to earn a living. They held up as ideal types heroic ascetics who had triumphed over rebirth by virtue of complete self-discipline. The last of these heroes, or "Jinas" was the historical individual known as Mahavira, whose period is thought to be around 600 B.C.E. It is from Mahavira, you will want to remember, that the contemporary Jaina community descends spiritually. Interpretations of his presentation of the Jaina philosophy are accepted as authoritative. It was under the influence of these theories that the Buddha developed an alternative conception of the obstacles to human spiritual freedom.

Briefly stated, the Jaina theory holds that there is nothing in the universe but matter. This idea is in marked contrast to Hindus and other religious believers who propose a separately existing spiritual element in man, such as a soul, and/or a supernatural being of a unique spiritual nature, such as a God or deities. These factors are completely reinterpreted in Jainism. Instead, in Jainism, there are two basic elements in the universe: Jiva and Ajiva. Jiva is the lightest form of matter. It is the luminous, self-subsisting element in all living things and in the gods. Ajiva is the matter of various kinds that creates a "shell" around the Jiva, whether at the psychological or physical levels. This shell makes it very difficult for the Jiva to know its true nature. Mahavira taught that through a heroic type of self-discipline—the elimination of all killing of sentient beings, being one of the most important purposes—you could gradually shed the Ajivic matter. When this shell had been shed completely, the Jiva would float free from the gross material world and rise to the top of the universe to remain forever in the perfection of its own purity.

To accomplish this goal meant the severest kind of restriction upon your body. For this reason, monastic life was an essential component of the discipline. Even the gods would have to be reborn for this purpose. Over time, the monk or nun was expected to develop increasing detachment from the body so that in exceptional cases he or she might develop such composure of mind as to leave the body without bad karmic effects, never to be reborn. This condition could only occur after a prolonged fast. Although it is not thought that many, if any, other persons after Mahavira have achieved such freedom, nevertheless, even today in India, there are some Jainas who undertake to fast unto death.

## Buddhism and the Early Life of Gautama

You will want to keep in mind the special viewpoint of the Jainas as you now consider the origin of Buddhism and its development through its formative period. You have already reflected upon some of the ways that Buddhism and Jainism differed from the Brahmanic religion that was their contemporary and which they "reformed" with original ideas and practices.

The Buddha, like Mahavira, was born into a Kshatriya or princely family. The story of the Buddha's life is told in great detail in the Jataka Stories translated by Henry Clarke Warren in *Buddhism in Translations*, and is illustrative of Buddha's pivotal role in human history. His birth was heralded by the gods as the most auspicious event of our age because it is only through a Buddha that the truth about human existence can be set forth. Indeed, after his Enlightenment, a Buddha has the further obligation of teaching the Way to Enlightenment to humanity at large.

The Buddha was born as prince Gautama of the Sakya clan in a small kingdom on the border of modern-day Nepal. At his birth, the astrologers predicted two possible destinies for the baby: (1) He would fulfill the warrior ideal and become a world conqueror or Chakravartin. (2) However, if Gautama came to realize the truth about human existence—that it is repetitive and dominated by such unpleasant events as death—he would renounce the world, seek emancipation, and become a Buddha.

You may want to view the subsequent long period of the prince's childhood and early manhood as an allegory on human experience in general. Consider the fact that his royal parents did everything possible to distract his attention away from the unpleasant realities of existence. He was raised in a pleasure palace from which every sign of mortality, down to dead leaves in the garden, was removed before Gautama could become aware of it. His every desire was met with alacrity while at the same time he was trained in the athletic skills and pastimes of his social class. What effect do you think such a life-style had on Gautama's development? When he was grown, he was married to a beautiful princess, and eventually they had a male child.

It was about this time that Gautama began to feel the pull of an inner sense of dissatisfaction. In contemporary terms we might say that he began to suffer from anxiety. It was the condition of his inauthentic existence that, in the artificial environment of the pleasure palace, created the anxiety. The latter is analogous to the condition in which most human beings are raised and live out their lives. They struggle to push the balance of life in the direction of pleasure, which is often equated with happiness, or at the very least toward an untroubled condition. Contrary to his father's instructions, Gautama managed to undertake an excursion outside the sheltering walls of his abode. This trip is equivalent in ordinary human terms to facing the reality of death and your own finitude. On the excursion, he experienced the four omens that would prompt him to renounce the world: these were a sick man, an old man, a dead man, and an ascetic with a face reflecting calm, inner repose.

## The Great Renunciation

Gautama, when he realized that old age, disease, and death were the common fate of humanity, immediately decided to leave his home and search for the solution to the misery of human existence that had been suggested to him in the omens, including the face of the ascetic. This decision was called The Great Renunciation and was the turning point in Gautama's life. It represents the choice that every human being has to seek greater maturity and personal freedom against the background of psychological and social entrapment. And like the subject of Campbell's *The Hero with a Thousand Faces*, Gautama would depart from familiar surroundings and achieve the goal of emancipation only after testing and triumphing over many obstacles. His experience also bears comparison with that of the Shamanic initiate and the magical journey of the heroes in the American Indian myth presented in Unit 2.

Gautama was about thirty years of age at this time. He spent his next six years as a wandering ascetic, going from one spiritual teacher to another. At last he joined a group of Jaina monks and became their leader in ascetic practices and fasting to such an extent that his body appeared to become a skeleton, clothed only in its translucent skin. However, in this condition Gautama did not experience that inner peace for which he was searching.

## The Enlightenment

While he was in a place called Gaya, in the modern Indian state of Bihar, he abandoned the fast. After taking food to restore his strength, he sat in meditation under a tree, famous as the Bo or Bodhi tree—the Tree of Enlightenment, where he experienced the transformative event of his Emancipation or entry into the condition of absolute freedom or Nirvana. This is the ultimate goal of the Buddhist religion for every human being.

The mythology of the temptation of the Buddha by Mara, the Buddhist equivalent of Satan, as he engaged in his inner struggle over the ordinary human condition, may be interpreted in psychoanalytic terms. You may wish to consider it as the final dissolution of the contents of the unconscious mind, which could be compared to breaking the chain which fetters human psychological freedom. Of course traditional Buddhist thought views the experience as absolute mystical transformation. It was after his Enlightenment Experience, at about the age of thirty-six, that the Buddha began his long career as a teacher of the Way to Freedom to others. His first converts were the monks with whom he had practiced the Jaina path just before his Enlightenment. He met them in the Deer Park at Sarnath outside the city of Banaras, where he preached the First Sermon, in which he set forth the principles upon which he based his claim to be the Enlightened One, the Buddha.

## The Buddha's First Sermon

A major point of the Buddha's First Sermon was that the central fact of human existence is suffering or Dukkha. You may be puzzled as to what kind of suffering he was referring to. Dukkha exists because nothing is permanent, the Buddha explained.

A second major point was that human beings remain trapped in the world of rebirth because of desire of Trishna, the thirst for existence. Contrariwise, human beings live in fear of the loss of existence and hence are caught between the fear of the loss of existence—characterized by possessions, personal traits, descendants—and the desire for more existence. These tendencies bring them back again and again into existence in succeeding lifetimes in the round of cosmic repetition or Samsara. Remember from the television program for this unit that Joseph Campbell compares the Eastern concept of reincarnation with the Catholic idea of purgatory. Both allow for a time of development after death before one is prepared to experience ultimate reality—although this is conceived of very differently in Catholicism and Buddhism.

You have also seen in the television program the architecture of the tower of the modern temple in Bodh Gaya, the place of the Buddha's experience of emancipation. Its different levels are meant to illustrate some of the possible intermediate states of "heaven" or "hell" that the Buddhist theory teaches. Between incarnations one may experience a period of reward and punishment in such states.

The Buddha taught, as the third point in his sermon, that the suffering arising out of this condition of essential impermanence could be terminated with the cessation of fear and desire. That state of cessation, with its concomitant freedom from rebirth, is Nirvana. Nirvana can be experienced in the midst of life, at any moment in life; and it is also the final state of the Emancipated One after death.

The fourth point in the Buddha's sermon was the Path to Nirvana. This is a type of yoga with eight stages. (For the full exposition of these four points, see the complete text of *What the Buddha Taught* by Walpora Rahula. A selection from this work is in the *Anthology of Readings*.)

The special vocation of a Buddha is to set in motion the Wheel of Dharma, which is the teaching of the Way to spiritual freedom. The Buddha lived to be eighty years of age and spent the remaining years of his life after his Enlightenment mainly in converting, organizing, and instructing the community of monks who were, like himself, to follow the disciplined life, which included celibacy and certain other restrictions. Remember that unlike the Jainas' way, the main emphasis of the Buddha's path was not upon severe bodily asceticism to become emancipated. The Buddha taught a middle path which was to free the monk or nun from the responsibilities of family life and attachment to the physical world, so that he or she could develop the psychological insight into the processes of mind, in order that freedom could be attained.

## The Chain of Causation

The Buddha's deeper teaching was an elaboration upon a theory of psychophysical process called the Chain of Causation with its twelve links and the associated theory of Dependent Origination of all the dharmas. (Consult the reading from Walpola Rahula's *What the Buddha Taught* in the *Anthology of Readings* for a full discussion of these and the following concepts.) In the latter teaching, the Buddha pointed out that what human beings experience in sensory and mental life is a continuous process of cause and effect. A dharma is comparable to a second's worth of experience arising in consciousness. The dharmas become instantaneously conscious in the mind and generally pass away rapidly. Due to the Chain of Causation, we mistakenly accept the psychophysical process so described as the reality of our identity. However, through the practice of awareness meditation you can gradually learn to be fully conscious of the stream of cause and effect and recognize a distinction between your awareness and the process itself. It is somewhere in the meditation act, as taught by the Buddha, that the experience of dissociation occurs that may convince you, if you are a meditator, of the reality of emanci-pation. Put another way, the Buddha taught the doctrine of Anatta (or Anatman) that there is no soul or self as understood in the Jaina or (differently) Hindu way. There is only the cause-and-effect process, and you can recognize that for what it is and transcend it.

During the Buddha's lifetime, many hundreds of men and, eventually, women joined the Order. After his death, the community remained united for several centuries. However, gradually, there grew up differences of interpretation of what the Buddha had taught and what he had demanded of his monks and nuns by way of discipline. There were also matters of differences that emerged because of the geographical separation of groups within such a large community. The teachings of the Buddha on theoretical and disciplinary issues were gathered together into two collections: The *Sutta* and the *Vinaya Pitaka* respectively. Later on, the *Abhidhamma Pitaka* was added to these to create the classical Buddhist canon of scriptures, *The Tipitaka*.

When differences arose among the monastics, on questions of discipline for example, a council would be held to settle the dispute. There were some monks, for instance, who wanted to have more ascetic disciplines and still others who wanted the discipline relaxed to make it easier for the laity to participate. Later on, scriptures were produced—apparently reflecting an earlier esoteric tradition of the Buddha's teaching—that were considerably different in content from the original *Tipitaka*.

## Theravada and Mahayana

All these distinctions eventually led to the emergence of two separate versions of Buddhism. These today have the names Theravada, "The Sayings of the Elders," and Mahayana, "The Great Vehicle." You will want to remember that the former follows the system which historically appears to be closest to the teaching and way of life of the historical Buddha, while the latter espouses a very elaborate theory of savior Buddhas and particularly emphasizes the Bodhisattva. You will find it useful to read Heinrich Zimmer's comparison of Theravada and Mahayana in the excerpt from *Philosophies of India* in the *Anthology of Readings*. This text was edited by Joseph Campbell. Zimmer refers to Theravada as Hinayana, which means, as noted below, "little ferry boat."

## The Mahayana

The Bodhisattva is a very advanced being, nearly emancipated, who takes the vow not to enter Nirvana until all sentient beings have been emancipated. There are, according to the Mahayana, innumerable universes with Buddhas and Bodhisattvas functioning as saviors on the path toward Emancipation. The Mahayana, in its various forms, became the prevalent Buddhism in regions to the North and Northeast of India, the homeland of Buddhism. Such countries as Tibet, China, Korea, and Japan remain under the influence of Mahayana today. South and Southeast Asian nations such as Sri Lanka, Thailand, Burma, and Cambodia retain the Theravada tradition. You can see the great variety in Mahayana by comparing the Pure Land sects of Chinese and Japanese Buddhism that teach faith in Amida, the cosmic Buddha of the West, and special devotion to the female Bodhisattva Kuan Yin as the means to salvation, with the meditation schools of Ch'an and Zen that teach an enlightenment experience similar to that of the Theravada school. Please consult the selection in the *Anthology of Readings* from *The Teachings of the Compassionate Buddha*, edited by Burtt, that presents parables helping you to understand the concepts of Skillful Means and Wisdom used by the Bodhisattva to assist deluded humanity toward the goal of Emancipation. The reading, entitled "Some Buddhist Concepts of Kuan Yin," by John Blofeld, in the *Anthology of Readings*, will give you a personal insight into the way the Chinese think about Kuan Yin.

Joseph Campbell, in the television program for this unit, quotes a modern parable about the Hudson River and the desire to cross to the New Jersey shore from Manhattan as a way of presenting the differences in metaphysics between the Theravada (Hinayana) and the Mahayana. For the Theravada, the trip to Jersey indicates an "absolute" change in location. Once arrived in Jersey, the traveler would not carry his ferry boat or raft about with him. He would be on the *further shore* for good. On the contrary, in Mahayana it is not so much changing your "location" as changing your perspective that is in question. For such a traveler, arrival on the Jersey shore would suddenly present the prospect of never having left Manhattan, for being Enlightened entails recognizing that there is no essential difference between one shore and the other, that there is no leaving and no arriving, and that what it all boils down to is that there is no difference between Samsara and Nirvana. That, according to the Mahayana teachers, would be the ultimate freedom.

## Parallel Developments in the Sixth Century B.C.E.

Campbell also makes comparisons with other developments in the spiritual traditions of East and West at the time of or shortly after the Buddha. For example, in the West, at about the same time or a little later, you should note the teaching of the Greek philosophers, culminating in Plato and Aristotle. The famous student of Aristotle, Alexander the Great, waged military campaigns in the Indo-Gangetic plain around 326 B.C.E. The aftermath of Alexander's conquests was to introduce Greek influences into India, for example in the techniques of sculpturing which were adapted to the presentation of the image of the Buddha. Likewise, Indian religious and philosophical influences spread westward.

The latter was accelerated under the great Buddhist king, Ashoka, who may have been of Greek descent. After a brilliant but bloody career as emperor and conqueror during which he put to death many of his close relatives in order to secure the throne, he renounced violence and became a devout Buddhist. This conversion was said to have occurred after his invasion and conquest of the southern kingdom of Kalinga, which was achieved at great cost in human lives and suffering. Throughout the rest of his life (from 261 to 232 B.C.E.) Ashoka devoted much of his energy to propagating Buddhism abroad and implementing Buddhist ideals within his kingdom at home. He sent missionaries to the West and to the Middle East; consequently, Buddhist ideas may have influenced the later development of Western religion, including Christianity.

In conjunction with the increasing mythologization of Buddhism in the centuries just prior to the Common Era, Campbell refers you to the idea of the divine king which had already been advanced in the case, for example, of Darius, king of the Persians. Alexander himself was affected by these ideas; but they also contributed to the twofold way in which the Buddha was regarded. His kingly role was absorbed into his role as the Enlightened One if for no other reason than by virtue of his birth and early life experience as a prince. His appeal as a teacher and charismatic sage has also been linked to his association with royalty and the upper classes. Campbell wants you to consider that there may be some parallels, perhaps, with the treatment of Jesus Christ in the mythology of the

West. Campbell is quite explicit in seeing the Buddha's spiritual quest and triumph over the suffering of the world as somehow analogous to the crucifixion.

In the same century that Buddhism began in India, there was a very important transformation in East Asian religion. The two great sages of China, Confucius and Lao Tzu, began to teach their philosophies of society and nature. Both teachers believed that there was a transcendent principle that underlay all the dimensions of the universe. It was the Tao, and if one lived in accordance with it in society, said Confucius, there would be harmony and happiness. Lao Tzu, whose picture you have also seen in the television program, emphasized the essential unity between human beings and nature. However, the unity was obscured by the effects of socialization and civilization. The mystic awareness that Lao Tzu and his followers cultivated toward nature may have influenced the development of the Mahayana view in East Asia that Samsara is the same as Nirvana.

The sage, you should notice, whether Buddhist or Taoist, could find in the contemplation of the simultaneous fullness and emptiness of nature—with its myriad forms and its vast spaces—the very symbol of Tao. Consider also the fact that Tao could be for the Buddhist the unmistakable sign of the Buddha nature which is in everything. For a flavor of the Taoist life as experienced by a contemporary student of Chinese philosophy and religion, read John Blofeld's *Taoism: The Road to Immortality* (noted in Unit Bibliography). In his book, Blofeld recounts his experiences among the Taoists of China prior to the imposition of Communist rule.

## ASSIGNMENTS FOR STUDY AND ANALYSIS

1. Discuss the basis upon which the Buddha formulated his theory of emancipation as set forth in the First Sermon.
2. Give your interpretation in Buddhist terms (as employed by Campbell) of the parable of the journey from Manhattan to the further shore of New Jersey.
3. Discuss the following statement from "The Doctrine of No-Soul: Anatta" in *What the Buddha Taught,* in the *Anthology of Readings*: "It [the idea of the soul or self] is the source of all the troubles in the world from personal conflicts to wars between nations. In short, to this false view can be traced all the evil in the world."
4. From your reading of the parables of "The Burning House" and "The Prodigal Son" in E. A. Burtt's *The Teaching of the Compassionate Buddha*, in the *Anthology of Readings*, discuss the means by which the Bodhisattva tries to help humanity toward Nirvana.
5. In Heinrich Zimmer's piece on the "Hinayana and Mahayana" in the *Anthology of Readings*, what is a main point that he makes about the distinction between Hinayana and Mahayana thought as valid philosophical viewpoints?

6. Now that you have seen the television program and read the selections in the *Anthology of Readings* for this unit, how would you explain the doctrine of No-Self or Anatta? This is the question raised by Campbell's assertion in the television program that though his physical body remained in the world after the Enlightenment, the Buddha himself was absent.

## FURTHER ASSIGNMENTS FOR WRITING AND REFLECTION

1. In the selection from Walpola Rahula in the *Anthology of Readings*, you will find a discussion of the Five Aggregates and the twelve "factors" of Paticca-samuppada, "Conditioned Genesis" or the "Chain of Causation." Describe in your own words the reality of human existence that is set forth in these concepts.
2. In the selection on "Hinayana and Mahayana," from *Philosophies of India* in the *Anthology of Readings*, Zimmer explains the disagreements between several Hinayana schools and Mahayana schools on whether and in what way the dharmas, "the winks" of material process, exist. Discuss your own understanding of what these different teachings are. Does Zimmer seem to favor one viewpoint over another? Discuss.
3. By comparing what you know now of Buddhist thinking about the "purpose and end of human life" and the reality of the physical world with the special viewpoints of Chinese religious thought, evaluate how the two approaches achieved a unique synthesis in China and Japan. Why was Mahayana especially attractive to the Chinese sensibility? You may want to consult additional authors before coming to your conclusion, for example, Richard H. Robinson and Willard L. Johnson, *The Buddhist Religion*, Third Edition; Stephan Beyer, *The Buddhist Experience: Sources and Interpretations*; and Laurence G. Thompson, *Chinese Religion: An Introduction*, Third Edition.
4. Having finished this unit, if you were asked to give an explanation of Buddhism to a group of Americans primarily of Christian and Jewish background, would you be able to give such an explanation? What points would you emphasize? What comparisons would you make?
5. What further information would you like to have about the role of Buddhism in the shaping of other Asian cultures, for example, that of Korea or Indonesia? Indonesia is now predominantly Muslim but was formerly Buddhist. Such scholars as Clifford Geertz believe that the influence of the former religion of Indonesia persists beneath the Islamic surface. See Clifford Geertz' *Islam Observed: Religious Development in Morocco and Indonesia*, New Haven, Yale University Press, 1968. Korea is rapidly becoming a Christian country. Against the Buddhist background, why is that happening? What about the role of Buddhism in Southeast Asian countries, such as Thailand, Cambodia, and Vietnam? Various works of Donald K.

Swearer would give you background for this question. For example: Donald K. Swearer's *Wat Haripunjaya: The Study of the Royal Temple, The Buddha's Relic, Lanyshun Thailand*. Missoula Scholar's Press, 1976.

6. What do you need to know about Buddhism in the modern world? How are Japanese attitudes shaped by the Buddhist heritage of Japan? How is Buddhism contributing to the evolution of future European and American societies and cultures? (Buddhism seems to be growing faster than other religions of Asian origin in the United States.) An important author on new Buddhist movements is Robert S. Ellwood. See Ellwood's *The Ego and the Rising Sun: Americans and the New Religions of Japan*. Philadelphia: Westminster Press, 1974.

7. Does the Buddhist psychology offer an alternative to the traditional religious systems of the West? Particularly, does the imaging of Mahayana meditation or the awareness meditation of Theravada offer an alternative to religion in the form of a kind of psychotherapy? The following texts may be consulted for further discussion of some of these issues: Robert C. Lester's *Buddhism: The Path to Nirvana*. San Francisco, Harper and Row, 1987 and Stephan Beyer's *The Buddhist Experience: Sources and Interpretations*. Encino, California, Dickenson Publishing Co., 1974.

## UNIT BIBLIOGRAPHY

Blofeld, John. "The Valley Spirit" from *Taoism: The Road to Immortality*. Boston: Shambala Publications, 1978. A study of the Taoist sages whose life-styles in certain respects parallels those of Buddhist monks.

Campbell, Joseph. *The Masks of God: Primitive Mythology*. New York: The Viking Press, 1976. Introductory section gives an interpretation of the possible origin of religious and mythological concepts.

———. *The Mythic Image*. Princeton: The Princeton University Press, 1981. Profusely illustrated introduction to myth-related iconography, architecture, including numerous references to the Buddha and Buddhism.

Coomaraswamy, Ananda. *Buddha and the Gospel of Buddhism*. New York: Harper and Row, 1964. Classic introduction to the subject by one of the founders of the Western Buddhological discipline.

Eliot, Sir Charles. *Japanese Buddhism*. London: Edward Ainold and Co., 1935. Classical presentation in limpid English of the principal types of Buddhism in Japan.

Fairservis, Walter A., Jr. "Epilogue" from *The Roots of Ancient India: The Archaeology of Early Indian Civilization*. London: Unwin Ltd., 1971. This selection describes several themes that appear in the background of Buddhist religion. It is the author's contention that Buddhism is the product of increasing urban malaise in ancient India.

Humphreys, Christmas. *Buddhism*. Hammondsworth, Middlesex: Penguin Books, 1951. A general, very readable introduction to Buddhism by a Western convert to Buddhism who was the founder of the Buddhist Society of London.

La Fleur, William R. *Buddhism: A Cultural Perspective*. Englewood Cliffs, N.J.: Prentice Hall, 1988. A good introduction to the Buddhist setting in different Asian nations. Includes a discussion of women in Buddhism.

Suzuki, Daisetz T. *The Essentials of Zen Buddhism*. New York: E. P. Dutton & Co., 1962. The foremost Japanese interpreter of Zen to the West, Suzuki's understanding of Mahayana influenced Joseph Campbell.

# NOTES

# NOTES

# NOTES

# From Id to the Ego in the Orient:
## *Kundalini Yoga Part I*

## UNIT STUDY PLAN

1. Read Unit 7 in your *Study Guide*.
2. Watch Program 7: "From Id to the Ego in the Orient: Kundalini Yoga Part I."
3. In your course notebook or journal, write a summary of Joseph Campbell's interpretation of Tantra, as the alternative life-affirming yoga of Indian spirituality.
4. Read the selections for this unit in the *Anthology of Readings*. These selections include excerpts from Agehananda Bharati, Herbert Guenther, and Charles S. J. White.
5. After reading the selections, comment in your notebook or journal on what you have read. Try to show the relationship between the readings and the essay in this unit.
6. Complete the assignments at the end of this unit as specified by your instructor.

## POINTS TO WATCH FOR IN THE TELEVISION PROGRAM

*This television program was delivered as a lecture by Joseph Campbell in New York City, in 1983.*

1. Follow Campbell as he traces the history of an "alternative-reality" concept in the West from Dionysius the Areopagite to Schopenhauer. Notice that he thinks in some Western philosophizing there is a "coming right together" with the Eastern metaphysical tradition.
2. Note the point that Campbell makes when he clarifies the difference between symbol and sign. This is especially important when we relate concepts about God, the divine, and ultimate reality to special theological positions.
3. A unifying thesis in this unit is that there are real "natural" laws that operate as much at the spiritual level as other such laws operate at the gross material level.
4. Visualize the relationship of Kundalini concepts to normal human anatomy.
5. Notice that the word "yoga," as used by Campbell, suggests a bridge between the spiritual realm and the material world.
6. Understand how Campbell, once again, can see parallels between Christianity and Kundalini Yoga. Campbell's thesis is that there are essential similarities between East and West.

## POINTS TO LOOK FOR IN THE *ANTHOLOGY OF READINGS*

1. In his historical exposition of Tantrism, Agehananda Bharati covers, in summary fashion, the history and structure of the Tantric movement in Hindu-Buddhist spirituality. Notice that he emphasizes Tantrism as marginal to Hinduism and Jainism but central to Mahayana (and particularly Tibetan) Buddhism.
2. The article entitled, "Swami Muktananda and the Enlightenment through Shakti-Pat" helps trace how Tantrism functions as an aspect of contemporary Hinduism. Everywhere, the development of paranormal powers, the performance of miracles, and the experience of unusual states of consciousness are powerful stimulants to religious enthusiasm. Thus, the Siddhis (the paranormal powers) of a spiritual master help to open the door to religious life to both the skeptic and the naive person. The Saint Shirdi Sai Baba, mentioned in the selection, used to say, "I give people the things that they want so that they will come to want the things I want to give them."
3. "The Way and the Apparent Eroticism of Tantrism" by Guenther is a sophisticated interpretation of the life-affirming aspect of Tantra or Kundalini Yoga. The practice of Kundalini meditation can involve actual erotic acts or their symbolic, meditative counterparts. The body of the yogi is the field in which the masculine and feminine forces replay the same transcendent game that is reflected throughout the world of time and matter. Guenther says it is difficult for Westerners to experience the full aesthetic value of the body's experiences because of the tendency to link sexuality to a mythology of power—a slave-master or master-slave ideology.

## UNIT GLOSSARY

**Chakra**: A spiritual center of the subtle body of humans according to Tantra Yoga.

**Ida**: The duct to the left of the Sushumna in the mystical physiology of Tantra. It is subtly connected to the left nostril and serves an important function in Tantra-Yoga breathing exercises.

**Kundalini**: The serpent-shaped element coiled sleeping at the base point of the Chakra system. It can be "awakened" by means of Tantric Yoga techniques.

**Lingam**: The phallic symbol of Shiva found in Indus-Valley religion and in contemporary Hinduism.

**Pingala**: The duct to the right of the Sushumna in the mystical physiology of Tantra. It is subtly connected to the right nostril and serves an important function in Tantra-Yoga breathing exercises.

**Siddhi (or occult power)**: Through yoga one can develop one's paranormal faculties such as telepathy, telekinesis, and "bilocation." The word "occult" means "hidden." Such powers remain hidden to others unless revealed by the yogi who is alleged to have them.

**Sthula**: Translated by Campbell as "gross matter," may be the physical, material world

**Sukshma**: Translated by Campbell as "subtle matter," also meaning "mind stuff."

**Sushumna**: The central channel of the occult physiology of Tantra which can be pierced by Kundalini.

**Sutra**: A brief "thread" of ideas (often previously memorized) used in the exposition of various ancient Indian "sciences."

**Tantra**: Campbell translates this term as "loom." It refers to the idea that the world is woven on a great loom of power, the Shakti. Understanding the processes of Shakti is essential to Tantra Yoga.

**Yoga**: A specific discipline (i.e., Raja Yoga) by means of which you can attempt to discover the reality of the spiritual realm.

**Yoni**: The symbolic representation of the female organ.

## UNIT PREVIEW

Yoga is the general term for spiritual discipline in the Hindu tradition. There are several traditional approaches to the goals of Hindu spirituality that have developed specific disciplines or yogas in this respect. This unit will compare and contrast the systems of yoga that grow out of the mainstream of Indian spirituality. In addition, there will be an introduction to the theory of Tantra, which is a special world view in the Hindu-Buddhist tradition. It was important and very influential but it remained a minority viewpoint because of its psychosexual theories and its reversal of the usual Indian view that the human body and the physical universe are obstacles to spiritual emancipation.

**The Traditional Yogas of Hinduism**: One purpose of the ancient Indian philosophies was, in addition to offering a metaphysical view of the place of human beings in the universe, to teach the means for the attainment of emancipation (Moksha). Hence, the philosophical teachings could form the basis of a particular yoga system. Some of the most significant of the yoga systems are Raja Yoga, Jnana Yoga, Karma Yoga, and Bhakti Yoga. Tantra Yoga was never as widely approved of as the other systems.

**Raja Yoga**: Of all the yogas, Raja Yoga has achieved the greatest clarity in the presentation of its technique for attaining Moksha. The discipline of Raja Yoga is divided into eight steps, called angas or "limbs." The terminology of the Raja Yoga system generally has influenced Indian religious practices.

**Tantra and Kundalini Yoga**: The origin of Tantra and Kundalini Yoga can be traced to passages in the Upanishads that indicate there is a "mystical physiology" that exists together with the gross physical body. From this and other sources, Tantra and Kundalini Yoga construct a complete theory of the universe that values the human body and the universe in a way that seems diametrically opposed to the usual disvaluing of the body and the physical universe in other areas of Indian thought.

The previous two units were introductions to the general context of the Hindu and the Buddhist religions with their special backgrounds. This included a discussion of the Jaina religion. In both Buddhism and Jainism, a culminating point in the development of early Indian religion can be seen.

Jainism and Buddhism proposed that the material universe was of negative value from the point of view of one's spiritual freedom. These religions are completely materialistic (i.e., in denying the separate existence of "spirit") in their respective understandings of the universe, and they do not place stock in the transcendent ultimate reality, commonly referred to as God in Western religions. Because of this notion of the universe as completely material, Buddhism and Jainism were regarded as heretical (nastika) by the religious authorities of the Brahmanic (Hindu) religion. Nastika in Sanskrit means something like, "who are of the 'is not'." This "is not" refers to the ultimate being of the Buddhist and Jainist creed that "is not."

The orthodox among the Hindus, from ancient times down to the present, "are of the 'is'" or Astika, which is to say that their creed is that ultimate reality—in the sense of soul, a universal spiritual power, or an individual spiritual reality—does exist.

In the television program for this unit, Campbell introduces some of the diverse teachings of the Hindu religion concerning the nature of ultimate reality. He focuses on the term yoga in this part of the discussion. His special interest is to elucidate the meaning of Kundalini Yoga. However, it will be helpful at this point to reflect on other Hindu theories of yoga and the philosophies that undergird such theories in order to understand what the special character of Kundalini Yoga may be.

# UNIT ESSAY

## Yoga and Indian Philosophy

As Campbell points out in the television program for this unit, the word "yuj" (the root of yoga) in Sanskrit means to yoke, or "to yoke something to something else." Yoga and yoke may be examples of Indo-European words that have a common origin. In the English translation of the New Testament, Jesus is quoted as saying, "My yoke is easy ... (Matthew 11:30). Similarly, the word in Sanskrit has the meaning of spiritual discipline or path.

One of the peculiarities of ancient Indian philosophies was that, in addition to offering a metaphysical view of the place of human beings in the universe, the means for the attainment of emancipation (Moksha) was a purpose of their teaching. Hence, philosophy was meant to provide the individual with an understanding of the universe that could be employed in a spiritual discipline or yoga. The individual could practice the particular yoga of the philosophy in an attempt to attain his or her own spiritual emancipation.

There are five principal yogas practiced by the Hindus. These are Raja Yoga, Jnana Yoga, Bhakti Yoga, Karma Yoga, and Tantra Yoga. They will be discussed briefly in this unit in context with their particular philosophical perspectives.

**Raja Yoga or the Royal Yoga**: This is the technical yoga taught by the author Patanjali, mentioned in the television program. He is the traditional source of the Yoga Sutras. You will find a discussion of Raja Yoga later in this unit. It is called "Royal" because it generally is regarded as the supreme expression of the yogas and its theories are points of reference for all the other forms of yoga.

**Jnana Yoga or the Yoga of Knowledge**: Shankara, the monist philosopher, taught that the Upanishads mainly were concerned with developing a discriminating mind. (An example of this theme is found in the passage from the Chandogya Upanishad, quoted in Unit 5, where the boy, Shvetaketu, is instructed in spiritual truths by his father Uddalaka.) With such discrimination, trained to the highest degree, you would be able to dissociate the mind from its own sensorially produced contents. Thereafter, you would become aware of the pure soul within you—the Atman. This would result in emancipation; for Atman and Brahman (the eternal, ultimate reality beyond the material world) are one; so Shankara taught.

**Bhakti Yoga or the Yoga of Devotion**: Later Hinduism emphasized the striking reality of the gods and goddesses such as Shiva, Krishna, Radha, and Durga. Through intense devotion to these images of the divine as real and a deep immersion in the mythology of their salvation stories, one could achieve the goal of spiritual emancipation. This yoga is not referred to specifically by Campbell in the television program, but this alternative path of devotion to God is intrinsic to the way that Hindus and Buddhists and those of other religions liberate the idea of sacred meaning in the universe from the exclusive control of the elite religious practitioners of more specialized disciplines. It would require living a monastic life or spending long hours in physical and psychological training on the path to the spiritual ideal. The goal of devotion is not immersion in Brahman or the Buddha nature, but communion with the chosen deity of religious faith.

**Karma Yoga or the Yoga of Action**: This yoga, made famous by Mahatma Gandhi in the twentieth century, teaches that your ordinary work may be done as an offering to the highest spiritual ideal. If you live the life of work this way, you can find the same kind of freedom that is the goal of other yoga paths. Though ancient philosophies did not elaborate on this yoga to the same extent that they did the other yogas, you might find some scholars who would argue that Karma Yoga is based on other well-developed theories of Yoga. The whole theory of Dharma, or socio-religious responsibility, including the caste system and the training in moral-ethical life of the Dharma Shastras (the ancient literature of formal teaching of social and political theory) conceivably provides the theoretical basis for Karma Yoga. The Bhagavad Gita's teaching (found in the Indian epic, *The Mahabharata*), of disinterested action—action undertaken without desire for the fruits of action—often is cited as the primary authority for the path of Karma Yoga.

**Tantra Yoga or the Yoga of the Divine Feminine Power**: This will be discussed later in connection with the special interpretation of this yoga in the Kundalini Yoga form. Since it is important throughout Tibetan Buddhism, it will be discussed further in Unit 9 on *The Tibetan Book of the Dead*. The word Tantra in Sanskrit can be translated as "loom." Remember that the implication of this meaning is that the universe is constructed on a great webbing of the divine feminine power. Through this loom the spiritual seeker can go beyond the realm of rebirth and suffering to complete freedom and emancipation from rebirth. It also suggests the continuously creative, dynamic nature of the universe.

## Patanjali's Yoga Sutras

It will be helpful to consider first the teaching of Patanjali's so-called Raja Yoga to appreciate the intimate link that some forms of Indian yoga acknowledge between the physical body and the goals of spiritual emancipation. The first thing to know about Patanjali's yoga philosophy is that it accepts the basic world view of Sankhya, which already has been introduced in Unit 5. Sankhya teaches that there are two irreducible elements in the world: Purusha and Prakriti. The former is the individual spiritual self and the latter is the physical world of cause and effect, time cycles, and rebirth.

In the television program for this unit, Campbell refers to the fact that the ideas in Indian philosophy are preserved in a special kind of text called a sutra. The word "sutra" means thread: the notion is that you can follow the thread of the teaching by knowing the sutras. Sutras connect to your memory, which was useful in former times, because all of this kind of literature was memorized. If you had the thread of the idea, that would provide you with the basis upon which to spell out the details.

Campbell quotes what he describes as the second of the sutras in Patanjali's work as follows: "Yoga is the intentional stopping of the spontaneous activity of the mindstuff." This gives you the key to the purpose of the yoga practices. It can be further explained this way: As long as the mind and body have primary control over the experiences made available to the spiritual self, or Purusha, the spiritual self will not recognize its true condition of freedom. A principal obstacle to this realization is the mind itself, which gives you a sense of autonomous, material existence, but does not necessarily give you an immediate intuition of the existence of the spiritual self.

However, if you follow the steps or "limbs" of Patanjali's yoga practices, you will develop sufficient control over the "mindstuff" and, thereby attain a stronger and stronger intuition of the spiritual self. When the reality of the spiritual self finally overpowers the last clinging of the mind to material existence, then emancipation occurs. At that time, the Self or Purusha is liberated forever from Prakriti and attains Kaivalya, the state of eternal freedom. This state is defined widely throughout Indian thought as Sat-Chit-Ananda: Being, Knowledge, and Bliss.

What the *Yoga Sutras* aim to do is to give you the technique necessary to achieve this goal. In all the practices of the different yogas that include mind-manipulation, it is essential for the student to have the expert guidance of a teacher. Students of yoga would want to be certain that they were not doing anything dangerous to their physical or mental health. The teacher has been through it before and can help students to avoid the pitfalls.

## The Eight Limbs of Yoga

With the foregoing in mind, you now are ready to look at the first example of the technique of overcoming the soul-body linkage. To return to Patanjali's phrase, students of yoga would be aiming for an "intentional stopping." Campbell suggests that it is not very easy to bring about this "stopping." In the television program for this unit, he says:

Suppose you wanted to hold in your mind one thought, or one image, something you think you might like to hold there. You will find that within four to five seconds that you are having associated thoughts. The mind is moving. The goal of this yoga is to make the mind stand still. . . . The image is given of a pond rippled by a wind. And the rippled pond with its waves is reflect-

ing images that are broken images, and they come and go, come and go. . . . What we do is identify ourselves with one of those broken images, one of those broken reflections on the surface of the pond. . . . Make the pond stand still. One image. What was broken and reflected is now seen in its still perfection, and that's your true being.

This process of calming the mind is divided into eight stages or "limbs" (angas in Sanskrit). They can be divided further into three groups that may be referred to as levels.

**Level One**: This level consists of two elements or limbs. They are: (1) Yama, translated as "self-restraint," which includes ahimsa or non-killing, truth-speaking, non-stealing, celibacy, and "possessionlessness." These precepts are in the realm of negative rules to improve the moral life; (2) Niyama, translated as "observances," which includes purity, contentment, right aspiration, study, and devotion to God or Ishvara. The last is thought of as a spiritual entity, separate from the world process, who can influence the soul to follow the path to emancipation. In classical yoga, the role of Ishvara no longer functions when the yogi has become free from rebirth. The point of the first two limbs is that the individual should be pursuing a moral way of life and cultivating wholesome mental qualities throughout the time of his or her yoga practice.

**Level Two**: There are two limbs to this level also: (3) Asana or postures and (4) Pranayama, the regulation of breath. The postures of this form of yoga sometimes are taught as a type of bodily conditioning and called Hatha Yoga. Such yoga classes are popularly advertised and even taught on television. The purpose of the postures and breath control is to strengthen the body and reduce the input of distracting sensory phenomena while trying to learn to control the mind. In addition, breath control is said to be an aid to changing the quality of consciousness. Both disciplines are thought to afford health benefits. In the television program, Campbell makes reference to breath control in these terms:

We begin by breath control, breathing to certain paces, and the breath is very curious. You begin breathing in one nostril, hold, etc. The notion is that emotion and feeling and state of mind are related to breath. When you are at rest, the breathing is in a nice even order. When you are stirred with shock the breathing changes. With passion the breathing changes. All right. Change the breathing and you change the state. So what we are trying to do is smooth the waters of the rippled stream. . . . When you see one of these priests breathing this way, the length of the breath is terrific, and the practiced yogi has a great chest full of breathing possibilities. So we're going to calm the waters.

**Level Three**: The last four limbs are contained in this final level of yoga. The first of the four is (5) Pratyahara, or withdrawal of the senses. This can be achieved by concentrating the mind on a single object or thought. Often the devotion to a god can be brought into play here. The various pictures or images that we have of our chosen deity can play a role in consciousness to free us from the attraction of other competing sensory stimuli. The next is (6) Dharana or steadying of the mind. With practice, the mind can be taught to concentrate for a long period of time on a single concept, such as the image of a chosen deity, to produce ekagrata, or one-pointedness. When this occurs, the external stimuli of the material world no longer intrude upon consciousness. Thus, limb six is the result of limb five. The foregoing state can be succeeded by (7) Dhyana, or contemplation. In this system, contemplation implies deep meditation without an object. Finally, (8) Samadhi can be reached. This is a profound contemplative trance in the realization of the Self or Purusha as ultimate reality. This condition can be temporary, as the fruit of the mystical experience, and abandoned to return to ordinary consciousness. Thus, the great yogis can control their whole body-mind mechanism and enter samadhi at will while also functioning in the world as teachers and spiritual masters. In such a condition they are jivan-mukti, "emancipated while alive." At the time of death, the emancipated yogi enters a final samadhi from which there is no return.

## Kundalini Yoga

It is against the background of the classical yoga of Patanjali that you can better understand the theory of Kundalini Yoga and its purpose within the Indian tradition. The ideas basic to this theory of yoga have contributed to both Hindu and Buddhist techniques of meditation with their accompanying world views. Nevertheless, ultimate philosophical distinctions remain between the two religions. These distinctions have been discussed in Units 5 and 6 and will be important in Units 8 and 9 as well.

Kundalini Yoga is an adaptation, by way of technique, of aspects of the philosophical notions of the type of Hindu thought identified with Tantra. Tantra is distinctive in the setting of Indian thought because of the greater value that it places upon physical embodiment, indeed upon the human body. This is a logical development of certain insights that pertain to Patanjali's Yoga and can be referred to even in the earlier Upanishadic literature. For example, in the Katha Upanishad there are references to the body's function in the case of the individual pursuing spiritual emancipation.

In one instance in the Katha Upanishad (II.5.11) the body is described as a city with eleven gates. The suggestion in that reference is reflected in the process of Raja Yoga in which the sensory inputs are brought under absolute control. The practitioner must control these gates of the body—the orifices that allow for sensory awareness, metaphorically speaking—to stream outward in order to gain direct access to the inner spirit.

Near the end of the Katha Upanishad, there is a verse that describes the passageway through which the soul exits from the body at the time of death:

There are a hundred and one arteries of the heart, one of them penetrates the crown of the head. Moving upwards by it, a man (at his death) reaches the Immortal; the other arteries serve for departing in different directions. (II.6.16).

If the dying person does not have control over the pathway, the soul may pass out of the body by an inauspicious avenue and be lost again in one of the lower worlds of rebirth. Whereas, if the soul can pass out of the body by the saggital suture, ("The deeply serrated articulation between the two parietal bones in the median plane of the top of the head"[1]), it will be free to be itself and not be reincarnated.

Tantra is a theory especially concerned about the means by which the material world can become the proper vehicle for the attainment of the highest goals of spiritual life. Kundalini Yoga is the particular adaptation to the Tantric view of the psycho-physical means to achieve complete self-mastery and spiritual freedom. As the passages from the Katha Upanishad suggest, there is a subtle physiology that is united with the gross physical body but also has its own distinctive organs and functions. Campbell says in his discussion of the underlying state, "This is all subtle substance. You won't find it on the operating table."

In this subtle physiology, the Kundalini power lies coiled in a serpent shape at the base of the Nadis, or spiritual channels, that lie adjacent to the physical spinal cord or column. The central channel, the Sushumna, which goes from the bottom to the top of the trunk of the body symbolically represents the universe from the bottom to the top. Along its length, from the bottom to the top, are situated a number of centers of spiritual energy and power. These are called lotuses (padma) or chakras, a term for which there is no precise equivalent in English, except perhaps "circular in shape." The human body itself, when it is seated in meditative posture, is a homologue of the structure of the universe.

The base of Kundalini is the region between the orifice of elimination and the orifice of reproduction. The top is the point at which the Sushumna passes through the saggital suture. The task of Kundalini Yoga is to awaken the spiritual power (Kundalini) coiled serpentlike at the lowest chakra and cause it, in a controlled fashion, to rise correctly along the Sushumna. As the Kundalini passes through or pierces each one of the chakras—if the technique is being performed correctly—the practitioner experiences a unique level of consciousness. Finally, when the Kundalini is raised successfully to the topmost chakra, the practitioner experiences final union with the unconditioned light of pure consciousness, which is the source from which the phenomenal world radiates. In reality you would directly know that Self which always had been in your possession, but of which you had been ignorant.

Many of the concepts previously discussed in the section about Raja Yoga apply also to the techniques of Kundalini Yoga. These include developing the right attitude and having the right understanding of the universe, having a controlled posture, breathing properly, and concentrating the mind to eliminate distracting elements. However, there are also some noteworthy special characteristics of the Kundalini or Tantra forms of practice.

There are three words in Sanskrit all beginning with the letter "M" that refer to these special techniques: (1) Mudras, ritualized gestures of the hands that are thought to be evocative of spiritual power; (2) Mantras, words or phrases identified with specific deities or states of consciousness that can alter consciousness and arouse an individual's latent divine power; and (3) Mandalas (also called yantras or chakras), often circular diagrams encompassing geometric shapes—but also pictures of deities or divine symbols—that are used in the process of meditation to make the human body a counterpart of the divine world. By using Mudras, Mantras, and Mandalas, the progress made in transiting the chakras, which will be discussed in detail in the next unit, brings about the development of paranormal powers. These powers are, in part, the aim of Tantra, which does not spurn the opportunity to enjoy in the physical world what is uniquely possible because of one's developed spiritual status. The occult powers that come to the practitioners of Tantra Yoga are called Siddhis. Since such powers can be used both positively and negatively, the Indian religious public has wisely been wary of some individuals who have the reputation of being Tantric practitioners.

### Joseph Campbell's Vision of Tantra

In the television program for this unit, Campbell presents a far-ranging interpretation of the background of Kundalini Yoga. One of the striking comparisons he makes is between the temptation of Jesus in the wilderness, recorded in the Gospel of Luke, 4:1–13, and the vision of the world that is promoted through Tantric theories and practices. Campbell goes through each one of the temptations and relates them to common human experience. In the first temptation, Satan challenges Jesus to turn stones into bread to assuage his hunger from fasting in the wilderness. Jesus refuses to be tempted by the "economic" solution to the problem of human existence. In the second temptation, Satan takes Jesus up into the air and shows him the world and offers him dominance if Jesus will fall down and worship him. Jesus rejects this "political" solution as well. Satan goes on to the third and last temptation; he challenges Jesus to throw himself from the pinnacle of the temple in Jerusalem. Campbell interprets Jesus' refusal to succumb to the last temptation—a kind of symbolic denial of the value of the physical—as a significant parallel to the Tantric rejection of the views of those Indian spiritual disciplines that hold the physical world to be an obstacle, a bondage to the spiritual. Campbell might go as far as to compare the heroic journey of Jesus (through his temptations and sacrifice on the cross to the Resurrection) with the Tantric Yogi's heroic journey, by way of the Kundalini, transforming the physical world into the divine Reality.

In Tantrism, the whole universe is thought to be the arena of the Goddess, who embodies the complementary force in the divine field of energy. As such, she is Shakti who complements the masculine power, personified in Shiva. Matter and spirit are united through these complementary elements in the divine field, with the feminine being the active and dominant in the material universe. Hence, everything that is good in the material world, perceived to be good in human physical existence, is good in the context of the divine existence. Madeleine Biardeau, a contemporary authority on Hinduism and Tantrism, has this to say of the concept of the goodness of the material world:

> Tantra is an attempt to place Kama, desire, in every meaning of the word, in the service of liberation... not to sacrifice this world for liberation's sake, but to reinstate it, in varying ways, within the perspective of salvation.[2]

## ASSIGNMENTS FOR STUDY AND ANALYSIS

1. Joseph Campbell makes some broadly based comparisons of Eastern and Western thought. Discuss your understanding of the underlying thesis behind them.
2. From your own or another Western religious tradition, what beliefs and practices can you find that compare with Raja, Jnana, Bhakti, and Karma Yoga? Explain.
3. In the article, "Swami Muktananda and the Enlightenment through Shakti-Pat," you have a description of a Hindu saint's life and practices within the Tantric tradition. What did you find out about the practical (i.e., "practiced") aspects of this yoga, taught by a modern Hindu teacher?
4. One of the features of Tantrism is the special place that sexual symbolism and sexual activity have in this system. Discuss some of the special features that you notice in the religious view of sexuality from another culture. Use the reading from Professor Guenther's *The Tantric View of Life* for further background information.
5. Discuss the comparison Campbell makes in the television program between the temptation of Christ and Tantric theory.

## FURTHER ASSIGNMENTS FOR WRITING AND REFLECTION

1. Choose one of the yogas mentioned in the essay (other than Tantric Yoga) and develop a bibliography of sources that discuss the topic. Write a two-page essay setting out the understanding you have of the yoga in your sources.
2. What are the principal differences between Tantric Buddhism and Tantric Hinduism? You may answer this in part by comparing materials on the subject from this unit with

Unit 9. You also may have to consult outside sources on the subject, such as those listed in the bibliography. The articles on Tantric Buddhism and Tantric Hinduism in the *Encyclopedia of Religion* (New York: Macmillan, 1987) will give you good orientation on the subject.

3. In this unit, we are faced with the claims of a religious way of life that believes in the possibility of the enhancement of parapsychological (occult) powers in the pursuit of religious goals. Western religions generally have forbidden such pursuits and have linked them to Satan, evil, or a more general negative force in the universe. Do you have any further reactions, positive or negative, to the Tantric insistence that there is nothing in the universe that is other than a manifestation of the goddess and hence is good? Tantra emphasizes the Hindu idea that the creative power of the divine is present in the world as Lila, play or sport. The universe is the divine dance of the god or goddess. Is it possible to translate the categories of play or sport into meaningful concepts or expressions for religious life in the contemporary world?

5. In many parts of the Western world today women are trying to develop ways to express their religious feelings within a feminine symbolism and worship system. Some men also join in this pursuit. For example, Margot Adler's *Drawing Down the Moon* (Boston: Beacon Press, 1986), second edition, contains reports of the growth of feminist paganism in North America. Discuss the larger issue of a "feminine religion" as an alternative to the traditional patriarchal religions of the West. Does Tantrism offer a model for the reconstitution of religion to take the feminist perspective into account?

## ENDNOTES

[1] "Saggital suture." *Webster's Third New International Dictionary of the English Language Unabridged.*

[2] "Tantrism." *Encyclopedia of Religion*, 1987 ed. 273.

## UNIT BIBLIOGRAPHY

Avalon, Arthur (Sir John Woodruff). *Principles of Tantra: The Tantratattva of Shriyukta Shiva Chandra Vidyarnava Bhattacarya Mahodaya.* Madras: Ganesh & Co., 1960. The classical study on the principles of Tantra but couched in indirect language, typical of its subject but not always helpful to students.

Avalon, Arthur (Sir John Woodruff). "Cit-Sakti" from *Shakti and Shakta.* New York: Dover Publishing Co., 1978. Sir John Woodroffe is the best-known Western scholar on the texts of the Tantric tradition, defines the relationship between spirit and matter.

Bhandarkar, R. G. *Vaishnavism, Shaivism and Minor Religious Systems.* Banaras: Indological Book House, 1966. Contains unique material from an earlier period of great historical interest and excellent background for contemporary religious life in India.

Biardeau, Madeleine. *L'Hindouisme: Anthropologie d'une Civilization.* Paris: Flammarion, 1981. One of the few comprehensive and authoritative studies of the whole Hindu tradition and Hinduism.

Das Gupta, Shashibhushan. *Obscure Religious Cults.* Calcutta: K. L. Mukhopadyhaya, 1969, third edition. A useful introduction to specialized aspects of the Tantric tradition.

Eliade, Mircea. *Yoga: Immortality and Freedom.* New York: Pantheon Books (Bollingen Series 56), 1958. The definitive work on yoga.

Kinsley, David. "The Sword, Kali, Mistress of Death" from *The Sword and the Flute: Kali and Krisna, Dark Visions of the Terrible and the Sublime in Hindu Mythology.* Berkeley: University of California Press, 1975. Kinsley explains the role that the feminine concept of deity has in the Hindu religion.

Padoux, Andre. "Hindu Tantrism." *The Encyclopedia of Religion.* New York: Macmillan, 1987. Vol. 14, p. 274 ff. A sensitive interpretation of its subject that points out the limitations of contemporary scholarship on Tantra. It clearly discusses what is presently known.

# NOTES

# NOTES

# NOTES

# UNIT 8

# From Psychology to Spirituality:
## *Kundalini Yoga Part II*

## UNIT STUDY PLAN

1. Read Unit 8 in your *Study Guide*.
2. Watch Program 8: "From Psychology to Spirituality: Kundalini Yoga Part II.
3. In your course notebook or journal write a summary of Joseph Campbell's interpretation of the yogi's spiritual journey through the chakras.
4. Read the selections for this unit in the *Anthology of Readings*. These selections include excerpts from works by Heinrich Zimmer, Mircea Eliade, Haridas Chaudhuri, and Edward Conze.
5. After reading the selections, comment in your notebook on what you have read. Show the relationship between the readings and the essay in this unit.
6. In your own words state what the chakras are in relation to the Kundalini.
7. Complete the assignments at the end of this unit as specified by your instructor.

## POINTS TO WATCH FOR IN THE TELEVISION PROGRAM

*This television program was delivered as a lecture by Joseph Campbell in New York City, in 1983.*

1. Notice the complex symbolism inscribed within each of the chakras. Of what use is the symbolism from the point of view of the yogi who is experimenting with Kundalini Yoga?
2. Remember to associate the Sanskrit name of the chakra with its English equivalent.
3. Visualize the chakras along the central axis of the human body. Link the interpretations given by Campbell with the chakras.
4. Make sure you follow the discussion about the alternatives to erotic symbolism in the different types of devotional yoga that Campbell discusses.
5. Notice comparisons between Vishnu and Jesus Christ. Campbell refers more than once in this television program to *The Cocktail Party* by T. S. Eliot as a secular literary version of the potent kind of ritual symbolism that absorbs Catholic Christianity, Hindu-Buddhist Tantra, and Kundalini Yoga.
6. Notice that the chakra system interpretation can lead to a total theory of the universe.

## POINTS TO LOOK FOR IN THE *ANTHOLOGY OF READINGS*

1. The selection from Haridas Chaudhuri's *Integral Yoga* in the *Anthology of Readings* includes the author's own conception of yoga, based on a synthesis of the distinct yogas presented in Unit 7 and Unit 8. Note how his modern interpretation of Tantra combines theories of ancient origin with modern scientific theories, such as those of physics. For example, the modern influence is seen in this statement from *Integral Yoga*, "Tantric Yoga is the art of splitting the spiritual atom in man. It is the technique of releasing the pent-up energies of the human psyche" (268).
2. You will want to note that one of the interesting elements in this unit is the repeated reference to the nineteenth-century Bengali Saint Ramakrishna in the selection from Heinrich Zimmer. Both Zimmer and Campbell felt a deep rapport with Ramakrishna, whose representatives run Hindu missions in the United States. Ramakrishna spoke to the educated Bengali public of his period. Bengal, in that era, was the center of British political and intellectual influence. Ramakrishna's Tantrism was a purified version of the theories and practices of Tantra carried on secretly in the India of those days.
3. Mircea Eliade, who is recognized today as the leading interpreter of the structures and meanings of religion, had his early scholarly training in India. He went from his native Rumania to Calcutta and, in the course of his education there, engaged in some of the yoga practices he wrote about in his definitive work called *Yoga*. Eliade is an especially important interpreter of yoga because he not only states the theories and describes the practices, but he also explains the meaning of the religious expression.
4. The collection of Buddhist texts edited by Edward Conze contains some excellent examples of the writings that are central to the Tantric tradition. The diagram of the Mandala should be noted particularly for it complements discussion in the three units (7, 8, and 9) that make reference to Tibetan Buddhism. In the excerpts, entitled, "The Fivefold Manifestation" and "An Evocation of Prajnaparamita," you will read more explicitly about the technique of meditation used in Tantrism. Campbell makes reference to these meditation practices in Units 7, 8, and 9.

## UNIT GLOSSARY

**Bhakti**: The mood of devotion, of love for one's chosen deity.

**Chakra**: A spiritual center of the subtle body of humans—according to Tantra.

**Kali**: The female deity-consort of Shiva. She is often depicted as fearsome, wearing a necklace of skulls and a skirt of severed human limbs. The "terrifying image" of Kali symbolizes the terror of time and the impermanence of the physical world. This is another view of Shakti.

**Krishna**: The most widely worshipped avatar ("descent form" or incarnation) of Vishnu. He is viewed as the supreme deity of devotional love in all its forms.

**Mahishasuramardani**: A name for Durga, one of the consorts of Shiva, signifying that she is the slayer of the demon Mahishasura.

**Maya**: The feminine symbol of the world of Samsara. Maya is equated with Shakti in the Tantric system.

**Shakti**: The feminine pole of the universal energy field of the universe. Shiva is the masculine pole. The image is analogous to a description of the magnetic field.

**Vishnu**: The deity who shares principal roles with Shiva in the Hinduism of Post-Vedic (after 600 B.C.E.) and modern times.

**Yab-Yum**: The stylized icons of Tibetan Buddhism that show the embrace of the masculine and feminine principles in the universe.

## UNIT PREVIEW

This unit discusses the implementation of the theory of Tantra by means of the Kundalini Yoga system. This yoga system teaches rituals and meditation practices to unite the spiritual power in human beings with the spiritual force in the universe. The system of chakras offers a complex, symbolic pattern of stages in the progress of the hero, called Vir in Sanskrit, toward the goal of universal consciousness.

**The Chakra System**: The spiritual centers of Kundalini Yoga are located along the axis of the human body. There may be some relation between the chakra theory and the actual human nervous system with its ganglia. The Indian genius tended toward the systematization of all aspects of religion and culture. The Kundalini Yoga system is an example of this.

**The Chakras and Their Interpretation**: The seven centers, or chakras, correspond to regions of the body as an image of the whole universe. Campbell sees the chakras linked to an evolving spiritualization of basic human drives. Through chakras one to three, the spiritual experience is allied closely with the physical world.

**The Remaining Chakras**: Those chakras numbered four to seven induce an increasing involution of the yogi's consciousness as Shakti turns away from the material world toward union with universal consciousness. When Shiva and Shakti are united, the distinction between them is obliterated.

**Sri Ramakrishna**: One of the greatest Tantric yogis, Ramakrishna cautioned against the overt use of sex on the part of the "Hero." He advocated the "Sattvic" or "Godlike, luminous" path of the saint. The best way to approach the goddess, he said, was in the mood of a child toward its mother. He was referring to the neutral attitude and the practices of the Tantric Yogi.

## UNIT ESSAY

### From Psychology to Spirituality: Kundalini Yoga Part II

In the television program for this second unit on Tantra and Kundalini Yoga, Joseph Campbell takes you on a tour of the chakras that lie along the central spiritual channel (Sushumna) of the mystical physiology. Campbell presupposes what you already have considered: the proposition that the microcosm reflects the macrocosm. By looking at each one of the chakras in turn, Campbell guides you first through some very significant aspects of the Buddhist-Hindu tradition. He also finds interesting correspondences between Kundalini theory and other religious traditions.

### The Chakra System

Having studied the Raja Yoga system with its eight limbs in Unit 7, you have learned to appreciate the Indian gift for organizing the content of a problem in a very systematic way. A part of the Indian genius was to create categories for almost every imaginable aspect of culture and some that no other cultures even considered. The ancient Indians were consummate grammarians, logicians, and dialecticians—meaning that they understood the structure of language, explanation, and argument. They also developed complete theories of the aesthetic experience, including such subjects as literary forms and the vocabulary of dance movement. They made sciences out of such subjects as socio-ethical behavior and temple ritual.

Seven Chakras of Kundalini Yoga

All these systems, taken together, are an amazing achievement—probably unmatched in any other ancient civilization.

With this in mind, the chakra system may not seem so incomprehensible even though it may be unusual. The theory of the chakras has some bearing upon actual human physiology. There are major nerve centers in the body called ganglia. Some of them are located along the central axis of the body and may have been discovered and interpreted in the light of certain experiences associated with meditation and other religious practices. The source of Tantra Yoga (an aspect of Hinduism) may come from the oldest strata of Indian history, perhaps back to the pre-Aryan period. There has been a continuing indigenous aboriginal culture, whose religious practices have been, at times, partially assimilated into the dominant Sanskrit-Hindu culture.

## Kundalini Terminology

The chakras are linked to specific areas of the body along the central axis as follows: the genital region—the Muladhara Chakra; the navel region—the Svadhishthana Chakra; the solar plexus—the Manipura Chakra; the heart region—the Anahata Chakra; the throat region—the Vishuddha Chakra; the mid-eyebrow region—the Ajna Chakra; the saggital-suture region (see Unit 7 for the definition of the saggital-suture)—the Sahasrara Chakra.

Draw a vertical line on a piece of paper and print the titles of the chakras to help visualize the location of the chakras while reading Campbell's analysis of the way these spiritual centers relate to different levels of spiritual awareness. The chakras also have corollaries with different qualities and expressions of Hindu religious theory. These, in turn, have general interpretive value in the way Campbell looks at comparative mythology. As in so much of Campbell's thought, the journey through the chakras makes of the yogi's practice a heroic voyage of self-discovery in which the human body is the vehicle for mastery of the universe and union with the universal spirit.

## The Interpretation of Kundalini

The Muladhara Chakra is the source from which the Kundalini, when awakened, starts its ascent through the universe and the yogi's subtle body. The Kundalini power, what it may be to the individual who attempts to experience it inwardly, is the fundamental reality of the universe. In Indian terminology, the basis of all that exists is described as feminine and given two conceptually fundamental names, not mutually exclusive. These are Prakriti and Maya. In Unit 5, Prakriti was introduced as the context in which Purusha (individualized spirit) finds itself trapped in the endless cycle of reincarnation. The idea of Prakriti remains fundamental to all discussions of the dynamics of the physical universe. The term Maya was promoted with special emphasis by the Advaitan philosopher Shankara, who espoused the prominent Indian view that the material world is a kind of veil thrown over ultimate reality. As long as attention is focused on the material world, one is not able to see the reality beyond.

Tantra philosophy, key to Kundalini Yoga, takes a somewhat different view of the character of Maya from that of Shankara. The Tantra philosophy posits that the universe is Maya-Shakti who is the "consort" of ultimate reality itself, personified as Shiva. At this point, review the selection from Heinrich Zimmer for this unit in the *Anthology of Readings*.

In the Sankhya system (as discussed in Unit 5), in addition to Purusha and Prakriti, the spiritual entity and the world in totality, there is a considerable list of factors related to different aspects of the material world. According to the Sankhya system, there are three gunas, the fundamental material elements. These are Tamas, Rajas, and Sattva. Each represents a characteristic of things in the world: Tamas is dense, heavy, opaque; Rajas is active, moving, dynamic; while Sattva is shining, peaceful, and quiet. Very often in the discussion of these qualities, Indian authors refer to various things in the world that have these qualities. For example, Indians are very concerned about the gunas in the food that they eat. In a spiritual milieu that places emphasis upon self-control and a calm mind, certain foods are thought to be stimulating or heavy in their effect. But certain other foods are thought to be light and more wholesome or Sattvic. Hence, a serious spiritual seeker should consume foods that are Sattvic in character since these will contribute to attaining one's spiritual goal of having a Sattvic mind. For example, vegetarian food is more Sattvic, in general, than meat and fish.

Similarly, human temperaments also tend to align with the gunas. In the overall perspective of the ideal of Indian spirituality, the Sattvic temperament is, therefore, the ideal because it would be less entrammeled in the more limiting and distracting characteristics of the material world.

Tantra, however, takes a different view from the Sankhya System of the desirable qualities of the guna-related temperaments. As Zimmer says in his book *Philosophies of India*: "In the Tantric vocabulary these three types are known respectively, as Vira [Rajas], the hero; Pasu [Tamas], the dark-witted animal of the herd; and Divya [Sattvic], the godlike, luminous saint."[1] The Tantric yogi is a hero, a Vira, who uses the five Ms in the pursuit of Kundalini awakening: These are Madya (wine), Mansa (meat), Matsya (fish), Mudra (parched grain), and Maithuna (sexual intercourse). But indulging in these foods and sexual relationships that would be forbidden according to the Sattvic tradition, the Tantric hero turns the world of ordinary limitations into a vehicle for union with the goddess, who is, after all, the base of everything in the world. The arousal of the Kundalini can occur under the stimulation of the "sacraments" when partaken of in a ritualized setting.

In nineteenth-century Bengal (a stronghold of goddess worship), one of the major figures of Hinduism in the modern period spoke in homely terms about the process of Kundalini arousal. His name was Ramakrishna. Saints like Ramakrishna eschewed the heroic path in favor of the Sattvic path to the same end. The following dialogue helps define the meaning of Kundalini arousal associated with the Muladhara Chakra. Someone is asking Ramakrishna a question. The form is this discussion is typical of the dialogue engaged in between spiritual teachers and disciples. The discussion is direct and unguarded:

"Isn't it true that the Tantra prescribes spiritual discipline in the company of women?"

"That," [Ramakrishna] had replied, "is not desirable. It is a very difficult path and often causes the aspirant's downfall. There are three such kinds of discipline. One may regard woman as one's mistress or look on oneself as her handmaid, or as her child. I look on woman as my mother. To look on oneself as her handmaid is also good; but it is extremely difficult to practice spiritual discipline looking on woman as one's mistress. To regard oneself as her child is a very pure attitude. . .

"The devotee assumes various attitudes toward Shakti in order to propitiate Her: the attitude of a handmaid, a 'hero' or a child. A hero's attitude is to please Her even as a man pleases a woman through intercourse. . .

"The worship of Shakti is extremely difficult. It is no joke. I passed two years as the handmaid and companion of the Divine Mother. But my natural attitude has always been that of a child toward its mother. I regard the breasts of any woman as those of my own mother. Women are, all of them, the veritable images of Shakti."[2]

The awakened Kundalini passes through the second chakra (the Svadhishthana Chakra) as it begins its ascent toward the goal of universal consciousness at the topmost chakra. Apparently the movement of the Kundalini varies. Ramakrishna described this variation as follows:

"Sometimes the Spiritual Current rises through the spine, crawling like an ant," Ramakrishna told a circle of his intimate friends. "Sometimes, in Samadhi [a state of mystical trance], the soul swims joyfully in the ocean of divine ecstasy, like a fish. Sometimes, when I lie down on my side, I feel the Spiritual Current pushing me like a monkey and playing with me joyfully. I remain still. That current, like a monkey, suddenly with one jump reaches the Sahasrara [the last chakra]. That is why you see me jump with a start.

"Sometimes, again, the Spiritual Current rises like a bird hopping from one branch to another. The place where it rests feels like fire. It may hop from Muladhara to Svadhishthana, from Svadhishthana to the heart, and thus gradually to the head. Sometimes the Spiritual Current moves up like a snake. Going in a zigzag way, at last it reaches the head and I go into Samadhi."[3]

Campbell's comments on this chakra are particularly rich since he associates the second chakra both with the ordinary division of men and women as sexual beings or partners (and hence the sexual bipolarism in nature at large) and with the sublimation of the sexuality of things into the distinct categories of love. Sexual relations are the expression of one category of love. As you might expect, the Indian theorists gave a good deal of thought to the relationship between the human capacity to love and the way that love is expressed in human terms. Campbell states that the second chakra is the chakra of Vishnu and that Vishnu is associated with the erotic.

Vishnu and Shiva are the principal deities of the Hindu pantheon today. In certain respects, both of them have an erotic dimension. Shiva is perhaps more associated with sex as we know it in the erotic motifs of literature, theater, or even pornography. The term "uninhibited" is usually associated with this version of sex. It is fair to say that this is not the only way that Shiva is linked symbolically to sex. The Kundalini Yoga theory of Tantra presents Shiva as the abstracted spiritual absolute, passive before the dynamic activism of the Shakti power in the universe. (This may be construed as a reversal of the customary male-female roles in sex.)

Vishnu, in the arena of love, plays a variety of roles, including the erotic. Campbell discusses the form of Vishnu known as Krishna, one of the most popular deities in later Hinduism. Krishna's beloved is Radha. The story of their love in union and separation is the basis of literary and philosophical works (for example, Jayadeva's Gita Govinda and the philosophical world of Shri Vallabhacharya). Distinct Hindu groups dispute the meaning of their love and create complete theological systems to defend a particular point of view.

In Unit 7, the different types of Yoga, including Bhakti Yoga, or the Yoga of Devotion, were discussed. In the television program for this unit, Campbell says that the second chakra, which also can be viewed as a certain stance in the structure of religion, is the elaboration of Bhakti Yoga within the Hindu tradition. It also relates to other religions.

Briefly put, Campbell says that Bhakti Yoga can project different moods. These are called rasas in the technical literature of Bhakti. Campbell uses the example of the woman who spoke to Ramakrishna and said, "I find that I do not love God." Ramakrishna asked her if there was something in the world that she did love. She replied that she loved her little nephew. Ramakrishna told her that this could be the focus of her love for God. One of the lessons of that anecdote is that the emotion of love tied to the second chakra can lead beyond the elementary form of the emotion to a cultural-religious expression, for example, from loving your nephew to loving God in the form of the Divine Child.

In the system of Bhakti Yoga, the emotions that can be separated include parental love for a child, the love of brothers (sibling love), the devotion of a slave or servant, marital love, the love of friends, and the love of female friends for the feminine divine image. Very often a charismatic leader expresses a unique reaction to a mythic story that he or she is able to make real in a special way for a group of followers. Ramakrishna could translate into modern terms the content of the Kundalini theory, making it respectable and even normative. Campbell once again sees a cross-cultural theme in the way that he interprets the second chakra. He says in the television program that, like Krishna, "Christ is a kind of Vaishnava incarnation. And there are many parallels as one studies Christianity in relation to. . .Vaishnavism." (Vaishnavism is the religious system with Vishnu at its center.)

In the third chakra, the Manipura Chakra, the symbolism is that of the negative side of sex. The positive side is the drive toward procreation of progeny and of love in its different forms. The negative side is characterized by the substitution of power for love. In its most extreme form it is symbolized by what Campbell calls, "Black time out of which all things come, back into which all things go." Time is the Goddess Kali who has terrifying attributes: lolling tongue, fangs, a necklace of human heads, and a skirt of human limbs. Just as love is the special province of Vishnu, the destructive character of the world is the arena of Shiva who acts through the Goddess.

Though terrifying, the ultimate purpose of the Goddess is the good of her devotees and of the universe. She is the special champion of the positive forces in the universe against the demonic forces. As Durga, consort of Shiva, she is called Mahishasuramardani, the slayer of the demon called Mahishasura. The demons are not only active in the cosmos but they can stand for our own psychological states, our drive for power, and our tendency to behave destructively in pursuing the goal of dominance by means of love. Campbell seems to say, also, that the third chakra is the region of self-interested goals in what often passes for religion in the popular mind. Health, wealth, and progeny form the constant petitions in the prayers of those who flock to some of the greatest shrines, such as the Basilica of the Virgin of Guadalupe in Mexico City or the Temple of Juggernaut in Puri, India. The power of the Goddess flows through the third chakra to serve several purposes, among them the maintenance of cosmic (and psychological) order through the destruction of the demonic and the fulfillment of the petitions of the mass of humanity. The third chakra is the source of occult power that serves a material purpose either for the yogi or for those who appeal for help by means of the yogi's siddhis or paranormal powers.

Campbell informs us that it is at the fourth chakra, the Anahata Chakra, of Kundalini awakening that the spiritual forms of religious life come into prominence. He says that the Anahata, which means "not hidden," refers to the concept in Indian spirituality of the "unsounded sound." Each of the chakras has a short mantra or sound phrase associated with it. These are called Bijamantras, or "seed mantras." Campbell especially associates the mantra, Om, with this chakra. Om is a sound symbol for the totality of the divine power in the universe. It also is understood to be Aum. In its latter guise you can experiment in private to understand better what he is talking about. The first letter "a" is said far back in the throat. There is no other sound that can precede it. In other words it is the beginning of creation. The sound of the vowel "u" is in the midst of the speech organ. The sound of "m" takes you to the very edge of the organ of speech with the closing of the lips. Since there is silence before the "Om" or "Aum" and silence afterward, these silences can be thought of as the pure spiritual void (in Buddhism) or being (in Hinduism) that precedes and succeeds all forms.

Campbell makes an interesting hook-up between the four stages of Aum and the four states of consciousness described in the Upanishads. Again this is a kind of "proof" that anyone can know from ordinary experience. The description of the four states of consciousness is meant to guide your thinking toward the goal of the apprehension of pure spirit. The "a" of Aum is analogous to the waking state, called Jagrat when we are completely conscious of the world. The "u" is analogous to the dreaming state or Svapna in which we are subject to many sensory experiences, but are detached partially from the full consciousness of the world. The "m" is analogous to the state of deep, dreamless sleep wherein we are not conscious of an object. That is called Sushupti in Sanskrit. Again, it is a common human experience that when we awake from dreamless sleep we have a special sense of happiness, of having almost been on a different plane of existence. So the Indian teachers want you to be guided by your own experience to explore various states of consciousness. The Kundalini technique, as well as others, can help you to arrive at the fourth state called simply, Turiya, the "fourth" or Amatra, the measureless. The Turiya state, which corresponds to the silence of Aum, can be reached only in meditation. In that state, there is no longer the subject-object dualism. The self shines with its own light.

Campbell explains that the fifth chakra, the Vishuddha Chakra, is the place of purgation. Its dark-petalled lotus is a companion of the dark-petalled lotus of the third chakra. Here the symbolism is that of Shakti (the feminine pole of energy) turning away from the material world to enter into the final embrace of union with Shiva (the masculine). This is presented for meditation in the Tibetan Buddhist erotic sculptures, some of great aesthetic appeal, called Yab-Yum. These sculptures represent the Bodhisattva in a ritualized sexual embrace with his own Shakti. Zimmer states the simultaneous dual and non-dual nature of this ultimate Tantric symbolism as follows:

> This Yab-Yum icon is to be read in two ways. On the one hand, the candidate is to meditate on the female portion as the Shakti or dynamic aspect of eternity and the male as the quiescent but activated. Then, on the other hand, the male is to be regarded as the principle of the path, the way, the method (upaya), and the female, with which it merges, as the transcendent goal; she is then the fountainhead into which the dynamism of enlightenment returns in its state of full and permanent incandescence.

And finally, the very fact that the dual symbol of the united couple is to be read in the two ways (with either the male or the female representing transcendent truth) signifies that the two aspects or functions of reality are of perfectly equal rank: there is no difference between samsara and nirvana, either as to dignity or substance. Tathata, the sheer "suchness," is made manifest both ways and for true enlightenment the apparent difference is nonexistent.[4]

Campbell shows us in other illustrations in the television program for this unit some of the further meanings of this chakra. Kali dancing on the prostrate body of Shiva is the symbolic act of renouncing the culturally conditioned images of divinity in favor of the elementary truth. Campbell talks about it in this memorable explanation: "Meister Eckhardt [a medieval Christian mystic] says the ultimate leave-taking is the leave-taking of God. That is to say, the folk-god, for God, that is to say, the elementary idea."

The second highest chakra, the Ajna Chakra, is representative of the first moment of union between pure spirit and the Shakti of the universe. The meaning of Ajna is unknowing or unaware, in the sense that Maya-Shakti in the embrace of Shiva is still unaware of the dualism that has come into existence. Its two petalled lotus is the symbol of the transformation of the One into the Two; in other words, the source of the dualism between spirit and matter. Campbell says it is symbolic also of the highest form of love. The symbolism of love in the second chakra, which took on so many guises but in its elementary form was the procreative energy of sex, is transmuted here into the highest form of love. In the television program for this unit, Campbell explains it under the imagery of a well-known Western literary character. "Chakra Two is brought up and turned into its sublime form of love for God. Now when Dante beheld Beatrice, it was in the way not of Chakra Two, but of Chakra Six. He saw her not as an object of lust, but as a manifestation of the beauty of God's grace and love for the world. And through contemplating her in that way, she was brought to the throne of final realization."

Something of the same perception may be in the background of the intense spiritualization of Sri Ramakrishna's love for the divine Mother Kali that you have seen expressed in the quotations in the discussion of the second chakra. Ramakrishna was perhaps the most articulate Tantric Yogi ever to explain his emotional life in detail. He saw Kali—through the disguise of her horrifying attributes—as the beloved on the analogy of Dante's love for Beatrice, wherein the erotic emotion had undergone a complete transformation into a kind of love that could not be compared with anything else.

The highest stage of chakra, the Sahasrara Chakra, has been reached when the Kundalini at last pierces the crown chakra, which is described as a one thousand petalled lotus. The moth, Campbell tells us, has at last attained union with the flame.

The power of Kundalini sometimes has been described as being possessed and its proponents, as experimenters with madness. This may have been true in some cases, but much of the interior experience of this unusual spiritual art can be accepted as metaphor and symbol for aspects of religious and aesthetic experience that you can, to some extent, relate your own experience. For example, to go back to a point that has been pursued throughout this discussion of Tantra, this Indian system accepts the physical world and the human body as valuable parts of the totality of the divine life in the universe. Religions try to communicate the relationship between the human and the divine by means of ritual, and Tantrism is highly ritualistic.

The practice of Kundalini Yoga is sometimes accompanied by very beautiful rituals. These are meant to intensify to the yogi his role as the image of the universe. Worship in other traditions sometimes has the same effect. We might close by quoting an interesting passage from Zimmer in which he compares Tantric ritual to the liturgical acts of the Western tradition:

> An example of nyasa (mantra) in Christian worship is the making of the sign of the cross, touching first the forehead ("in the name of the father"), then the breast ("and of the son"), the left shoulder ("and of the Holy"), right shoulder ("Ghost"), and finally bringing the palms together in the position of salutation known to the Hindus as anjali, which is the classic Christian mudra of prayer ("Amen").[5]

Zimmer, as he continues the quotation, cites a proclamation of the Council of Trent (1545–1563 C.E.), edited by Arthur Avalon in *The Principles of Tantra*, to show the parallel vocabulary from the ritualistic aspect of Tantra:

> The Catholic Church, rich with the experience of the ages and clothed with their splendor, has introduced mystic benediction (mantra), incense (dhupa), water (acamana, padya, etc.), lights (dipa), bells (ghanta), flowers (pushpa), vestments and all the magnificence of its ceremonies in order to excite the spirit of religion to the contemplation of the profound mysteries which they reveal. As are its faithful, the Church is composed of both body (deha) and soul (atman). It therefore renders to the Lord (Ishvara) a double worship, exterior (vahya-Puja) and interior (manasa-puja), the latter being the prayer (vadana) of the faithful, the breviary of its priest, and the voice of Him ever interceding in our favor, and the former the outward motions of the liturgy. (Interpolations by authors of *The Principles of Tantra*.) [The Sanskrit words, following their English equivalents in the passage above, are a part of the common vocabulary of liturgy in Indian religion, inspired by Tantric ideas.][6]

## ASSIGNMENTS FOR STUDY AND ANALYSIS

1. In your own words write a description of the gunas. Think about the different classes of things in the world: things close to you and things far away. How would you fit them into the guna system?

2. Tantra and Kundalini Yoga use vivid imagery to focus the meditation of the yogi. From your own reflections on the Kundalini system what would you expect the mechanism of this yoga to be? How does it affect the mind? Can you think of devices that are used in contemporary culture to induce mental absorption in vivid imagery? Discuss.

3. What do you understand about Campbell's use of the second chakra to call attention to the different types of Bhakti (devotional) Yoga? Do you think that sexual imagery can have a valid role in religious life? What are the problems in this question? Explore the differences in cultural attitudes on this question. Campbell says that the sublimated emotions of parent-child love, love between friends, or love of a servant for his or her master, to give some examples, can be associated with your religious faith as a vehicle for devotion to God. This comes out of the Indian religious tradition. Discuss.

4. Discuss the use of repetitive devout speech, such as the invocation of the Trinity or the Lord's Prayer (in Christianity) or the mantra of Kundalini Yoga. Are their purposes comparable?

5. You have studied in Unit 5 and Unit 6 the Hindu-Buddhist theory of the necessity to put the world of matter aside in the pursuit of spiritual freedom. The Kundalini and Tantric theories, discussed in Unit 7 and Unit 8, advise using the material world as a positive means for self-transcendence. Discuss your understanding of these theories, including their relationship to one another as well as their differences.

## FURTHER ASSIGNMENTS FOR WRITING AND REFLECTION

1. Joseph Campbell sees the hero's journey as an important motif in world religions. Discuss any comparisons you find between the "heroic" journey of the Kundalini Yogi and the Navajo tale of "Where the Two Came to Their Father" in Unit 2.

2. Initiation is another important element in mythology and ritual. Can you see any parallels between the initiatory aspect of Kundalini Yoga theory and the initiatory element in Native American religion or in the Greek Mystery Religions? You will be studying the Mystery Religions in Unit 10. To answer this question you may need to consult other sources. *The Encyclopedia of Religion*, published by Macmillan in 1987, is a good place to find articles on the Mysteries and, also, on Kundalini Yoga.

3. In your own words, formulate a systematic presentation of the interrelationship between (1) the eight limbs of Patanjali's Yoga; (2) the three gunas of Sankhya, and (3) the seven chakras of Kundalini Yoga.

4. Kundalini Yoga and other yoga systems in Hinduism and the practices of Buddhism, in both Hinayana and Mahayana forms, suggest that the world can be viewed from a completely novel perspective, based on the creative experience of meditation. This concept bears comparison with trends in modern art and literature wherein a new "vision" of self and the world is presented through the "eye" of the painter, the writer, or the poet. Jesus says in the Bible, "Unless a man be born again he cannot enter the Kingdom of God" (John 3:3). Discuss in ordinary human terms some of the implications of the "born-again" motif in these different spiritual traditions. In other words, what can it possibly mean?

5. Some avant-garde Western writers of the twentieth century, such as D. H. Lawrence and Henry Miller, have advocated an uninhibited sexual life as a form of secular salvation. Find a work of literature in this genre and compare its thesis with what you understand about the viewpoint of Kundalini Yoga.

6. In the *Anthology of Readings* you will find an excerpt from Haridas Chaudhuri's *Integral Yoga*. Chaudhuri attempts to relate the developmental character of Tantra's Kundalini (and devotion to the Goddess) to ordinary life:

Worship of the Divine Mother implies appreciation of the presence of profound wisdom in nature, both external and internal. There is a principle of cosmic intelligence operative in external nature. It controls the process of cosmic evolution. Similarly, there is deep wisdom inherent in man's inner nature, in his unconscious psyche. It secretly determines his inner evolution. If a person intelligently follows the bent of his own nature, his desires become more and more refined and lofty. Base desires gradually yield place to noble desires. Lower impulses are replaced by higher impulses. When a child's natural desire to play with toys is duly satisfied, it is soon outgrown yielding place to a keen interest in books or living playmates. When a man's natural desire for sex is lawfully satisfied, it gives rise to a growing interest in social welfare or humanitarian service. When his desire for enjoying the world is duly satisfied on the basis of intelligent self-organization, one day it gives rise to a deeper longing for Transcendence.

So Tantric Yoga prescribes what is called desireful prayer and worship (*sakama upasana*). All natural desires are accepted as modes of manifestation of the creative spirit of nature. The problem is to organize them intelligently with a view to the maximum satisfaction and fulfillment of one's nature. There is divine sanction behind such self-fulfillment. One can also invoke divine blessings in such self-fulfillment. One places one's desire before God, and then, with God's sanction and sanctification, proceeds to fulfill them in a spirit of self-offering to the Divine. This brings about an increasing refinement and spiritual transformation of one's desire-nature. A constructive channelling of the libido toward the higher ends of existence takes place (269).

Discuss some significant aspect of contemporary life experience that would seem relevant to the world-affirming aspect of Kundalini Yoga.

## ENDNOTES

[1] Heinrich Zimmer, *The Philosophies of India* (Princeton, New Jersey: Princeton University Press, 1951) 588.

[2] Zimmer 590–91.

[3] Zimmer 593.

[4] Zimmer 557.

[5] Zimmer 586.

[6] Zimmer 586.

## UNIT BIBLIOGRAPHY

Avalon, Arthur. *The Principles of Tantra*. 2 vols. London: Luzac & Co., Ganesh & Co., 1914–1916.

————. *The Great Liberation* (Mahanirvana Tantra). 2nd Edition. Madras: 1927. Definitive works on Tantra and its yoga by the foremost interpreter of Tantra to the West.

Beane, Wendell Charles. *Myth, Cult and Symbols in Shakta Hinduism*. Leiden: E. J. Brill, 1977. An elaborate reduction of the complex content of the Shakta tradition but with many perplexities of its own.

Bharati, Agehananda. *The Tantric Tradition*. London: Rider and Co., 1965. An account of Tantra by a U. S. academic who has a personal acquaintance with the subject.

Blofeld, John. "Kuan Yin's Indian and Tibetan Genesis" from *Bodhisattva of Compassion: The Mystical Tradition of Kuan Yin*. Boston: Shambhala Publications, n.d. Provides an introduction to the way in which the pantheon of Buddhas and Bodhisattvas interrelate.

Dasgupta, Shasi Bhushan. *An Introduction to Tantric Buddhism*. Berkeley: Shambhala Publications, 1974. A scholarly study of the theory of union that underlies the Kundalini Yoga system of chakras by one of the great modern authorities in the field.

Lhalungpa, Lobsang P. *The Life of Milarepa*. Boulder: Prajna Press, 1982. Reveals the importance that the tradition places upon the demonstration of one's attainments in yoga through paranormal abilities.

Mookerjee, Ajit. *Tantra Art: Its Philosophy and Physics*. New Delhi: Ravi Kumar, 1971. A striking study in color of paintings and diagrams that illustrates the Indian practice of Tantra and Kundalini Yoga.

Wayman, Alex. *The Buddhist Tantras*. New York: Samuel Weiser, 1973. A complex introduction to the symbolism and rituals of Tantrism—some of them witnessed by the author. Professor Wayman is the foremost U. S. authority.

# NOTES

# NOTES

# NOTES

# The Descent to Heaven:
## The Tibetan Book of the Dead

## UNIT STUDY PLAN

1. Read Unit 9 in your *Study Guide*.
2. Watch Program 9: "The Descent to Heaven: The Tibetan Book of the Dead."
3. In your course notebook or journal write a summary of Joseph Campbell's interpretation of the way that the life-stream ("soul") entity passes through the various stages between death and possible rebirth in a human form. (These stages are called the three Bardos, according to *The Tibetan Book of the Dead*.)
4. Read the selections for this unit in the *Anthology of Readings*. These selections include excerpts from *The Tibetan Book of the Dead*, and sections by Giuseppe Tucci, Heinrich Harrer, and Fokke Sierksma.
5. After reading the selections, comment in your notebook on what you have read. Show the relationship between the readings and the essay that follows in this unit.
6. In your notebook, analyze the special way that Joseph Campbell approaches a discussion of death through the spiritual outlook of Tibetan Buddhism.
7. Complete the assignments at the end of this unit as specified by your instructor.

## POINTS TO WATCH FOR IN THE TELEVISION PROGRAM

*This television program was delivered as a lecture by Joseph Campbell in New York City, in 1983.*

1. Notice how Campbell introduces the topic with reference to the country of Tibet. Note on a map Tibet's geographical linkage to India and China.
2. Campbell compares the present situation in Tibet to what happened to Buddhism in India in the early Indo-Islamic period. Be certain you understand that comparison.
3. Campbell implicitly relates the theory of the chakras (Tantra and Kundalini) with the cosmography of *The Tibetan Book of the Dead*. Pay attention to those relationships.
4. Consider the theory of the Bodhisattvas, heavens and hells, presented by Campbell, as a rational way of structuring the totality of the mythic universe. (Reread the introduction to the essay in Unit 5 with reference to "acute and chronic cognitive concern.")

5. Notice the comparisons Campbell makes between Tibetan-Buddhist "psychoanalysis" and that of Freud and Jung.
6. Be aware that Campbell makes a special effort to indicate the way that feminine symbolism and mythology figure in Tibetan religion. Some of this is adapted from Hinduism.

## POINTS TO LOOK FOR IN THE *ANTHOLOGY OF READINGS*

1. You will observe that the selection from *The Tibetan Book of the Dead* in the *Anthology of Readings* has been translated into an old-fashioned English style to resemble the Tibetan original. Read through the short passage from the Evans-Wentz edition to get the sense of the practical nature of the instruction. According to this reading, there is no doubt about the reality of the postmortem experience.
2. The selection from Sierksma on Tibet's terrifying deities gives you a good background on the contribution made by Shaivism (Shaiva cult) and Tantrism to the origin of Tibetan Buddhism. The author has an interesting case to make for the low-class origin of the movement. (This may go all the way back to the suppression of the original Indus-Valley people.) The erotic cult does not disappear in Tibet. However, the Dalai Lama's sect, the Gelug-Pa, or "Yellow Hats," completely prohibited overt eroticism.
3. It is worthwhile to read the excerpt from Tucci's *Tibet* to get a flavor for the great fascination Tibetology (the study of Tibetan language and culture) has had for some Westerners. It truly seems that for some Westerners Tibet represents an alternative reality. Tucci's chapter on "Birth, Marriage, Sickness and Death" will give you a simplified version of the Bardo teaching as well.
4. Heinrich Harrer's writings on his return to Tibet in the 1980s—30 years after his previous sojourn—afford touching comparisons between the way matters were then and the way they are now. The title of his chapter, "I am recognized," suggests the happiness he felt in the midst of the alienation of the Communist Chinese occupation.

## UNIT GLOSSARY

**Akshobhya** (uhk-sho-byuh): The Dharmakaya (cosmic) Buddha of the East. Campbell's defines him as "can't be moved."

**Amitabha (Amida)** (uh-mee-tuh-buh): The Dharmakaya (cosmic) Buddha of the West. Campbell defines him as "the Buddha of immeasurable radiance."

**Amoghasidda** (uh-mo-guh-si-duh): The Dharmakaya (cosmic) Buddha of the North. Campbell's definition is "who will not be turned from the achievement of his aim."

**Animistic**: Comes from the Latin word amina, meaning "soul." Term used to describe early stratum of religion wherein many things in nature are thought to possess spirits.

**Avalokiteshvara** (uh-vuh-lo-kee-tas-huh-rah): The Bodhisattva form of Amida Buddha. Called by Campbell, "The Bodhisattva of Infinite Compassion."

**Bodhisattva** (bo-dee-sut-vah): A prominent role for the "Buddha-to-be" which exists in Mahayana Buddhism. A Bodhisattva delays emancipation in order to help other suffering beings to achieve emancipation. Often the concept of Bodhisattva implies a transcendent spiritual being (one among many), comparable to the gods and goddesses of Hinduism.

**Bon**: The animistic religion of Tibet, partially assimilated to the dominant Buddhist cults.

**Dakini**: Female spirit of terrifying visage.

**Dalai Lama**: The chief monk or (former) ruler of the classical Tibetan state, which was a theocracy. According to Tibetan Buddhism, he is the incarnation of the Bodhisattva Avalokiteshvara.

**Hallaj** (huh-luj): A Muslim Sufi (mystic) of early Islam, (858–922 C.E.) whose full name is Husayn Ibn Mansur al-Hallaj. He was martyred by the orthodox Muslim for the excesses of his devotion to Allah.

**Ishtadevata** (ish-tuh-da-vuh-tah): One's chosen deity. Equals yiddam in Tibetan.

**Kuan Yin** (kwan-yin): The Chinese version of the feminine manifestation of Avalokiteshvara.

**Lama**: The Tibetan name for a Buddhist monk or priest. The religion of Tibet sometimes is called Lamaism.

**Mahavairocana** (muhuh-veye-ro-chu-nuh): The Great Sun Buddha at the top center of the universe.

**Maitreya** (meye-tra-yah): The Buddha who will come at the end of the cosmic age.

**Mandala** (mun-duh-lah): A diagram used for meditation in Tibetan Buddhism (also in Hinduism). It may be purely geometric or contain symbolic representations of Buddhas, animals, humans, and many other elements. (For a further discussion of mandalas, see Unit 2.)

**Parinirvana** (puh-ree-nir-vah-nah): The final Nirvana (i.e., the death of the Buddha). The Buddha is shown lying on his side as he enters parinirvana.

**Potala** (po-tuh-lah): The palace of the Dalai Lama in Lhasa.

**Shunyata**: The state of emptiness. From the Sanskrit word Shunya, meaning "empty." The term refers to the absolute difference between Nirvana (i.e., shunyata) and Samsara.

**Sukhavati** (su-kuh-vuh-tee): The paradise of Amitabha.

**Tara**: The Tibetan version of the feminine manifestation of Avalokiteshvara.

**Thanka** (thun-ka): Paintings (some of enormous size) that Tibetans use to illustrate theological and mythological concepts.

**Vajrayana** (vuj-ruh-yuh-nah): A name for the type of Mahayana Buddhism practiced in Tibet. "Vajra" means thunderbolt.

**Yama** (yu-muh): The Hindu god of death, also represented in the Buddhist pantheon. He represents the essential impermanence of everything that exists.

## UNIT PREVIEW

Tibetan Buddhism combines elements from the earlier Bon religion, perhaps of Shamanic origin, with a Tantric form of Buddhism that was introduced into Tibet in the seventh century C.E. Tibetan Buddhism employed the vivid imagery of mythology, ritual, painting, and even stylized bodily movements and gestures to assist the serious practitioner to overcome the entrapment of the physical world. Among the unique features of this form of Buddhism was the development of a theory of the after-death state of the transmigrating life-stream entity. (It is more appropriate to use the expression "life-stream entity" than "soul" because Buddhism denies the existence of a permanent spiritual element.) The life-stream's causal process leads to subsequent incarnations unless spiritual emancipation occurs. The latter is identified with what Buddhist's call Nirvana.

**Transmigration and Karma**: *The Tibetan Book of the Dead* is a manual principally to be used by an assisting lama, or Buddhist priest, to guide the dying person from his or her present incarnation to an auspicious after-life or next-life state. Buddhism teaches that there is no action without a consequence either in the present life or in a subsequent life. The fate that awaits each person in the after-life or next-life depends on the karma that is, so to speak, stored in one's "account." The "science of death and dying," which is taught in *The Tibetan Book of the Dead*, is meant to help the life-stream to navigate successfully the perils of the transition. Much depends upon karma, but there is a magical element of intervention, as well, that is provided by the Tantric methods of the priest.

**The Stages of the After-life Experience**: To understand what is proposed in the transition between one life and another, something must be known about the Tibetan Buddhist cosmology. According to this cosmology, there are celestial Buddha or Bodhisattva forms that provide assistance to humanity in the realm of Samsara—rebirth of the cosmos and individual reincarnation. The dying person will face a gradual descent through the levels of the universe into the next rebirth (and will encounter the different realms of Buddhas and Bodhisattvas) unless he or she has earned the right to immediate emancipation because of the efforts made in this or prior lifetimes. The guidance of the lama can assist the life-stream to embrace emancipation without fear if it is appropriate. Failing that, the lama can assist the life-stream to avoid unfortunate after-life states of punishment or other inauspicious rebirths. A successful rebirth in a human baby will assure the life-stream of another opportunity to try to attain Nirvana.

# UNIT ESSAY

Tibet was, until 1959, the repository of a special kind of Mahayana Buddhism ("The Big Ferry boat") adopted from India by the ancient ruler of the country. Buddhism traditionally became Tibet's official religion during the reign of King Srong-brtsan-sgam-po (620–649 C.E.) who married two princesses of Buddhist faith. Since 1959, the country has been ruled by the Communist Chinese government in Peking and the Buddhist character of Tibet has changed considerably. However, there are many signs that Buddhism still is struggling to maintain the traditional ethos of the country. The Dalai Lama, the former religious and political leader of Tibet, lives in exile in India from which he encourages an international effort to restore independence to the land.

## Tantrism and Buddhism

As Joseph Campbell points out, the type of Mahayana Buddhism that came into Tibet is called Tantric Buddhism because it incorporates elements of the Tantrism that was prominent in Indian religion at the period of its adoption. This was, traditionally, from the seventh century C.E. onward. Tantrism was and is an aspect of the Hindu religion as well. The distinctive character of Tantrism arises from its emphasis upon the ultimate reality (whether Buddhist Nirvana, or Hindu Brahman) as a field of energy, polarized between masculine and feminine and celestial and demonic.

## The Right-Hand and Left-Hand Paths

The devotee of Tantrism needs spiritual emancipation by the right-hand or the left-hand paths. The right-hand path employs startling imagery, visualizations, sounds, and bodily movements to manipulate that energy toward the goal of transcending all material and mental phenomena. Beyond these lies Nirvana, the emancipated state, defined as the Void or Shunyata because it is incapable of being conceptualized. (Alternatively, Mahayana proposes that the Buddha nature is ultimate reality.)

The left-hand path abandons the merely mental plane as the location of its practices and acts out what purely is imagined in the other path. This results in activities that are regarded, at times, as immoral and may involve crimes of violence. There is great variety in the practices of Tantra, but whether of the right-hand or of the left, the meditations or the actions have, as their final purpose, the transcendence of time, space, and matter. The transcendence consists of everything that constitutes the physical universe, wherein the course of human existence is characterized by transmigration from one incarnation to the next. (See Units 5 and 6 for further discussion of transmigration in the earlier Indian context.)

## Paranormal Powers

Because of the belief that the practice of Tantrism may result in the development of occult or paranormal powers, Tantrism often is regarded by the adherents of other Eastern spiritual paths as more dangerous and less certain in its outcome. The belief in Tantra's ability to stimulate occult powers arises from the theory that Tantra gives one control over Shakti, or access to Shakti, which is the underlying power in the universe. This distrust of Tantrism occurs because occult powers have a great fascination in and of themselves. The argument follows that if you possessed such powers, you would be sorely tempted to use them for your own benefit. To do so would lead you to even greater delusion in this life and in subsequent lives. However, the followers of Tantra would argue that under the guidance of a pure spiritual teacher—a guru—you successfully may avoid becoming trapped in the occult powers.

## Transmigration and Karma

The idea of transmigration seems to appear in Indian religion during the later Vedic period and is clearly the accepted position of the authors of the Upanishads. (For a discussion of the Upanishads see Unit 5.) Reincarnation is closely associated with the moral-ethical theory of karma. Campbell compares the Eastern theories of reincarnation with the Western Catholic teachings about purgatory in several instances. (For an example of this, see Unit 6 of this course.) In both these theories, the concept is put forth that most human beings are not ready for the direct experience of ultimate reality at the time of death. In the theory of purgatory, the soul goes to an intermediate state where it prepares itself for eventual entry into paradise. Very often the imagery of purgatory was that of a place of suffering where you had to pay the price for your sins even though you had asked for forgiveness and been forgiven through the offices of the Church. It seems evident that purgatory in this conceptualization was not very different from hell, only of fixed duration; whereas, hell was for eternity.

In the theory of karma, Hinduism and Buddhism taught that the imperfections of moral-ethical life and the immaturity of the higher mind prevented the soul or life-stream entity in human beings from realizing its true nature. Failing such realization, the subtle body (mind and emotions, etc.) was destined to reincarnate endlessly and to carry with it the spiritual or life-stream entity until such time as karma was completely controlled and eliminated. In such a situation, the constant repetition of life-stream experiences (inevitably leading to suffering, sorrow, and death) could be analogous to a living hell, although there would be periodic episodes of great pleasure and happiness. (You may want to review these points already discussed in Unit 6.) The desire for existence itself, however miserable at times, would be sufficiently motivating to draw you back again and again into new lives.

## The Tibetan Book of the Dead

As Campbell explains, *The Tibetan Book of the Dead* was a manual to be used by a lama, a Tibetan Buddhist monk, to guide the life-stream of the dying person from the current incarnation through the various stages that awaited him in the after-life state. Emancipation might be a possibility there, but for most reincarnating human life streams, the principal objective would be to avoid an extended period of time in one of the purgatorylike hells of the Buddhist after-life in favor of a good rebirth in human form. For all of the ancient Eastern faiths of Indian origin, rebirth in human form was a prerequisite for a try at emancipation from karma and continual rebirth.

A fundamental preconception of *The Tibetan Book of the Dead* is that the universe is impermanent. In particular, a general concept in Mahayana Buddhism is that what exists in the universe can best be understood as occurring in the mind or consciousness. This is true even when talking about parts of the universe such as heaven, the earth plane, or hell. It is also true when referring to the great celestial beings, the Buddhas and Bodhisattvas, the subjects of Mahayana mythology, and symbolism. All phenomena, whether of the material world or of the spiritual, are transitory appearances in the consciousness. However, the one permanent reality of the universe is the Buddha nature against which the mental phenomena occur.

In *The Tibetan Book of the Dead,* called the *Bardo Thodol* (hereafter called the Bardo) in Tibetan, you will find instruction for a dying or recently deceased person, concerning the proper means by which to make the transition between the present existence, which he or she is leaving, and the next existence. The text provides specific instructions to the deceased for a period of forty-nine days after death. (The time period should be understood, literally, but the role of the lama throughout the period varies.) The assumption is that the deceased may go through a determined set of intervening stages but will reincarnate at the end of the process.

To understand what Campbell is talking about in the television program for this unit and to put yourself interpretatively into the situation that is described in the Bardo, you must imagine that there is an absolute continuity between consciousness in the physical body and consciousness transmigrating to its next incarnation. The teaching of the Bardo is an hypothesis and a map. Drawing on the information in the Bardo, you, as a living person, could orientate your life toward certain after-death experiences.

If you are well prepared for death, on the basis of the Bardo teachings you may experience a more successful transition between lives than if you are not equipped with the Bardo knowledge. Irrespective of whether you are prepared, the lama priest can help you to have a better experience in the transition after death.

## The Shape of the Bardo

What the Bardo provides and what Campbell discusses in the television program is a step-by-step description of the way that the transmigrating soul experiences the three after-death states. These states are set forth in the three subdivisions of the Bardo (these categories are derived from *The Tibetan Book of the Dead,* edited by W. Y. Evans-Wentz): (1) The First Bardo, "The Chikhai Bardo," translated as "Transitional State of the Moment of Death"; (2) The Second Bardo, "The Chonyid Bardo," "Transitional State of (the Experiencing or Glimpsing of) Reality"; (3) The Third Bardo, "The Sidpa Bardo," "The Transitional State of (or while seeking) Rebirth.[11]

## Mahayana Cosmology

Before you can fully understand the particular phases described in the above three categories, you should have a basic view of the universe as set out in the Mahayana theories of cosmology. The three levels of the universe correspond in a significant way with the three stages of the after-death experience as outlined above.

First note that there is a point of origin for the world of transmigration, called Samsara. (You have already been introduced to the Hindu views of Samsara in Unit 5.) This point of origin is sometimes personified as the Adibuddha, or primordial Buddha. Structurally speaking, this figure or concept corresponds with the idea of a creator in other religious systems. The difference is that beyond the Adibuddha there is the pure nonmaterial condition of Nirvana—the ultimate goal of all sentient beings beyond the realms of the vivid imagery presented for contemplation in Mahayana mythology.

Imagine yourself at the very topmost, central point of the universe and able to gaze all around and below to view the denizens of other regions. From that vantage point you would see that the universe is composed of three levels, each of which is dominated by certain Buddha or Bodhisattva forms.

The highest region below the point of origin is identified as the dharma–body region or Dharmakaya level. Campbell refers to some of the names of the transcendent forms of the Buddhas and Bodhisattvas that inhabit this region. Among the most important ones usually found are Vairochana ("the Sun Buddha"), Ratnasambhava ("Born of a Jewel"), Amitabha ("The Buddha of Immeasurable Radiance"), Amoghasiddhi ("Undistracted from his aim") and Akshobya ("can't be moved"). These are the Celestial Buddhas, the most potent beings in the realm of Samsara. They also symbolize certain possible states of consciousness as well as realms of existence most remote from the crude characteristics of earth life. Some sects of Buddhism in the Far East focus upon the celestial Buddhas, who function both as spiritual ideals and almost in the capacity of deities who grant favors to the devotees or provide them with a satisfactory after-life. Given the underlying Mahayana theory that the universe is but the field of the universal consciousness or Buddha nature, these great beings can be likened to concepts in the mind or to symbols of your own spiritual potentiality.

Some scholars theorize that the origin of these five transcendent beings lies in the Zoroastrian religion. The Zoroastrians first postulated the Amesha Spenta, the "Immortal Holy Ones," analogous to the Dharmakaya or Dhyana Buddhas, before such ideas had entered Buddhist metaphysics. The great angels of the Middle Eastern faiths of Judaism, Christianity, and Islam also may have originated in the Zoroastrian system. Zoroaster, the purported founder of the Zoroastrian religion may have lived in Iran around 600 B.C.E. The religion of Iran was in existence before Zoroaster, but he clarified its teachings. Iran became a Muslim state in the seventh century C.E.

From your imaginary vantage point, transiting the cosmos from above, you will perceive that there are close links between the highest Buddhas of the Dharmakaya realm and those just below them in the hierarchy. These enjoyment body or Sambhogakaya forms of the Bodhisattvas occupy a middle realm between highest heaven and earth. Among these intermediate beings, five correspond and link structurally with the five Dhyana Buddhas already mentioned. These are Samantabhadra ("Untroubled Joy"), Ratnapani ("Holding a Jewel"), Padmapani (or Avalokiteshvara) ("Holding a Lotus"), Vishvapani ("Holding the World"), and Vajrapani ("Holding the Thunder-bolt").

Campbell calls special attention to Avalokiteshvara, whose name means "The Glancing Lord." His eyes are averted from their straightforward heavenly gaze to look downward to the realm of suffering beings on the earth plane. This is symbolic of compassion and concern—in the sense of searching out the means to help. (You should be aware that within the system of Tantric Buddhism, each of the masculine forms—as mentioned above—is accompanied by a feminine form, its Shakti. In some of these symbolic representations, especially the terrifying type, there is a strongly suggested sexual element.) In the case of Avalokiteshvara, a very popular "non-sexually-suggestive" feminine counterpart is depicted as the goddess Tara. Tara, the playful young maiden, gives rise in East Asia to the elegant motherly Kuan Yin who is a goddess of help to all who call on her. Campbell can thus refer to the Mother or Goddess as constituting a significant element in the after-death experience of the Bardo.

Finally, the lowest level of the cosmos is that of the earth plane, the Nirmanakaya or the appearance body. It is there (or here) that the historical Buddha taught his doctrine of enlightenment and where the possibility of emancipation of the life-stream became actual. Moreover, according to the beliefs of Tibetan Buddhism, certain high-ranking lamas actually are incarnate forms of the spiritual beings above them in the cosmic hierarchy. Most important among these incarnations is the erstwhile ruler of Tibet, the Dalai Lama, who is believed to be the incarnation of Avalokiteshvara. The special technique of embalming the deceased Dalai Lamas, whose bodies were mummified and restored to a lifelike shape and painted with a gold-containing substance, was indicative of their precious status. Afterward, they were enshrined and worshipped in their mortal remains. (A child born in the same year as the death of the previous Dalai Lama would be chosen to succeed to the position. He was chosen by tests to prove that he was the incarnation of the previous Dalai Lama.)

The religion of Tibet is an amalgam of Buddhism with the old religion, called Bon or Bon-po. Bon's origins go back to the pre-Buddhist period and some of its traits are incorporated into the form of Mahayana Buddhism found in Tibet. Bon was a shamanic faith, perhaps in its early forms similar to the later shamanism recorded as widespread throughout northern Asia and existing in other parts of the world. (For a further discussion of shamanism, see Unit 2.) A typical characteristic of shamanism is its concern with spirits and communicating with the other world through various devices. Shamans were men and women who were especially gifted (or trained) to experience the passage from the world of the living to the world of the departed spirits. Their craft included healing and exorcism. It seems likely that this dimension of Bon or the earlier shamanism is at the basis of the special interest that Tibetan Buddhism exhibited in the process of death and the fate of the dead.

## Joseph Campbell's Interpretation of the Bardo

With the foregoing information in mind you will realize that the story of the life-stream's progress in the Bardo, as interpreted by Campbell, is a journey related to the cosmos as described above.

In Units 7 and 8 of the television programs, Campbell discusses the theory of energy linked to the concepts of the Kundalini and the chakras. These, too, have bearing upon this final interpretation of the Bardo. You will want to reflect upon the underlying mystical and occult theories of the Buddhist religion, and in particular of the Bardo, that the inner and outer structures of samsara (the world of transmigration) are profoundly interconnected. This would lead you to realize that when talking about the mystical cosmology of the Trikaya or "Three Bodies" (that just have been traversed imaginatively in the three layers of Buddha-Bodhisattva realms), it is not a reference to something "out there." That cosmology is equally "in here," (i.e., within the mystical physiology of the Kundalini system). Hence, as Campbell does, the after-death experience can be described by relating it to the system of chakras.

However, since the chakras normally are identified with the living body of a yogi, it may be more meaningful to imagine the journey of the deceased as a departure from the body to metaphysically located states of postmortem experience or consciousness.

## The Bardo Experience

With the preceding theory and information you should be able to follow the general theory of the intermediate, after-death experience of the life-stream as depicted in the Bardo.

As the person lies dying, the attending lama is concerned to establish the exact moment of death, so that the departing life-stream can react appropriately and in the most favorable manner to the postmortem experience. Buddhism primarily is concerned with creating the circumstances in which you would not have to be reborn. Hence, the after-death experience begins with the most desirable option from the Buddhist point of view. The Bardo is written to show the steps by which the departing individual can face the most desirable option and, failing the ability to take that opportunity, to show how the individual can cope with the succeeding experiences. Some of the succeeding experiences are dangerous and/or terrifying. You could become trapped in one of the very undesirable intermediate states. With proper guidance during the forty-nine-day postmortem period you may be able to pass to rebirth successfully. However undesirable rebirth may be, it at least would provide a fresh opportunity to prepare yourself for emancipation from samsara, the world of transmigration.

For purposes of greater clarification, the description of the three stages of the departed should be associated with the tripartite structure of the cosmos as set forth in various Mahayana treatises. The postmortem experiences do not need to be correlated with the system of chakras. However, Campbell's discussion of the Buddha-Bodhisattva relationship to the chakras in the television program for the unit does correlate with the cosmology.

**The First Bardo, "The Transitional State of the Moment of Death":** The life-stream rises to the top of the universe and is presented with the opportunity to merge with what Campbell calls "The Mother Light." In strictly Buddhist terms, the option of merging with the universal Buddha consciousness or nature is at stake. If you have residual karma that inclines your life-stream to desire more existence, you will not be able to choose the option of final emancipation. However, the vision of the pure "Mother Light" will operate unconsciously to draw you to itself, however long or however many lifetimes it may take.

**The Second Bardo, "The Transitional State of [the Experiencing or Glimpsing of] Reality":** The passage from one Bardo to the next is comparable to a temporary rebirth, and it is accompanied by loss of consciousness of the previous stage. Hence, if you have lost the opportunity to merge with the light of pure Buddha consciousness, you swoon into the second stage wherein the Bardo describes the encounter you will have with both benign and malevolent cosmic beings. These may be construed to be your own earned karma in personified form. The Second Bardo reveals a fall from the highest regions of the spiritual universe, which remain cut off from you for this transition period. The following quotation from W. Y. Evans-Wentz's introduction to the Bardo summarizes the very complex possibilities of experience in these intermediate regions of the spiritual universe:

> The chief deities themselves are the embodiments of universal divine forces, with which the deceased is inseparably related, for through him, as being the microcosm of the macrocosm, penetrate all impulses and forces, good and bad alike. Samantra-Bhadra, the All-Good, thus personifies Reality, the Primordial Clear Light of the Unborn, Unshaped *Dharma-Kaya*. Vairochana is the Originator of all phenomena, the Cause of all Causes. As the Universal Father, Vairochana manifests or spreads forth as seed, semen, all things; his *shakti*, the Mother of Great Space, is the Universal Womb into which the seed falls and evolves as the world-systems. Vajra-Sattva symbolizes Immutability. Ratna-Sambhava is the Beautifier, the Source of all Beauty in the Universe. Amitabha is Infinite Compassion and Love Divine, the Christos. Amogha-Siddhi is the personification of Almighty Power or Omnipotence. And the minor deities, heroes, *dakinis* (or 'fairies'), goddesses, lords of death, rakshasas, demons, spirits, and all others, correspond to definite human thoughts, passions, and impulses, high and low, human and sub-human and superhuman, in *karmic* form, as they take shape from the seeds of thought forming the percipient's consciousness-content.[1]

If your Karma demands it in the second Bardo, you may be rewarded with rebirth in a paradisal state or severe punishment in one of the purgatory like hells. The description of these states and the tendencies that draw one toward them are set forth in vivid Tankhas (religious theme paintings, including diagrammatic mandalas, typical of Tibetan art.)

**The Third Bardo, "The Transitional State of [or while seeking] Rebirth":** If your Karma destines you to rebirth in the human world, toward the end of the whole intermediate state—symbolized by the forty-nine-day interval—you will experience the desire for another birth and be drawn in a visionary way to scenes of copulating couples. In one of these episodes you will be caught in such a copulation and cast into a human womb. Having forgotten everything about your previous life-stream experience and about the visionary experiences of the Bardo, you will be born into another life and go through another cycle similar to the one described. (To savor the style of the Bardo, see the excerpt from it in EvanWentz' *The Tibetan Book of the Dead* in the *Anthology of Readings.*

## ASSIGNMENTS FOR STUDY AND ANALYSIS

1. Heinrich Harrer has written a classic travel story about his experiences in Tibet before the Communist takeover. Much has been written about the current Dalai Lama's attempt to restore his country's independence. What are your views about the close linkage of politics and the Tibetan Buddhist religion in Tibet? Are there other contemporary examples of the religious state in the modern world? Compare and contrast. (It may be helpful to consult recent newspapers and periodicals to gather information for this answer.)
2. Tibetan religion makes use of highly vivid mythology and ritual to communicate its meanings. Illustrate and discuss these phenomena.
3. Death is fearful and mysterious. Explain the pros and cons of a belief in the after-life such as you find in *The Tibetan Book of the Dead*. Compare the Tibetan theory with your own beliefs about death and afterwards.
4. In your own words describe the Tibetan Buddhist cosmology.
5. How would you explain to someone unfamiliar with these ideas the Tibetan theory of what happens to an individual in the process of reincarnating? Make comparisons and use illustrations, based on the television programs for this unit, the unit essay and this unit's selections in the *Anthology of Readings*.

## FURTHER ASSIGNMENTS FOR WRITING AND REFLECTION

1. Joseph Campbell illustrates the transmigration theory of Tibetan Buddhism by linking it to the chakra system studied in previous units. What is your understanding of the Tantric idea that the human body is a mirror of the universe? This is sometimes stated as, "The macrocosm is in the microcosm."

2. In what ways do you think a highly "spiritualistic" religious system, such as Tibetan Buddhism, answers basic human needs? You should read about and make comparisons with the American Spiritualist movement that began in this country in the early nineteenth century.
3. Do you think the occult or paranormal aspects of Tibetan beliefs about the after-life use other than nonscientific speculations? What scientific literature or popular "scientific" literature do you know of that discusses life after death? Do research to develop a short bibliography and annotate it (i.e., give a paragraph summary of the principal statements of each book in your bibliography).
4. Discuss the probable fate of Tibetan Buddhism if the Dalai Lama is not able to return to rule in his capital in Lhasa. Many Tibetan monks live abroad in India, Switzerland, and the United States. Do you think that Tibetan religion can survive in such a far-flung diaspora? (It may be helpful to research current periodicals for the answer to this question.)
5. The previous five units illustrate what is problematic for many Eastern religions: The material world is a barrier to human freedom and happiness. The semitic religions (Judaism, Christianity, and Islam) generally are more accepting of the material universe as the sign, at least, of the existence of a powerful, creator God. This God is affirmed as "good" and hence His creation is also "good." Do you have any different views on your own philosophy (ethical or metaphysical) after studying aspects of Campbell's presentation of Eastern mythology and symbolism? Discuss the possibility of a real antithesis between Eastern "spirituality" and Western "materialism."
6. The practice of one's religion is linked closely to such factors as national and cultural identity. Tibet is an example of the tragedy of loss of identity that the loss of full religious freedom entails. Make comparisons with the situations involving deep religious conflicts in other parts of the world today. What common elements emerge in religious cultures attempting to preserve their identities?
7. What do you think are the ramifications of the inclusion of the horrifying and demonic within the normative spiritual perspective of Tibetan Buddhism? How do other religions cope with the negative aspects of the religious understanding of the world? (The Bardo seems to suggest that the negative aspects of divine beings are merely their reverse and they are an essential part of their natures [and ours]). Do you have any thoughts on the propriety of affirming both the divine and the demonic as essential values in the same religious system? Answers to this question address the issue of the existence of evil. Discuss how Campbell's discussion in the television program of the traits associated with the chakras and their attendant Bodhisattvas points up this dichotomy.

## ENDNOTES

[1]W. Y. Evans-Wentz, *The Tibetan Book of the Dead* (New York: Oxford University Press, 1960) 32.

## UNIT BIBLIOGRAPHY

Bell, Sir Charles A. *The Religion of Tibet*. Oxford: The Clarendon Press, 1931. Account in the heydey of the British Raj of the author's experience as British Political Representative to Tibet, Bhutan, and Sikkim.

Campbell, Joseph. "The Spontaneous Animism of Childhood." From *The Masks of God: Primitive Mythology*. New York: The Viking Press, 1987. This selection illustrates how children's thought about such things as dreams and birth reflect the spontaneous way in which these universal ideas may have been generated at the very origin of the different world cultures.

Chang, Garma C. C. (Translator). *The Hundred Thousand Songs of Milarepa, Vol. I & II*. New Hyde Park, N.Y.: University Books, 1962. The life story, together with translations, of Tibet's great poet-saint.

David-Neel, Alexandra. *Magic and Mystery in Tibet*. New York: Dover Publications, 1971. The work of a giant in scholarship that founded the field of Western Tibetology.

Harrer, Heinrich. *Seven Years in Tibet*. New York: Dutton, 1954. A vivid account of life in Tibet before the Communist Chinese takeover.

Hicks, Roger. *Great Ocean: An Authorized Biography of the Buddhist Monk Tenzin Gyatso, His Holiness the Fourteenth Dalai Lama*. Longmead, Dorset: Element Books, 1984. A discussion of the many tragedies and triumphs in the life story of the current Dalai Lama.

Jung, C. G. "The Tibetan Book of the Dead: Psychological Commentary," from W. Y. Evans-Wentz, "The Bardo of the Moments of Death," from *The Tibetan Book of the Dead*. New York: Oxford University Press, 1960. Jung is credited with discovering certain archetypes that exist in the mind and that are commonly shared by humanity. These, Jung believes, may bear comparison with some of the psychic structures that are proposed in the Bardo theory.

Nebesky-Wojkowitz, Rene de. *Oracles and Demons of Tibet*. The Hague: Mouton, 1956. An exhaustive study of the Tibetan pantheon.

Paul, Robert A. *The Tibetan Symbolic World: Psychoanalytic Explorations*. Chicago: University of Chicago Press, 1982. Relates the psychoanalysis of Tibetan religion to modern psychoanalytic interpretations.

Rijnhart, Susie Carson. *With the Tibetans in Tent and Temple*. New York: Fleming H. Revell Co., 1901. A memoir of one of the first women to visit Tibet.

Tucci, Giuseppe. *The Religions of Tibet*. Berkeley: University of California Press, 1980. An overview of Tibetan religion by the most renowned contemporary scholar in the field.

Tucci, Giuseppe. *The Theory and Practice of the Mandala*. New York: Samuel Weiser, 1973. Perceptive analysis of the effects of Tantric meditation upon consciousness.

# NOTES

# NOTES

GEORGE DEFOREST LORD
ROBERT MERRILL

# UNIT 10

# From Darkness to Light:
## *The Mystery Religions of Ancient Greece*

## UNIT STUDY PLAN

1. Read Unit 10 in your *Study Guide*.
2. Watch Program 10: "From Darkness to Light: The Mystery Religions of Ancient Greece."
3. In your course notebook or journal write a summary of Campbell's interpretation of the Greek mystery religions as presented in the television program. What is the symbolism of food and agriculture? As soon as you have finished watching the program, make a note of points that may be unclear as well as your own reactions and observations.
4. Read the selections for this unit in the *Anthology of Readings*. These include *The Hymn to Demeter*, a selection from Euripides' play *The Bacchae*, *The Teachings of Pythagoras*, and a chapter from Walter Burkert's *Greek Religions*.
5. After reading the selections, comment on what you have read in your notebook. Show the relationships between the readings and Campbell's insights about the initiation process and the final stage of acceptance into the mysteries. Comment especially on the human's relationship to the earth and god (or the gods).
6. Complete the assignments at the end of this unit as specified by your instructor.

## POINTS TO WATCH FOR IN THE TELEVISION PROGRAM

*This television program was delivered as a lecture by Joseph Campbell in Santa Fe, New Mexico, in 1982.*

1. The essence of the spiritual experience of Eleusis is a shift in consciousness from the ordinary phenomenal aspect of one's life to the deep eternal aspect. Consider how the myth of Eleusis and its mysteries mediate between a familiar world and the underworld experience of death.
2. Note why Campbell says that the fall of Adam and Eve was, in the long run, a happy one because it led to God's decision to redeem man through the voluntary death of Jesus Christ. In the long-run view, good and evil are necessary parts of a larger totality.
3. Be sure that you understand the role of Pluto as both death and a source of fertility. Campbell says that the Greeks stored food underground to preserve it from the summer heat, thus food of life sustenance comes from underground. Be sure to note the spiritual meaning of this symbolism.

4. Demeter and Persephone comprise a dual goddess. Note how Demeter as a goddess of agricultural fertility is also the mother of the Queen of Death.
5. Observe that Dionysus is occasionally shown holding a wine cup or chalice. Campbell identifies this cup with the Mass Chalice and the Holy Grail. (The Grail is discussed in Units 11, 12, and 13).
6. Follow carefully Campbell's linking of the symbology of the Pietroasa Bowl to Christianity. In the second and third centuries C.E., however, under the leadership of Clement of Alexandria, Christianity turned away from the Greek mystery religions and aligned itself more closely with Mosaic traditions of the Hebrew Old Testament.
7. In connection with the shift in Christianity, notice the two possibilities for the interpretation of scripture: the Hermetic (symbolic) and the Mosaic (historical).

## POINTS TO LOOK FOR IN THE *ANTHOLOGY OF READINGS*

1. Pythagoras is well known as the founder of mathematics (as in the Pythagorean theorem) but he was also the founder of astrology and a theoretician of music. He believed that numerical relationships exist between all things of the earth: the stars, human psychology, religion, history, and most importantly music. Knowledge of such relationships was the science of harmony, a science best reflected in the harmony or the music of the stars. *The Teachings of Pythagoras* included in the *Anthology of Readings* are not outwardly mathematical, but the sense of relation between all things is foremost. Note his conclusions about the proper harmony among humans, the animals, and the earth.
2. Walter Burkert, in the chapter titled "Mysteries and Asceticism," presents an overview of Greek mystery religions. Note the chief concerns of each different cult and the concern for the process of initiation, growth, and eventual transmigration of the soul.
3. Euripides' *Bacchae* is a play about the worship of Dionysus (or Bacchus). It is set in Thebes, which is ruled by Pentheus, who attempts to prevent the Theban women from continuing their yearly rituals. Pentheus argues against frenetic and irrational religious practices, offering the Apollonian or rational approach to religion. In his attempt to prevent the rituals he is attacked by the women and torn to pieces. Note the connection between his death and Campbell's point in the television program about the dismemberment of the gods who enter time (i.e., Orpheus and Christ).

4. The *Hymn to Demeter* is the most significant evidence now existing for the nature of the mysteries of Eleusis. While it is impossible to know just how much of the mysteries are revealed by the poem, you should read it in the spirit of Campbell's symbolic representation. Think of the way he interprets the figures on the Pietroasa Bowl. What is the figurative vocabulary of this story of abduction, rape, the sorrowful mother, famine, and finally reunification. As Campbell did with the Pietroasa Bowl, pay careful attention to the descriptions of events and characters.

5. The great challenge in reading mythological tales is that of interpretation and symbolism. Hermeneutics, the Greek word for interpretation, has been one of the principal branches of philosophy beginning precisely in the period of the flourishing of mystery religions. As you read, think of ways that these stories can mean something which is not present in the narrative itself. Symbolism is a way of presenting what is ineffable or inexpressible: the presentation of what cannot be presented.

## UNIT GLOSSARY

**Anodos:** A rising upward.

**Apollo:** The god of sun, prophecy, music, medicine, and poetry. Associated with the oracle at Delphi.

**Apollonian:** Relating to Apollo. In art the, qualities of being clearly defined, and reasoned.

**Chthonic:** Relating to the gods and spirits of the underworld.

**Demeter:** (Roman, Ceres) The goddess of agriculture, fertility, and marriage. Mother of Persephone.

**Dionysus:** (Roman, Bacchus) The god of wine, associated with an orgiastic religion celebrating the power and fertility of nature.

**Epiphany:** To show forth, a moment of sudden intuitive understanding or revelation from the gods.

**Epoteia:** A mystical vision.

**Gnosis:** Intuitive apprehension of spiritual truths.

**Hades:** (Roman, Pluto) The god of the underworld and distributor of earthly riches.

**Hermetic:** Relating to the gnostic mysteries of the first to third centuries C.E. and attributed to Hermes Trismegistus. The works of Hermes are called the *Corpus Hermeticum*.

**Hermeneutics:** The branch of philosophy and theology dealing with methods and theories of interpretation.

**Kathodos:** (Cathodos) The path downward or descent into the underworld.

**Maenad:** (Roman, Bacchae) A woman of the orgiastic cult of Bacchus.

**Moses:** The legendary founder of Israel and of Yahwism, the form of the Hebrew religion whose God is the mover behind history.

**Mystery Religions:** Name for a group of religious cults popular in Hellenic and Roman periods in Greece (third century B.C.E.–third century C.E.). The mysteries centered around a dying and rising savior and the process of purification of initiates. Chief cults include the mysteries of Eleusis, Isis-Osiris, Orpheus, Dionysus, and Mithra.

**Occidental:** Of the west, particularly Europe.

**Persephone:** (Roman, Proserpina) The daughter of Demeter and wife of Hades.

**Satyrs:** Woodland gods in ancient Greek and Roman mythology, in human form but having a goat's ears, tail, and legs.

**Telestrerion:** Place where the higher mysteries of Eleusis were performed.

## UNIT PREVIEW

In this unit you will be introduced to the mystery religions of Greece. You will learn the significance and meaning behind the religions and their importance in an agriculturally based society, as represented in the myth of Demeter and Persephone.

**The Mystery Religions of Greece:** The symbolism of the mystery religions was based upon the paradox of the germination of seeds, thought to depend upon their death and burial for sprouting and growing. Thus, life emerges from death. The cults celebrated the annual death and rebirth of a divinity who symbolized the seasonal cycle of agricultural fertility. The mystery religions led initiates through a process of self-purification and participation in the devine pattern of descent into the underworld and ascent into the world above.

**The Influence of The Mystery Religions:** The mystery religions of Greece and Rome had a profound influence on European culture and religion, especially Christianity. The central mystery of a divinity who dies and is reborn in order to insure the spiritual life of mankind is taken by Christianity from the Greek mysteries.

**The Myth of Demeter and Persephone**: The sacred rites at Eleusis were the best known and the most widespread of the mystery religions in the ancient world. Great political figures such as Peisistratos, Kimon, Perikles, Hadrian, Marcus Aurelius, and Cicero were all initiated into the mysteries at Eleusis. You will read about these mysteries in some detail as well as in the *Hymn to Demeter*, the best surviving evidence about the contents of the mysteries.

# UNIT ESSAY

At the outset of *Masks of God: Occidental Mythology*, Joseph Campbell identifies what he considers the unique deep structure of all that falls under the very broad rubric of Western Civilization or Western Mythology. This underlying structure will be the subject of the last four units, covering the period of the Greeks and Romans (1500 B.C.E.–400 C.E.), the Christian Dark Ages (400–1050 C.E.) and the High Middle Ages (1050–1500 C.E.). Campbell writes on the fundamental difference in Oriental and Occidental world views,

> In the Western ranges of mythological thought and imagery… whether in Europe or in the Levant, the ground of being is normally personified as a Creator, of whom Man is the creature, and the two are not the same; so that here the function of myth and ritual cannot be to catalyze an experience of ineffable identify. . . . The high function of Occidental myth and ritual, consequently, is to establish a means of relationship—of God to Man and Man to God.[1]

This idea of a radically transcendental God—separate from this world—means inevitably that within the foundations of Western myth lies a fundamental paradox or tension, an unresolvable dualism. Campbell describes it this way,

> Certain exclusively Occidental complications result from the fact that, where two such contradictory final terms as God and Man stand against each other, the individual cannot attach his allegiance wholly to both.[2]

All of Western mythology, religion, and philosophy, Campbell goes on to explain, can be seen in terms of a grandiose interplay of these two poles or pieties: Man and God. On the side of Man lie the early Greek mystery religions and the tradition of humanism which continues to this very day. On the side of the God are the Hebrew tradition of Mosaic Law and Christianity which teach a renunciation of Man's judgment and experience in favor of the majesty and power of God. In the philosophical tradition of Plato, Plotinus, St. Augustine, and most Christian thinkers up to St. Thomas Aquinas, human existence is radically dependent upon the deity. The ground of being lies not in this earth or with mankind, but elsewhere, with the gods and a more real life after death. In this viewpoint, the eternal soul is imprisoned in the temporary house of the body and, therefore, life is worth nothing. Each pole has the inevitable effect of denying the intrinsic dignity and being of the other.

You should remember this point as you read the next four units, for these sections on Western mythology will move toward the relationship of an equal allegiance to man and God and frank recognition of the dualism in the figure of Parzival, the Grail knight, whose name, as the author Wolfram von Eschenbach tells us, means *perce a val*—that is, "pierce through

the valley" or the middle. Parzival's life quest moves toward identification with his half-brother, the pagan/Christian Feirefiz who is half-white and half-black. In addition, the great high medieval legends of Arthur and the Grail are, in fact, a rebirth of many of the mythological archetypes, spiritual processes, and symbols of the Greek mystery religions.

This unit concerns the recognition of the dualism in the mystery religions of ancient Greece and how those mysteries were rejected by the early Fathers of the Roman and Eastern church in favor of the Hebrew tradition of Mosaic Law and a renunciation of the human side of the dualism. It also concludes, as Campbell makes clear in the television program, with the always open potential of recognizing the roots of Christianity in Greek mysticism.

## An Overview of Greek Religion

Chronologically, the period of the Greek mystery religions follows the period of the Olympic gods. We can locate the high point of worship of the Olympic pantheon at around the time of Homer's writing of the *Iliad* and *Odyssey* and Hesiod's three poems on the origin of the gods, *Theogony*; the creation of men, *Works and Days*; and *The Shield of Herakles* on the deeds of hero-men or demi-gods. This period dates from about 800 B.C.E. (the first Olympic games were held in 776 B.C.E.) to the Classical period of the great Greek city-states, philosophy, art, and drama (*c.* 400 B.C.E.). In the accounts of Hesiod and Homer, the original Olympian gods, led by Zeus, were interested in power and manipulating the fate of humans. In these accounts, there is very little sense of the developing spiritual energy that would characterize the mystery religions. In fact, the Olympic gods are anti-mystical, and their natures are fully revealed by writers such as Homer and Hesiod.

In a quite controversial and stimulating book titled *The Origin of Consciousness in the Breakdown of the Bicameral Mind*, Princeton psychiatry professor Julian Jaynes locates the emergence of rational consciousness in human evolution precisely in this period of Homeric or Olympian Greece. The Olympic gods are the sort of theism that results from rational consciousness. They are not personally related to individuals as interior gods, though they may favor the fate of some particular person. Their natures are universals known to all. Odysseus's ability to think of the gods, other men, and experiences in the abstract—that is, apart from his immediate experience—is the substance of Jaynes's assertion of a new consciousness. Preconscious man could not think abstractly, be introspective, or lie. He could also not conceive of a system of virtues and values in universalized categories apart from his immediate actions.[3]

Perhaps this new form of consciousness is why the classical period in Greece was also a time of religious crisis. It became increasingly difficult to explain the gods of Homer in terms of universal praise. Homer simply revealed too many situations in which the gods appeared to have base motivations. Satiric and comic dramatists presented the gods in the morally unworthy situations that we know so well from myth writers such as the Roman Ovid, whose *Metamorphoses* (*c*. 19 C.E.) makes no attempt to justify the actions of the Gods. Society had to develop explanations that supported continued respect for the gods and deterred criticism. Remember that Socrates was put to death in 399 C.E. because the new rationalism he preached in the Athenian Agora, or marketplace, tended to undermine faith in the gods. The function of Greek tragedy, as opposed to satire and comedy, was to explain the motivations of the gods. Aristotle argues in *The Poetics* that the tragedies had the effect of purging human arrogance and instilling piety.

In Sophocles' *Oedipus Rex*, Oedipus is a rationalist similar to Socrates, and Sophocles makes very clear the theological implications of humanism. A close reading of the Oedipus Trilogy (*c*. 425–400 C.E.) reveals that Oedipus's crime of killing his father is, symbolically, the very act of denying the gods. One kills a god by denying his truth and by denying the origin of human life in the gods. The results of this denial were shown in the fertility plague that devastates Thebes at the opening of the play. In the second play of the trilogy, *Oedipus at Colonus*, Oedipus comes to discover that his true father is neither Polybos nor Laios, but the god Apollo whose truth he had denied at Delphi only moments before meeting and killing his biological father. As Oedipus's experience reveals, the Greeks of the classical period were losing the literal and historical sense of the fatherhood of the gods, the connection between the gods and the vitality and fertility of nature and human life. What was emerging in classical Greece in response to the loss of the historical and literal Greek religion was a mystical sense of the fatherhood—and importantly, motherhood—of the gods. The evolution of Greek religion is a movement from polytheism to mysticism, but it is well to remember that the roots of the mystical religions go back to the origins of the Olympic gods.

The Greek Mystery cults flourished from the third century B.C.E. to the third century C.E.—at least this is the period of temple building, though many of the writings, such as the important *Hymn to Demeter*, go back to about 600 B.C.E. Any discussion of the mystery religions must be prefaced with a caveat that it is impossible to know just how much of our knowledge of the mysteries actually represents the mysteries themselves and not merely the symbols and figures used both to conceal the mystery from outsiders and simultaneously to reveal it to initiates who know how to interpret the sacred symbols. With that caveat in mind, it appears that these religions centered around the death and rebirth of a savior god whose sacrifice makes possible continued natural fertility. Thus the mystery religions also center upon the interdependence of life and death, symbolized in the agricultural process of planting or burying of seed. On the surface the myth is agrarian and sexual, but these outward images symbolize the spiritual process of the death of the ego (i.e., rational consciousness) and the rebirth or transcendence to a higher level of spiritual existence. That is, a rebirth of a higher existence in the mystical knowledge of the mysteries, as Campbell describes in the television program for this unit.

## Branches of Mystery Religions

Scholars generally recognize five main branches of the mystery religions: the Eleusinian mysteries; the mysteries of Isis-Osiris, Cybele-Attis, and Aphrodite-Adonis; the Orphic mysteries; the mysteries of Dionysus; and Mithraism. Very briefly, the Eleusinian mysteries derived from the myth of Demeter and Persephone. Demeter was the goddess of harvest and Persephone, her daughter, was abducted and taken to the underworld to be the wife of Hades. The myth concerns the succession of the seasons in Persephone's movements back and forth between and under- and upper-worlds, and the rebirth of life in Spring. Gradually it came to symbolize personal rebirth and initiation into the spiritual and eternal aspect of life.

The Isis-Osiris, Cybele-Attis, and Aphrodite-Adonis mysteries are very similar to those of Eleusis but their origin is ultimately Egyptian, Phrygian, Semitic, or Syrian and can be traced back to about 1700 C.E. Isis, Cybele, and Aphrodite are all earth-mother godesses, while Osiris, Attis, and Adonis are resurrection gods. These cults spread throughout the Mediterranean area and were powerful in Rome until extirpated by Christians in the second century C.E. (For further discussion of the Isis-Osiris myth see Unit 4.)

The Orphic mysteries also contained a symbolic death or sojourn to the underworld, and like the Isis-Cybele-Aphrodite cults, involved frenzied music and the mutilation of the god's body. Orpheus, as the popular myth tells, descended to the underworld to bring back to life his beloved wife Eurydice. The religious experience of Orpheus's music had the power to halt the eternally futile and senseless labors of the underworld. In Orphic mystery religions, the music was the key and power to harmony of spirit and nature. The mysteries of Dionysus were the most ecstatic, seeking union with the god through wine, dance, song, and the ritualistic slaughter of a sacrificial animal. And finally, there were the mysteries of Mithra which were particularly prevalent among Roman soldiers and involved achievement of a spiritual enlightenment in the slaying of a bull. They involved a seven-stage process of purification for the initiate symbolizing the seven heavens through which one must ascend in order to pass into paradise. This discussion will not cover Mithraism, but you have probably seen the Mithric ritual in the ending section of Francis Ford Coppola's

*Apocalypse Now*. Mithraism is the mystical religion of military forces; thus it is the process into which Colonel Kurtz has entered. The ritual hacking into pieces of the bull and of Colonel Kurtz occurs within a context of the elevation of the soul to an understanding of the mystery of death as the mystery of life. From the death of the bull, or from any death, emerges new life. Death is the fertility. Colonel Kurtz, of course, forgets to take the rituals symbolically and spiritually, and rather takes literally the idea that one can kill everything in order to start a new and more beautiful form of life.

An initiate in these religious cults bore the name of "mystes"; that is, one who participates in the mysteries of god. This mysticism, in general, represented a nondiscursive or nonrational way of approaching an ineffably transcendent god. Its opposite tradition is the Mosaic tradition of Judaism, in which the religious experience was codified in a body of laws and commandments. This contractual or covenental relationship between God and man is well demonstrated in the Old Testament book of Exodus in which the Ark of the Covenant is given to the Israelites by Yahweh who reveals his commandments to them (Exodus 25:22). One gains access to the godhead by fulfilling certain requirements and cultivating a certain commanded selfhood. Religion, in this sense, creates a social and political identity constructed around a body of laws.

In contrast, mystery religions might be thought of as negative religions, as does Dionysus the Areopagite ("Via Negationis" [The Way of Negation] in *Mystical Theology*). Dionysus wrote that one reaches an understanding of god by denying all of god's doctrinal attributes. One reaches the godhead by losing the self, by dying to this world and rising in spiritual radiance. As Campbell phrases it in the television program for this unit, by going down into the abyss and coming out again mystically filled with the gods. In this sense, the experience of God is ineffable or impossible to put in words. Only symbolic or mythic representations are capable of translating these experiences or concepts to us. There is almost never any direct social and political consequences of mysticism, but it rather remains a personal experience of god. Every religion based in rational doctrine also has its mystical aspects. In Islam, it is called Sufism, and in Judaism it is called Cabalism and Hasidism. It is important to note that while the Eleusinian mysteries were a vital part of the civic life of Athens, the rational Olympian religious practices remained the official religion of the city-state.

## The Mysteries at Eleusis

Eleusis lies at the edge of the Aegean Sea, some fourteen miles down a fertile valley from Athens. It is here that the story of Demeter and Persephone takes place. (See the *Hymn to Demeter* in the *Anthology of Readings* for the full telling of this myth.) The poem begins one beautiful spring day as Persephone, the daughter of Demeter, is out picking flowers. She is particularly attracted to a glorious Narcissus with a hundred blossoms. The beauty of the maiden compounded with the beauty of the flowers sets the fire of love ablaze in the heart of Hades (the Roman god Pluto, as he is frequently called by Campbell in the television program for this unit). Hades, one of the sons of Cronos (father time) and the brother of Zeus, is the lord of the underworld. His name means "the unseen one" or "the wealthy one", wealthy in the sense of fertility and numbers of those who are with him. The realm of Hades and those who inhabit it in the afterlife are called Chthonian, that is, of the earth and darkness as opposed to the Olympians, who are of light and of bright air. According to the poem, Hades seizes Persephone and, in spite of her cries to Zeus for help, bears her off in his golden chariot to his home in the underworld. The *Hymn to Demeter* thus represents a struggle between Zeus and Hades for possession of mankind.

On a heap of rocks by a well just outside of the village of Eleusis, Demeter ceases her futile wanderings over the face of the earth in search of her lost daughter. Having learned the truth about Persephone's abduction by Hades, Demeter has left the company of the gods for the remoteness of Eleusis where she, disguised as an old woman, sits beside a well to vent her grief. Demeter commands the people of Eleusis to build an altar and a great temple from which she will teach them her sacred rites. Demeter is the goddess of agriculture and harvest, the goddess who gave the gifts of the earth in season. Closed within her temple, apart from all the gods and mourning the loss of her daughter, she withholds these gifts from mankind. In vain, the poem tells us, do the oxen and men plow the fields and sow barley. Famine rages throughout Greece and the gods in Olympus are deprived of their gifts and sacrifices. One after another the gods come to her entreating her to relent, but she vows that seed will never again sprout on earth until she beholds her daughter face to face. Thus death holds sway.

Because Hades is sometimes addressed in mythology as the Chthonian Zeus, the other side of Zeus, and all that is opposite to what is clearly seen and known, the *Hymn to Demeter* represents a struggle between Zeus and Hades for possession of mankind. As long as Hades holds Persephone, mankind will surely die and all will become Chthonians. For this reason, Zeus grants the demand of Demeter and promises to bring Persephone back from the underworld and reunite her with Demeter at Eleusis. As Persephone is about the leave the underworld, Hades forces into her mouth a pomegranate seed, the effect of which is that Persephone will have to spend three months of each year in the underworld and nine months above in the world of the living. Once reunited with her daughter, Demeter lifts her curse on the land, and we are told in the *Hymn* that fruit springs up throughout the fertile valleys and the wide land is laden with leaves and flowers. As Campbell describes in the television program for this unit, Demeter is often depicted in the art of the Greco-Roman world embracing Persephone and holding a sheaf of grain, barley, in her hand. Demeter, moreover, goes on to tell the rulers of Eleusis that she will teach them the holy mysteries and the performance of sacred rites. These ceremonies must not be questioned, violated, or expressed to anyone who has not been invited to participate in the rites themselves.

The *Hymn to Demeter* is our best evidence as to the contents and the religious import of the mysteries of Eleusis. The second best evidence is the ruins of the site itself. The cult spread in popularity rapidly throughout Greece so that what began as a single temple in the *Hymn* grew to a complex of many vast temples covering the hillsides of Eleusis. George Mylonas, in his *Eleusis and the Eleusinian Mysteries*, surveys the history of the building of temples and examines in detail the findings of numerous archaeological excavations beginning in 1882. His book includes fascinating photographs of the temple remains that give some clues to the intricate process and levels of secrecy that initiates had to pass through. (Note again the importance of the process of initiates as discussed in Unit 1.) One building, called the Telesterion, apparently served as an inner sanctuary where the final secrets might have been revealed to initiates who had followed a prescribed course though several outer temples. Apparently temple construction continued at Eleusis right up to the period of the Roman Emperor Theodosius (ruled, 379–95 C.E.) who declared Christianity the only permitted religion in the Roman Empire and who issued strict laws against the mystery cults. The archaeological record indicates that at this time the destruction of the temples began, as non-Athenian and non-Eleusinian priests were placed in charge of the sacred area.

## Interpreting the Eleusinian Mysteries

The *Hymn* attributes to Demeter the origin and the secret nature of the rites. Now the problem we face is one of interpreting this *Hymn* in a way that tells us something about the religious beliefs and practices of ancient Greece. What can Demeter mean for human life? In the television program for this unit, Campbell tells us that the use of agricultural imagery or symbols is one way of rendering a spiritual message. "It is not the object," Campbell says, "it's the reference that is the sense of the ritual." St. Paul explains spiritual or mystical interpretation of objects this way, "The Spirit scrutinizes all matters, even the deep things of God. . . . The natural man does not accept what is taught by the Spirit of God. For him, that is absurdity. He cannot come to know such teaching because it must be appraised in a spiritual way. The spiritual man, on the other hand, can appraise everything." (1 Corinthians 3:10–16.) Our problem, as St. Paul tells the Corinthians in a later epistle, is to learn to understand not with the eyes and ears of the body or of the rational consciousness, but with the eyes and ears of the spirit.

How are we, therefore, to understand the strange story of the rape of Persephone, her mother's anger and grief, the nine months of exile, and the joyous reunion. Studying the rituals of

the mysteries of Demeter will reveal the significance of this story. Literary, archaeological, and epigraphical evidence suggest the following general reconstruction of the Eleusian mysteries. The rites at Eleusis fell into three stages: 1) participation in the Lesser Mysteries or preparatory stages, 2) advancement to the Greater Mysteries or the full initiation, 3) the *Epopteia*, mystical vision, or full revelation of the secrets of Eleusis. The Lesser Mysteries were held in Athens each year during the early spring, and the Greater Mysteries once every four years during September and October. The Lesser mysteries lasted for nine days (recall that Demeter spends nine days searching for her daughter and Persephone spends nine months in life with her mother) and included various activities such as cleansing oneself in the sea, a similar cleansing of a piglet to be sacrificed later, and long periods of prayer.

On the fifth day, the procession to the temples of Eleusis began. The initiates carried a statue of Iacchus (probably Bacchus or Dionysus, in some accounts he is seen as the son of Persephone and Hades) and chanted his name the whole way. At the temple, the initiates fasted and prayed. The fasting ended with the drinking of the ceremonial drink, the Kykeon, a mixture of barley, water, and mint—just what Demeter drank as she made her stand against the Olympian gods. In the television program for this unit, Campbell alludes to the theory that this drink contained some sort of hallucinogen, possibly Ergot, which prepared the initiates to experience the ineffable. Whether this is true or not, it is clear that this period of fasting was designed mentally to prepare the initiates for an experience directed to the spirit, and not to the bodily senses. The ceremonies in the temple proper involved three stages: a dramatic enactment, the revelation of sacred objects, and the pronouncement of secret words. We cannot know very much about these activities in the inner sanctum, but very likely they reenacted the events of the *Hymn to Demeter*; that is, in symbolic representation, the initiates experienced for themselves just what Demeter and Persephone experience in the poem. At the end, the initiates emerged from the temple carrying a single ear of wheat or barley.

Campbell tells us in the television program for this unit that this discovery, this epiphany, must have been the revelation of the deep, energetic aspect of life, experienced after one has learned not to focus exclusively on the perceptible and phenomenal aspects of life. He goes on to point out that, among the Greeks, the richness of life came from underground, as in the model of agriculture and the planting of seed in the ground from which new life emerges. Thus the entrance to the inner sanctuary replicated the kathodos (descent into the ground or underworld) and the anodos (ascent or rebirth) of the sacrificial Persephone. In the mystery religions, the abyss, the chthonic, the darkness was the realm of spiritual truth. On a vase now in the Naples Museum, Campbell shows an initiate being led by Herakles into a dark chamber. On a sarcophagus in the same museum, the descent into darkness, or the unknown, is symbolized by an initiate wearing a hood over his head and face, thus blinding him to aspects of the world that are seen and known by the eyes and the conscious reason. In the *Oedipus Rex* of Sophocles, blinding serves this same function. The blind seer, Tiresias, is the model for seeing with the eyes of the spirit. And Oedipus, in blinding himself, exclaims that he has attained a new way of seeing.[4]

The revelations of the gods (epiphanies) can only be made to those who have overcome the blinding light of sight and rational consciousness. The rational mind organizes and sorts life into useful categories. This is true for Aristotle and classical philosophy in general. It is also true for Christianity in the Dark Ages, sorting out good from evil and elaborating on a set of authorized practices while condemning others. The divine aspects of beings are drained away as things take on a use-value, even a spiritual use-value, in saving one's soul. Slaves, according to Aristotle, did not have souls; their being was defined by their use-value. But at Eleusis, even slaves could participate in the mysteries. No one was excluded. Once in darkness, the initiate learned the divinity of all that existed on earth and of every part of life. Evil and good, the light and the dark, life and death were welcome parts of the same whole.

It is reported that initiates were required to bring a piglet with them. Apparently the piglet was washed and purified in the same manner as the initiate. At the height of the ceremony the piglet was sacrificed; it died instead of the initiate and provided the initiate with a tangible symbol of the experience of death he was undergoing.

As Campbell makes clear in the television program for this unit, the Eleusis revelations were that everything is a part of the divine. He remarks that the simple act of eating is also the taking of divine substance into our bodies. Our whole lives are supported by the powers and energies of the gods which flow into us at every moment and in everything we do. The rational consciousness cannot comprehend this with its eyes and ears, but the spirit can. Campbell concludes that the essence of the mysteries is the realization of "the dynamic of inexhaustible nature which pours its energy into the field of time and with which we are to be in harmony in both its destructive and its productive aspects." Clement of Alexandria reported that the initiates of Eleusis emerged from the temple carrying a single ear of wheat. Although, as Campbell makes clear in the television program, Clement's intent in telling this detail was to belittle the Eleusinian mysteries, the ear of wheat contains the mystery of life. As Clement could not understand, it is as much a Christian mystery as a Greek pagan one. The Gospel of John phrases it this way:

> I solemnly assure you, unless a grain of wheat falls to the earth and dies, it remains just a grain of wheat. But if it dies, it produces much fruit. (John 12:24)

This theme of mystical interpretation is the subject of *The Teachings of Pythagoras* (see The *Anthology of Readings*), in which the nature of god is the unity of all things of the world, including death and life.

*The Teachings of Pythagoras* present a vision of the world of someone who has been initiated in the mysteries, and these teachings bring us as close to the gnosis as we are likely to get. Pythagoras was a mathematician and an astrologer who sought to know the nature of god, and what he discovered was that the nature of god is in all things. The soul of an individual links him with all other animate things. Pythagoras developed a theory of the transmigration of souls: "Our souls are deathless; always, when they leave our bodies, they find new dwelling places. . . . All things are always changing, but nothing dies" (*Anthology* 368). Nothing dies because it lives again in a changed form. Thus the food that is eaten by an animal or a human takes on a new life in that form. We are potentially a part of everything. The conclusion of Pythagoras's teachings is a profound respect for the earth and all that lives on it. The earth is living and all living things emerge from it. He enumerates many instances of spontaneous generation, such as the sudden emergence of frogs from mud. Man is brother to all the animals and therefore must not eat meat of any sort. But at the same time, Pythagoras knows that life is what sustains life and the new life is born from the "chewing and mangling" of another life.

## The Apollonian and the Dionysian

In Greek mythology, Apollo and Dionysus are opposites. Dionysus represents the dark, chthonic, irrational, frenzied, orgiastic, and energetic. Apollo, in contrast, is the serene, rational, light, and well ordered. Both gods are associated with music, and their differences can be seen in the kinds of music they prefer. Apollo is often portrayed with the harp or lyre, instruments of formal music characterized by Pythagorean harmony and restrained elegance. The Apollonian is also the spirit found in Greek architecture, sculpture, and political philosophy. Dionysian music is the furious screaming of the Bacchae as they flail and dance with their heads thrown back in the orgiastic expression of uncontrollable primal energy (see the selection from Euripides' *The Bacchae* in the *Anthology of Readings*).

Friedrich Nietzsche cited this dynamic of the Apollonian and the Dionysian as the origin of tragedy in his famous work, *The Birth of Tragedy*. One cannot understand either of these two poles without a full comprehension and recognition of the existence of the other. Greek tragedy, Nietzsche felt, portrays the Apollonian harnessing and restraining of the energy of the Dionysian. What tragedy shows is the tremendous force exerted by mankind and, ultimately, the Olympian gods to impose a rational order on life, that is, to understand life as productive and not destructive. Tragedy in its mystical sense depicts the human desire to deny death. This is the tension in *The Bacchae* (*c.* 406 C.E.), a play that seeks to overcome the mystery of the Dionysian cults. The cult of Dionysus held that the soul (Greek, psyche) pre-existed the body and was called by Zeus from a pradisiacal realm into bodily existence. The soul was chained in the body and longed to escape into its former state of ecstasy and pleasure. Through wine, dancing, and wild singing, the soul briefly escaped into the ecstasy of freedom. This frenzied state was also regarded as possession by the god. Thus one died to this world in order to live in the spiritual world of the gods. The rites normally ended in the death of an animal that was torn to pieces by the hands of the participants and eaten raw as a sacramental meal. It was believed that the god was present in the wild animals chosen for this sacrifice, and in this manner the Maenads, as female devotees were often called, took the god into themselves.

In Euripides' play, *The Bacchae* (in the *Anthology of Readings*), Pentheus, king of Thebes, believes that it is sufficient and good for humans to live by reason alone. As king of Thebes, he feels that political life is superior to all else, and thus the fundamental ground of human existence. He wants to put an end to the yearly rituals in which the women of Thebes go into the woods for a week to drink wine, sing, dance, and revel with Dionysus. Significantly, Pentheus binds Dionysus in chains when he arrives in Thebes to call the women out. Of course, Dionysus cannot be so restrained. In the end of the play, Pentheus sneaks into the forest camp disguised as a woman but is soon recognized and torn to pieces by the frenzied women, his own mother among them. Pentheus's mother, Agave, triumphantly dances around with what she believes to be a lion's head. Later on, in a calmer mood, she realizes that it is the head of her son and immediately renounces the Dionysian orgies. Thus Pentheus's initial aim is achieved; the women now, as represented by his mother, renounce the chthonic side, but the cost of this suppression is surely greater than even Pentheus bargained for. The subject of tragedy is just such agony.

Euripides' play is not exactly a fair representation of the Dionysian mysteries. But we can infer from the play some of the content of the annual visit to the woods with the god Dionysus. As discussed earlier, the mystery religions reasserted the value and power of the irrational side of human life, while tragedy was more of a state sponsored event that asserted the power of the Olympic gods and instilled in the viewers piety and humility with regard to established political and theological orders. In the story of Pentheus, we see the cost of that order.

The world of light, or the world that is known by the eyes and the operation of the ordering capacities of the mind, is only half of the world that exists. We too often take it for the true aspect of life because all of our sciences, philosophy, religious doctrines, and social institutions are part and parcel of the Apollonian piety. The task of these institutions is the suppression of the dark, chthonic side with the corresponding assumption that the public or civic life of a person is all that exists. The women go out into the woods, symbolically a wild place in opposition to the order of the city. In the selection from *Greek Religion* by Walter Burkert (in the *Anthology of Readings*), the point is made that the Dionysian mysteries were also a vehicle

by which an individual separated himself from the "polis" (Greek for city). But the retreat can also be individual. In this manner, a selfhood is attained beyond and in contrast to the group. The mysteries teach that fertility, or new life, originates beyond the purview of the city and reason, from the darkness of the body and the earth. The fertility of the women of Thebes is established by these yearly sojourns in the woods with Dionysus. In this manner, the earth is made sacred.

## Christianity and the Mystery Religions

Toward the end of the television program for this unit, Campbell presents a slide showing a crucified Orpheus and Bacchus. His point is that Orpheus, Bacchus, Persephone, Jesus, Osiris, and many others are resurrection gods and goddesses whose stories are all the same. They all identify humans with the great and eternal power of the universe. The death of the god and his or her descent to the underworld occurs so that the knowledge of the divine in all things can be returned to humans after it has been lost in the ego-restricted world of fear, pride, and desire. This suggests, as Campbell points out, that Christianity had its beginnings in Greek mystery religions. As a religion, Christianity centered around the mythic experience of the death and rebirth of a Savior whose sacrifice insures the flow of spiritual energy in the world, as well as the process of initiation of members into a higher state of spiritual purity and knowledge of sacred mysteries. Campbell also shows the remarkable number of similarities between the Greek religions and Christian rites, such as the elevation of the wheaten host and the symbolic eating of the body of the sacrificial victim.

By the third century C.E., however, under the influence of the Eastern Fathers of the Church, particularly Clement of Alexandria and his most precocious student Origen (who became head of the Catechetical School at Alexandria, Egypt, at age eighteen), the mystery religions were set in opposition to Christianity. In Rome, Gnosticism, as mystery religions were called (from the Greek word gnosis for secret knowledge), was condemned as heresy, and its influence upon Christian doctrine waned as attacks upon Gnostics mounted, often to the point of violent destruction of life and of sacred temples.

The Alexandrian School of Clement and Origen embraced the Hebrew Old Testament with its historical and messianic deep structure. Clement (175–202 C.E.) reinterpreted the stages of individual initiation presented in mysticism as symbolic of stages of development in world history. The history of the Israelites provided the model: first a period of exile and wandering, then the birth and redemption of Christ, and finally the growth of the Church as the body of Christian Truth and a world power on earth. Such a mythos fit better with the growing power of the Roman papacy. It provided the rationalization for declarations such as that of Theodosius that Christianity was the only legitimate religion on earth; all others were preliminary and superseded.

Origen (186–254 C.E.) produced an edition of the Scriptures with facing Greek and Hebrew texts, and thus began the long tradition in Christianity of biblical exegesis. He is said to have written more than a thousand books interpreting every passage of the Bible. The effort of this kind of biblical scholarship was, as Campbell suggests, to show the point for point relationship between the Old Testament and the New Testament; that is, to show how the life of Christ fulfills the prophesies of the Old Testament once and for all. For these writers, Jesus is not a mystical or symbolic savior in whose sacrifice devotees can participate to fill themselves again and again with the god. Rather Jesus is a historical savior whose sacrifice accomplishes the redemption once and for all. Christianity, under the early Church Fathers, demanded that the mythological parts of the Apostles, Creed Campbell recites at the end of the television program for this unit be taken both literally and historically. Christians were required to believe that the events actually did happen. The events were not mysteries, but literal fact. To this day, Catholic doctrine requires belief in its essential doctrines, such as the virgin birth, the assumption of Mary, and transubstantiation, as literal fact. In this way, Christianity divorced itself from its mystical roots.

Origen was also responsible for the theoretical development that would become a major weapon in the Christian suppression of mystery religions and some Christian dualistic sects such as Manichaeism, a religion in which equally powerful God and Satan fought for allegiance of mankind. Origen asserted that good and evil were not opposites and that dualism was not a fundamental principle of being. Rather, as Origen argued, evil was nonbeing; that is, what we call evil, darkness, or the irrational is only a lacking or privation of goodness, light, and reason. This idea would gain even more power in the hands of St. Augustine, two centuries later. But here we can see the crucial theoretical possibility for denying a large part of what the mystery religions sought to teach. The whole realm of the chthonic is relegated to nonbeing, a lacking in the realm of the upper world of light and reason. Initiation in this Christian sense meant a process of freeing oneself from the chthonic and the earthly in order to become more purely spiritual. The meaning of spirit takes on, as a result of Origen's theory, its modern sense of opposition to the earthly, the bodily, or the temporal. In Greek mysteries, however, the spiritual must be understood as the full awareness of the inseparability of the chthonic and the ethereal, of light and dark. The spirit, the mystery of the "breath of life," is held in the seed of wheat.

Though Christianity did turn away from the Greek mysteries, we can, as Campbell points out in the television program for this unit, read back into Christian doctrine and ritual the foundations of the original mysteries. This is the Hermetic tradition of sacred and mystical writing rather than the Mosaic tradition promulgated by the early church Fathers. And Campbell suggests the rediscovery of the *Corpus Hermeticum*, a mystical interpretation of the Greek and Roman heroes, was a major inspiration for Renaissance painters. They were now able to make connections between pagan deities and Christian doctrine, while formerly all pagan deities were condemned as devils. They could see, Campbell says, "that the symbolic imagery of the pagan world was equivalent in its mystic meaning to the mystically interpreted symbology of Christianity." Campbell goes on to describe a picture by Pinturicchio in the Bordieu room of the Vatican showing Isis, the Great Mother Goddess of Egypt, on her throne instructing two disciples—the two just happen to be Moses and Hermes. All you have to do, Campbell suggests, is spend a little time with the sacred images and they will sing to you.

The mystical and spiritual meaning of life, Campbell's work shows, is not held in the teachings and doctrines of institutions, but in the individual's acceptance of his or her own experience as the absolute ground of meanings. In the mysteries, the recognition of the absoluteness of individual experience is symbolized by the confrontation with death, an initiation which changes forever they way one understands the images and appearances of life whether presented by Christianity or the mythologies of various peoples of the world.

## ASSIGNMENTS FOR STUDY AND ANALYSIS

1. Compare the Hermetic (symbolic) and the Mosaic (historical) interpretation of scripture and myth. Explain the general principles of each hermeneutical method.
2. Why does Demeter adopt the guise of an old woman when she takes her stand at the well in Eleusis? Give a symbolic interpretation of her disguise.
3. Read a few selections of the Epistles of St. Paul from the New Testament. Does St. Paul encourage a symbolic interpretation of Christian belief? Do the same thing with the parables narrated in the Gospels of John.
4. Explain the relation of the annual agricultural cycle to the experience of Persephone and the mystery of Eleusis. What specifically is the symbol (vehicle) and what is the meaning (the content).
5. Myth is a symbolic language that comprehends and harmonizes fundamental oppositions or dualities in experience: youth/age, past/present, temporal/eternal, and life/death. Show how these dualities are harmonized in the Greek mystery religions.
6. Explain Pythagoras's general views about the earth, animals, and human life in *The Teachings of Pythagoras* (in the *Anthology of Readings*).

## FURTHER ASSIGNMENTS FOR WRITING AND REFLECTION

1. Hermetic (symbolic) and Mosaic (historical) interpretation are not limited to discussion of scripture and myth. The same principles operate in discourse about any nation. Write an analysis of the way that key events or persons at the founding of the United States are presented. Do you see the principles of symbolic and historical interpretation at work?

2. We frequently hear today references to the Dionysian-Apollonian dualism in our own cultural practices. Explain what this dualism is and show how it operates in things such as contemporary music, dance, or public rituals such as sports and elections.

3. The experience of Persephone and her death and rebirth can be interpreted psychologically as a maturation myth. What does her fascination with the Narcissus flower suggest? (For more background read the story of Narcissus in a book of myths.) How does her descent to the underworld and her marriage to Hades complete the maturation process? What is the meaning of the process according to the myth?

4. Campbell's *Hero with a Thousand Faces* identifies the death/resurrection experience as the monomyth of the hero. Examine the general outlines of the hero's quest Campbell presents, and show how the experience of Persephone and the initiates at Eleusis follow the pattern.

5. This unit began with Campbell's belief that the unique feature of Western myth is its preservation of dualities, manifest in the polarity of God and Man. Myth serves the function of relating the two without denying one or the other. How does Christianity deal with dualities? What was the method of Origen and St. Augustine?

6. *The Teachings of Pythagoras* represents a mystical understanding of life and the world. How much do the views expressed by Pythagoras relate to our world today? We accept Pythagoras's mathematics, but can we accept what he thought mathematics should be used for—that is, the understanding of the unity of all things? Are the ecology and animal rights movements outbreaks of neo-Pythagorean thought?

7. *The Bacchae* has rather overt sexual overtones. From the point of view of a rationalist like Pentheus, what is the connection of sex with the chthonic? In this regard also, what might be a mystical interpretation of sex?

8. Campbell refers to the Christian Dark Ages as a period when the mysteries and symbolic meaning of sacred images were lost. Generally, this means a loss in the ability to see the Dionysian or chthonic aspect of life. In our own times, how well do we acknowledge the Dionysian aspect? In what ways is this impulse manifest in our rituals?

9. In your library, find a book on Renaissance paintings. Look at Renaissance painters' depictions of Christian figures along side pagan heroes. Look up the stories of each of the figures in the Old Testament and Ovid's *Metamorphoses*, and explain the significance of these figures appearing in the same pictures.

## ENDNOTES

[1] Joseph Campbell, *The Masks of God: Occidental Mythology*, (New York: Penguin Books, 1976) 4.

[2] Campbell 4

[3] Julian Janes. *The Origin of Consciousness in the Breakdown of the Bicameral Mind*, (Boston: Houghton Mifflin, 1976) 270–85.

[4] Sophocles, *The Oedipus Cycle*. Trans. Dudley Fitts and Robert Fitzgerald. (New York: Harcourt Brace Jovanovich, 1939) 75.

## UNIT BIBLIOGRAPHY

Burkert, Walter. *Greek Religion*. Cambridge: Harvard University Press, 1985. An overview of Greek religion.

Clinton, Kevin. *Sacred Officials of the Eleusinian Mysteries*. Philadelphia: American Philosophical Society, 1974. A study of the rites of Eleusis and the roles of people involved.

Haining, Peter. *Ancient Mysteries Reader*. Garden City, NY: Doubleday, 1975. An anthology of sacred writing of Greek mystery religions.

Frazer, Sir James George. *The Golden Bough: A Study in Magic and Religion*. New York: Macmillan, 1922. The classic interpretation of mythology.

Guthrie, W. K. C. *Orpheus and Greek Religion: A Study of the Orphic Movement*. New York: W. W. Norton, 1966. A scholarly examination of Orphism.

Hermes Trismegistus. *Hermetica*. Trans. Walter Scott. Boston: Random House, 1985. Ancient Greek and Latin writings which contain religious and philosophical teachings ascribed to Hermes Trismegistus. Generally called the Corpus Hermeticum. English and Greek texts.

Hesiod. *The Works and Days, the Theogony and the Shield of Herakles*. Trans. Richmond Latimore. Ann Arbor: University of Michigan Press, 1959. The eighth-century B.C.E. story of the birth of the gods, the creation of the world, and the trials of the heroes.

Jaynes, Julian. *The Origin of Consciousness in the Breakdown of the Bicameral Mind*. Boston: Houghton Mifflin, 1976. An interpretation of Greek myths and religion in the light of contemporary theories of the brain.

Kerenyi, Karl. *Eleusis: Archetypal Image of Mother and Daughter*. New York: Pantheon Books, 1967. An interpretation of the cult of Eleusis.

Kerenyi, Karl. *Dionysus: Archetypal Image of the Indestructible Life*. Princeton: Princeton University Press, 1976. Presents the myths of Dionysus in relation to fertility and nature.

Kerenyi, Karl. *The Gods of the Greeks*. New York: Thames and Hudson, 1979. An overview of Greek Religion by one of the foremost Greek scholars.

Meyer, Marvin. *Ancient Mysteries: A Sourcebook of Sacred Texts of the Mystery Religions of the Ancient Mediterranean World*. San Francisco: Harper and Row, 1987. An anthology of sacred writings.

Morford, Mark and Robert Lenardon. *Classical Mythology*. New York: David McKay and Company, 1971. A standard textbook of Greek and Roman mythology.

Mylonas, George. *Eleusis and the Eleusinian Mysteries*. Princeton: Princeton University Press, 1961. A comprehensive survey of the knowledge about Eleusis. Contains discussion and photographs of archaeological work on the site of Eleusis as well as historical, religious, and philosophical problems.

Nietzsche, Friedrich. *The Birth of Tradegy*. Trans. Walter Kaufman. New York: The Viking Press, 1967.

Ovid. *The Metamorphoses*. Trans. Rolfe Humphries. Bloomington: Indiana University Press, 1955. The most famous retelling of the Greek myths by the first-century Roman.

Watts, Alan. *Myth and Ritual in Christianity*. London: Thames and Hudson, 1954. Watts traces many Christian rituals and feasts back to their origins in pagan and Hebrew rites.

# NOTES

# NOTES

# NOTES

# Where There Was No Path:
## Arthurian Legends and the Western Way

## UNIT STUDY PLAN

1.  Read Unit 11 in your *Study Guide*.
2.  Watch Program 11: "Where There Was No Path: Arthurian Legends and the Western Way."
3.  In your course notebook or journal, write a description of the process of migration taking place in Western Europe as Campbell describes it in the television program. What happens as different peoples mix together? Note the areas of Europe that are of central importance to the emergence of the Arthurian myths. Make a list of points that are unclear and a list of your reactions to particular points.
4.  Read the selections for this unit in the *Anthology of Readings*. These include selections from historical chronicles by the Roman Gildas, the Anglo-Saxon Nennius, and the Welshman Geoffrey of Monmouth. Also, there are two selections from Thomas Malory's romance, *King Arthur and His Knights*; and two essays by the Arthurian scholar, Roger Sherman Loomis.
5.  After reading the selections, think about the historical conditions described and comment on them in your notebook. Discuss the relationship between Campbell's presentation of this history and the depictions in the chronicles and legends. Also, comment on the overlay of the three cultures: Christianity, pagan-Germanic war ethos, and Celtic mythos.
6.  Complete assignments at the end of this unit as specified by your instructor.

## POINTS TO WATCH FOR IN THE TELEVISION PROGRAM

*This television program was delivered as a lecture by Joseph Campbell in San Fransisco, California, in 1984.*

1.  In the television program, Campbell cites as his main theme for this unit the rediscovery of individualism—"the divine power operative in your own heart"—the mythology and world view of the original European people. Notice how this mythic and religious center is destroyed or buried by successive migrations of peoples with different religions and myths.
2.  The original European myths were preserved in areas not invaded and settled by Indo-Europeans, Aryans, Romans, Germans, or Norsemen. Note where these areas are (Ireland, Cornwall, Wales, and Brittany) and note also that the basic stories for Arthurian Romance come from these same places. Campbell calls these areas "the Celtic

matrix." Notice, in the slides that Campbell uses, that there still exists evidence of Celtic and pre-Celtic myths in certain areas of Europe.
3.  Make clear to yourself Campbell's insight about the fundamental tension between the social order that is imported or imposed on people and the individual life or path that grows out of the heart. This is Campbell's criticism of Christianity, Judaism, and Islam. As religions, they are intolerant of other gods and other paths of life. You can see how serious this point is in Campbell's discussion of Tristan's reaction to the love potion.
4.  Arthur is rediscovered by the Normans, or Norsemen, who were interested in stories to tell at court. Notice how they are initially attracted to the military or warlike aspects of the stories but rather quickly become more interested in the individual careers of knights and especially in love. In the next unit, Unit 12, you will learn how the theme of love was introduced into these essentially warlike stories.
5.  The title of this unit is "Where There Was No Path: Arthurian Legends and the Western Way." Be sure that you notice how Campbell connects the concept of fulfillment of individual potential with the stories of Arthur, Parzival, Lancelot, Tristan, Gawain, and others. These are the uniquely western myths—the Western Way.

## POINTS TO LOOK FOR IN THE *ANTHOLOGY OF READINGS*

1.  The historical selection from Geoffrey of Monmouth and "Merlin" by Thomas Malory tell of essentially the same events: the parentage, birth, and early battles of Arthur. While there are differences in historical legend and romance, notice the similar desire for a king who will unite his people against their enemies and create a secure nation. Is this also the crisis in *King Arthur and His Knights*?
2.  Welsh writer, Geoffrey of Monmouth (1100–1154), exhibits in his *Historia Regum Britanniae* (History of the Kings of Britain) a great deal of pride in his Celtic origins. The whole story is an attempt to prove that the British Celts are the descendents of Brutus, grandson of Aeneas of Troy, by tracing the history of British kings from Brutus down to the present day. This book was written 70 years after the Norman conquest of England. As Campbell mentions in the television program for this unit, the Normans were deeply interested in Celtic stories and held the English (Anglo-Saxons) in great contempt. Look for the ways in which Geoffrey is promoting British or Celtic peoples.

3. Roger Sherman Loomis's two essays, "The Mabinogion" and "The Intermediaries," discuss important Welsh and Cornish folk tales that became the prototypes for many later Arthurian Romances. These essays help fill in some of the connections, alluded to by Campbell, between Celtic folk stories and the first great romance writer, Chretien de Troyes.

4. Nennius, in the *Historia Brittonum*, mentions a certain Anir. This is the Celtic form for the name Mordred, the son of Arthur, who eventually kills him (as in *The Death of Arthur*). Mordred is mentioned in almost every account of Arthur. Campbell mentions the importance of Judas and of the killer of the bull or bear in mythology. Does Mordred have a similar mythological function?

## UNIT GLOSSARY

**Amor**: French for love (also, amour).

**Aryans**: Indo-European peoples who migrated into what is now Germany and northern Europe. They split up into various tribes including the Angles, Jutes, Frisians, and Saxons.

**Bard**: Briton story teller or singer of folk tales. Generally, tales were sung with accompaniment of a harplike instrument.

**Britons**: A group of Celtic people who migrated into the British Isles. They were driven into remote areas of Wales, Scotland, and Ireland by the Anglo-Saxon invasions.

**Celts**: An Indo-European people who began migrating to central and western Europe in the tenth century B.C.E. Most Celts were assimilated by the Romans, but notably, the Britons preserved separate cultures in Cornwall, Wales, Scotland, and Ireland.

**Danes**: People from Denmark and Sweden who invaded the British Isles during the ninth and tenth centuries. They drove many Celts or Britons into Brittany in northwest France (little Britain as opposed to Great Britain).

**Druids**: An order of priests, magicians, or prophets among the Celts.

**English**: General name for the Germanic tribes, Angles, Saxons, Frisians, and Jutes, who migrated from northern Europe into the British Isles from 450 until 700. Sometimes simply referred to as Anglo-Saxons. Arthur was a Celtic war-leader against the English.

**Gothic**: Medieval romanticism, as opposed to classicism or the Romanesque in artistic and literary styles. The Gothic period is generally the twelfth and thirteenth centuries.

**Lais**: (singular lay) The Britons were well known in the Middle Ages for their wealth of myths and stories and their skill in singing tales called "lais" with the accompaniment of any sort of harplike stringed instrument.

**Merlin**: Arthur's chief counselor, reputed to have magical powers, but the legends vary greatly on the extent of his magic. He is associated with the Druids.

**Minstrals**: Wandering lyric poets and story tellers, similar to troubadours, but who flourished in northern Europe and England.

**Troubadors**: Wandering lyric poets who flourished in Provence and Aquitaine in the south of France during the eleventh and twelfth centuries. Adulterous love and chivalry were the favorite poetic themes—and often real-life preoccupations.

## UNIT PREVIEW

This unit begins a subject that will be continued and developed through Units 12 and 13. The subject is Arthurian and Courtly Romance, two themes that were to emerge suddenly, then combine in the middle of the twelfth century and remain even to this day as the central myth of Western Civilization.[1] This unit covers the legends of Arthur as warrior-king and the reemergence in the eleventh century of Celtic myth. Arthur, as you will see, is the king who, in legend, unites all of England and becomes the head of the Round Table.

Unit 12 shows how, in the writings of Chretien de Troyes, chivalry is combined with Courtly Love to present fully developed the theme latent in much of Celtic myth: the irresolvable tension between the individual and the society or group to which he or she belongs. This theme reaches its highest expression in the story of Tristan and Isolde, whose own lives and personal salvations reside in a love that is against the law. Unit 13 examines how these themes of love and chivalry are raised to a psychological and spiritual level in the Quest for the Holy Grail (remember that "psyche" is the Greek word for "soul" so that the spiritual is always also the psychological).

It is important, therefore, to think of these three last units as tightly related and forming a progression in Western Culture's understanding of the relations and tensions between individuals and their societies—and ultimately, as Campbell points out over and over again, between the individual and God. The twelfth century and Arthurian Romance, in particular, mark the moment in Western Civilization at which the individual becomes, as Campbell puts it, "the mythogenic zone"[2]—in other words, the individual heart becomes the origin of the group, the gods, and the life-giving powers of myths and the Grail.

**The Historical and Legendary Arthur**: Arthur, a battle leader mentioned briefly in Latin chronicles beginning in the sixth century, gains sudden importance in Geoffrey of Monmouth's *Historia Regum Britanniae* (1136 C.E.), *The History of the Kings of Britain*. You will see in these units that with the shift to Arthur, comes a corresponding shift in the interest of the romance writers from the obligations of the knight to fulfill the goals of his commander to the nature of the experience of the quest itself—that is, as Campbell points out in the television program, to the career and path of life of the individual knights. Unit 11 explains the prominent position of Arthur in Briton folklore and shows how his stories were transmitted to French courtly writers.

**The Cycle Romances**: We think of Arthurian Romances today as vast and interwoven narratives that include all the adventures of any knight who might belong to the Round Table.

Actually, the progression toward the compilation of a single comprehensive romance required several centuries. We will see how the inherent themes of the folk-tales implied a universal story and also how the combinations developed between 1180 and 1470, the high points certainly being the *Vulgate Cycle* in the thirteenth century and Malory's *Le Morte D'Arthur* in 1470.

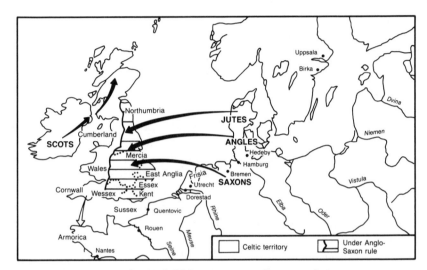

Invasions in the Mid-fifth Century to the Seventh Century

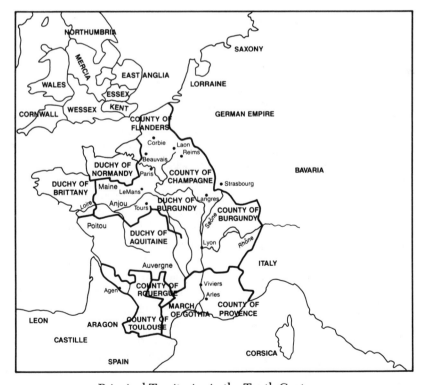

Principal Territories in the Tenth Century

## UNIT ESSAY

### The Arthur of History

Joseph Campbell believed that the rebirth of the spirit of individualism occurred with the emergence of Celtic folk tales into the dominant Anglo-Norman culture of the twelfth century. Central among these folk-tales was the story of Arthur, the "dux bellorum" or war-lord, who lead the Celtic Britons in twelve battles against the invading armies of Angles, Saxons, and Jutes from northern Europe. Equally central to the myth is the promise that Arthur will come again; he is "Rex quondam et futurus"—the once and future king. As Campbell mentions in the television program for this unit, "this is the hope of Briton." Certainly, the resurgence of tales not only of Arthur but of other Celts such as Tristan, Parzival, Gawain, Yvain, Kay, or Bedivere into the mainstream of the Christian West is nothing short of a prophecy fulfilled. We will first consider the historical accounts of Arthur and then the accounts in legend and folk tales.

Research by Arthurian scholars in recent years has shown with ever greater certainty that early references to Arthur in chronicles and histories are, indeed, based upon historical fact. He is first mentioned by Gildas in his *De Excidio et Conquestu Britanniae* written about 540, a chronicle of the slaughter of the Britons at the hands of the Angles and Saxons. The English translation of Gildas's book is The Cutting-up and Conquest of Britain. Gildas himself, as other legends tell us, was a Welshman who fled to Brittany from the marauding Saxons. It is clear that he hates the Saxons, whom he calls "hangdogs." In the earliest reports, Arthur is a pagan leader, Christianity not having been brought to England until the year 597.

All early accounts cite Arthur as the leader of the important victory over the Anglo-Saxons at Mount Badon. At this battle, according to Nennius in the *Historia Brittonum*, Arthur single-handedly killed 960 Saxons. This is the event that enshrined Arthur in the British collective memory forever (see Nennius and Gildas in the *Anthology of Readings*). The *Annals of Wales*, another early chronicle written about 950 dates the battle of Mount Badon at 518 and mentions the death of Arthur and Mordred at Camlann (possibly the original for Camelot) in the year 539. Gildas tells us only that the battle occurred in the year of his birth, which would have been around the year 500.

While Mount Badon has never been located, the story of an important battle halting the march of the Anglo-Saxons matches well with the known history of southern England. Around the year 500, the invading Anglo-Saxons are known to have penetrated southward as far as the Salisbury Plain in Berkshire and Hampshire and then stopped, not to resume fighting in the area for another half-century. And even then, the Anglo-Saxons left the Celts to relative peace and independence along the southwestern edge of England, in the principalities of Wales and Cornwall along the coast of the Irish Sea. Some Celts at this time migrated to Brittany in northwest France. We know also that the name Arthur, or in Latin, Artorius, was common enough at the time. A Welsh poem, *Gododdin*, which has been clearly dated in the year 600, seems to refer to Arthur's military prowess as if it were common knowledge. Aneirin, the author, praises a contemporary hero for his fighting prowess, but adds as an afterthought "though he was not Arthur."

### Celtic Britain

In order to understand why Arthur would assume such a central place in the folklore and national consciousness of the British, we need only think of the conditions of the Celtic Britons during the thousand years between the first Roman invasions of Claudius Caesar in the year 43 and the Norman invasion under William the Conquerer in the year 1066. Roman domination of Britain—of which a firsthand account has been preserved in Tacitus's *Agricola*, named after the Roman general who led the invasion—lasted from the year 43 until 410, when troops were recalled to protect Rome itself from southward marauding Visigoths. The partially Romanized Celts were left without political unity and totally without military organization, except for a few officers trained by the Romans (perhaps Arthur was a son of one of these). Within fifty years of the Roman departure, there were invasions by the Angles, Saxons, Jutes, and Frisians, and thus began another period of domination. This is commonly called the Anglo-Saxon period, and the English language derives from the speech of these people.

During the reign of the Saxon Egbert (802–839), the principality of Wessex attained some political sovereignty over other Anglo-Saxon principalities, and thus some stability and a cessation of war. But Egbert's successors fell victim to another wave of invading migrants. This time the migrants were the fierce Norsemen, invaders from Scandinavia, especially Denmark and Sweden. The northern Anglo-Saxon kingdoms of Mercia, Northumbria, and East Anglia were destroyed by the year 870. In the year 878, fearing his own destruction, Alfred the Great of Wessex signed a treaty with the Danes dividing Britain into two parts with "Watling Street," the road from London to Chester, marking the boundary between the kingdom of Wessex and northern England which would now be a part of Denmark. "The Danelaw," as the treaty was called, held until the early eleventh century when Norman (Norsemen who had settled in the part of France now called Normandy) pressure began to be felt. The last Anglo-Saxon king was Edward the Confessor who died in the year 1066 without leaving a son as heir. The throne of England was then disputed by two men, Harold and William, whose disputed claim was settled quickly and fatefully on the battle field at Hastings in 1066 with William emerging as victor.

The Norman invasion of England marks both the end of the Anglo-Saxon period and the beginning of the return of Celtic peoples to the center of political and social power. You will recall from the television program for this unit, that the Normans were ruthless in repressing and destroying Anglo-Saxon traditions. Anglo-Saxons were stripped of land and political power. Part of this process created an indirect opening for the reemergence of Celtic culture. It was the Normans who brought the feudal social system to England and built the first castles there, as many as three hundred in the lifetime of William the Conquerer. These great castles became social centers where the reemergence of the Celts could begin with the introduction of myths and folklore as entertainment in the feudal castles of the Normans. The Normans, moreover, had been in frequent contact with the Celts in Brittany, where many Britons spoke French and fought alongside the Normans in the invasion of 1066. As a result, some of the land taken from Anglo-Saxons was given to Britons who, quite naturally, were eager to reestablish relations with their Welsh and Cornish kinsmen and were even more eager to hear the old tales in their own castles.

It is important to remark, before turning to the folk tales themselves, upon the pent-up tribal or national energy invested in the myths of Arthur as the king who would come again to restore life to his people. Having undergone 1,000 years of subjugation and destruction by foreign rulers, we can well understand "the hope of the Britons" and the hope that lay for so long at the center of myth and folktale. For the Normans, Arthur was perhaps just a magnificent fighter who opposed the Anglo-Saxons, as they themselves did. But for the Celts, he was the one who would return to the world the spiritual energy of life. In *The Hero with a Thousand Faces*, Campbell writes, "It has always been the prime function of mythology and rite to supply the symbols that carry the human spirit forward."[3]

When you read "Merlin" by Thomas Malory in the *Anthology of Readings*, be sure to notice the depth of despair among both common people and lords after Uther Pendragon's death: "Then stood the realm in great jeopardy long while, for every lord that was mighty of men made him strong, and many weened to have been king" (393). Surely, this recalls the long years of Saxon and Danish domination and the constant battles among war-lords for territory and power. And note as well Malory's depiction of the zeal among the common people when Arthur is proclaimed king: "all the commons cried at once, 'We will have Arthur unto our king! We will put him no more in delay, for we all see that it is God's will that he shall be our king, and who that holdeth against it we will slay him" (395).

## The Legendary Arthur: Geoffrey of Monmouth's *Historia*

It was into this highly charged atmosphere that Geoffrey of Monmouth (1100–1154) released his *Historia Regum Britanniae*. Little is known of Geoffrey's life, except that he was a Welsh clerk (minor religious order) who spent most of his life in Oxford, returning to Wales in 1151 as Bishop of St. Assaph. He was probably educated at Oxford and, from his writing, seems to have been extremely wellread. His appointment as Bishop in his native Wales also suggests that he enjoyed the favor of some highly placed religious officials and perhaps even of King Henry I and later King Stephen.

That Geoffrey's purpose was to glorify the Celtic Britons is perfectly clear from his tracing of the race of Britons back to Brutus and the royal family of Troy. This was a ploy derived from the Roman Virgil who provided the same genealogical valorization for Augustus Caesar. Virgil's *Aeneid* traces the journey of Aeneas, the youngest son of Priam, from Troy to Italy where he becomes the founder of Rome. Geoffrey tells us that Brutus, the grandson of Aeneas, left Rome and settled in Albion, the legendary name of the British Isles. Brutus was the progenitor of the Britons. The name Britain is derived from Brutus. Geoffrey tells us that he is merely translating into Latin a very old book in the Briton language. While it is doubtful Geoffrey worked from a single source, it is clear that he knew of the accounts of British history recorded by Gildas, Nennius, and Bede, and he drew upon vast amounts of Welsh legends recounting the history of Arthur, Merlin, Bedivere, Kay, and numerous others who would become the heroes of Arthurian Romance. Essentially, in Geoffrey we have the first fully developed account of Arthur and his principal knights. Probably Merlin is largely a product of Geoffrey's imagination, though some few references to Merlin (Myrddin in Welsh) before Geoffrey are known, but none so well developed as we find him in the *Historia*. Geoffrey's particular interest in Merlin was also the subject of another book, *The Prophetiae Merlini*, or *The Prophesies of Merlin*, in which Geoffrey develops even more the messianic import of Arthur, the king who will come to restore the Briton people.

Geoffrey's great theme is "the hope of the Britons." He tells of past British kings—Brutus, Belinius, Brennius, and Arthur—who had reduced their enemies to vassalage and achieved true independence for the Britons. And he laments the sorry present in which Britons are subject to the rule of others. The *Historia* ends with Geoffrey's repeating Merlin's prophesy that a time will come when the Britons will again rule the island—that Arthur will come again: "God had willed that Britons should no longer reign in Britain before that time should come whereof Merlin had prophesied unto Arthur.... The voice [of an angel] told him that the people of the Britons should again possess the island by merit of their faith when the appointed time should come."[4]

Geoffrey's *History of the Kings of Britain* is Arthur's greatest promotion. Completed in about 1136, the *Historia* was translated from Latin into French by Robert Wace in 1155. Wace is important because of his connection to the royal families of France and England (the English kings were, of course, also French and French speaking at this time). Wace's *Roman de Brut*, *The Story of Brut*, (also known as the *Geste des Britons* or the *History of the Britons*) was dedicated to, and very likely presented to, the famous wife of Henry II, Eleanor of Aquitaine, mother of Marie de Champagne and patroness to both Andreas Capellanus and the first great romance writer Chretien de Troyes (both discussed in Unit 12). Wace's poem was immensely popular and influential. It survives today in eighteen complete manuscripts, an astonishing number considering that we feel fortunate to have but fragments of manuscripts for many of the more important romances. In addition to its circulation in French, Wace's *Roman* was translated around 1200 into a Middle English poem, *Brut*, by Layamon. Now the legendary history of Arthur was circulating in Latin, French, and English. Within a hundred more years, this list would include Spanish, Italian, Icelandic, Russian, and German— practically the entire European world of 1300.

It is important to note what Wace did. He introduced French nobility to the "matter of Britain"; in short, he hooked them on the stories of Arthur. Their intuitive appetite for these stories and myths is the immediate cause of the great outburst of Arthurian and Courtly Romance in the 100 years following Geoffrey and Wace. Not at all ignorant of his ploy, Wace prefaces his *Roman de Brut* thus: "I address myself to rich folk who possess revenues and silver, since for them books are made and good words are composed and well set forth."[5] And indeed they did have books made. As Chretien de Troyes tells us at the opening of his "Lancelot or the Knight of the Cart," he wrote the romance at the request of Marie de Champagne who had given him a copy of some folk tale.

Not everyone, however, was as happy about this pseudo history as were the French nobility, and Geoffrey's myth-making was clear to some. William of Newburgh, writing in 1198, commented that "disguised under the honourable name of history, thanks to his Latinity, the fables of Arthur … he took from the ancient fictions of the Britons and increased out of his own head."[6] William goes on later to say that Geoffrey made the little finger of Arthur thicker than the thighs of Alexander the Great. What is important in this sour remark is William's acknowledgment of the long and creative tradition of story telling among the Britons.

## Welsh, Briton, and Celtic Story Tellers

In this section we are going to examine briefly the traditions of popular folk tales in Wales and Cornwall on the western coast of England and in Brittany, on the northwest coast of France. As has been noted before, these are the regions into which the Celts had been driven by various invasions, and it is from these regions that the seminal stories for Arthurian romance emerge. We are interested now in the kind of stories that eventually are transmitted to the great romance writers, beginning with Chretien de Troyes and ultimately leading to the *Vulgate Cycle* and Thomas Malory. In connection with this discussion, you should consult the two essays by Roger Sherman Loomis in the *Anthology of Readings*.

The Britons were well known in the Middle Ages for their wealth of myths and stories and their skill in singing these tales called "lais" with the accompaniment of any sort of harplike stringed instrument. One of Geoffrey Chaucer's Canterbury Pilgrims tells a Briton lay and pays a compliment to these people known for their stories:

> Thise olde gentil Britouns in hir dayes
> Of diverse aventures maden layes,
> Rymeyed in her firste Briton tonge,
> Whiche layes with hir instrumentz they songe,
> Or elles redden hem for hir pleasaunce;
> And oon of hem have I in remembrance.[7]

Most storytelling in the Middle Ages was oral. Accounts as old as the Anglo-Saxon *Widsith* (*c.* 600) describe wandering gleemen, scops, minstrals, bards, or storytellers, and the pleasure and wisdom they would bring to the hearers of their tales. Chaucer's own Canterbury Pilgrims preserve this tradition as they take turns telling tales to help pass the time during their travel to Canterbury Cathedral. Unlike Chaucer's tales, however, very few of these tales were written down, and so far more stories have been lost than we now possess. One of the best collections of Welsh or Briton tales, however, survives in a compilation of eleven stories called *The Mabinogion*, a name meaning "tales of a hero's birth, infancy, and youth." In these stories and certainly in many others that are now lost, can be found the prototypes or the mythogenic narratives that are later found in a highly developed form in Arthurian romance.

Before the reemergence of Arthur, most European heroic literature dealt with heroes modeled upon Germanic fighters such as Attila or Frankish leaders such as Charlemagne and his principal fighters, most notably Roland and Oliver.[8] The theme was always, as Campbell suggests in the television program for this unit, the submission of the individual to the good of the kingdom or society. Thus, Roland and Oliver stay behind Charlemagne's main force and give up their lives blocking the path through the Pyrenees from Spain into France against the pursuing Moors. But in Celtic mythology a new theme emerges: it is the tale of the hero's birth, infancy, and growth. In short, we are now confronted with a set of myths in which the path of personal development and growth is far more important than one's usefulness to society. In fact, as we see in the case of Tristan and Isolde, one's position in society is often directly opposed to personal development and exists as a source of death for the individual life. W. P. Ker in his classic study,

*Epic and Romance*, notes that the transition in literature around the year 1100 from predominantly epic literature to predominantly romance literature was also a transition in the interests of writers from the public virtues and values of their heroes to their private lives as individuals. The public virtues of the epic heroes such as prowess in war, honor, and civic leadership are replaced by the hero's career as a lover. The new romances sought to probe the depths of the human psyche, and quite often the imposed political order represented the greatest obstacle in the path of the fulfillment of psychic potential. As Campbell mentions in the television program, this period is the birth of psychology.

Loomis's essay in the *Anthology of Readings* will give you a detailed discussion of the contents of *The Mabinogion*; here it is more important to consider the relation of the stories to the beginnings of romance proper with Chretien de Troyes. In Unit 12, Campbell discusses in detail each of Chretien's five romances, and so this discussion sets a context for the next unit. Almost all of the major characters in Chretien's romances appear also in their own stories in *The Mabinogion*. "Peredur" is Perceval. "Gereint and Enid" is Chretien's story "Erec and Enid." "Owein or the Countess of the Fountain" is Chretien's story of Yvain who has to choose between his love for the lady of the fountain and his loyalty to Arthur. While all information about exactly how Chretien came into possession of these tales is hopelessly lost, we can surmise that the stories, all Welsh and set in Wales, made their way from Wales into Brittany sometime in the eleventh century, and from there to southern France where the lively Provençal culture picked them up (see the discussion of Provence in Unit 12 of the *Study Guide*).

Chretien was a court poet in the employ of Marie de Champagne, daughter of the famous Eleanor of Aquitaine. Eleanor, as Campbell points out, was the granddaughter of William of Poitiers, himself a troubador from the Provence region of southern France. William's court, like Eleanor's to follow, was a very popular place for wandering minstrals and bards. Their stories were always welcome to a family with eager ears and hearts for legends. It is not at all unlikely that these stories and many others were commonly known in the family of Eleanor and thus given for rewriting and development to Chretien. On several occasions Chretien credits Marie or the Count of Flanders with giving him the stories that he merely turned into poetry.

Chretien adds a great deal of courtly overlay to the stories. To be sure, the stories had undergone many revisions by other bards in the oral tradition before Chretien received them, but he is responsible for adding the themes of courtly love. This subject will be discussed in Unit 12 in connection with *Tristan and Isolde*; here we must return for one further point with regard to the new thematic interest of Welsh folk tales. The figure of Arthur is present throughout the stories of *The Mabinogion*, as he is in Chretien's versions, but he is in the background. He is the established and powerful king, already married to Gwenhwyvar (Guinevere) and settled in his role of patriarch and gravitational center for younger knights. In the foreground of any story is a particular knight and his strange and often mysterious quest to fulfill himself as in individual. This interest in the individual path, as we shall see more fully in Units 12 and 13, becomes the central theme of Arthurian Romance and, as Campbell makes clear in the television program for this unit, is the unique, western way.

## The Vulgate Cycle and Thomas Malory

With Arthur's position as gravitational center, the separate stories concerning the quest for the Holy Grail, Tristan, Lancelot, Galahad, Parzival, and many more gradually came to be subsumed into a vast master-romance with Arthur and the Round Table serving as an architectonic social structure against which the careers of individual knights might be reflected. This is first manifest in Chretien de Troyes's combination of the codes of Courtly Love with the codes of Chivalry. A knight had to be both a fighter and a lover. The first great combination of separate romances is the *Vulgate Cycle* (c. 1230), which brings together the legends of Merlin, Lancelot, the Grail Quest, and the Death of Arthur into a single romance of some 1,200 manuscript folios.

This encompassing spirit ends with Malory's insertion of even the Tristan material into the stories of Arthur, Lancelot and the Grail. Malory is quite aware of what he has done. He ends *Le Morte D'Arthur* this way: "Here is the end of the whole book of King Arthur and of his noble knights of the Round Table, that when they were whole together there was ever an hundred and forty."[9] Furthermore, as Malory tells us at one point in his Grail Quest, "Merlin made the Round Table in tokening of the roundness of the world, for all men should by the Round Table understand the roundness signified by right. For all the world, Christian and heathen, repaireth unto the Round Table, and when they are chosen to be of that fellowship they think themselves more blessed and more in worship than if they had gotten half of the world."[10] Malory's comment here is a translation from the French *Queste del Saint Graal*, but it suggests very clearly that the stories of Arthurian Romance are world constructing myths. The Round Table is the world in which all of mankind is called to live. How well or how poorly one lives in that world is the quest and the challenge of life.

## ASSIGNMENTS FOR STUDY AND ANALYSIS

1. Discuss the "hope of the Britons" as a dream or myth of other oppressed people you know about from other historical periods. Some examples might be the Hebrews or African people living in the United States.
2. Recall Campbell's discussion of Judas in the television program for this unit and give your interpretation of the role of Mordred in Malory's "The Day of Destiny" a selection in the *Anthology of Readings*.
3. Write out your analysis of the way stories are modified as they are passed from one person to another. You might think of some examples you know from your personal experience. Apply the principles you observe to the ways in which Briton stories filtered into the courtly culture of France.
4. Think about the role of heroes in society. You may have read Campbell's *Hero with a Thousand Faces*, but if not, use your experience with film and contemporary legend. Comment on the attitudes of Nennius, Gildas, and Geoffrey toward Arthur.
5. Having watched the television program and read the selections in the *Anthology of Readings* for this unit, what do you think of Campbell's assertion that what is unique about western culture is the role of the individual in society? Discuss how this theme is present in these readings in ways that it is not present in other readings for earlier units in this course.
6. Describe in your own words the migrations of different people during the period Campbell discusses in the television program. What are some of the things that happen as different cultural groups mix together? What problems can this process cause?

## FURTHER ASSIGNMENTS FOR WRITING AND REFLECTION

1. Joseph Campbell says in the television program that individualism is uniquely the western myth. You recall that the Grail knights each entered the forest on their own paths. And yet we also know that nationalism or extreme patriotism is a dominant feature of modern western society. Discuss the ways in which these two poles, the individual and the group, exist side by side. Do you see them together in the early Briton myths and the histories of Arthur?
2. Merlin is a character who has fascinated readers and moviegoers in our own times. But his role in the original legends is much more ambiguous than that often depicted in modern popular accounts. Look at how he is represented by Malory and Geoffrey, and then think about Campbell's remarks about him in the television program. Write an essay analyzing Merlin's role in the readings which accompany this unit.

3. In this unit, a reference was made to W. P. Ker's *Epic and Romance* which makes the point about a fundamental shift in literary themes from the presentation of public virtues to the examination of private thoughts and feelings. Read the essay on *The Mabinogion* by Loomis and write your thoughts on the foundations of this shift. You will see it developed much more fully in the next two units, but for now reflect on this change as a possible reason for the sudden interest in Celtic myths in the twelfth century. Why were they no longer interested in the tales of Charlemagne? What did they see in stories like those of *The Mabinogion*?
4. In the television program for this unit, Campbell suggests that the intolerance of Christianity is the cause of the Dark Ages. Consult the readings for this unit and develop your own ideas based on the reading of what early British writers thought of Christianity.
5. Consider the extent to which the themes of the legends (such as the hope of the Britons) has contributed to the shaping of British history in the post medieval world. Tatlock's *Legendary History of Britain*, listed in the Unit Bibliography, is a good place to start.
6. Compare the portraits of Arthur in Gildas (*c*. 640), in Nennius (*c*. 800), and in Geoffrey (1136). Do you see an evolution in the understanding of his character? What are his characteristics that attract each writer? J. D. Bruce in *The Evolution of Arthurian Romance*, argues that an evolutionary process in the development of the characters can be seen. Write your analysis of the growth in Arthur's character.

## ENDNOTES

[1]Denis de Rougement, *Love in the Western World* (Princeton: Princeton University Press, 1940) 15–22.

[2]Joseph Campbell, *The Masks of God: Creative Mythology* (New York: Viking Press, 1980) 677.

[3]Joseph Campbell, *The Hero with a Thousand Faces* (Princeton: Princeton University Press, 1949) 11.

[4]Richard L. Brengle ed., *Arthur, King of Britain: History, Chronicle, Romance, and Criticism* (New York: Appleton-Century-Crofts, 1964) 262.

[5]Charles Foulon, "Wace" *Arthurian Literature in the Middle Ages* Ed. R. S. Loomis (Oxford: The Clarendon Press, 1959) 94.

[6]John J. Parry and Robert A. Caldwell, *Geoffrey of Monmouth* (Oxford: The Clarendon Press, 1959) 65.

[7]Geoffrey Chaucer, "The Franklin's Tale" *Chaucer's Major Poetry* Ed. A. C. Gaugh (Englewood Cliffs, New Jersey: Prentice Hall, 1963) 470.

[8]*The Song of Roland* Trans. Patricia Terry. (Indianapolis: Bobbs-Merrill, 1965).

[9]Thomas Malory, *Works* Ed. Eugene Vinarer. (London: Oxford University Press, 1984) 726.

[10]Malory 541.

# UNIT BIBLIOGRAPHY

Ashe, Geoffrey. *The Discovery of King Arthur*. New York: Doubleday, 1985. Ashe is a world renown authority in historical and geographical research on the Arthurian legends.

Brengle, Richard L. Ed. *Arthur, King of Britain: History, Chronicle, Romance, and Criticism*. New York: Appleton-Century-Crofts, 1964. Includes selections from the principal works that refer to Arthur from the very earliest through Malory. The section of critical essays provides valuable background.

Bruce, J. D. *The Evolution of Arthurian Romance: From the Beginnings down to the Year 1300*. 2 vols. Gloucester, MA: Peter Smith, 1958. A standard history of romance. This is the study Campbell cites most often in his books.

Gantz, Jeffrey. Trans. *The Mabinogion*. Harmondsworth, UK: Penguin Books, 1976. A collection of eleven Welsh folk tales which feature many of the heroes and events that later on figure prominently Arthurian Romance. The word Mab inogion means, the birth, youth, and development of a hero.

Geoffrey of Monmouth. *History of the Kings of Britain*. Trans. Sebastian Evans. New York: E. P. Dutton and Co., 1958. Complete edition of Geoffrey's *Historia*.

Ker, W. P. *Epic and Romance*. New York: Dover, 1957. A classic study on the transition from heroic literature of the Dark Ages to the courtly romance of the High Middle Ages.

Loomis, Roger Sherman. Ed. *Arthurian Literature in the Middle Ages: A Collaborative History*. Oxford: The Clarendon Press, 1959. The standard scholarly history of Arthurian Romance.

Loomis, Roger Sherman. *The Development of Arthurian Romance*. New York: W. W. Norton, 1963. A brief but comprehensive history of Arthurian romance by one of the subject's preeminent scholars.

Malory, Thomas. *Works*. Ed. Eugene Vinaver. London: Oxford University Press, 1984. This is the standard edition of the Winchester Manuscript of Malory's King Arthur and His Knights, a name attached to the romance by William Caxton when he published it in 1485.

Rumble, Thomas C. Ed. *The Briton Lays in Middle English*. Detroit: Wayne State University Press, 1965. A collection of eight Briton lays with a valuable introduction.

Tacitus. *The Agricola and the Germania*. Trans. H. Mattingly. Harmondsworth, UK: Penguin Books, 1948. A first-century account of the Roman conquest and occupation of Britain and Germany. Agricola was the general in charge of Britain. This book provides information on life-styles of the early Celts.

Tatlock. J. S. P. *The Legendary History of Britain*. Berkeley: University of California Press, 1950. A comprehensive and scholarly history of early Britain.

# NOTES

# NOTES

# NOTES

# A Noble Heart:
## The Courtly Love of Tristan and Isolde

## UNIT STUDY PLAN

1. Read Unit 12 in your *Study Guide*.
2. Watch Program 12: "A Noble Heart: The Courtly Love of Tristan and Isolde."
3. In your course notebook or journal, write a summary of the common theme Campbell finds in the five poems by Chretien de Troyes and in the *Tristan* of Gottfried von Strassburg. Discuss the way in which this theme comprises a definition of courtly love. As soon as you have finished watching the program, make a list of points that may be unclear. List also your reactions to the stories Campbell tells and the interpretations he gives.
4. Read the selections for this unit in the *Anthology of Readings*. These include selections from Andreas Capellanus's *The Art of Courtly Love* and two romances: "The Knight of the Cart" and selections from *Tristan*.
5. After reading the selections, comment on what you have read in your notebook. Discuss the connections between Campbell's insights and the stories you read. Reflect upon the differences or similarities between conditions of love and marriage in the twelfth century and right now in the twentieth century.
6. Complete the assignments at the end of the unit, as specified by your instructor.

## POINTS TO WATCH FOR IN THE TELEVISION PROGRAM

*This television program was delivered as a lecture by Joseph Campbell in San Francisco, California, in 1984.*

1. Pay careful attention to the psychological definition of love that Campbell develops.
2. Note that the name of Eleanor of Aquitaine's daughter is Marie de Champagne. She is the very important patroness of both Chretien de Troyes and Andreas Capellanus.
3. Chretien's best story according to Campbell is the "Lancelot." Note especially his interpretation of the Sword Bridge.
4. Wounds are frequently symbolic in romance. In Campbell's retelling of the stories, note how and where people are wounded. This is a theme which will become even more important in Unit 13 in connection with the maimed Fisher King and the Quest for the Grail.

5. The love potion that Tristan and Isolde drink will also be their death. Campbell spoke about this early in the television program for Unit 11 and for this unit. Refer to your notes to refresh your memory about the love-death theme in the television program for Unit 11.
6. Be sure you understand the tension of honor against love and love against marriage. Recall that Campbell is not talking about lust but something entirely different. Look for the definition of love that emerges in Campbell's retelling of the stories.

## POINTS TO LOOK FOR IN THE ANTHOLOGY OF READINGS

1. Gottfried sees the world as a paradox. He writes of the love-death. Love is always called a death. Notice that when Tristan is conceived, Blancheflor, his mother, takes away from the bed her own death: "death she received with the child." But love is also life. Try to resolve this paradox in your own mind. *Tristan* ends tragically because Gottfried could conceive of no resolution, but Parzival ends happily largely because Wolfram can. Keep this point in mind when you come to Unit 13.
2. In the *Art of Courtly Love*, Andreas says some very puzzling things about love: it has nothing to do with marriage, it is a sickness, and it makes a person chaste. What is the context for this? Think about the religious and social contexts mentioned by Campbell and in the readings for this unit, and see if you can come to an understanding of what Andreas is talking about.
3. Notice in all the readings the importance of the eyes, or of seeing one's beloved. The eyes are the pathways to the heart. This is also important in the context of medieval Christianity which condemned the senses as false means for learning the truth about one's self and the world.

## UNIT GLOSSARY

**Charity:** The virtuous form of human love, according to the tradition of Christian doctrine beginning with St. Augustine. Charity is the love of others or anything of the world for the sake of God.

**Cupidity:** The form of love opposite to charity; that is, love of another or anything of the world (even one's self) for its own sake, or at least any sake other than God's. Lust or the enjoyment of something for its own sake.

**Courtly Love:**  The general name for the cult of passionate and adulterous love that began in the eleventh century in southern France. Courtly love became assimilated with Arthurian Romance in the works of Chretien, but flourished in the non-Arthurian romances of Dante or Petrarch. Courtly love remains the intensely passionate romantic love of much contemporary literature and film.

**Eros:**  Not to be confused with lust or cupidity. Eros is passionate energy which is expended in the quest to fulfill oneself as an individual. Christian doctrines about human love for God are often erotic, deriving ultimately from Plato's ideas about divine eros or enthusiasm in his *Symposium*.

**Langue D'oc:** The name of the language of southern France. So-called because the word for "yes" is "oc" and not the "oui" ("oil" in old French spelling) of northern France.

**Transcendence:**  Literally "to pass beyond or above." The ability to rise above life negating conditions of social identification to mythic association.

**Transgression:** Literally "to step across." The act of breaking laws or rules, in medieval Christian terms transgression is sin, but in courtly love it refers to breaking laws of marriage and becomes, in this way, a great virtue.

## UNIT PREVIEW

This unit introduces you to the principal themes of the great romance writers Chretien de Troyes and Gottfried von Strassburg. You will learn about the emergence of the movement called courtly love and how this practice of love came to be joined with the military careers of the great knights of Arthurian Romance.

**Chretien De Troyes—Courtly Love and Heresy:** In the television program, Campbell discusses five of Chretien's romances. It is worthwhile to consider "The Knight of the Cart" in a closer connection with Roman Catholic doctrine since much of the archetype upon which the romance is built specifically invokes religious themes, but the romance itself violates those themes. At the final trial of Guinevere, God is invoked to judge the battle, but the conclusions is Lancelot's truth, not God's.

**The Legend of Tristan and Isolde:** This story, by all accounts, is the great love story of the Western World. The love here is passionate, erotic, and transgressive. It is a love story that is a tragedy, like the more familiar *Romeo and Juliet*. The lovers are destroyed in the end, but in their destruction we are able to identify the social forces that their love challenged.

## UNIT ESSAY

### Eleanor of Aquitaine and the Culture of Provence

Under the leadership of Eleanor of Aquitaine (1122–1204), the idea of the "lady" was born in the south of France in the second half of the twelfth century. As Campbell mentions in the television program for this unit, Eleanor was the daughter of William of Poitiers, an early troubador, and before her long life ended she had been the wife of the two most powerful kings in Europe and the mother of two more. But even more important than that, Eleanor supervised a cultural revolution that C. S. Lewis in the *Allegory of Love* has called one of the three or four fundamental shifts in human sentiment of all human history. By changes in human sentiment, Lewis means the great shifts in the way humans understand themselves and their purposes on earth. These shifts are associated in the west with Socrates, Jesus, courtly love, and the rise of science. One historian puts it this way:

> Europe's conversion to the courtly way of life, the birth of the roman courtois and the flowering of Troubador poetry were all intimately connected with Eleanor and the rise of the Angevin Empire.... The day when monks and clerks were the custodians of a man's soul was past; a man's hope of felicity now lay in the hands of his *dompna* (Provencal for *domina*), his lady. With the lady as mentor, the two together could build up the inner kingdom of courtly love outside the bonds of wedlock.[1]

You might want to remember when studying Unit 13 and the Parzival legends, that Parzival comes from Anjou or the Angevin empire, and he seeks in his quest just the sort of inner kingdom that the historian Heer attributes to Eleanor. As important as the Briton legends, the south of France contributed to this rebirth or renaissance of the twelfth century, the intense interest in adulterous love, and a flair for heresy and nonconformism. The area south of the Loire River extending to the Pyrenees Mountains is sometimes called the "langue d'oc" because the dialect of French spoken there differed greatly from the French spoken in the north, the "langue d'oil." The names derive from the different pronunciations of the French word for "yes": in the south "oc" and in the north "oil," now spelled "oui." The langue d'oil was the language of Paris and as the political and economic center of France in the late Middle Ages, the langue d'oil won out over the langue d'oc. The southern area is also known as Provence. It was an area in which the deep pagan roots of the people had not been fully supplanted by Christianity.

It was in the cultural center of Provence that Eleanor's grandfather, William of Poitiers, began to sing love songs about women in terms and with an emotional fervor that had previously been used only for man's love for God. After the breakup of her first marriage to Louis VII, in 1152, Eleanor settled in Angers, the chief town of Anjou, and for the first time was able to organize her court after her own tastes. Her court became a safe haven for troubadors such as the famous Bernard de Ventadour, whose over-ardent wooing of the wife of the count of Ventadour nearly cost him his life. Bernard then fell to writing love poems for Eleanor, saying that Tristan and Isolde never suffered for love as much as he did.

Later on around 1170, Eleanor moved to Poitiers, and her following of troubador poets increased to what can be called a school whose influence spread eventually to Italy, England, northern France, Spain, and eastern Europe. The "chanson d'amour" or the "love songs" followed a fairly set pattern. The subject was love itself; the lady was represented by a symbol such as a rose in the famous *Romance of the Rose* by Guillaume de Lorris. She was typically married to a man of social rank higher than the poet-lover. Her reputation was of great concern and stood as an obstacle to the affair. In the hopeless situation of separation, the poet rehearsed the full range of emotional outpourings, eulogy, grief, hope, despair. You will recall from the television program for this unit Campbell's emphasis on the heart. In these poems—coexisting in a world of constant warfare from the crusades to baronial skirmishes—the ideal conception of the gentle heart is born.

## Love and Heresy

In this same area of southern France flourished also a heresy known as Catharism. While very little is known about the Cathars, for reasons that will be clear in a moment, it seems that their religious practices centered around a single sacrament, the "consolamentum" or the consolation for the suffering of this life. Candidates for the religion had to undergo at least a year of fasting, testing, and penance before receiving the sacrament, the laying on of the hands by one of the "perfect." Legends have it that the sacraments were performed by women, thus women hold both the quality of being "perfect" and the consolation. More legends still suggest that troubador love poetry was a secret expression of longing and ritualistic preparation for the consolamentum. Love might well have been a code word for the sacrament of the Cathars which replaced the Mass and all other Catholic sacraments.

On the surface, the similarities seem convincing since the love poetry did, in fact, elevate women to a godlike status, and both the lover and sacramental candidate were expected to put themselves through all manner of tests and sufferings before being accepted by the lady or into the "Church of the Pure." In the television program for this unit, Campbell describes some of the trials, tests, and sufferings a knight might have to endure before receiving "merci" from his lady. Here is a stanza of Bernard de Ventadour's "The Joy of Being in Love":

It is no marvel, that I should sing

Better than any other singer;

For my heart more draws me toward Love,

And I am likelier made to her command.

Heart and body, wisdom and wits,

Strength and power, have I wagered:

The bridle so draws me toward Love

That I attend to nothing else.[2]

We might suppose that Bernard could just as well be secretly or allegorically describing a religious process of self-purification in anticipation of the sacrament of consolation.

Unfortunately, however, we are not likely ever to solve the riddle of Catharism, for its practices spread so rapidly from Provence to adjacent parts of France that the Catholic church began a series of crusades against the Cathars in 1171. The Dominican Order was largely responsible for refuting Catharism through a series of debates, trials, and refutations. In 1205, Pope Innocent III declaring that "actions rank higher than words" gave the order to "exterminate" the heretics. The so-called Albigensian wars lasted until about 1229 with the result that the culture of the south established by Eleanor was all but destroyed. The extermination was especially savage against women who were regarded as free spirits and evil. All writings of the Cathars and much love poetry was burned. Some reports hold that as many as sixty-thousand Cathars were put to death. Eleanor herself had died in 1204, but fortunately for Western civilization, the romantic spirit of Provence had long been exported and assimilated into the heroic Arthurian poetry by Chretien, the court poet of Eleanor's daughter Marie.

## Poetry, Love, and Philosophy

It is difficult to make much of a philosophy out of troubador love poetry, but in the hands of two more systematic writers of the same period, we are able to see the final direction that troubador innovations would take. The first is Peter Abelard, the great and revolutionary philosopher, and what he discovered in the course of his love affair with Heloise. The second is the first philosopher of love, Andreas Capellanus, connected closely to Eleanor's court as the personal chaplain to Marie.

Peter Abelard was one of those volatile and competitive personalities that seems bound to change the course of history. In his autobiography, *Historia Calamitatum* (best translated as The History of My Misfortunes), Abelard describes his ascent from the humble origins of a middle-class family in Brittany to a position of the most powerful professor at the University of Paris. His skill in teaching and argument made him the enemy of almost every established scholar of theology and philosophy at the time. He was just too young and too daring in his methods, and he seemed to lack the proper deference for his superiors and elders.

While in Paris, in about the year 1116, in his mid-thirties, Abelard fell in love with another of the truly remarkable women of the Middle Ages, Heloise, the seventeen-year-old niece of Fulbert, from whom Abelard had rented rooms. Their affair was to change the face of history and is certainly as famous as the love of Tristan and Isolde or even Shakespeare's Romeo and Juliet. Campbell mentions in the television program for this unit that Abelard and Heloise served as a model for the Tristan and Isolde story. When Heloise became pregnant, the two refused to marry on the grounds that marriage was little more than a degrading form of slavery. In their letters, written during their forced separation of the next thirty years, Heloise explains her preference for the name of "mistress" since that would connote a love freely given. The two would be bound only by "gratia"—love given without contract or compulsion. The concept of "gratia" or free-love as opposed to the contractually binding love of marriage they derived from Cicero's treatise on friendship, *De Amicitia*. In her letters, Heloise, even after thirty years of isolation, affirms her preference for "love to wedlock and freedom to chains."

At this time, however, Abelard's enemies and rivals were many and they used this opportunity to inflame the anger of Fulbert and destroy Abelard. At first they claimed a marriage would satisfy them and save Abelard and Heloise from further persecution and even possibly a condemnation to death. After much effort, Abelard persuaded Heloise to accept a marriage. Heloise saw from the beginning, as Abelard did not, that a marriage would not appease the anger of Fulbert and Abelard's enemies. Shortly after a private wedding ceremony, Abelard was attacked by his enemies and castrated. Eventually Heloise, against her will, joined a convent of nuns and was prevented from seeing Abelard for most of the rest of their lives. What survives of the affair is a series of letters written over the course of thirty years. They are one of the most remarkable records of long suffering and strong wills that we have.[3]

What the letters show is that neither Abelard nor Heloise will renounce their love, their sin as they are now forced to call it. Here are Heloise's words on the subject written some twenty years after their forced separation:

> How can it be called repentance for sins, however great the mortification of the flesh, if the mind still retains the will to sin and is on fire with its old desires. It is easy enough to anyone to confess his sins, to accuse himself, or even to mortify his body in an outward show of penance, but it is very difficult to tear the heart away from hankering after its dearest pleasures.... In my case the pleasures of loves which we shared have been too sweet—they can never displease me, and can scarcely be banished from my thoughts. Wherever I turn they are always before my eyes, bringing with them awakened longings and fantasies which will not even let me sleep.[4]

All of this had a profound effect on Abelard's thought and writings. He was universally hated by other philosophers, especially the Dominican St. Bernard of Clairvaux who succeeded finally in the year 1140 at the Council of Sens in having Abelard's work condemned as heretical. (It is interesting to note that Bernard was also instrumental in the divorce of Eleanor and Louis VII. For Bernard this was a convenient way of getting of Eleanor out of the seat of power in France.) Abelard's treatise on ethics, titled *Scito te ispum*, which means Know Yourself, certainly presented a problem for Catholic theology. Abelard was the first to argue for an ethics of pure intention; that is, actions must be judged good or bad solely on the spirit or on the intentions in which they are preformed. No act can be good or bad in itself. In a letter to Abelard, Heloise reflects on Abelardian ethics in her judgment of herself: "Wholly guilty though I am, I am also, as you know, wholly innocent. It is not the deed but the intention of the doer which makes the crime, and justice should weigh not what was done but the spirit in which it is done."[5]

Campbell makes a point similar to this with regard to the love potion Tristan and Isolde drink. In the television program for this unit, he poses the theological problem: if the magic of the potion takes intention away, can there be sin? It is not a far leap in reasoning to turn this proposition around and say that if the intention is love, and not lust, can there be sin? Here in the story of Abelard and Heloise, as Campbell says, the new spirit of love or the psychology of love and the shift to the woman as the guiding force in men's lives is found. This is a love that is intensely personal, and in that sense it is also a human psychology. Love becomes the revelation and the means of fulfillment of the heart or of the whole person. This is what is important in the stories of Tristan and Parzival.

In his letters, Abelard reverses the traditional medieval male-female hierarchy that had assigned all women to an inferior status associated with irrationality and Eve as the temptress. He paraphrases a typical medieval formula that held that a woman's head is man, man's head is God. Abelard told his fellow monks, knights, and clergymen—obsessed with power, war, violence, honor here on earth and in Heaven, and finally truth according to reason—that woman was a higher form of humanity. She possessed a refined spirit and soul and was thus capable of conversing with God in the inner kingdom of the heart on terms of intimate friendship. Abelard stressed the point that Christ's women disciples stood closer to him than his male disciples and that the most favored human was Mary, the mother of God. Campbell suggests that the final meaning of troubador love poetry is precisely this: the discovery of the divine in another person. Certainly Abelard and Heloise were the pioneers in that discovery.

## Andreas Capellanus and the Courts of Love

About the year 1170, Eleanor moved her household to Poitiers and there her court became, as one historian has put it, "the academy of Western Europe for teaching the arts of courtesy."[6] Eleanor and her daughter Marie began the practice known as "the courts of love." Lovers from all over Europe would bring their troubles in love to the court for a ruling by the queen or some of her ladies. The great teacher in Eleanor's academy was Andreas Capellanus, or Andrew the Chaplain, whose *Art of Courtly Love* would set down in clear rules and exemplary cases the process of molding passion under the direction of a man's mistress. Andreas addresses his book to a certain Walter whom he calls "a new recruit of Love." The book itself is a sort of manual of etiquette for the proper pursuit of an adulterous relationship. In a sense, Andreas establishes a set of laws parallel and opposite to the Church's laws regarding love and marriage. This is a counter-cultural project. It is very clear from the thirty-one "rules for love" Andreas lists at the end of the treatise, that he has in mind a love that is against marriage (see *The Art of Courtly Love* in the *Anthology of Readings*). Rule One states, "Marriage is no real excuse for not loving" (448)—that is, a woman cannot give the excuse that she is married to put off the advances of a lover. This is the principle Campbell refers to in the television program in this unit.

Andreas was interested in a different kind of love than was possible in the typical medieval marriage. The sections of *The Art of Courtly Love* which have been reprinted in the *Anthology of Readings* contain a case presented before the Queen and her court that concerns the differences between married love and unmarried love. This is an important case because the lady's answer is that "Marital affection and the true love of lovers are wholly different and arise from entirely different sources" (447). The Latin title of Andreas's work is *Del Arte Honeste Amandi* which means the "art of honest or honorable love." But what is this true love? Andreas calls it "a certain inborn suffering derived from the sight of and the excessive meditation upon the beauty of the opposite sex, which causes each one to wish above all things the embraces of the other and by common desire to carry out all of love's precepts" (*Anthology* 444). What is being defined is Eros, something almost unknown in the philosophies of love in the Christian Middle Ages. The Christian tradition from St. Augustine had taught that humans are capable of two kinds of love: charity and cupidity. He described both of these as "motions of the soul." Charity is a motion of the soul toward God, while cupidity is a motion of the soul toward one's self or any other created thing. Cupidity is, of course, the root of all sin; his Latin phrase is "radix malorum est cupiditas." Charity, on the other hand, means that one should only love another person or anything in the world for the sake of God, never for its own sake.[7]

Eros is a very important concept and should never be confused with the popular and journalistic use of the word "erotic" in our own times to describe pornography or merely sexually explicit materials. Eros is Sigmund Freud's concept of libido or Carl Jung's psychic energy—for both, eros is the energy of the body required to confront and adjust to the external world and therefore to maintain some happiness. In this sense it is the energy required to create oneself every day. In *The Masks of God: Creative Mythology*, Campbell calls eros "the passion for life" and a little later "the affirmation of an individual, regardless of worth."[8] The best way to understand eros, however, is to look back to Plato who, in a dialogue called

*The Symposium*, recounts the story of the creation and fall of man as the story of the origin of eros.

*The Symposium* is Plato's dialogue on love. At the house of Alcibiades, the famous hero of the Peloponnesian War, Socrates and a few others gather to discuss love. Each takes a turn telling a myth and explaining what love is. Aristophanes tells the story of the golden age when there were no men or women, but rather androgenous beings in whom the sexes were not divided. These beings had two heads, four arms, four legs, and the sexual organs of both male and female. They were round in shape and very fast and strong. They were so happy and so much fulfilled within themselves that they had little interest in worshipping or listening to the words of the gods. After a while the gods became jealous of their creation. They believed that the humans had grown too powerful and might attack the heavens. After much counsel and concern, Zeus devised a plan whereby each human was cut in two, down the middle, and ever after the halves lived in great anxiety looking for their missing other halves.

For Aristophanes, the fall of mankind is a psychic fragmentation; Campbell's term for this would be "mythic dissociation" or the loss of the sense of godliness and autonomy of each individual. Beings that were once complete in themselves now needed the company of another in order to feel complete. The priests, of course, always offered religion (literally *re + ligare*: to bind back) to bind people back to their origin in god. But the myth makes it perfectly clear that human wholeness originated in human beings themselves. When one half finds its other, Aristophanes tells us, it would cling to it in memory of an earlier condition and, in that way, recover an earlier state of psychic wholeness and happiness. This conception of eros is what Campbell means when he remarks in the television program for this unit that sex is a sacrament.

Aristophanes's explanation of the origin of love in psychic fragmentation and sex is something with which the medieval world was not prepared to deal. If we think of Andreas's comment about the two different sources for married love and for honest or true love, it should now be clear that true love, the love of Tristan and Isolde, arises from the psychic urge to complete oneself as an autonomous individual by recognizing and affirming the self in another; that is to say, the divine in another. Abelard tried to tell the monks of Europe that he saw this in women. But married love in the Middle Ages was largely an economic relationship and a strategy for preventing sin. Sex was regarded by the church as sinful in all cases, but less sinful in marriage than outside of marriage. Only when sex resulted in the birth of a child could it be excused, but even then only on the frank recognition that the birth of a child meant one more virgin in the world. Two of the most important fathers of the Church, St. Paul and Origen, castrated themselves so they would never be tempted to have anything to do with sex and women. The whole of Church ideology was a vast process of repression of eros; that is, of fracturing and denying self-fulfillment in order to make people more dependent upon God and the rituals of the Roman Church as the sole source of psychic fulfillment. In this sense, the Church is similar to Aristophanes' depiction of Zeus who thought that by destroying eros he might make humans devote more of their time and attention to the gods. In *The Flight of the Wild Gander*, Campbell has described this process as "mythic dissociation":

> God in this system is a kind of fact somewhere, an actual personality to whom prayers can be addressed with the expectation of a result. He is apart from and different from the world: in no sense *identical* with it, but *related* to it, as cause to effect. I call this kind of thinking 'mythic dissociation.' The sense of an experience of the sacred is dissociated from life, from nature, from the world, and transferred somewhere else—an imagined somewhere else—while man, mere man, is accursed. . . . The sacred is not now the secular.[9]

As Freud and Jung have taught us, however, the repressed returns. What we witness in the rebirth of love in the twelfth century is the return of repressed eros, the energy and desire to make oneself whole, both psychologically and spiritually, and the frank recognition that the power to do this does not lie with God, but resides within another human being. One redeems oneself by loving another. This is not at all the self-sacrificing kind of love advocated by medieval moralists, but an erotic and passionate seizing the world and remaking it after one's own image. Eros is the desire to create oneself, no longer to renounce the self.

## Lancelot

With good reason, Campbell in the television program for this unit calls "The Knight of the Cart," sometimes simply called "Lancelot," Chretien's finest romance. It is a romance remarkably rich in layers of signification. The version reprinted in the *Anthology of Readings* is Malory's fifteenth century rewriting of a thirteenth century prose rewriting of Chretien's twelfth-century poem. It is very likely that there were even more intermediary rewritings between Chretien and Malory, but Malory's presents you with all the essentials of the romance.

Chretien based his story on the apocryphal gospel of Nicodemus, the story of Christ's descent into hell, battle with the demons, and rescue of the people confined there since the fall of Adam. The archetype here invoked by Chretien is the redemption of mankind, the monomyth of the hero who unlocks the gates of death and returns the flow of life into the body of the world (see Campbell's *Hero with a Thousand Faces*, Chapter 1 and the discussion of the *Hymn to Demeter* in Unit 10). On numerous occasions, Lancelot is identified as a type of Christ: "Sir this is the man who will deliver us all from exile and the dire misfortune in which we've languished for a long time; and we should do him great honour when, to free us from

imprisonment, he has come through so many perilous places and will pass through many more."[10]

The first of these perilous adventures is the cart that Lancelot mounts in order to rescue Guinevere and all the people being held captive in the land of Gorre—"the kingdom from which no stranger returns, but is forced to stay in that land in servitude and exile."[11] Mounting the cart symbolizes the humiliation and crucifixion of Christ, something Christ had to willingly submit to in order to accomplish his redemption. Chretien says that at that time there was only one cart such as this one, and it was used to carry all those who had committed any crime to the place of punishment. Symbolically, when he mounts the cart, Lancelot takes on himself the sins of the world. In order to arrive in Gorre, Lancelot must cross the Sword Bridge, a single razor's edge spanning the chasm between life and death. Once across, Chretien remarks that Lancelot has now received five wounds in his quest: in his hands and feet from crossing the bridge and in his side from the sword of the Perilous Bed. It is with these five wounds, the wounds of Christ, that Lancelot arrives in Gorre to confront Meleagant, the captor of Guinevere and the king of the land where people are held in exile and servitude.

Campbell's interpretation of the Sword Bridge shows precisely where Chretien deviates from the doctrinal portrayal of Christ, though not from the mythic archetype of Christ's redemption. "Any trip," Campbell says in the television program for this unit, "along your own path is a razor's edge. It really is, nobody's done it before."

The scene of Lancelot's reunion with Guinevere, their night together, and the blood smeared bed is well narrated by Malory in the *Anthology of Readings* so needs no summary here. What is important to address is the final battle with Meleagant. Meleagant formally accuses Guinevere of adultery or of faithlessness to the king. He points to the blood-stained bed and to the wounded Sir Kay (another captive knight) who has been sleeping in the room next to Guinevere as proof. Guinevere's honor will have to be tested in a trial by combat. Meleagant will fight whomever dares to defend the Queen.

Now it is important to see that Meleagant counts on having God on his side in this battle (of course, theologically it is also God's judgment that sends a person to hell—Meleagant merely hopes to act out God's judgment). According to medieval theories of trial and justice, God would protect from physical harm anyone who swears a true oath in his name. If the person is injured in the trial or ordeal, then the oath is judged to be false. Campbell alludes to this principle when he retells the story of Isolde who is made to swear an oath that she has never lain with any man other than her husband and then made to take hold of a red hot iron bar. Meleagant swears upon holy relics that Guinevere has slept with Sir Kay. Lancelot swears the contrary, that she has not slept with Sir Kay—knowing full well that she had slept and had sex with Lancelot, and that the blood staining the sheets was from Lancelot's wounds.

The judicial battle takes place before King Arthur and the assembled court. Guinevere sits at his side. The last scene is crucial. Chretien describes the Queen:

> Never before had she been so jubilant as she is now on his [Lancelot's] return. Would she not have gone up to him? Indeed she has: she is so close to him that her body virtually came within an ace of following her heart. Where, then, is her heart. It was kissing and making much of Lancelot. Why, then, was her body hiding? Why, is her joy not complete? Is it, then, mingled with anger or hatred? Certainly not in the least; but it is possible that the king or some of the others there, who have eyes on everything would have quickly become aware of the whole situation if she had been prepared to follow the promptings of her heart under the public gaze.[12]

The terms Chretien has set up here are quite complex. Through the trial, a public performance, Guinevere and Lancelot seek to ratify the truth of their love, which is not public but rather a secret matter for their own hearts. By killing Meleagant with the blessing of God's miracle or intervention, as is implied in all judicial battles, Lancelot proves publicly that he and Guinevere are right and true, that Meleagant's charges are false and wicked. But we know, as do Lancelot and Guinevere themselves, that they are guilty of adultery, and we would have to be pretty naive to think that God does not know it as well. We should recall Heloise's comment that "Wholly guilty though I am, I am, you know also wholly innocent." What Lancelot achieves as a result of his reenactment of the redemption monomyth is the establishment of his truth, of the truth in his and Guinevere's hearts that even while they know themselves to be guilty of the public charges, they also know themselves to be innocent of any sin. The truth in their hearts becomes, due to Lancelot's killing Meleagant and freeing the captives, the public truth, although the public represented by Arthur cannot understand it and is not yet ready to hear it—the truth of true love which has the power to free those once held captive.

## Tristan

The transgressive nature of the Lancelot story has proven to be a source of great upset for many medieval scholars. Among them, D. W. Robertson has argued vigorously that we are meant to see Lancelot and Guinevere as hopelessly corrupt and their portrait at the end of *Knight of the Cart* as a satire on the extent to which passion corrupts the truth.[13] Such a reading as this makes good sense only if we assume that orthodox doctrines of love and morality were, without problem, a standard for all. But given the heterodox context for the emergence of courtly love and Arthurian romance, it is much more likely that the transgressions were indeed intended by Chretien as well as Andreas and the host of other poets of the twelfth century. Toward the very end of the television program for this unit, Campbell mentions the "Wasteland" and the story of Parzival or of the Grail as the answer or solution to the conditions of the Wasteland. The Wasteland is the romance writers' representation of orthodoxy and Christian mythic dissociation in the Middle Ages, of the sum of teachings which required the renunciation of eros.

We come now to Gottfried von Strassburg's *Tristan*, a romance that elevates transgression to levels never dreamed of by poets and readers squeamish in the face of institutional authority. Campbell is certainly correct in noting that the Grail Quest is the resolution of the wasteland condition. The Tristan poems are without doubt the most profound analysis of that condition, for this legend is of the love-death, love that means death in life or, perhaps more clearly, life that means the death of love and eros. In the television program for this unit, Campbell concludes, "So this is the situation: love against marriage. And you might call it counter-culture against culture. How do we bring these things together?" First, a little background on the Tristan legends.

## The Diffusion of the Legend

Earlier in this unit, it was pointed out that the troubador Bernard de Ventadour compared his love for Eleanor to that of Tristan and Isolde. Numerous comments like this one have led scholars to believe that a fully developed romance of Tristan and Isolde circulated throughout the courts of France and England as early as the year 1150. (Notice here, as in so many places, the prominence of Eleanor of Aquitaine.) The earliest existing romances are all from the period 1160–1180. They include the romances of Thomas of Britain, who wrote in French, probably at the court of Henry II (Eleanor's second husband); Beroul, a Norman who wrote in a Norman dialect but who shows an unusual knowledge of the geography of Cornwall; and Eilhart von Oberge, who wrote in German at the court of Henry Duke of Saxony (husband of Eleanor's daughter, Mathilda). These are the early poems that exist. All are fragmentary and all seem to be based upon different originals.

What might be called a second generation of Tristan poems includes Gottfried von Strassburg's poem, composed about the year 1210, and a Norse *Tristrams Saga*, written by Friar Robert in the year 1226 at the request of King Hakonarson of Norway. Both of these poems are fairly close to the version of Thomas, more so in the case of the Norse poem. The third generation is much more difficult to describe and in many ways less important for us as modern readers. By the year 1250, the diffusion of the poem extended into Czechoslovakia, throughout Germany, Britain, and Italy, and most importantly into numerous French prose versions designed for a more popular audience. These prose "Tristans" began the process of assimilating Tristan with the court of Arthur so that Tristan and Lancelot become best comrades and have many adventures together. In some versions, Tristan even goes on the Quest for the Holy Grail.

The problem for modern readers is that of the hundred or more manuscripts and printed medieval versions almost none of the French prose "Tristans" have been published in modern editions or translated into English. Thomas Malory's fifteenth-century *Le Morte D'Arthur* relies principally on three distinct versions of the French prose *Tristan*, and is thus the most accessible version of that branch of the legend.

## Tristan and Eros

In the television program for this unit, Campbell recounts how Tristan comes to live with his Uncle Mark only to discover that the custom exists in Cornwall of surrendering young boys up as a tribute to the King of Ireland (Campbell includes girls, but the story clearly says "There were no girls, only boys" *Anthology* 420). This is important for what it suggests about Cornwall. We are told by Gottfried that Cornwall is an extremely rich and courtly land and yet at the same time that its strength is yearly depleted by this tribute paid to Ireland: "Now the Cornish and English were unable to obtain justice by means of open warfare since their lands had declined in strength" (*Anthology* 420). The decline, of course, results from giving up its supply of young males who might grow up to be fighters. We are meant to see that the social status quo in Cornwall, that is to say the well-being of Mark and the barons, is maintained by the yearly sacrifice of young men. This is incomprehensible to the naive Tristan, who remarks, "After all, fathers should give their lives for their children, since their lives are one and indivisible" (*Anthology* 421). And yet, this sacrifice proves true, for even Tristan volunteers to risk his life in fighting the monster Morold to save the lives of those in Cornwall who will not fight.

Initially, he is no different from any other Cornish son who goes to his death so that the fathers might live well. This sacrifice is the first indication of the life that means the death of love and of eros. The wound Tristan receives from Morold, a deep gash in the thigh, symbolizes as all such wounds do in Arthurian romance—and they occur quite frequently—castration. In various versions, Lancelot and Parzival suffer such wounds. You should remember this symbology in the next unit, since Wolfram says that the Wasteland begins when King Amfortas receives a lance-wound in the testicles, making him impotent and the land that he rules infertile. The son's, in this case Tristan's, giving of his life for Cornwall is a giving up of his eros and is therefore, in symbolic terms, a castration. In Freudian terms, the repression of eros is always a castration, which symbolizes the sum of prohibitions and regulations that civilizations place on individuals in order to provide for the stability of institutions and the maintenance of the civilization's ideology.

Only Isolde can heal the wound Tristan receives from Morold, and symbolically from King Mark of Cornwall, since it is for Mark that Tristan entered the fight. And what does Tristan learn from Isolde? He learns transgression. He learns to transgress honor, which always implies a person's standing within the community and the responsibilities one has to social superiors like Mark who, as it turns out, are simply interested in the death of younger males. One is honored by others when one does things that benefit the group, that is, when one sacrifices oneself. Tristan learns to defy Mark. This theme becomes more and more clear as the Tristan legend develops over the centuries. In the early poetic versions, Mark appears to be a decent man who has some genuine affection for both Tristan and Isolde. As the tale progresses into the French prose versions and to Malory, the portrait of Mark becomes more and more hateful, so much so that in Malory's *Tristram*, Mark appears to have little other interest in life than the destruction of Tristram. In Malory's version, Tristram openly defies Mark. Such open rebellion would not have been thinkable in the early poems such as Gottfried's, except in the veiled and symbolic form, as we shall see.

Near the end of Gottfried's Tristan, he plays with a typical bit of medieval antifeminism about the transgressive character of women, which is far different from the transcending understanding we find in Abelard and Heloise. He writes, "Women do many things just because they are forbidden, from which they would refrain were it not forbidden. . . . Women of this kind are the children of Eve, who flouted the first prohibition."[14] A page later, he turns the antifeminism back against itself: "For when a woman grows in virtue despite her inherited instincts and gladly keeps her honour, reputation, and person intact, she is only a woman in name, but in spirit she is a man!"[15] It seems that traditional morality would have women become men. Would men then approve of the woman's nature? He concludes this long and deeply ironic passage, "When a woman acts against herself and so directs her thoughts that she becomes her own enemy—who, in the face of this is going to love her?"[16] The upshot is that there is no use in women trying to be like men, and what Tristan learns from Isolde, as Campbell points out in the television program, is that honor is a trap designed to force people, men or women, to give up their unique and individual potential for the goals or status quo of the group. Honor asks them to renounce their natures. And so to be healed, Tristan has to learn to be like Isolde.

He transgresses his love for Isolde to marry the Isolde of the White Hands. Then he transgresses that marriage by refusing to consummate what he promised to do at the altar. He reasons to himself, Thomas tells us, for Gottfried's version has broken off now and we have to resort to Thomas for the end of the story, "If the good thing [i.e. Isolde] that he has were not his, he would not be averse to it; but in his heart he cannot like what he must perforce own. If he could not have what he possesses, he would have longed to acquire it."[17] This is almost word for word the antifeminist cant Gottfried used to construct in his indirect and ironic way a principle of feminist transcendence. Now it is Tristan who is doing it! It is not that Tristan ceases to love Isolde; on the contrary, he has to go through this process of denying whatever is in himself in order to find out who he is before he can love her on terms that are wholly and uniquely theirs. As long as he remains the champion of Mark, he will never be able to love Isolde except in the manner of the love-death.

The romance by Gottfried and Thomas is a tragedy. It concerns characters confined in a world that is too small for the energy of their souls, and so the world closes in around them and stifles them. In the end, Mark, in a mirror image of Tristan's whole life, kills Tristan. Here transgression is not enough to escape the rules and restrictions of society. The occasion of Tristan's death is a symbolic return to the scene at Cornwall. A neighbor significantly called Dwarf Tristan (you might want to look at Carl Jung's theory of the shadow or the apparition of ourselves that we at crucial moments see acting out behaviors that we cannot consciously face) requests Tristan's help in rescuing his mistress who has been forcefully carried off by Estult l'Orgillus of Castel Fer. Here the Dwarf Tristan's situation looks powerfully like the situation of Tristan whose lover Isolde is taken by force in marriage to Mark.

In the battle that ensues, Dwarf Tristan is killed and "the other Tristan [is] wounded through the loins by a lance bated with venom" (*Anthology* 432). The implications of this wound should be clear. It is the conditions of Tristan's entire life. What is most remarkable, however, is that Tristan kills Estult. If we think of this structurally, we cannot help concluding that Estult symbolically represents Mark. If we think about this in mythic terms rather than in personal ones, it is, as Campbell describes in *The Hero with a Thousand Faces*, the son's confrontation and atonement with the father. There Campbell writes, "there is a new element of rivalry in the picture: the son against the father for the mastery of the universe."[18] Who will the world belong to: the older generation or will it be passed to the sons along with the power to recreate it after their own fashion? This romance is a tragedy and Tristan dies unfulfilled. There is no atonement with the father, but the romance itself points to the general cultural condition understood by the naive Tristan when he tells the cowardly Barons, "After all, father should give their lives for their children, since their lives are one and indivisible" (*Anthology* 421).

## ASSIGNMENTS FOR STUDY AND ANALYSIS

1. Explain the meaning of eros in your own words. How does it relate to Campbell's emphasis on "your own path." Is the Catharist religion an "erotic" religion?
2. Write two interpretations of the last scene of *The Knight of the Cart*: one from a Christian point of view and one from the point of view of courtly love.
3. From your reading of Andreas's *The Art of Courtly Love*, develop a description of the kind of relationship that is implied in the rules and in the cases. Does this seem like the cultivation of emotions and the sensitivities of the heart?
4. Campbell says in the television program that our tradition of psychology begins in courtly love. From your understanding of psychology, can you explain the connection between our tradition of psychology and courtly love?
5. The problem of morality is always also a problem of who's morality. When Campbell says that love and honor are opposed, he is also saying that two perspectives on morality are competing. Explain what these two forms of morality are. Where do we stand on this issue in our society today? Is it a beneficial thing for there to be a pluralistic morality?

## FURTHER ASSIGNMENTS FOR WRITING AND REFLECTIONS

1. Some scholars, such as Georges Duby in *The Knight, the Lady, and the Priest* (cited in the Unit Bibliography), trace modern ideals about love and marriage to courtly love and its absolute requirement of an erotic commitment to the marriage partner. Discuss the ideals of modern marriage and love and relate them to the ideas in Andreas's *The Art of Courtly Love* and *Tristan*.
2. Read more about Abelard and Heloise through their very interesting autobiography and letters. In addition to introducing a new ethics of intention, Abelard was instrumental in introducing a new logic. To what extent do people today subscribe to an ethics of intent? How is it viewed by the legal system? It is clear that an act cannot be good or evil in itself, since the same act is regarded differently on different occasions, i.e., the state is permitted to kill but individuals are not. How are differences in justifications rationalized, if not by an ethics of intent?
3. The scenes of trial by combat or ordeal were popular in romance. Campbell described the ordeal of Isolde, and the trial of Guinevere is recounted in "The Knight of the Cart." What is your interpretation of these scenes?
4. Campbell's notion that sex is a sacrament is both daring and profound. The chapter in Tristan on "The Cave of Lovers" is certainly the proof-text for any theory of sex as sacrament. Read that chapter carefully and develop an explanation of the idea that you would present to your associates or classmates.
5. If the theme of much romance is love against honor or love against marriage, then lovers must transgress honor and marriage in order to fulfill their loves. Discuss this theme of transgression and its place in both the romances and in contemporary society. What does Campbell mean when he implies that transgression is the first step in an "authentic" life?
6. Contemporary depictions of love in novels and movies seem to have stories that are much more developed in their portrayals of romance. But with the medieval love

stories, the key is their struggle with the forces that oppose love. Explain the way in which the loves of Lancelot and Guinevere and Tristan and Isolde are the personal commitments that Campbell suggests.

# ENDNOTES

[1] Friedrick Heer, *The Medieval World* Trans. Janet Sondheimer (New York: New American Library, 1961) 165.

[2] Joseph Campbell, *The Masks of God: Creative Mythology* (New York: Penguin Books, 1976) 179.

[3] *The Letters of Abelard and Heloise* Trans. Betty Radice (Harmondsworth, UK: Penguin Classics, 1974).

[4] *Letters* 132–33.

[5] *Letters* 115.

[6] Heer 170.

[7] St. Augustine, *On Christian Doctrine* Trans. D. W. Robertson (Indianapolis: Bobbs-Merrill, 1958) 62.

[8] Campbell, *Creative Mythology* 331–32.

[9] Joseph Campbell, *The Flight of the Wild Gander* (New York: The Viking Press, 1969) 204.

[10] Chretien de Troyes, "The Knight of the Court," *Arthurian Romances* Trans. D. D. R. Owen (London: J. M. Dent & Sons, 1987) 217.

[11] de Troyes 211.

[12] de Troyes 276–277.

[13] D. W. Robertson, *A Preface to Chaucer: A Study in Medieval Perspectives* (Princeton: Princeton University Press, 1962) 87–91.

[14] Gottfried von Strassburg. *Tristan* (New York: Penguin Books n. d.) 277.

[15] Strassburg 278.

[16] Strassburg 278.

[17] Strassburg 304–305.

[18] Joseph Campbell, *The Hero with a Thousand Faces* (Princeton: Princeton University Press, 1949) 136.

# UNIT BIBLIOGRAPHY

Campbell, Joseph. *The Masks of God: Creative Mythology*. New York: Penguin Books, 1976. For Campbell's discussion of the myth of Tristan see Part I, pages 1–171 of this book.

Capellanus, Andreas. *The Art of Courtly Love*. Trans. John J. Parry. New York: W. W. Norton, 1941. A manual commissioned by Marie de Champagne for the instruction of young men in the arts of love.

Duby, Georges. *The Knight, the Lady, and the Priest: The Making of Modern Marriage in Medieval France*. Trans. Barbara Bray. New York: Pantheon, 1983. Traces marriage customs in the Middle Ages and shows how modern views of love and marriage were innovated in the twelfth and thirteenth centuries.

Kelly, Amy. *Eleanor of Aquitaine*. New York: Vintage Books, 1950. A fascinating biography of one of the world's most influential women. Details Eleanor's relations with all the important kings between the years 1137 and 1204 (Eleanor lived to the age of 84) and her life as a patroness of the arts, especially the emerging romance.

Lewis, C. S. *The Allegory of Love*. London: Oxford University Press, 1938. A sociological and psychological study of romance that argues that a fundamental change in human sentiment, and thus in manners and life-style, occurred in the twelfth century.

Plato, *The Symposium*. Trans. Benjamin Jowett. Indianapolis: Bobbs-Merrill, 1948. *The Symposium* is Plato's dialogue on love and presents five views by prominent Greek philosophers and dramatists on love.

Rougement, Denis de, *Love in the Western World*. Princeton: Princeton University Press, 1940. A controversial study of love based largely on the Tristan legends which argues that Christian love in the Middle Ages had brought men to such a psychological dead end that passionate love arose as a cult of death. Love is love of death.

St. Augustine. *On Christian Doctrine*. Trans. D. W. Robertson. Indianapolis: Bobbs-Merrill, 1958. St. Augustine's most important treatise on interpretating the Bible.

Strassburg, Gottfried von, *Tristan*. Trans. A. T. Hatto. Harmondsworth: Penguin Classics, 1960. Contains the best translation of Gottfried's romance along with the romance of Thomas of Britain so that the story is complete.

Troyes, Chrtien de, *Arthurian Romances*. Trans. D. D. R. Owen. London: John M. Dent & Sons, 1987. Contains all extant romances by Cretien.

# NOTES

# NOTES

GEORGE DEFOREST LORD
ROBERT MERRILL

# UNIT 13

# In Search of the Holy Grail:
## The Parzival Legend

## UNIT STUDY PLAN

1.  Read Unit 13 in your *Study Guide*.
2.  Watch Program 13: "In Search of the Holy Grail: The Parzival Legend."
3.  In your course notebook or journal, write a summary of Joseph Campbell's interpretation of the Grail Quest as presented in the television program. Make notes on points in the program that are unclear, and keep a record of your own reactions and observations to the stories and events as Campbell retells them.
4.  Read the selections for this unit in the *Anthology of Readings*. These include selections from Wolfram von Eschenbach's *Parzival*, which complement Campbell's retelling of the legend. They also include Thomas Malory's alternative explanation for the origin of the Wasteland and Carl G. Jung's essay on his own Grail Quest to discover his personal myth.
5.  After reading the selections, comment on what you have read in your notebook. Show the relationships between the readings and Campbell's insights about the personal quest.
6.  Complete the assignments at the end of this unit as specified by your instructor.

## POINTS TO WATCH FOR IN THE TELEVISION PROGRAM

*This television program was delivered as a lecture by Joseph Campbell in San Francisco, California, 1984.*

1.  Campbell emphasizes that the Grail Quest is the solution for the problem of the love-death or death in life that the Tristan story presents. Pay careful attention to this connection.
2.  Campbell seems very pleased that Lancelot could never feel contrition for his affair with Guinevere. Think about this in relation to Christianity and Campbell's basic interpretation of life.
3.  The Neutral Angels are a key to the interpretation of Parzival. Be sure you understand their position. They are the keepers of the Grail, in Wolfram's *Parzival*.
4.  Throughout the television program, Campbell refers to the Christian belief that nature is fallen or corrupt. Wolfram takes a different view about nature. Be sure that you follow Campbell's several references to nature.
5.  Keep track of Campbell's theoretical development of the Grail Quest. It involves a process of compassionate responses to others, commitment, and a rejection of the authority of the culture to control one's life.

## POINTS TO LOOK FOR IN THE *ANTHOLOGY OF READINGS*

1.  Thomas Malory's "Balin, or the Knight with Two Swords" is largely his own invention to explain the origin of the Wasteland. It differs sharply from the origin in Chretien and Wolfram which ascribe the Wasteland to, as Campbell phrases it in the television program for this unit, "the spiritual ideals of the Middle Ages which have castrated Europe." Malory knew only the *Queste del Saint Graal* where the Wasteland is caused by sin (remember that the *Queste* was written by Cistercian Monks). Malory must have been dissatisfied with that explanation, for he presents Balin, a super-socialized knight whose overzealous desire to accomplish socially determined goals, as opposed to searching for his own path, destroys every land he visits. Notice Balin's motivations in his knightly career.
2.  Read very carefully the selections from *Parzival* that have to do the wounding of King Amfortas and the origin of the Wasteland. Think about what is happening here in comparison to Malory's story of Balin. Is there a similarity in these two understandings of the Wasteland, even though Malory knew nothing of the version of the story by Wolfram or Chretien?
3.  In Unit 12, you were introduced to the idea of the shadow or double in the episode of Tristan and the Dwarf Tristan. Balin has a brother named Balan. Do you think Malory, too, is working with a doubling theme here? What does the shadow show about Balin that he is unable to see consciously in himself?
4.  The same theme of the shadow or double is apparent in the brothers Parzival and Feirefiz. What shows in this doubling? Think about the opening pages of the romance in which Wolfram says that heaven and hell have equal parts in man.
5.  Carl Jung concludes his essay, "The Confrontation with the Unconscious" with a statement that is very reminiscent of Parzival's quest. He writes, "When I parted with Freud, I knew that I was plunging into the unknown. Beyond Freud, after all, I knew nothing; but I had taken the step into darkness. When that happens, and then such a dream comes, one feels it as an act of grace" (492). Jung was a disciple of Freud for many years. Freud was a brilliant but over-dominant master. You might want to look up some more about their relationship in a biography of Jung or Freud. Think about Jung's decision to launch out on his own in relation to Parzival's similar decision and also in relation to Campbell's insights about the hero's journey and what myths have to teach us.

## UNIT GLOSSARY

**Alchemy**: From Arabic al-Khimia meaning chemistry. The belief that everything was composed of varying proportions of air, earth, fire, and water. The discovery of the proportions of each would enable one to transmute one substance into another, such as lead into gold. The knowledge of secret proportions, written on the philosopher's stone or tablet, would also mean complete control of nature by man.

**Condwiramurs**: Parzival's wife, queen of Brobarz. The name is old French for "guide of love": conduire + amor.

**Fisher king**: Sometimes identified as Amfortas, other times as Pellam, and still in other legends as Alain or Brons. He is the wounded and impotent king of the Wasteland. The name is rich with Christian and pagan symbolism: Christ as the fisher of men and in Celtic myth the fish as a fertility symbol, i.e., the king seeking fertility. Also the old French pun *le roi pécheur* translates as "the king who has sinned" and *le roi pêcheur* as "the king who fishes." Robert de Boron in *Joseph of Arimathea* says that Brons, the fisher king, catches the fish that is served at the Last Supper.

**Galahad**: The Grail knight in the Cistercian *Queste del Saint Graal* and the *Estoire del Graal*. The name comes from the biblical "Galeed," meaning "a heap of testimony."

**Grail**: Old French, Graal, from "gradale," meaning a dish used to serve successive courses in a meal. Robert de Boron says the Grail is the cup used at the Last Supper and that was filled with Christ's blood at the Crucifixion. Wolfram says that the Grail is a large stone, the "lapis exilis" (see below).

**Lapsit Exillis** or **Lapis Exilis**: The Grail in Wolfram's *Parzival*, but in no other version. Lapis Exilis is the philosopher's stone, the much sought after substance in alchemical research that had power to transmute lead into gold.

**Magna Charta**: A charter limiting the rights of the monarch, forced upon King John I by English barons in 1215.

**Munsalvaesche**: The mysterious land where the Grail Castle is located. The name means "Mount Savage" or wild mountains.

**Mythic Dissociation**: Campbell's term for the separation of the realms of nature and spirit. It is the notion that divinity and transcendence do not exist within individuals, but only "out there," separate from the world.

**Neutral Angels**: Angels who took neither God's side nor Lucifer's side in the battle in heaven. In Wolfram they are the guardians of the Grail.

**Social Identification**: Campbell's term for a social or political condition when myths lose their connection to people's lives.

## UNIT PREVIEW

In this unit, you will be introduced to the theme of the Wasteland, or death-in-life, and to its two origins in medieval literature. The great goal of the Quest for the Grail is to restore life to this spiritually and psychologically dead land, and it is up to Parzival to discover that the source of life resides within himself. In the Quest for the Holy Grail, the terms of self-creation, by looking within oneself instead of outside of oneself to cultural authorities, are finally clearly recognized.

**Branches of the Grail Legends**: Grail stories spread throughout Europe like wild-fire. The mix of Christian and pagan symbolism is quite complex and often hard to follow. This unit will provide you with a map of the development of Grail legends from Chretien in the twelfth century to Malory in the fifteenth century. It is important to notice how the legend evolved and changed, as each writer seemed to understand more clearly the nature of the symbol of the Grail.

**Origins and Nature of the Wasteland**: Campbell mentions that the Grail Quest is the solution for the conditions of life symbolized by the Wasteland. There are several conceptions of the origin and nature of the Wasteland, each deriving from different writers of the legend. Christian writers, such as the Cistercian Monks who wrote the *Queste del Saint Graal* clearly regard the Wasteland as the condition of sin in the world and the soul. The Quest, therefore, is the process of repentance and can be achieved only by one who is without sin. Wolfram, on the other hand, portrays the Wasteland as the result of the castration of Amfortas, the Fisher King. In all versions, the land is a reflection of the spiritual/psychological/physical condition of the knights.

**Wolfram von Eschenbach's Parzival**: Campbell regards Wolfram's *Parzival* as the highest literary and mythic achievement of the Middle Ages. In many ways it is also the most radical. It ends, as Campbell notes in the television program for this unit, with the hermit Trevrizent telling Parzival that he has forced God to change his laws. Campbell reads this as an indication of Wolfram's discovery that the God within the self is the true legislator for one's life and for the world.

**The Grail Myth and Psychoanalysis**: Contemporary psychoanalysis derives a great deal of its insights and its approach to healing from medieval myths. The Grail is the great myth of psychological and spiritual healing. Both Carl Jung and Sigmund Freud were well versed in the Grail legends and their descriptions of the development of psychoses can be seen in terms of the origin of the Wasteland and the healing provided by Parzival. The question Parzival must ask in order to heal the symbolically sick king is "Uncle, what is troubling you?" Just as in psychoanalysis, the question itself contains the answer, that is, questioning itself provides the healing.

## In Search of the Holy Grail: The Parzival Legend

Perhaps the most effective way to understand the development of the Grail legends is to trace the evolution of the meanings ascribed to the mysterious Grail. As Campbell suggested in Unit 12, the point of these romances was to take a story from some earlier writer and develop it; that is, make it, in the judgment of the new writer, a better expression of the true account. The Grail was certainly one theme that each writer felt obliged to modify according to his own mythic sensibility. Because the meaning of the Grail is central, when it changes meaning or manifestation, we also get corresponding changes in the nature of the Wasteland and the identity of the Fisher King.

### Chretien's *Conte Del Graal* and His Continuators

It is to Chretien de Troyes that we owe the story of the Grail. Nothing is known of how or where Chretien derived his story of the richly ornate platter from which is served every sort of sumptuous food, but it is likely that he knew of some myth (perhaps Celtic) of a food producing vessel, such as a cornucopia or a cauldron of plenty. In Chretien, the vessel is clearly described. Perceval (Chretien's spelling) is seated on a couch beside the Fisher King and sees a magnificent procession enter through a door at one end of the hall and exit at the opposite end. The procession is led by a young knight who carries a bleeding lance. He is followed by young men with candelabras. Finally, a lady enters bearing in her hands "un graal" which was worked with fine gold and many precious stones. The Grail maiden passes before Perceval several times, but he does not ask who is to be served from the Grail.

It is clear at this point that Chretien has in mind a Grail, "un graal," that is no more than a richly ornate serving dish. The term derives from the medieval Latin word "gradale," meaning "by degrees or in stages" and when applied to a dish suggests that the food was brought in stages or courses. This is just what happens when Perceval first sees the Grail. All manner of foods are brought to the table one course at a time: "The first course was a haunch of venison in hot pepper sauce."[1] While they eat, the Grail maiden passes in front of the table, and Perceval restrains himself from asking who is served from the Grail and what is the meaning of the bleeding lance.

Much later, five years to be exact, Perceval is told by a hermit that this Grail does not contain pike, salmon, or lamprey, fish which might ordinarily be served on a Grail, but rather a single consecrated Host from the Mass which is given to the Fisher King and has been his only sustenance for twelve years. Perceval also learns that the Fisher King is his uncle. By this time, Perceval understands that the Grail is clearly the Christian form of spiritual nourishment. The hermit goes on to say that the host supports the Fisher King in full vigor, so spiritual a life he leads and so holy a thing is the Grail.

Chretien's romance breaks off mysteriously at the point of Perceval's second entrance into the Grail Castle. In the television program for this unit, Campbell suggests that Chretien may not have liked where the story was leading to, but there was no shortage of others who felt compelled to complete the story and make explicit facts about the Grail that Chretien had left as mystery. In Chretien, we are still in connection with the pagan roots of some fertility myth, involving the impotent king who turns out to be the hero-knight's grandfather or uncle. In some versions, the bleeding lance must actually be inserted into the Grail, thus suggesting a sexual symbology. The roots of the story in fertility myths have been well explored by a number of writers you might be interested in researching, particularly Jessie L. Weston's *From Ritual to Romance*, a book that aroused T. S. Eliot's interest in the Grail Legends and inspired his poem, *The Wasteland*, and Roger Sherman Loomis, *The Grail: From Celtic Myth to Christian Symbol*.

### The Continuators

In Chretien's continuators, however, the story is stripped of its pagan mythic roots and invested with the lore of the New Testament. Robert de Boron, writing in about the year 1205, fifteen years after Chretien, makes the Grail the chalice of the Last Supper which Christ passed to Judas. This same cup was used by Joseph of Arimathea to catch the blood of the crucified Christ as it poured from the lance wound given him by the Roman soldier; thus the bleeding lance which precedes the Grail in the processions. In Robert's hands, Chretien's "un graal" becomes "le Saint Graal"—the Holy Grail—a Christian treasure carried from Jerusalem to England by the descendents of Joseph of Arimathea. It is thus the original for the Mass chalice that contains the body and blood of Christ.

In the monastic versions produced by Cistercian Monks, the *Estoire del Graal* and the *Queste del Saint Graal*, the Grail becomes an experience of the Beatific Vision. Perceval is dropped as the Grail knight and instead the pure and ethereal knight Sir Galahad is substituted. Galahad is the son of Lancelot and a woman, Elaine, who tricks him into sleeping with her. Thus from such sinful beginnings is born the knight who will achieve the spiritual perfection his parents could not. An important point about these monastic versions is their intention of showing the corruption of all the Arthurian knights. Gawain, Lancelot, Perceval, even Tristan in later versions, fail in the Grail Quest because of old sins they cannot relinquish. Campbell mentions in the television program for this unit the case of Lancelot who is struck unconscious by God because of his love for Guinevere. He cannot give up Guinevere.

Galahad, on the other hand, is completely without sin. He is often tempted but resists on every occasion. Roger Sherman Loomis has traced the name Galahad (Galaad in old French) to the biblical "Galeed" that refers to a pile of stones set up by Jacob and Laban as a "heap of testimony" to their convenant of loyalty to each other. In achieving the Grail, Galahad's life is also a heap of testimony to the value of a chaste and virtuous life, for it is to him alone that the vision of the Grail is revealed. As the *Queste del Saint Graal* has it:

> The other day, when we saw in part the wonders of the Holy Grail which Our Lord of His gracious mercy deigned to show us, as I was looking on the hidden mysteries that are not disclosed to common view, but only to them that wait on Jesus Christ, in the moment that revealed to me those things that the heart of mortal man cannot conceive nor tongue relate, my heart was ravished with such joy and bliss, that had I died forthwith I know that no man ever breathed his last in such beatitude as then was mine … I was translated in that moment from the earthly plane to the celestial, to the glorious martyrs and the beloved of Our Lord.[2]

The monastic Grail legends are filled with long quotations of scripture and scriptural interpretations. While in Arthurian romance, we become used to a knight meeting another knight to fight at almost every turn, in the *Estoire* and the *Queste* we meet a monk or a hermit who is more than willing to explain at length just why a particular knight's sinful life is keeping him from achieving the Grail. The stories are filled with prophesies and parables all pointing to the sinfulness and corruption of this world and urging the ascetic life of renunciation of this world and full devotion to Christ. This monastic approach became the source of Malory's fifteenth-century *Tale of the Sankgreal* ("Sankgreal" is Malory's literal spelling of "Saint Graal"). It should be clear to you that the spirit of Wolfram von Eschenbach's *Parzival* has almost nothing to do with the direction of Chretien's continuators or with the monastic version. It is the same case with Malory, who was an actual fighting knight like Wolfram.

Malory worked with the only version of the Grail story he knew, but his sensitivities were sharp enough to lead in the same direction that Wolfram took when he encountered the story. Malory drops almost all of the sermonizing and places the Grail Quest squarely in the middle of a social crisis within the Round Table. Factions are developing. The kin of Lancelot are plotting against Tristram because he is now winning more fame than Lancelot. The family of Gawain is plotting against Lancelot because he has, they feel, too much of Arthur's favor. When the Grail Quest is presented, Arthur clearly sees that it will be the end of the Round Table. It will lead his knights off on a chase for something that has little to do with this world and will distract them from resolving the real problems they face.

Malory, more clearly than any other writer, shows that the search for the transcendental God robs people of the power and inclination to resolve the problems they face in the here and now. Campbell says in the television program for this unit that "the spiritual ideals of the Middle Ages which distinguished supernatural from natural grace had castrated Europe." Nothing could be closer to what Malory presents in his Grail Quest. One after another, the Grail knights undergo some form of castration or renunciation of eros (for a full development of this point see Robert Merrill, *Thomas Malory and the Cultural Crisis of the Late Middle Ages*, 301–390). For Malory, the Quest is an utter failure. Those knights who do return, come back with their ideals broken and their spirits embittered. Slander, rivalry, and strife grow steadily within the Round Table until the outbreak of the great civil war which leaves only three or four of the original knights alive.

## The Wasteland

Because he knew only the monastic versions of the Grail Quest that gave sin as the cause of the Wasteland, Malory felt compelled to invent a new story that would locate the cause elsewhere, that is, not in sin but in the over-dependence upon institutional authority for the determination of meaning and value in one's life. Campbell notes several times that the Grail Quest is the cure for the condition of the Wasteland, which he calls "mythic dissociation" in *The Masks of God: Creative Mythology*. "Social identification," Campbell also points out, "is the corresponding social or political condition when the myths lose their connection to men's lives." It is quite interesting to observe that in Wolfram's thirteenth-century Grail story, the cause of the Wasteland is mythic dissociation, while in Malory's fifteenth-century version, it is social identification. We will examine these two stories rather closely and simply assume that the logic of the Christian story of original sin, as the model for all sin, is well enough known. In the Christian versions, sin is the corruption of nature and the condition from which men must be healed.

The motif of the Wasteland very likely is Celtic in origin, though the backgrounds are far from clear or simple. You might want to consult the books by Loomis and Weston mentioned above for a fuller development of the origins in folklore. The chief components of the Wasteland myth are a king who suffers a wound in the genitals making him impotent (i.e., a castration); a barren land; extraordinary dangers to be overcome in the quest to find the king's castle; and a question that must be asked in order to heal the king and free his kingdom from the enchantment of infertility. The myth turns upon the belief that the natural fertility of a land is related to the potency of the king; in more general terms, that the world is a function of the psychological health of mankind. The land we call a kingdom is land invested with the value and meaning of human origin. Thus we see that the king's wound is the crucial cause for the conditions of the land and the event that makes the quest necessary. How the king receives the wound tells us much.

Different legends assign different names to this king. In Wolfram he is called Amfortas, in Malory he is Pellam, and still in other legends, for example, that of Robert de Boron, he is Brons. In all of the legends he is the Fisher King, a name rich with Christian and pagan symbolism. It may be that the identification of the king with fishing was only the result of a confusion of words in old French oral recitation. The words for fishing and sinning have nearly the same sound in French: thus *le roi pécheur* means "the king who has sinned" and *le roi pêcheur* means "the king who fishes." The same similarity exists in modern French for the word "sinner" and "fisherman": *pécheur* means sinner and *pêcheur* means fisherman. The king is a sinner, given the moral standards of Christianity. Nevertheless, it was a confusion pregnant with possibilities. Christ announced to Peter that he had come to be the fisher of men. And in Catholicism, the fish is frequently the symbol for the Eucharist or the sacrificed Christ. In some Celtic myths, the fish appears as a fertility symbol; in this case, the king is seeking or fishing for fertility. Robert de Boron in *Joseph of Arimathea* says that Brons, the fisher king, catches the fish that is served at the Last Supper. Wolfram, more uniquely, notes that fishing is a humiliating pastime for a king, but he only does it to relieve some of the pain of his wound and to be out in fresh breezes which blow away some of the stench of the festering wound that, in spite of all manner of medicines, will not heal.

## Wolfram's Wasteland

Campbell retells the event of the wounding of Amfortas according to Wolfram. As a young knight, Amfortas rides forth from his castle to win his fame under battle cry, "Amor!" In his first fight, he kills another knight but receives a lance wound in the testicles. This story is told to Parzival by Trevrizent, Amfortas's brother who, upon learning of the wound, gives up the world for the life of a hermit. He urges Parzival to take the same path of life. Trevrizent is an important character because he comes to stand for all the wrong views; that is, his kind of thinking is an intellectual rather than emotional response to the infertile and dead land. When confronted with a frightening wound such as Amfortas's, Trevrizent's reaction is to give up his life to prayer and penance. He believes, as medieval Christianity taught, that nature and the flesh are corrupt and that a person's only hope in life is to aim his life at purity or virginity. The full context of the following passage is reprinted in Wolfram's *Parzival* in the *Anthology of Readings*; here let us simply look at how he understands nature:

> The earth was Adam's mother, by her fruits Adam was nourished. The earth was still a virgin then. It remains for me to tell you who took her maidenhead. Adam was father to Cain, who slew Abel for a trifle. When blood fell upon the pure earth her virginity was gone, taken by Adam's son. This is the beginning of hatred among men, and thus it has endured ever since. There is nothing in the whole world so pure as an honest maiden.

> Consider the purity of maidens: God himself was the Virgin's child. Two men were born of virgins: God Himself took on a countenance like that of the first virgin's son, a condescension from his sublimity (462).

What Trevrizent is saying is a repudiation of what Campbell calls the energy of nature, which is tapped into by myth. He rejects nature as a fertile location for human life or as a source of fertility and seeks, ironically, fertility in renunciation and virginity. Amfortas is doing precisely the same thing, for this is what medieval Christianity taught. He regards his wound as a punishment for a sinful life or as the corrupt body to which the pure soul is chained. When Amfortas confronts the pain of life, he, unlike Tristan, does not accept it as his life but rather condemns all of life itself. The judgement that his life has been and is sinful is his own self-judgement. He cannot be cured of the wound until he learns to see himself differently—but that will require an entirely different and revolutionary outlook on nature. This new outlook is symbolized in the sacramentalization of sex. Sex can only be a sacrament in a world where nature is filled with the mythic energy of creation. This is what Parzival shows to the people of Munsalvaesche, the proper name of the Wasteland, which means savage or wild land. After healing Amfortas by simply asking "Uncle, what ails you?" Parzival again meets Trevrizent who, in astonishment, tells him that he has forced God to change his laws.

In *The Masks of God: Creative Mythology* Campbell writes:

> The life-desolating effects of this separation of the reigns of nature and the spirit in such a way that neither touches the other but destructively, remains to this day an essential psychological problem of the Christianized world; and since it is at the root a consequence of the basic biblical doctrine of an ontological distinction between God and his universe, creator and creature, spirit and matter, it is a problem that has hardly altered since it first became intolerably evident at the climax of the Middle Ages. In briefest statement, the Christian is taught that divinity is transcendent not within himself and his world, but 'out there.' I call this mythic dissociation.[3]

## Malory's Wasteland

Wolfram's origin of the Wasteland is mythic dissociation; the other origin presented by Malory is social identification. Campbell's definition for that is the:

> totalitarian dogma of "society"—almost any quorum, it seems, will do: a "people," a "church," even a trade union, or anything calling itself "the state"—as the only vehicle of value, through association with which an individual life can achieve worth, when actually the truth is the other way round, that whatever human worth a social group may claim, it will have gained only by grace of the great and little individuals of its membership.[4]

Social identification is the death of a self, or a castration, because it locates the source of mythic energy in institutions, and not in people. The worst form of it is the excessive patriotism that leads zealots to the extermination of other people in the name of national security and national interests. Whose interests? The abstract interests of the state. You might want to refer again to Malory's story of "Balin, or the Knight with Two Swords" for this part of the discussion. The story of Balin is a very densely and richly written story and attention to even the smallest detail is important.

Malory tells us that into Arthur's court came a knight who was poorly dressed and who had spent the last half-year in prison, but "in his heart," Malory goes on, "he was fully assured to do as well, if his grace happed him, as any knight there was" (*Anthology* 472). He begs that he be given an adventure that will prove his worth, but no one is much interested in such an undistinguished looking knight. To support his case, Balin argues that "worthiness and good tatches [qualities] and also good deeds is not only in array-ment, but manhood and worship is hid within a man's person: and many a worshipful knight is not known unto all people" (*Anthology* 472). Balin voices precisely what Campbell regards as the key insight of Arthurian romance—that the individual is the source of whatever value and order exists in the world, and that the recognition of this creative divinity within each person is the great quest of life. But even Balin, after his own statement of his self worth, feels that he has to gain the recognition of the Round Table as a worthy knight. This story is about who—the individual or the insti-tution—determines the meaning of worth.

At this time, Arthur's Round Table is at war with a group named only by Malory as the Eleven Kings. Arthur does not yet rule all of England but is in the midst of his conquest. The war is going badly for Arthur, whose troops are outnum-bered by the Eleven Kings. Balin cannot seem to do anything right. He manages to pull a magical sword from its scabbard, but then on an impulse kills the lady who brought the sword. Arthur is furious with Balin and thinks he shames the whole court; he says, "I am right wroth with Balin. I would he were quit of the despite that he hath done unto me and my court" (*Anthology* 473), and sends him away from the court, sug-gesting that he not return until he has redeemed his wrongs.

We need to look at Balin's next actions as a sociologist would. Balin leaves Camelot determined to win Arthur's admiration. Everywhere he goes, he imagines to himself what Arthur would want done in this situation. And then he does it. Sociologists call this sort of imagining and behavioral self-control the internalization of the "significant other."

At this point, Balin meets his brother who previously had not been mentioned. The brother's name is Balan, and we should think of this meeting in the same way as Tristan's meeting the Dwarf Tristan. Balan is more of a shadow or a double of Balin than he is a brother, but a brother is accurate

enough. Balin tells his brother, "I am right heavy that my lord Arthur is displeased with me, for he is the most worshipful-lest king that reigneth now in earth; and his love I will get other else I will put my life in adventure" (*Anthology* 474). In effect, Balin is trading his life as an unique individual with the power to create his own worth in the world for the worship that Arthur can give him. As we shall see, his brother, Balan—his other self—symbolizes the uniqueness of the individual. All of Balin's instinctual energy is given over to his fantasies of what Arthur would want done in this case or that. He becomes totally identified with Arthur's society. More and more, his understanding of himself is in terms of Arthur's interests. Balin becomes a fighting ma-chine, killing and overrunning the troops of the Eleven Kings and establishing Arthur as king throughout England.

Arthur asks when these two marvelous knights, Balin and Balan, are going to come to court. Merlin answers that Balin will not be long in coming, but, he says, the other brother, Balan, will depart and you will never see him. In the process of socialization, Balin has given up so much of himself that is unique and individual that this part of him, symbolized by Balan, ceases to exist at all. In this sense, Balin is very much like Trevrizent and Amfortas, who because of the pain they encounter in the world adopt toward them-selves the condemning attitude of God. They renounce and deny any potential they might have for curing themselves.

With Balan as the presocial or inner self gone, Balin becomes the scourge of the earth. Everywhere he goes, pure destruction lies in his wake. He argues with King Pellam (the Fisher King) and gives him the wound that originates the Wasteland: "And King Pellam lay so many years sore wounded, and never might be whole till that Galahad the Haut Prince healed him in the quest of the Sankgreal" (*Anthology* 478). Malory shows a Balin wandering aimlessly through a world bereft of all value: "And so he rode forth through the fair countries and cities and found the people dead and slain on every side, and all that ever were on live cried and said, "A Balin! Thou has done and caused great damage in these countries. For the Dolorous Stroke thou gave unto King Pellam these three countries are destroyed. And doubt not but the vengeance will fall upon thee at the last" (*Anthology* 478).

"Balin, or the Knight with Two Swords" is Malory's most penetrating critique of social identification, which in the Middle Ages meant identification with the Christian Church. While an institution is bound to appear more worthy than a mere individual, seeking self-fulfillment only within the institution's goals and values is nothing short of death for all. As we saw in the case of Lancelot and the Sword Bridge, your own path is the only path to redemption. In the context of a Roman Church increasingly faced with heresies that led to the Inquisition, the more closely you were connected to the Church, the more apt you were to take actions that were a scourge to the rest of the world. It is for this reason, that Parzival, as he leaves the hut of the hermit Trevrizent, mutters to himself that he hates God and that he no longer even believes in Him. Parzival is denying the institutionally conceived and defined God who, as seen by Amfortas and Trevrizent, only condemns. To deny this misconception of God is a profound act of faith in the God within. By transgressing the institutional God, one transcends the Wasteland condition and discovers, as Campbell entitles the last chapter of *The Masks of God: Creative Mythology*, "All the Gods within you."

Balin and his brother Balan do meet again at the end of the story. They meet as mortal enemies and in a tremendous battle give each other a wound which soon means their death. They are enemies because they do not even recognize each other, so changed are they by the process of social identification.

## Healing the Maimed King

In Wolfram's version, the question Parzival must ask in order to heal the Fisher King is "Dear uncle, what ails you?" (*Anthology* 468); in the original middle German "Oeheim, waz wirret dir?" The German verb "wirren" does mean "to trouble" but not with the implications of disease that "ailing" suggests. It is closer to "what is bewildering or confusing you?" The verb carries the sense of someone being muddleheaded and disordered. In all other versions of the Grail Quest, the knight must ask "why does the lance bleed?" and "whom does one serve with the Grail?" These questions ask for the secrets of redemption and locate the knowledge of redemption in some authority outside of the individual knights. For the Middle Ages, the secrets or mysteries of religion were the exclusive province of the Church and its canon lawyers. Individuals did not make doctrine; this was the message of the Fourth Lateran Council of 1215 which restated the essentials of the Christian faith and asserted for the first time that no salvation at all is possible outside of the Catholic faith. But in Wolfram, Parzival's question about what is befuddling Amfortas locates the problem squarely within Amfortas. Parzival achieves the Grail Quest through his commitment to the earth when he asks Amfortas to reexamine his own beliefs to see what among them is causing this renunciation of life.

It turns out that the physical wound is nothing at all. The real wound is in Amfortas's mind, which has accepted the notion that truth is held somewhere else and that to attain it one must give up the present life. When Parzival comes to him, Amfortas wishes not to be healed but to die: "If you are a man of reputation and honour, ask the knights and maidens here to let me die, and so end my agony" he says to Parzival (*Anthology* 468). Amfortas is befuddled because he thinks that life is a form of death or because he has confused life and death. As the church taught, sin is equal to spiritual death, and so the life he has been living and, indeed, the Wasteland are death. These notions of life exhaust the potential of life. These notions are not far from the Christian teaching that the true life and true potential of mankind is the eternal life with God. Balin, too, thought his true life was with Arthur and the Round Table. The present life and the present self are condemned. In fact, Amfortas and Balin are living death because they have chosen to focus on some power outside of themselves (the Church or Arthur) and have renounced life.

Immediately following the healing of Amfortas, Parzival suggests that he wants to see Condwiramurs, his wife from whom he has been absent for five years. As Campbell emphasizes in the television program for this unit, before Parzival can reach her, Trevrizent rushes in exclaiming that Parzival's defiance (transgression) has forced God to change his laws. But just as important is Trevrizent's subtle accusation that Parzival is one of the Neutral Angels. It was Trevrizent who told the story of the Neutral Angels to Parzival. Trevrizent concludes by saying that God placed the Neutral Angels as the guardians of the Grail until he would accept them back into heaven. Now Trevrizent changes his story:

> I lied as a means of distracting you from the Gral and how things stood concerning it. Let me atone for my error—I now owe you obedience, Nephew and my Lord. You heard from me that the banished angels were at the Gral with God's full support till they could be received back into His grace. But God is constant in such matters: He never ceases to war against those whom I named to you here as forgiven. Whoever desires to have reward from God must be in feud with those angels. For they are eternally damned and chose their own perdition (*Anthology* 469).

So the Angels are not so neutral after all. Or could it be that Trevrizent is lying this time! What is the issue here? Trevrizent is suggesting to Parzival that one must choose either God or damnation. We have seen that choosing God is what has befuddled Amfortas and Balin. The great triumph of Parzival, then, is in becoming like the Neutral Angels and not choosing between God and himself; that is, not placing one above the other, but finding the one within the other. Trevrizent's last words to Parzival are a stern command that he should seek humility—meaning renounce the world and become a hermit. Parzival's answer is that he wants to see his wife, and Wolfram moves into one of the most beautiful descriptions imaginable of the reunion of the mother and father and two children and of the love-making that lasted through the night until morning. Sex as a sacrament. Campbell says it really is. This is Parzival's choice.

## Myth and Psychoanalysis

Even a cursory reading of Campbell's books reveals his deep debt to the traditions of psychoanalysis in this century. In the *Anthology of Readings* is an essay by Carl Jung entitled "Confrontation with the Unconscious" in which he describes his own crossing of the Sword Bridge and the path of his own life. Both Jung and Freud, though they quarreled, saw psychoanalysis as the process of discovery of the energy or the divinity within the human heart. Jung describes a process of self-analysis. He asks himself Parzival's question: "What is troubling or confusing you?" In the process he learns that he cannot seek answers in inherited knowledge or the experience of others. He tells us that he had to abandon his academic career, for that knowledge stood in the way of the growth of his inner personality: "I therefore felt confronted with the choice of either continuing my academic career, whose road lay smooth before me, or following the laws of my inner personality" (*Anthology* 488). This is the Sword Bridge, the path of the unknown. It takes a great deal of courage to let go of the secure and known to allow the unconscious to unfold. In the television program for this unit, Campbell stresses that when Parzival rides out on the quest, he allows the horses reins to lie slack. The conscious reason is not in charge here. One must not choose this path or that path that is offered by the world's institutions for a secure and easy life.

In *The Masks of God: Creative Mythology*, Campbell phrases the problem of the Wasteland this way:

> The Wasteland, let us say then, is any world in which (to state the problem pedagogically) force and not love, indoctrination, not education, authority, not experience, prevail in the ordering of lives, and where the myths and rites enforced and received are consequently unrelated to the actual inward realizations, needs, and potentialities of those upon whom they are impressed.[5]

The Wasteland, then, is our contemporary neurotic world. Sigmund Freud tells us that what we call our civilization is largely responsible for the misery of our lives. People become neurotic, he goes on, because they cannot tolerate the frustration which society imposes upon them in the service of its cultural ideals.[6]

We cannot, therefore, fulfill the cultural goals we inherit from the past without losing our sanity in the process. It is legitimate to ask why this should be so, for the insights of both Campbell and Freud seem to suggest that the wisdom of the conservative to preserve tradition is as foolish and destructive as Trevrizent's attempt to trap Parzival into choosing between God and himself. What we often fail to see is that our traditional values were in their day innovations and often radical departures from the traditions of even older times. The world marches forward, whether for good or ill we can never be sure. Every innovation successfully employed changes the world we know, so we cannot truly say that our experience is the same as that of our forebears. A good example of this principle is the role that science as a system of cultural values or mythology plays in our society.

Science emerged in the late Middle Ages as a genuine need to confront and understand nature in ways that would materially benefit mankind. In this sense, it was a revolution against the sort of Christian teachings one finds in, for example, the *De Contemptu Mundi* (On Contempt for the World) of Pope Innocent III (though this was a very popular topic for medieval writers). Pope Innocent advises having as little to do with nature as possible, for it is hopelessly corrupt and only a path to sin. Concentrate on the spirit, he advises. But later it was felt and discovered that mankind could relate differently to nature. Francis Bacon's *Novum Organum* is a proposal for the different ways one might think about nature for the benefit of mankind. Thus modern science was born, and in the eighteenth century, philosophic voices said that men should aim at constructing lives in harmony with nature. (For further discussion of these viewpoints, read Voltaire, Diderot, Rouseau, Pope.) This is the mythology and the values of science.

In our own century, the values of science have become old, and rather than placing us in greater harmony with nature they produce the opposite condition of dire alienation from the world. We live in a world now saturated with the values of science in the same way that Wolfram's world was saturated with medieval Christian values and meanings. As Campbell's description of the Wasteland (quoted above) would suggest, science is that world in which force, indoctrination, and authority order our lives. Yet love, education, and experience, as the work of psychoanalysis and the study of myth show, must be the sources for new ways of relating people to each other and to nature. Plato's myth of love in *The Symposium*, mentioned in Unit 12, shows us the deep necessity of relating to others, of finding ourselves in others. Our modern scientific values simply do not work well at doing that any longer.

In his essay, Jung tells us that after letting go of his academic career (setting himself on his own hero's journey) and allowing his unconscious to unfold itself through dreams and the interpretation of myths and mythic images (note his mention of mandalas), he discovers that he is able to relate to others in ways never before possible. He writes, "That was the first event which broke through my isolation. I became aware of an affinity; I could establish ties with something and someone" (491). He was learning the ability to love genuinely, which is, after all, what Arthurian romance, especially Wolfram's *Parzival* is all about. Loving is something that must come from the heart, but first one must let go of those institutionalized selves in order to let the heart seek its other. While the love of Condwiramurs and Parzival is quite obvious and the individual aspects of it well discussed by Campbell in the television program for this unit, Parzival's discovery of his half-white, half-black brother, Feirefiz, is perhaps even more revealing.

Feirefiz is Wolfram's ultimate symbol for the Neutral Angel who will not choose an institution over a person. As Campbell says at the end of the television program, "The God in us is the one that gives the laws and makes the laws and it is within us." Campbell makes it clear that Feirefiz chose to be a Christian because that is the religion of Repanse de Schoye, the Grail maiden with whom he has fallen in love. While this may be a shallow reason for conversion, it nevertheless places things in the right order: experience and love come first. It is Parzival's meeting and fighting with his brother that first shows us how his long wandering among the unknown paths of the unconscious has taught him how to love, how to see himself in the other and the other in himself. He is fully identified with the other person, not a social institution:

> If I lay hold of truth, both my father and you, and I, too, were but one, though seen as three distinct entities. No wise man in search of truth counts father and children as related. On this field you were fighting with yourself. I came riding to do battle with myself and would gladly have slain myself. By fighting on so doggedly you defended my own life from me.[7]

## ASSIGNMENTS FOR STUDY AND ANALYSIS

1. Write out an explanation of the problem to which the Grail Quest is the solution as Campbell discusses it in the television program.
2. Discuss the background of the Neutral Angels. They are not often mentioned in typical Christian teaching. Can you discover a reason why?
3. What is the typical attitude of medieval Christianity towards nature? Is this attitude different now that we have had the Protestant Reformation? What is the difference between the Christian attitude toward nature and the scientific attitude?
4. What is Campbell's understanding of compassion? He makes a significant point about it in the television program. You might want to think of Tristan and Isolde as well in this connection.
5. Summarize Malory's insight about the process of socialization as it is portrayed in "The Knight with Two Swords." Read the story carefully and discuss the symbolism of the two swords.
6. How is the Fisher King actually healed? Explain the significance of the different questions. Why would he be healed with a question? What can it mean to be healed?

## FURTHER ASSIGNMENTS FOR WRITING AND REFLECTION

1. Write an essay discussing alternative attitudes toward nature, that is, attitudes that get beyond the problems inherent in the scientific and the religious attitudes. Use the Parzival myth to help develop your answer.
2. Write a discussion of the three notions of the Wasteland: the monastic Wasteland, Malory's, and Wolfram's. It might help to know that in the *Estoire*, it is also the failings of the knights that helps perpetuate the impotence of the king and the curse on the land.
3. Read a copy of T. S. Eliot's *The Wasteland*. Explain how the Grail myths operate in this poem. What does Eliot see as the cause of the twentieth-century wasteland?
4. Jung says that the three years he spent discovering himself, or finding his own path in the world, were the most valuable years of his life. Why do you think that in our society so little emphasis is placed upon a process of self-discovery like the one Jung describes?
5. If you were asked to give an explanation of the Grail Quest to people who only knew the name from the Monty Python movie, what would you say? Write a presentation for people who have never been introduced to the mythic and symbolic importance of the subject.
6. Jung writes in the essay in the *Anthology of Readings* that when he had to leave his studies with Freud it felt like a step into darkness. He also writes that he felt he had to resign from his academic career. Think about the way that Parzival conducts his quest for the Grail Castle, with his horse's reins slack. Use what you have learned about the Grail Quest to write an analysis of Jung's decisions.
7. In *The Hero with a Thousand Faces* Campbell writes that psychoanalysis is now the master of the mythological realm in that it teaches us how to read dreams and images (9–11). Think about the relation between psychoanalysis and myth. Also think about the Fisher King and healing. What is aimed at in these relationships? What does it mean to be healed in the mythic and psychoanalytic sense? In this connection, think about Campbell's idea of the discovery of the God within.

## ENDNOTES

[1]Chretien de Troyes, "Perceval," *Arthurian Romances*, Trans. D. D. R. Owen. (London: J. M. Dent & Sons, 1987) 417.

[2]*Queste del Saint Graal*, Trans. P. M. Matarasso, (Harmondsworth, UK: Penguin Classics, 1969) 279-280.

[3]Joseph Cambell, *The Masks of God: Creative Mythology* (New York: The Viking Press, 1968) 393.

[4]Campbell 637.

[5]Campbell 388.

[6]Sigmund Freud, *Civilization and Its Discontents* Trans. James Strachey (New York: W. W. Norton & Co., 1961) 33-44.

[7]Wolfram von Eschenbach, *Parzival* Trans. A. T. Hatto (Harmondsworth, UK: Penguin Classics, 1980) 374.

## UNIT BIBLIOGRAPHY

Campbell, Joseph. *The Masks of God: Creative Mythology*. New York: The Viking Press, 1968. See pages 405–570 for Campbell's discussion of the Parzival legend.

Eschenbach, Wolfram von. *Parzival*. Trans. A. T. Hatto. Harmondsworth, UK: Penguin Classics, 1980. The best-known medieval legend of Parzival and the Grail.

Freud, Sigmund. *Civilization and Its Discontents*. Trans. James Strachey. New York: W. W. & Sons Norton, 1961. Freud's attempt to introduce a psychoanalytical study of human institutions and cultures.

Jung, Carl G. *Memories, Dreams, and Reflection*. New York: Random House, 1962. Jung's autobiography that recounts his parting with Freud and his own journey into the study of archetypes.

Loomis, Roger Sherman. *The Grail: From Celtic Myth to Christian Symbol*. Cardiff: University of Wales Press, 1963. Loomis, one of the best-known scholars of Arthurian romances, traces the Grail legends to their origins in mythology and rituals.

Malory, Thomas. *Works*. Ed. Eugene Vinaver. London: Oxford University Press, 1982. The work of Thomas Malory was the complete and final medieval compilation of all the Arthurian Romances.

Merrill, Robert. *Sir Thomas Malory and the Cultural Crisis of the Late Middle Ages*. New York: Peter Lang, 1987. Merrill has written a key psychoanalytic study of Arthurian romances.

*Queste del Saint Graal*. Trans. P. M. Matarasso. Harmondsworth, U. K.: Penguin Classics, 1969. The very religious, thirteenth-century version of the Grail written by Cisterian monks. Galahad replaces Parzival as the Grail knight.

Weston, Jessie Laidley. *From Ritual to Romance*. Cambridge: University Press, 1920. This book, a deeply religious and symbolic interpretation of the Grail legends in terms of fertility myths, was the inspiration of T. S. Eliot's *The Wasteland*.

# NOTES

# NOTES

## GENERAL BIBLIOGRAPHY

Alcock, Leslie. *Arthur's Britain*. New York: Penguin Books, 1973.

Allen, Paul Gunn. *The Sacred Hoop: Recovering the Feminine in American Indian Traditions*. Beacon, Mass: Beacon Press, 1986.

Ashe, Geoffrey. *All About King Arthur*. London: W. H. Allen, 1969.

———. *The Quest for Arthur's Britain*. New York: Paladin Books, 1968.

Ashe, Geoffrey and Norris J. Lacey. *Arthurian Encyclopedia*. New York: Garland Publishing, 1986.

———. *The Virgin: The Myth and Cult of Mary*. London: Routledge and Paul, 1976.

Auden, W. H. "The Quest Hero." *Perspectives in Contemporary Criticism*. Ed. Sheldon Norman Grebstein. New York: Harper and Row, 1968.

Baigent, Michael, Richard Leigh, and Henry Lincoln. *The Holy Blood and the Holy Grail*. London: Johnathan Cape Ltd., 1982.

Barber, Richard W. *King Arthur: Hero and Legend*. Woodbridge: Boydell Press, 1987.

———. *King Arthur in Legend and History*. Woodbridge: Boydell Press, 1971.

Basso, Keith. "Stocking with Stories." *Text, Play and Story: Construction and Reconstruction of Self*. By Edward M. Bruner. Washington, D.C.: American Ethnological Society, 1984.

Bauman, Richard. *Verbal Art as Performance*. Rowley, Mass: Newbury House Publishers, 1978.

Bettelheim, Bruno. *The Uses of Enchantment: The Meaning and Importance of Fairy Tales*. New York: Random House, 1976.

Beyer, Stephan. *The Cult of Tara: Magic and Ritual in Tibet*. Berkeley: University of California Press, 1973.

Briggs, Charles L. *The Wood Carvers of Cordova, New Mexico: Social Dimensions of an Artistic "Revival."* Knoxville: University of Tennessee Press, 1980.

Brown, Joseph Epes. "The Roots of Renewal." *Seeing with a Native Eye*. Ed. Walter Holden Capps. New York: Harper and Row, 1976.

Brown, Arthur C. L. *The Origins of the Grail Legend*. Cambridge: Harvard University Press, 1943.

Bryant, Nigel. *The High Book of the Grail*. Cambridge: D. S. Brewer, 1982.

Chant, Joy. *The High Kings*. New York: Bantam, 1984.

Christ, Carol P. and Judith Plaskow. Ed. *Weaving the Visions*. San Francisco: Harper and Row, 1989.

———. ed. *Womanspirit Rising: A Feminist Reader in Religion*. San Francisco: Harper and Row, 1979.

Cohen, Perry S. "Theories of Myth." *Man*. N.S. 4, (September 1969): 337–53.

Detieenne, Marcel. *The Gardens of Adonis: Spices in Greek Mythology*. Atlantic Highlands, N.J.: Humanities Press, 1977.

Dodds, E. R. *The Greeks and the Irrational*. Berkeley: University of California Press, 1951.

Doty, William G. *Mythography: The Study of Myths and Rituals*. University, Alabama: University of Alabama Press, 1986.

Dundes, Alan. *The Study of Folklore*. Englewood Cliffs, N.J.: Prentice-Hall, 1965.

Eggan, Dorothy. "The Personal Use of Myth in Dreams." *Myth: A Symposium*. By Thomas Albert Sebeock. Bloomington, Indiana: Indianna University Press, 1965.

Eliade, Mircea. *From Primitives to Zen: Sourcebooks of the History of Religions*. New York: Harper and Row, 1967.

———. *Myth and Reality*. New York: Harper and Row, 1963.

———. *Rites and Symbols and Initiation*. New York: Harper and Row, 1958.

———. *Shamanism: Archaic Techniques of Ecstasy*. New York: Pantheon Books, 1964.

Falk, Nancy Auer and Rita M. Gross. *Unspoken Worlds: Women's Religious Lives*. New York: Wadsworth Publishing, 1989.

Frankfort, Henri. *Kingship and the Gods: A Study of Ancient Near East Religion as the Integration of Society and Nature*. Chicago: Chicago University Press, 1948.

Geertz, Clifford. *The Interpretation of Cultures*. New York: Basic Books, 1973.

Georges, E. *Studies on Mythology*. Homewood: Dorsey Press, 1968.

Gimbutas, Marija Alseikaite. *The Gods and Goddesses of Old Europe: 7000 to 3500 B.C. Myths, Legends and Cult Images*. Berkeley: University of California, 1974.

———. *Language of the Goddess*. New York: Harper and Row, 1989.

———. *Bronze Age Cultures in Central and Eastern Europe*. The Hague: Mouton, 1965.

Guthrie, W. K. C. *Orpheus and Greek Religion: A Study of the Orphic Movement*. London: Methuen, 1952.

Hillman, James. *Revisioning Psychology*. New York: Harper and Row, 1975.

———. *The Dream and the Underworld*. New York: Harper and Row, 1979.

Hymes, Dell H. *Reinventing Anthropology*. New York: Pantheon Books, 1972.

Ihle, Sandra Ness. *Malory's Grail Quest—Invention and Adaptation in Medieval Prose Romance*. Madison: University of Wisconsin Press, 1983.

Jackson, W. T. H. *The Anatomy of Love: The Tristan of Gottfried von Strassburg*. New York: Columbia University Press, 1971.

Jung, Carl Gustav. *The Archetypes of the Collective Unconscious*. Zurich: n.p., 1954.

———. *Four Archetypes: Mother/Rebirth/Spirit/Trickster*. Princeton, New Jersey: Princeton University, 1969.

Kempe, Dorothy. *The Legend of the Holy Grail—Its Sources, Character and Development*. London: Oxford University Press, 1905.

Kinsley, David R. *Hindu Goddesses: Visions of the Divine Feminine in the Hindu Religious Tradition*. Berkeley: University of California Press, 1986.

Kirk, G. S. *Myth: Its Meaning and Functions*. Berkeley: University of California Press, 1975.

Kluckholn, Clyde. "Myths and Rituals." *Harvard Theological Review* 35 (1942): 45–79.

Larson, Gerald James. *Myth in Indo-European Antiquity*. Berkeley: University of California Press, 1974.

Leori-Gourhan, Andre. *The Dawn of European Art: An Introduction to Palaeolithic Cave Painting*. New York: Cambridge University Press, 1982.

Lessa, William A. and Evon Z. Vogt. *Reader in Comparative Religion*. New York: Harper and Row, 1965.

Lincoln, Bruce. *Myth, Cosmos, and Society: Indo-European Themes of Creation and Destruction*. Cambridge: Harvard University Press, 1986.

Long, Charles H. "The Dreams of Professor Campbell: Joseph Campbell's *The Mythic Image*." *Religious Studies Review* 6:4 (October 1980): 261–72.

Loomis, Roger Sherman. *The Development of Arthurian Romance*. London: Hutchinson and Company, 1963.

Lord, Albert B. *The Singer of Tales*. Cambridge: Harvard University Press, 1960.

Maranda, Pierre. *Mythology: Selected Readings*. New York: Penguin, 1972.

Marshack, Alexander. *The Roots of Civilization*. New York: McGraw Hill, 1972.

Matarasso, Pauline. *The Quest of the Holy Grail*. Trans. P. M. Matarasso. London: Penguin Books, 1969.

Mookerjee, Ajit. *Tantra Art: Its Philosophy and Physics*. Basel: R. Kumar, 1971.

Mylonas, G. E. *Eleusis and the Eleusian Mysteries*. Princeton, New Jersey: Princeton University Press, 1961.

O'Flaherty, Wendy Doniger. *Dreams, Illusion, and Other Realities*. Chicago: University of Chicago Press, 1984.

———. *Other People's Myths: The Cave of Echoes*. New York: Macmillan, 1988.

Oppenheim, A. Leo. *Ancient Mesopotamia: Portrait of a Dead Civilization*. Chicago: University of Chicago Press, 1964.

Preston, James. *Cult of the Goddess: Social and Religious Change in a Hindu Temple*. New Dehli: Vikas, 1980.

Radin, Paul. *The Trickster*. London: Routledge and Paul, 1956.

Raglan, Lord Fitzroy *The Hero: A Study in Tradition, Myth and Drama*. London: Methuen and Co., 1936.

Rank, Otto. *A Psychological Interpretation of Mythology*. Trans. Drs. F. Robbins and Smith Ely Jellife. New York: The Journal of Nervous and Mental Disease Publishing Company, 1914.

———. *The Myth of the Birth of the Hero, and Other Writings*. New York: Vintage Books, 1959.

Ruether, Rosemary Radford. *Sexism and God-talk: Toward a Feminist Theology*. Boston: Beacon Press, 1983.

Silko, Leslie. *Ceremony*. New York: Viking Press, 1977.

Spretnak, Charleene. *Lost Goddesses of Early Greece*. Boston, Mass: Beacon Press, 1981.

Swain, Brian and Arnold Krupat, eds. *Recovering the Word: Essays on North American Literature*. Berkeley: University of California Press, 1987.

Talayesva, Don C. *Sun Chief: The Autobiography of a Hopi Indian*. New Haven: Yale University Press, 1963.

Tedlock, Dennis. trans. *Popul Vuh: The Definitive Edition of the Mayan Book of the Dawn of Life and the Glories of Gods and Kings*. New York: Simon and Schuster, 1985.

Tedlock, Dennis. *Finding the Center: Narrative Poetry of the Zuni Indians*. Lincoln: University of Nebraska Press, 1972.

———. *The Spoken Word and the Work of Interpretation*. Philadelphia: University of Pennsylvania Press, 1983.

Toelken, Barre. *Dynamics of Folklore*. Boston, Mass: Houghton Mifflin, Co., 1979.

Turner, Victor. *The Forest of Symbols: Aspects of Ndembu Ritual*. Ithaca: Cornell University Press, 1967.

———. *The Ritual Process: Structure and Anti-Structure*. London: Routledge and Paul, 1969.

Witherspoon, Gary. *Language and Art in the Navajo Universe*. Ann Arbor: University of Michigan Press, 1977.

Zimmer, Heinrich Robert. *The King and the Corpse: Tales of the Soul's Conquest of Evil*. New York: Pantheon Books, 1948.

# GENERAL GLOSSARY

**Abstract Design**: A design that has only intrinsic form with little or no attempt at realistic pictorial representation.

**Adze**: A cutting tool with a thin arched blade set at right angles to the handle.

**Aesthetic Field**: An enclosed area in a work of art that is separated from the space outside in which the work is organized.

**Ajiva**: Contaminating, non-living, karmic matter that Jainas believe prevents emancipation. (J)°

**Akshobhya**: (uhk-sho-byuh) The Dharmakaya (cosmic) Buddha of the East. Campbell's definition, "Can't Be Moved." (B)

**Alchemy**: From Arabic al-Khimia meaning chemistry. The belief that everthing was composed of varying proportions of air, earth, fire, and water. The discovery of the proportions of each would enable one to transmute one substance into another, such as lead into gold. The knowledge of secret proportions, written on the philosopher's stone or tablet, would also mean complete control of nature by man.

**Amitabha (Amida):** The Dharmakaya (cosmic) Buddha of the North. Campbell's definition, "the Buddha of Immeasurable Radiance." (B)

**Amoghasiddhi**: The Dharmakaya (cosmic) Buddha of the North. Campbell's definition, "who will not be turned from the achievement of his own." (B)

**Amor**: French for love (also, amour).

**Animistic**: Comes from Latin anima, meaning "soul." Term used to describe early stratum of religion wherein many things in nature are thought to possess spirits. (H)

**Anodos**: A rising upward.

**Apollo**: The Greek god of sun, prophecy, music, medicine, and poetry. Associated with the oracle at Delphi.

**Apollonian**: Relating to Apollo. In art or reasoning, the qualities of being clearly defined and ordered.

**Archetype**: A word similar in meaning to Campbell's "elementary ideas." It was used by the psychologist Jung to refer to a common psychic heritage of symbolic forms that all human beings share in the collective unconscious.

**Aryan**: The word, meaning "Noble" in Sanskrit. This term is used by high-caste Hindus to refer to their ancient ancestors. (H)

**Aryans**: Indo-European peoples who migrated into what is now Germany and northern Europe. They split up into various tribes including the Angles, Jutes, Frisians, and Saxons.

**Atum**: The Egyptian sun god in the aspect of the setting sun portrayed in the figure of an old man.

**Avalokiteshvara**: (uh-vuh-lo-kee-taysh-vuh-rah) The Bodhisattva form of Amida Buddha. Called by Campbell, "The Bodhisattva of Infinite Compassion." (B)

---

°An H, B, or J designates that the term applies to Hinduism, Buddhism or Jainism.

**Axial Tree**: A symbol of absolute reality, that is, of the center of the world. (See "World Axis.")

**Axis Mundi**: "The axis of the world." A mythological concept that can be represented by a tree, such as the Bodhi Tree under which the Buddha attained Enlightenment, a mountain, or any conceived center of reality. The Buddha seated in meditation under the Bodhi Tree, therefore, is at the center of the universe or is the center of the universe. Campbell has used the term "Immovable Spot" to refer to the same conept. (B)

**Ba**: A combination of the soul and intelligence in ancient Egypt.

**Bard**: Briton story teller or singer of folktales. Generally, tales were sung with the accompaniment of a harp like instrument.

**Bhakti**: The mood of devotion, of love for your chosen deity. (H,B)

**Bhumi Sparsha**: (boo-me spar-sha) "Touching the earth." The gesture used in depicting the Buddha in iconography wherein he touches or points toward the earth. This is to call mother earth as witness to his resolve to persist in his final pursuit of emancipation in spite of the temptations of worldly and material existence, symbolized in the temptations of the Buddha by Mara. (B)

**Bodhisattva**: (bo-dee-sut-vah) A prominent role for the "Buddha-to-be" that exists in Mahayana Buddhism. A Bodhisattva delays emancipation in order to help other suffering beings to achieve emancipation. Often the concept of Bodhisattva implies a transcendent spiritual being (one among many), comparable to the gods and goddesses of Hinduism. (B)

**Bodh-Gaya**: (bod with a silent 'h' and gai-a) The place in the contemporary Indian state of Bihar where the Buddha attained Enlightenment. (B)

**Bon**: The animistic religion of Tibet, partially assimilated to the dominant Buddhist cults. (B)

**Brahmanas**: The highest Hindu social caste—the priesthood. In ancient times this caste dictated the rules of religious and social behavior in Hinduism. (H)

**Britons**: A group of Celtic people who migrated to the British Isles. They were driven into remote areas of Wales, Scotland, and Ireland by the Anglo-Saxon invasions.

**Celts**: An Indo-European people who began migrating to central and western Europe in the tenth century C.E. Most celts were assimilated by the Romans, but notably the Britons preserved separate cultures in Cornwall, Wales, Scotland, and Ireland.

**Chakra**: One of seven centers, along the Sushumna, wherein the human body connects to higher and higher levels of the spiritual power in the universe. (H, B)

**Charity**: The virtuous form of human love, according to the tradition of Christian doctrine beginning with St. Augustine. Charity is the love of others or anything of the world for the sake of God.

**Chthonic**: Relating to the gods and spirits of the underworld.

**Condwiramurs**: Parzival's wife, queen of Brobarz. The name is old French for "guide of love": conduire + amor.

**Cosmogony**: The creation or origination of the world or universe or a theory of the origin of the universe.

**Courtly Love**: The general name for the cult of passionate and adulterous love that began the the eleventh century in southern France. Courtly love became assimilated with Arthurian romance in the works of Chretien, but flourished in the non-Arthurian romances of Dante and Petrarch. Courtly love remains the intensely passionate romantic love of much contemporary literature and film.

**Cupidity**: The form of love opposite to charity; that is, love of another or anything of the world (even one's self) for its own sake, or at least any sake other than God's. Lust or the enjoyment of some thing for its own sake.

**Cycles of the Heavens**: The fascinating transit of the heavenly bodies according to strict laws of time and motion. One of the earliest sources for the religious imagination, according to Campbell. (H,B)

**Dakini**: Female spirit of terrifying visage. (B)

**Dalai Lama**: The chief monk or (former) ruler of the classical Tibetan state, which was a theocracy. According to Tibetan Buddhism, he is the incarnation of the Bodhisattva Avalokiteshvara. (B)

**Danes**: People from Denmark and Sweden who invaded the British Isles during the ninth and tenth centuries. They drove many Celts or Britons into Brittany in northwest France (little Britain as opposed to Great Britain).

**Demeter**: (Roman, Ceres) The goddess of agriculture, fertility, and marriage. Mother of Persephone.

**Desacralized**: Without spiritual or sacred implications.

**Dionysus**: (Roman, Bacchus) The god of wine, associated with an orgiastic religion celebrating the power and fertility of nature.

**Druids**: An order of priests, magicians, or prophets among the Celts.

**English**: General name for the Germanic tribes, Angles, Saxons, Frisians, and Jutes, who migrated from northern Europe to the British Isles from 450 until 700. Sometimes simply referred to as Anglo-Saxons. Arthur was a Celtic war-leader against the English.

**Epiphany**: To show forth, a moment of sudden intuitive understanding or revelation from the gods.

**Epoteia**: A mystical vision.

**Eros**: Not to be confused with lust or cupidity. Eros is passionate energy that is expended in the quest to fulfill oneself as an individual. Christian doctrines about human love for God are often erotic, deriving ultimately from Plato's ideas about divine eros or enthusiasm in his *Symposium*.

**Fisher King**: Sometimes identified as Amfortas, other times Pellam, and still in other legends as Alain or Brons. He is the wounded and impotent king of the Wasteland. The name is rich with Christian and pagan symbolism: Christ as the fisher of men and in Celtic myth the fish as a fertility symbol, i.e., the king seeking fertility. Also the old French pun *le roi pécheur* translates as "the king who has sinned" and *le roi pêcheur* translates as "the king who fishes." Robert de Boron in *Joseph of Arimathea* says that Brons, the fisher king, catches the fish that is served at the Last Supper.

**Galahad**: The Grail knight in the Cistercian *Queste del Saint Graal* and the *Estoire del Graal*. The name comes from the biblical "Galeed," meaning "a heap of testimony."

**Gnosis**: Intuitive apprehensive of spiritual truths.

**Gothic**: Medieval romanticism, as opposed to classicism or the Romanesque in artistic and literary styles. The Gothic period is generally the twelfth and thirteenth centuries.

**Grail**: Old French, Graal, from "gradale," meaning a dish used to serve successive courses in a meal. Robert de Boron says the Grail is the cup used at the Last Supper and that was filled with Christ's blood at the Crucifixion. Wolfram says that the Grail is a large stone, the "lapis exilis."

**Gynocratic**: Related to the political supremacy of women.

**Hades**: (Roman, Pluto) The god of the underworld and distributor of earthly riches.

**Hallaj**: (huh-luj) A muslim Sufi (mystic) of early Islam, 858–922 C.E. whose full name is Husayn Ibn Mansur al-Hallaj. He was martyred by the orthodox Muslims for the excesses in his devotion to Allah.

**Hammurabi**: (2100 B.C.E.) King of Babylonia. His code of laws is one of the most famous of ancient documents.

**Hermeneutics**: The branch of philosophy and theology dealing with methods and theories of interpretation.

**Hermetic**: Relating to the gnostic mysteries of the first to third centuries C.E. and attributed to Hermes Trismegistus. The works of Hermes are called the *Corpus Hermeticum*.

**Herodotus**: (c. 484–425 B.C.E.) Greek historian known as the father of history. His work, the first comprehensive attempt at secular narrative history, is the beginning of the writing of history in the Western world.

**Iconography**: The representation of religious or legendary objects by conventional images and symbols.

**Ida**: The duct to the left of the Sushumna in the mystical physiology of Tantra. It is subtly connected to the left nostril and serves an important function in Tantra yoga breathing exercises. (H, B)

**Ikhnaton**: (c. 1375–1358 B.C.E.) King of Egypt. He was the son of Amenhotep III and began his reign as Amenhotep IV. But he changed his name when he undertook a complete reform in an attempt to unify political, social, and artistic life under a monotheistic cult centered around the sun god Aton. The priests opposed him and gradually he was brought to ruin, but his period was one of the greatest in Egyptian art.

**Ishtadevata**: (ish-tuh-day-vuh-tah) One's chosen deity. Equals yiddam in Tibetan. (H)

**Jaina**: One who is a follower of a Jina. (J)

**Jina**: "The Victor" refers to the Jaina hero (or heroine) who has become emancipated and teaches others the way. (J)

**Jiva**: The life monad in Jainism. Term also used in Hinduism to refer to the living, personal soul. (J, H)

**Johann Wolfgang von Goethe**: (1749–1832) German poet, dramatist, and novelist. Author of *Faust*, a rarely performed play, completed just before his death and very important in the history of German literature.

**Ka**: To the ancient Egyptian, a kind of "double" of the deceased that had been with the person since he was born, but functioned at his death to guide the individual in the realm of the dead. At death one was said to have "gone to his ka."

**Kachinas**: The masked gods of Pueblo ritual, who appear especially in dances of the winter season.

**Kali**: The female deity-consort of Shiva. She is often depicted as fearsome, wearing a necklace of skulls and a skirt of severed human limbs. She represents the destructive nature of time. (H)

**Kathodos**: (Cathodos) The most widely worshipped avatar ("descent form" or incarnation) of Vishnu. He is viewed as the supreme deity of devotional love in all its forms. (H)

**Kuan Yin**: (Kwan–Yin) Chinese version of the feminine manifestation of Avalokiteshvara. (B)

**Kundalini**: The serpent-shaped element coiled sleeping at the base point of the chakra system. It can be "awakened" by means of Tantric Yoga techniques. (H, B)

**Lais**: (singular lay) The Britons were well known in the Middle Ages for their wealth of myths and stories and their skill in singing tales called "lias" with the accompaniment of any sort of harplike stringed instrument.

**Lama**: The Tibetan name for a Buddhist monk or priest. The religion of Tibet is sometimes called Lamaism. (B)

**Langue D'oc**: The name of the language of southern France. So-called because the word for "yes" is "oc" and not the "oui" ("oil" in old French spelling) of northern France.

**Lapsit Exillis or Lapis Exilis**: The Grail in Wolfram's *Parzival*, but in no other version. Lapis Exilis is the philosopher's stone, the much sought after substance in alchemical research that had power to transmute lead into gold.

**Libation Vase**: A vase used for pouring a liquid as a sacrifice to a diety.

**Liminal**: Reference to the threshold between two states of being.

**Lingam**: The symbolic representation of the male sexual organ. (H)

**Little Ferryboat and Big Ferryboat**: Campbell's and Heinrich Zimmer's translations of the Hinayana and Mahayana respectively: the two principal types of Buddhism. (B)

**Macrocosm**: The universe.

**Maenad**: (Roman, Bacchae) A woman of the orgiastic cult of Bacchus.

**Magna Charta**: A charter limiting the rights of the monarch, forced upon King John I by English barons in 1215.

**Mahavairochana**: (muhuh-veye-ro-chu-nuh) The Great Sun Buddha at the top center of the universe. (B)

**Mahavira**: The most recent Jina and founder of Jainism. (J)

**Mahishasuramardani**: A name for Durga, signifying that she is the slayer of the demon Mahishasura. (H)

**Maitreya**: (meye-tray-yah) The Buddha who will come at the end of the cosmic age. (B)

**Maize**: Indian corn.

**Mandala**: (mun-dah-lah) The Sanskrit word for a circle symbolic of the cosmic order. A diagram used for meditation in Tibetan Buddhism (also in Hinduism). It may be purely geometric or contain symbolic representations of Buddhas, animals, humans, and many other elements. (H, B)

**Martin Buber**: (1878–1965) Jewish philosopher whose theological writings have had an influence throughout the world.

**Matriarchy**: A social organization marked by the supremacy of the mother in the clan or family, the legal dependence of husbands or children, and the reckoning of descent and inheritance through the female line.

**Maya**: Common term in Hinduism to refer to the transitory, "illusory" nature of the material world. It is the feminine symbol of the world of samsara. In the Tantric system, Maya is equated with Shakti. (It has some relationship to the philosophical issue of how you determine that what you perceive with your senses really exists.) (H)

**Merlin**: Arthur's chief counselor, reputed to have magical powers, but the legends vary greatly on the extent of this magic. He is associated with the Druids.

**Mesocosm**: A culture or large social grouping; that which exists between the universe and the individual human being.

**Minotaur**: A monster shaped half like a man and half like a bull.

**Minstrals**: Wandering lyric poets and story tellers, similar to troubadors, but who flourished in northern Europe and England.

**Moses**: The legendary founder of Israel and of Yahwism, the form of the Hebrew religion whose God is the mover behind history. Also the lawgiver of Israel and the prophet who led his people out of bondage in Egypt to the edge of Canaan, the Promised Land. Through Moses, God gave the Ten Commandments, the criminal code, and the liturgical law to the people. Therefore they are called Mosaic law.

**Munsalvaesche**: The mysterious land where the Grail Castle is located. The name means "Mount Savage" or wild mountains.

**Mycenae**: An ancient city in Greece that reached its height of development about 1600 B.C.E. Excavations here in 1876 helped to rewrite the history of Greece.

**Mystery Religions**: Name for a group of religious cults popular in Hellenic and Roman periods in Greece (second century B.C.E. – third century C.E.). The mysteries centered around a dying and rising savior and the process of purification of initiates. Chief cults include the mysteries of Eleusis, Isis-Osiris, Orpheus, Dionysus, and Mithra.

**Mysticism**: Dimension beyond religion in which the claim is that a human being experiences union with God (or Spirit).

**Mythic Dissociation**: Campbell's term for the separation of the reigns of nature and spirit. It is the notion that divinity and transcendence do not exist within individuals, but only "out there," separate from the world.

**Nefertite**: The Queen of Iknaton's rule. A statue bust of her is one of the greatest treasures of world art.

**Neophyte**: A new convert involved in a ritual experience.

**Neutral Angels**: Angels who took neither God's side nor Lucifer's side in the battle in Heaven. In Wolfram they are the guardians of the Grail.

**Occidental**: Of the west, particularly Europe.

**Paleolithic**: A period of the prehistoric era known as the Stone Age. Historians have divided the prehistoric times into the Stone, Bronze, and Iron Ages. The Stone Age was further divided into Paleolithic, Mesolithic, and Neolithic on the basis of the kind of hunting done and the types of artifacts used.

**Pantheon**: The collective deities of a people.

**Papyrus**: Ancient Egyptians used the roots of this plant for fuel, the pith for food, and the stem for boats, cloth, twine, and sheets for writing material.

**Parinirvana**: (puh-ree-nir-vah-nah) The final Nirvana, i.e., the death of the Buddha. The Buddha is shown lying on his side as he enters Parinirvana. (B)

**Patriarchy**: A social organization marked by the supremacy of the father in the clan or family, the legal dependence of wives and children, and the reckoning of descent and inheritance through the male line.

**Perennial Philosophy**: Concept linking together all mystical experience in spite of the religious and cultural differences in which mystics arise.

**Persephone**: (Roman, Proserpina) The daughter of Demeter and wife of Hades.

**Petrafact**: A myth that has become "petrified"; one that is no longer alive for the culture in which it exists.

**Pharaoh**: The biblical title of the kings of Egypt.

**Pingala**: The duct to the right of the Sushumna in the mystical physiology of Tantra. It is subtly connected to the right nostril and serves an important function in Tantra-Yoga breathing exercises. (B, H)

**Potala**: (po-tah-lah)The palace of the Dalai Lama in Lhasa. (B)

**Pythagoras**: (c. 582–c. 507 B.C.E.) Greek philosopher and mathematician who believed that the essence of all things was number and that all relationships could be expressed and understood numerically.

**Ra**: The sun god worshipped in Egypt. Through this deity the concept of supreme rule became associated with the sun cults in Egypt.

**Ratnasambhava**: (rutha-sum-ba-vuh) The Dharmakaya (cosmic) Buddha of the South. Campbell's definition, "born of a Jewel". (B)

**Realm of Karma**: The world of cause and effect, i.e., Samsara. (B, H, J)

**Samsara**: The cosmic system of constant change because of the inexorable law of cause and effect. It refers to the constant recreation of the universes and the reincarnation of souls or life-stream entities. (B, H, J)

**Sankhya**: One of the six classical Hindu philosophies, accepted by orthodox Hindus as authoritative. (H)

**Sanskrit**: The alleged language of the Aryan invaders of India (c. 1800 B.C.E.) who first introduced the special cultural perspective and religion that transformed Indian culture. (H, B)

**Satyrs**: Woodland gods in ancient Greek and Roman mythology, in human form but having a goat's ears, tail, and legs.

**Shakti**: The feminine pole of the universal energy field of the universe. Shiva is the masculine pole. (H, B)

**Shamanism**: A religious phenomenon, most clearly characteristic of Siberia and Central Asia, in which a religious figure or medicine man, a "Shaman" moved through trace into the supernatural for the purpose of healing or resolving the problems of his people.

**Shiva**: One of the two principal deities of Hinduism. (The other is Vishnu.) His symbols, the trident and lingam, are found in the earliest strata of Indian civilization. (H)

**Shunyata**: The state of emptiness. From the Sanskrit word Shunya, meaning "empty." The term refers to the difference between Nirvana (i.e., shunyata) and samsara at a higher level, however, they are the same. (B)

**Siddhi (or occult power)**: Through yoga one can develop one's paranormal faculties, such as telepathy, telekinesis, and "bilocation." The word "occult" means "hidden." Such powers remain hidden to others unless revealed by the yogi who is alleged to have them. (H, B)

**Sigmund Freud**: (1856–1939) Austrian psychiatrist and author of *Moses and Monotheism*.

**Social Identification**: Campbell's term for a social or political condition when myths lose their connection to people's lives.

**Sthula**: Translated by Campbell as "gross matter," may be the physical, material world. (H)

**Stupa**: Originally a mound-shaped structure within which were preserved the relics of the Buddha. The Stupa was the inspiration in other parts of Asia for the temple structures of Buddhism such as the Pagoda.

**Sukhavati**: (su-kah-vah-tee) The paradise of Amitabha. (B)

**Sukshma**: Translated by Campbell as "subtle matter," also meaning "mind stuff." (H, B)

**Sushummna**: The central channel of the occult physiology of Tantra that can be pierced by Kundalini. (H, B)

**Sutra**: A brief "thread" of ideas (often previously memorized) used in the exposition of various ancient Indian "sciences." (H, B, J)

**Symbol**: A word, a picture, a gesture (and other things) that open the religious imagination from the physical, mundane world toward the spiritual or higher world. (The word may have other meaning in other disciplines, for instance literature).

**Syncretism**: The combination of different forms of belief or practice.

**Tantra**: Campbell translates this term as "loom." It refers to the idea that the world is woven on a great loom of power, the Shakti. Understanding the processes of Shakti is essential to Tantra yoga. (H, B)

**Tara**: Tibetan version of the feminine manifestation of Avalokiteshvara. (B)

**Telestrerion**: Place where the higher mysteries of Eleusis were performed.

**Thanka**: (thun-kah) Paintings (some of enormous size) that Tibetans use to illustrate theological and mythological concepts. (B)

**The Tao**: (dah-oh) A concept in Chinese religion and philosophy that there is an impersonal source from which everything that exists arises. It also is the source of order and harmony in human society and nature if understood properly.

**The Long Body**: The body in its entire course of existence from birth to death as opposed to the physical body existing at any given moment.

**The Buddha Nature**: A theory especially prominent in Mahayana Buddhism that the whole universe is permeated by the essential characteristics of Buddhahood. This gives rise to the further theory that every human being is potentially a Buddha. It also implies that Samsara, the world of transmigration of persons and the continuous cycles of the universe, and Nirvana, the condition of complete spiritual freedom (or ultimate reality) are the same. (B)

**Transcendence**: Literally "to pass beyond or above." The ability to rise above life negating conditions of social identification to mythic association.

**Transgression**: Literally "to step across." The act of breaking laws or rules, in medieval Christian terms transgression is sin, but in courtly love it refers to breaking laws of marriage and becomes, in this way, a great virtue.

**Transmigration**: The passing of a person's soul into another body after death.

**Trefoil**: An ornament or symbol in the form of a stylized leaf of a leguminous herb.

**Trishula**: The trident symbol of Shiva that, Campbell points out, was also the symbol of Poseidon, the Greek god. (H)

**Troubadors**: Wandering lyric poets who flourished in Provence and Acquitaine in the south of France during the eleventh and twelfth centuries. Adulterous love and chivalry were the favorite poetic themes — and often real-life preoccupations.

**Tutankhamen**: (c. 1355 B.C.E.) King of ancient Egypt of the XVIII dynasty. He was the son-in-law of Ikhnaton and revised the latter's policy by returning to the worship of Amon. His tomb was opened in 1922 by Howard Carter.

**Upanishads**: The literature of the first period of historical Hinduism that presented many of the ideas that led to the later Hindu emphasis upon spiritual emancipation as the final goal of religious life. (H)

**Vajrayana**: (vuj-ruh-yuh-nah) Name for the type of Mahayana Buddhism practiced in Tibet. "Vajra" means thunderbolt. (B)

**Varna**: The Sanskrit word (basic meaning is "color") for the castes of classical Hinduism. Castes are social divisions determined by birth. (H, B)

**Vedic**: Referring to the scripture, called the Veda, upon which the Hindu religion is based — also, the period from about 1800 to 600 B.C.E. when the Veda was composed. (H)

**Vishnu**: The deity who shares principal roles with Shiva in the Hinduism of Post-Vedic and modern times. (H)

**World Axis**: The imagined axis linking the earth's surface with the lower world (hell) and the upper world (heaven) at the metaphoric center of the earth. The world axis is often metaphorically a tree, with its crown in the upper world and its roots in the lower.

**Yab-Yum**: The stylized icons of Tibetan Buddhism that show the embrace of the masculine and feminine principles in the universe. (B)

**Yahweh**: The Hebrew name for God in some books of the Old Testament.

**Yama**: (yu-muh) The Hindu god of death, also represented in the Buddhist pantheon. He represents the essential impermanence of everything that exists. (H, B)

**Yoga**: A specific discipline (e.g., Raja Yoga) by means of which you can attempt to discover the reality of the spiritual realm. (H, B, J)

**Yogi**: A term coming from Indian religion for the individual who attempts to control body and mind to become attuned to the inner spiritual center opening to ultimate reality.

**Yoni**: The symbolic representation of the female organ. (H, B)

**Ziggurat**: An ancient Babylonian temple tower consisting of a lofty pyramidal structure built in successive stages with outside staircases and a shrine at the top.

# LIST OF *ANTHOLOGY* ESSAYS

**Unit 8 From Psychology to Spirituality: Kundalini Yoga Part II**

**Haridas Chaudhuri "The Synthesis of Yogas: Hatha, Raja, and Tantra"** *from Integral Yoga: The Concept of Harmonious and Creative Living*

**Heinrich Zimmer "Tantra"** *from Philosophies of India, Joseph Campbell, editor*

**Mircea Eliade "Yoga: Immortality and Freedom"** *from Yoga: Immortality and Freedom*

**Edward Conze "Buddhist Texts Through the Ages"** *from Buddhist Texts Through the Ages*

**Unit 9 The Descent to Heaven: The Tibetan Book of the Dead**

**Giuseppe Tucci "Birth, Marriage, Sickness, and Death"** *from Tibet: Land of Snows J. E. Stapleton Driver, translator*

**W. Y. Evans-Wentz "The Bardo of the Moments of Death"** *from The Tibetan Book of the Dead*

**Heinrich Harrer "I am Recognized"** *from Return to Tibet*

**Fokke Sierksma "Buddhism: Mantrayāna and Vajrayāna"** *from Tibet's Terrifying Deities: Sex and Aggression in Religious Acculturation, G. E. Van Baaren-Pape, translator*

**Unit 10 From Darkness to Light: The Mystery Religions of Ancient Greece**

**Euripides "The Bacchae"** *from An Anthology of Greek Drama, Charles Alexander Robinson, Jr., editor*

**Walter Burkert "Mysteries and Asceticism"** *from Greek Religion*

**George deForest Lord** "The Hymn to Demeter" *from The Hymn to Demeter, George deForest Lord, translator*

**Ovid "The Teachings of Pythagoras"** *from Metamorphoses, Rolfe Humphries, translator*

**Unit 11 Where There Was No Path: Arthurian Legends and the Western Way**

**Gildas "De Excidio et Conquestu Britanniae"** *from Arthur, King of Britain: History, Chronicle, Romance, and Criticism, Richard L. Brengle, editor*

**Nennius "Historia Brittonum"** *from Arthur, King of Britain: History, Chronicle, Romance, and Criticism Richard L. Brengle, editor*

**Geoffrey of Monmouth "Historia Regum Britanniae"** *from Arthur, King of Britain: History, Chronicle, Romance, and Criticism, Richard L. Brengle, editor*

**Sir Thomas Malory "King Arthur and His Knights"** *from King Arthur and His Knights, Eugene Vinaver, editor*

**Roger Sherman Loomis** "The Development of Arthurian Romance" *from The Development of Arthurian Romance*

**Unit 12 A Noble Heart: The Courtly Love of Tristan and Isolde**

**Gottfried von Strassburg "Tristan"** *from Tristan, A. T. Hatto, translator*

**Sir Thomas Malory "The Knight of the Cart"** *from King Arthur and His Knights, Eugene Vinaver, editor*

**Andreas Capellanus "The Art of Courtly Love"** *from The Art of Courtly Love, John Jay Parry, translator*

**Unit 13 In Search of The Holy Grail: The Parzival Legend**

**Wolfram von Eschenbach "Parzival"** *from A. T. Hatto, translator*

**Sir Thomas Malory "Balin or the Knight with the Two Swords"** *from King Arthur and His Knights, Eugene Vinaver, editor*

**C. G. Jung "Confrontation with the Unconscious"** *from Memories, Dreams, and Reflection*

## COPYRIGHTS AND ACKNOWLEDGMENTS

## ILLUSTRATION CREDITS

A 9
B 0
C 1
D 2
E 3
F 4
G 5
H 6
I 7
J 8